PLATO'S *PARMENIDES* AND ITS HERITAGE
VOLUME 2

Society of Biblical Literature

Writings from the Greco-Roman World Supplement Series

John T. Fitzgerald
Series Editor

Number 3

PLATO'S *PARMENIDES* AND ITS HERITAGE, VOLUME 2

PLATO'S *PARMENIDES* AND ITS HERITAGE
VOLUME 2:

ITS RECEPTION IN NEOPLATONIC, JEWISH, AND CHRISTIAN TEXTS

Edited by

John D. Turner and Kevin Corrigan

Society of Biblical Literature
Atlanta

PLATO'S *PARMENIDES*, VOLUME 2

Copyright © 2010 by the Society of Biblical Literature

All rights reserved. No part of this work may be reproduced or transmitted in any form or by any means, electronic or mechanical, including photocopying and recording, or by means of any information storage or retrieval system, except as may be expressly permitted by the 1976 Copyright Act or in writing from the publisher. Requests for permission should be addressed in writing to the Rights and Permissions Office, Society of Biblical Literature, 825 Houston Mill Road, Atlanta, GA 30329 USA.

Library of Congress Cataloging-in-Publication Data

Seminar, "Rethinking Plato's Parmenides and its Platonic, Gnostic, and Patristic Reception" (2001–2007)
  Plato's Parmenides and its heritage : history and interpretation from the old academy to later platonism and gnosticism / edited by John D. Turner and Kevin Corrigan.
     p. cm. — Society of Biblical Literature writings from the Greco-Roman world supplement series ; v. 2)
  Includes bibliographical references and index.
  ISBN 978-1-58983-449-1 (paper binding, vol. 1 : alk. paper) — ISBN 978-1-58983-450-7 (paper binding, vol. 2 : alk. paper)
  1. Plato. Parmenides—Congresses. I. Turner, John Douglas. II. Corrigan, Kevin. III. Title.
  B378.S46 2016a
  184—dc22

2009041812

Printed on acid-free, recycled paper
conforming to ANSI/NISO Z39.48-1992 (R1997) and ISO 9706:1994
standards for paper permanence.

Contents

Abbreviations   vii

Introduction   1

Section 1: *Parmenides* Interpretation from Plotinus to Damascius

1. Plotinus and the *Parmenides*: Problems of Interpretation   23
   Matthias Vorwerk
2. Plotinus and the Hypotheses of the Second Part of Plato's *Parmenides*   35
   Kevin Corrigan
3. The Reception of the *Parmenides* before Proclus   49
   Luc Brisson
4. Is Porphyry the Source Used by Marius Victorinus?   65
   Volker Henning Drecoll
5. Porphyry and the Gnostics: Reassessing Pierre Hadot's Thesis in Light of the Second- and Third-Century Sethian Treatises   81
   Tuomas Rasimus
6. Columns VII–VIII of the *Anonymous Commentary on the Parmenides*: Vestiges of a Logical Interpretation   111
   Luc Brisson
7. Iamblichus's Interpretation of the *Parmenides*' Third Hypothesis   119
   John F. Finamore
8. Syrianus's Exegesis of the Second Hypothesis of the *Parmenides*: The Architecture of the Intelligible Universe Revealed   133
   John M. Dillon
9. Damascius on the Third Hypothesis of the *Parmenides*   143
   Sara Ahbel-Rappe

10. Metaphysicizing the Aristotelian Categories: Two References to the *Parmenides* in Simplicius's Commentary on the *Categories* (75,6 and 291,2 Kalbfleisch) 157
    Gerald Bechtle

    SECTION 2: THE HIDDEN INFLUENCE OF THE *PARMENIDES* IN PHILO, ORIGEN, AND LATER PATRISTIC THOUGHT

11. Early Alexandrian Theology and Plato's *Parmenides* 175
    David T. Runia

12. Christians and the *Parmenides* 189
    Mark Edwards

13. Origen's Platonism: Questions and Caveats 199
    Mark Edwards

14. Plato's *Parmenides* among the Cappadocian Fathers: The Problem of a Possible Influence or the Meaning of a Lack? 217
    Jean Reynard

15. The Importance of the *Parmenides* for Trinitarian Theology in the Third and Fourth Centuries C.E. 237
    Kevin Corrigan

16. Pseudo-Dionysius, the *Parmenides*, and the Problem of Contradiction 243
    Andrew Radde-Gallwitz

References 255

Contributors 269

Subject–Name Index 273

Index Locorum 289

Abbreviations

General

ca.	circa
cf.	compare
conj.	conjecture
e.g.	for example
i.e.	in other words
frg.	fragment
MS	manuscript
parr.	parallel passages
prop.	propositions in Proclus, *Institutio Theologica*
Ps.	Pseudo-
rev. ed.	revised edition
sc.	that is to say
test.	Testimonium

Primary Sources

Const. ap.	*Apostolic Constitutions*
Alcinous	
Intr.	*Introductio in Platonem*
Didask.	*Didaskalikos*
Anon. in Parm.	*Anonymus Taurinensis in Platonis Parmenidem commentarium*
Ap. John	*Apocryphon of John*
Aristotle	
Int.	*De interpretatione*
Metaph.	*Metaphysica*
Arnobius	
Adv. nat.	*Adversus nationes*
Athanasius	
Adv. Ar.	*Adversus Arium*
Decr.	*De decretis Nicaenae synodi*

Syn.	De Synodis
Athenagoras	
Leg.	Legatio sive Supplicatio pro Christianis
Augustine	
Civ.	De civitate Dei
Faust.	Contra Faustum Manichaeum
Barn.	Barnabus
Basilius Caesariensis	
Eun.	Adversus Eunomium
Spir.	De spiritu sancto
Clement	
Exc.	Excerpta ex Theodoto
Strom.	Stromata (Miscellanies)
Cod. bruc.	Codex brucianus
Const. ap.	Constitutiones apostolicae
Corp. herm.	Corpus hermeticum
Damascius	
Dub. et sol.	Dubitationes et Solutiones
In Parm.	In Parmenidem
In Phaed.	In Phaedo
Princ.	De principiis
Vit. Isid.	Vita Isidori
Did.	Didache
Diogn.	Diognetus
Dexippus	
In cat.	In Aristotelis categorias commentarium
Epiphanius	
Pan.	Panarion
Eunomius	
Apol.	Apologia
Eusebius	
Praep. ev.	Praeparatio evangelica
Gregory of Nyssa	
Ad abl.	Ad ablabium
An. res.	De anima et resurrectione
Antirrh.	Antirrheticus adversus Apolinarium
Eun.	Contra Eunomium libri
Graec.	Ad Graecos, Ex communibus notionibus
Hom. Beat.	Homiliy on the Beatitudes
Hom. Cant.	Homiliae in Canticum canticorum
Hom. Eccl.	Homilies on Ecclesiastes
Opif. hom.	De Opificio Hominis
Vit. moys.	De vita Moysis

Hermias
   In Phaedr.   *In Platonis Phaedrum Scholia*
Hierocles
   In aur. carm.   *In aureum carmen*
Hippolytus
   Ref.   *Refutatio omnium haeresium*
Iamblichus
   An.   *De Anima*
   Mys.   *De Mysteriis*
   Theol. Arith.   *Theologoumena arithmeticae*
Irenaeus
   Adv. Haer.   *Adversus Haereses*
John Lydus
   Mens.   *De mensibus*
L.A.E.   *Life of Adam and Eve*
Marius Victorinus
   Adv. Ar.   *Adversus Arium*
   Cand.   *Ad Candidum*
Origen
   Cels.   *Contra Celsum*
   Comm. Jo.   *Commentarii in evangelium Joannis*
   Comm. Rom.   *Commentarii in epistulam ad Romanos*
   Dial.   *Dialogus cum Heraclide*
   Hom. Cant.   *Homiliae in Canticum*
   Or.   *De oratione*
   Philoc.   *Philocalia*
   Princ.   *De principiis*
Philo
   Cher.   *De Cherubim*
   Deus   *Quod Deus sit immutabilis*
   Fug.   *De fuga et invention*
   Leg.   *Legum allegoriae*
   Mut.   *De mutatione nominum*
   Post.   *De posteritate Caini*
   Prov.   *De providentia*
   Sobr.   *De sobrietate*
   Somn.   *De somniis*
   Spec.   *De specialibus legibus*
Philostorgius
   Hist. Eccl.   *Historia ecclesiastica*
Photius
   Epit. Phot.   *Epitoma Photiana*

Plato
  Parm.   *Parmenides*
  Phaed.   *Phaedo*
  Phaedr.   *Phaedrus*
  Resp.   *Respublica*
  Symp.   *Symposium*
  Tim.   *Timaeus*
Plotinus
  Enn.   *Enneads*
Porphyry
  Abst.   *De abstinentia*
  Antr. nymph.   *De antro nympharum*
  Gaur.   *Ad Gaurum*
  Hist. phil.   *Historia philosophiae fragmenta*
  Isag.   *Isagoge sive quinque voces*
  Marc.   *Ad Marcellam*
  Sent.   *Porphyrii Sententiae ad intelligibilia ducentes*
  Vit. Plot.   *Vita Plotini*
Priscianus
  An.   *De anima*
Proclus
  Inst. theol.   *Institutio Theologica*
  In Alc.   *In Alcibiadem*
  In Parm.   *In Parmenidem*
  In Tim.   *In Timaeum*
  Theol. Plat.   *Theologia Platonica*
Ps.-Dionysius
  Div. nom.   *Divine Names*
  Myst.   *De mystica theologia*
Sextus Empiricus
  Math.   *Adversus Mathematicos*
Simplicius
  In cat.   *In Aristotelis categorias commentarium*
  In phys.   *In Aristotelis physica*
  Steles Seth   *Three Steles of Seth*
Syrianus
  In Metaph.   *In Metaphysica*
Tertullian
  An.   *De Anima*
  Val.   *Adversus Valentinianos*
Theodoret
  Haer. fab. comp. *Haereticarum fabularum compendium*
  Zost.   *Zostrianos*

SECONDARY SOURCES

AMP	Ancient and Medieval Philosophy
ANRW	*Aufstieg und Niedergang der römischen Welt*
Armstrong	Armstrong, A. H. *Plotinus: Ennead II.* LCL 441. Cambridge, Mass.: Harvard University Press, 1966
BCNH	Bibliothèque copte de Nag Hammadi
BG	*Codex Berolinensis Gnosticus*. Edited by C. Schmidt and W. C. Till, Die gnostischen Schriften des koptischen Papyrus Berolinensis 8502. Texte und Untersuchungen 60. Berlin: Akademie, 1955. Rev. ed. edited by H.-M. Schenke, 1972
BETL	Bibliotheca Ephemeridum Theologicarum Lovaniensum
Bidez	Bidez, J. 1913. *Vie de Porphyre: Le philosophe néo-platonicien*. Reprinted 1980. Hildesheim: Georg Olms.
Busse	Busse, A. *Isagoge et in Aristotelis categorias commentarium*. CAG 4.1. Berlin: Reimer, 1887
CAG	Commentaria in Aristotelem Graeca
Cousin	Cousin, V. 1864. *Procli philosophi Platonici opera inedita, pt. 3*. Paris: Durand, 617–1244. Repr. Hildesheim: Olms, 1961
CQ	*Classical Quarterly*
CSEL	Corpus scriptorum ecclesiasticorum latinorum
CUF	Collection des Universités de France
de Falco	de Falco, V., ed. *[Iamblichi] theologoumena arithmeticae*. Leipzig: Teubner, 1922
des Places 1973	des Places, É. 1973. *Numénius: Fragments*. Collection des Universités de France-Association Guillaume Budé. Paris: Les Belles Lettres
Diehl	Diehl, E. *Procli Diadochi in Platonis Timaeum commentaria*, 2. Leipzig: Teubner, 1904. Repr. Amsterdam: Hakkert, 1965
Diels 1882	*Simplicius. In Aristotelis physicorum libros quattuor priores commentaria*. Edited by H. Diels. CAG 9. Berlin: Reimer, 1882
Dörrie 1959	Dörrie, H. 1959. *Porphyrios' Symmikta Zetemata*. Monographen zur Klassischen Altertumwissenschaft 20. Munich: Beck
Dodds	Dodds, E. R. *Proclus: The Elements of Theology: A Revised Text with Translation, Introduction and Commentary*. Oxford: Clarendon, 1963
Einarson-De Lacy	Einarson, B. and P. H. De Lacy, trans. Reply to Colotes in Defence of the Other Philosophers. Pages 190–315 in *Plutarch's Moralia in seventeen volumes*. Vol. XIV with an

	English translation by Benedict Einarson and Phillip H. De Lacy. Cambridge, Mass.: Harvard University Press; London: Heinemann, 1967.
Finamore and Dillon	Finamore, J. F. and Dillon, J. M. *Iamblichus De Anima: Text, Translation, and Commentary*. Leiden: Brill, 2002
Fowler	Fowler, H. N., trans. *Plato in Twelve Volumes*. Vol. 9 translated by Harold N. Fowler. Cambridge, Mass.: Harvard University Press; London: William Heinemann, 1925
GCS	Die griechischen christlichen Schriftsteller der ersten drei Jahrhunderte
Heil-Ritter	Heil, G. and A. M. Ritter. *Pseudo-Dionysius Areopagita. De Coelesti Hierarchia, De Ecclesiastica Hierarchia, De Mystica Theologia, Epistulae*. Patristische Texte und Studien 36. Berlin: de Gruyter, 1991
Hermann	Hermann, C. F. *Platonis Dialogi secundum Thrassylli tetralogias disposili. Ex recognitione Caroli Frederici Harmanni*. Leipzig: Teubner, 1850–1853
Hiller	*Theon of Smyrna. Expositio rerum mathematicarum ad legendum Platonem utilium.* Edited by E. Hiller. Leipzig: Teubner, 1878
HSCP	*Harvard Studies in Classical Philology*
HTR	*Harvard Theological Review*
JAC	*Jahrbuch für Antike und Christentum*
JHS	*Journal of Hellenistic Studies*
JTS	*Journal of Theological Studies*
Kalbfleisch	*Simplicius. In Aristotelis categorias commentarium*. Edited by K. Kalbfleisch. CAG 8. Berlin: Reimer, 1907
Klostermann	Klostermann, E. *Eusebius' Werke* 4. GCS 14. Leipzig: Hinrichs, 1906, 1–54. Revised by G. C. Hansen. GCS 14. Berlin: Akademie, 1972 and 1991.
Koetschau	Koetschau, P. *Origenes Werke V. De principiis*. GCS 22. Leipzig: Hinrichs, 1913
LCL	Loeb Classical Library
LSJ	Liddell, H. G., R. Scott, H. S. Jones, *A Greek-English Lexicon*. 9th ed. Oxford, 1996
Morrow-Dillon	Morrow, G. R. and J. M. Dillon. *Proclus' Commentary on Plato's Parmenides*. Princeton: Princeton University Press, 1987
Musurillo	Musurillo, H., ed. *From Glory to Glory: Texts from Gregory of Nyssa's Mystical Writings*. Crestwood, N.Y.: St. Vladimir's Seminary Press, 1995.
NHC	Hag Hammadi Codex
NHS	Nag Hammadi Studies

PG	*Patrologia Graeca*
PGL	*Patristic Greek Lexikon*. Edited by G. W. H. Lampe. Oxford: Clarendon, 1968
PL	*Patrologia latina* [= Patrologiae Cursus Completus, Series Graeca]. Edited by J.-P. Migne. 161 vols. Paris, 1856–1866.
REG	*Revue des études grecques*
RHE	*Revue d'histoire ecclésiastique*
Rousseau-Doutreleau	*Irénée de Lyon: Contre les hérésies*, Livre 1, vol. 2: *Texte et traduction*. Edited by Adelin Rousseau and L. Doutreleau. SC 264. Paris: Cerf, 1979
RThPh	*Revue de théologie et de philosophie*
Ruelle	Ruelle, C. É. 1899. *Damascii successoris dubitationes et solutions. De primis principiis in Parmenidem*. 2 vols. Paris: Klincksieck, 1899. Repr. Brussels: Culture et Civilisation, 1964; Amsterdam: Brepols, 1966
Saffrey-Westerink	Saffrey, H.-D. and L. G. Westerink 1968–1997. Proclus, Theologie Platonicienne. Texte etabli et traduit par H.D. Saffrey and L.G. Westerink. 6 Vols. Collection des universités de France. Paris: Les Belles Lettres.
SBLSymS	SBL Symposium Series
SC	*Sources chrétiennes*. Paris: Cerf, 1943–
Segonds	Segonds, A.-Ph. *Proclus: Sur le Premiere Alcibiade de Platon*. 2 vols. CUF. Paris: Les Belles Lettres, 2003
Smith	Smith, A. Porphyrian Studies since 1913. ANRW 36.2:717–73. Part 2, 36.2, Edited by H. Temporini and W. Haase. Berlin: de Gruyter, 1987
Sodano	Sodano, A. R. *Porphyrii In Platonis Timaeum Commentariorum fragmenta*. Naples: Istituto della Stampa, 1964.
Suchla	Suchla, B. R. *Corpus Dionysiacum I: Pseudo-Dionysius Areopagita. De divinis nominibus*. Patristische Texte und Studien 33. Berlin: De Gruyter, 1990
VC	*Vigiliae Christianae*
Von Balthasar	Von Balthasar, H. U. 1984. Origen, Spirit and Fire: A Thematic Anthology of His Writings. Trans. R. Daly. Washington, D.C.: Catholic University of America Press
Wachsmuth	Wachsmuth, C. and O. Hense. *Ioannis Stobaei anthologium*. 5 vols. Berlin: Weidmann, 1884–1909. Repr. 1958
Westerink-Combès	Westerink, L. G. and J. Combès. *Damascius, Traité des premiers principes*. 3 vols. CUF–Association Guillaume Budé. Paris: Les Belles Lettres, 1986–1991
Westerink-Combès	Westerink, L. G. and J. Combès. *Damascius: Commentaire du Parménide de Platon*. 4 vols. CUF–Association Guillaume Budé. Paris: Les Belles Lettres, 1997–2003

WSNT	Wissenschaftliche Studien zum Neuen Testament
WUNT	*Wissenschaftliche Untersuchungen zum Neuen Testament*
ZAC	*Zeitschrift für Antikes Christentum*
Zintzen	Zintzen, C. *Damascii vitae Isidori reliquiae*. Hildesheim: Olms, 1967
ZKG	*Zeitschrift für Kirchengeschichte*
ZNW	*Zeitschrift für die Neutestamentliche Wissenschaft und die Kunde der älteren Kirche*

Introduction

These two volumes collect the work of twenty-two scholars from ten different countries presented in a seminar, "Rethinking Plato's Parmenides and Its Platonic, Gnostic and Patristic Reception," that was held during six annual meetings of the Society of Biblical Literature from 2001 to 2006 and that has broken new ground on several fronts in the history of interpretation of Plato's *Parmenides*. There was also a special conference, "Mittelplatonisches im nachplotinischen Diskurs bis Augustin und Proklos," held at the end of July, 2007 in Tübingen, Germany, organized and hosted by Volker Drecoll, whose results were published in the *Zeitschrift für Antikes Christentum* (*ZAC*) 12, 2008. Four of those papers have been included in vol. 2 of this collection by kind permission of the editors and publisher (Walter de Gruyter) of *ZAC*.

Two of the most impressive features of this extended enterprise have been the excellent, free spirit of international collaborative scholarship, still quite rare in the Humanities, and the dedicated commitment of our small community to sustain the project over what has effectively been a six-year period. Since not only Plato's *Parmenides* itself but also the various traditions or instances of its interpretation are difficult and highly complex, we provide here a detailed survey of the contents of the two volumes so as to make this collaborative, interdisciplinary work as accessible as possible to students and scholars in many fields.

The overall theme of vol. 1 is the dissolution of traditionally rather firm boundaries for thinking about the tradition of *Parmenides* interpretation from the Old Academy up to and including the beginnings of what has become known as Neoplatonism. The volume suggests a radically different interpretation of the history of thought from Plato to Proclus than is customary by arguing against Proclus's generally accepted view that there was no metaphysical interpretation of the *Parmenides* before Plotinus in the third century C.E. Instead, this volume traces such metaphysical interpretations, first, to Speusippus and the early Platonic Academy; second, to the Platonism of the first and second centuries C.E. in figures like Moderatus and Numenius, who began to uncover various metaphysical realities in the "hypotheses" of the second part of the *Parmenides*; third, to the emergence of an exegetical tradition that read Aristotle's categories in relation to the Parmenides; and fourth, to important Middle Platonic figures and texts. The volume also casts further doubt upon several commonly held theses: 1) it provides evidence to suppose that the *Anonymous Commentary on the Parmenides* (attributed for the last forty years to Porphyry, but perhaps even pre-Plotinian) is probably itself dependent upon an earlier, now lost, commentary or commentaries available to both late-second- and early-third-century Gnostics and Platonists; 2) it suggests that the "Middle Platonic" provenance usually assigned to Moderatus's "Neopythagoreanism" (via Porphyry's testimony in Simplicius) has undergone interpolation with a much later Neoplatonic set of ideas; and 4) it also shows that, despite the undoubted importance of Plotinus, the traditional view of Plotinus as the "father" of Neoplatonism and "originator" of the doctrine of the three "Ones," should be seriously rethought on the basis that not only Plotinus, but also Gnostic and Platonic thinkers that preceded him, seem to be the joint inheritors of a tradition that may well go back to the early Academy.

Volume 1 focuses on the earlier period from Plato and the Old Academy up to Middle Platonism and Gnosticism, with a critical eye upon direct or indirect testimonies from the later Neoplatonists and others. Volume 2 first examines the Neoplatonic tradition itself from Plotinus to Damascius and then takes a broader comparative view of the reception of the *Parmenides* by such important figures as Philo, Clement, and certain other Patristic authors up to Pseudo-Dionysius.

Volume 1: Plato's *Parmenides*: History and Interpretation from the Old Academy to Later Platonism and Gnosticism

Section 1: Plato, from the Old Academy to Middle Platonism

Kevin Corrigan sets the scene by problematizing the place of the *Parmenides* in Plato's writings and by providing an overview of some of the major interpretations ranging from the time of Proclus's *Commentary on the Parmenides* to contemporary scholarship. Corrigan suggests that, despite Proclus's apparent view that there were no metaphysical interpretations before Plotinus, the intrinsically thought-provoking nature even of an aporetic dialogue such as the *Parmenides* (when put beside its earlier counterpart dialogue of ideas, the *Symposium*) makes it unlikely that such metaphysical interpretations arose only in late antiquity, especially when one considers hints of such interpretations in earlier authors: in the "episodic" system of Speusippus, in Moderatus, Eudorus, and Nicomachus of Gerasa, in the apparently pre-Plotinian Sethian Platonizing Gnostic texts, and in Middle Platonic thought in general, especially the *Anonymous Commentary on the Parmenides*, attributed to Porphyry by Pierre Hadot, but possibly composed even earlier than Plotinus.

There then follow three different perspectives on Speusippus. Gerald Bechtle asks what "points of contact" between Plato's Parmenides and Speusippus's metaphysical system might have meant, especially since such points of contact do not necessarily imply a paraphrase or a definite system of principles in either Plato or Speusippus, and since such contact may have been bidirectional, as has been proposed by Andreas Graeser, who has hypothesized that Plato wrote the Parmenides as a reaction against Speusippus's theory of principles. Bechtle then undertakes a brief reconstruction of Speusippus's doctrine of principles (the One and Multiplicity) on the basis of both Aristotelian material and later Platonist texts. He argues that the tenet of the One as smallest principle does not necessitate a view of the One as deficient negativity or as (Neoplatonic) transcendent non-being or beyond-being, but it should rather be interpreted in a neutral way according to which the One is not any determinate being in the stereometric, planimetric, linear, or mathematical dimensions deduced from it. He concludes that there are clear links between Speusippus's metaphysics and the *Parmenides*. First, the dichotomic method of the second part of the Parmenides and Speusippus's equally exhaustive diairetic semantics are conducted exactly on the same logical principles. Second, the first and third Parmenidean deductions (about the one in relation to itself and the others in relation to the one, on the hypothesis that the one exists) and Speusippus's views on the relation between the one and the many are genuinely comparable and concern exactly the same topic, namely, they explore possibilities of how to conceive and render functional the principles necessary to explain how all of reality comes about.

Luc Brisson tackles the question from a different perspective. He starts with a fragment attributed to Speusippus in the *Anonymous Commentary on the Parmenides*. By means of a critical analysis of texts in Damascius, Proclus, Iamblichus, Porphyry (as attested in Cyril of Alexandria), and Plotinus that seem to refer to it, Brisson, following Carlos Steel, argues that this fragment does not go back to the historical Speusippus, but instead derives from a Neopythagorean apocryphon that reveals a Neopythagorizing interpretation of the Parmenides proposed in the first two centuries C.E. that is used by the Neoplatonists (perhaps Amelius or Porphyry) to interpret the first series of deductions of the second part of the Parmenides. We are therefore deprived of what looked at first sight to be quasi-direct access to Speusippus himself even though tantalizingly closer to relatively early Parmenides-interpretation, albeit through the lens of Neoplatonic spectacles.

Finally, John Dillon argues that an ontological interpretation of Plato's argument in the second hypothesis (about the generation of number at *Parm.* 142d–144a, and especially 143c–144a) may have been behind Speusippus's theory about the way the universe is generated from a radically unitary and simple first principle, and that this theory has actually left traces in Plotinus's doctrine of numbers in 5.6 [34]. This view seems, on the one hand, to contradict the consensus (based on Proclus) that earlier generations of Platonists took the Parmenides simply as a logical exercise, but, on the other hand, to render Moderatus's derivation of a system of hypostases from the first three hypotheses of the Parmenides more comprehensible.

What ultimately interests Plotinus is an insight derived from Speusippus, namely, that the first product of the union of the primal One and Multiplicity is not the Forms, but Number. Being is prior to Number (as against Speusippus), but Number is prior to beings or the multiplicity of the Forms (as Speusippus asserted). Plotinus finds room for forms as well as numbers, whereas Speusippus wanted to relegate forms to the level of the World Soul. However, if we are prepared to suppose that Speusippus assigned an ontological value to the first two hypotheses, then we may well go further (on the understanding that we cannot know definitively whether or not this was actually the case) and suggest that, since Speusippus seems to have posited a five-level universe, he probably took the first five hypotheses as representing levels of reality, while the last four hypotheses simply reinforced—in negative terms—the necessity of there being a One. Hence the matching of the first five hypotheses with levels of reality is an entirely plausible interpretation as early as Speusippus, Plato's own nephew.

The three following contributions that make up the first major section of vol. 1 broaden the focus so that we can see some of the deep complexities of interpretation involved in our assessment of the historical period between the times of Speusippus and Moderatus.

Thomas Szlezák explores the question of the indefinite dyad in Sextus Empiricus's report at *Math.* 10.248–283, setting forth initially good reasons for considering this report to be a Neopythagorean version of an older report on Plato's famous lecture, "On the Good." How does this relate to the interpretation of the *Parmenides* that we find in Simplicius's quotation from Porphyry's testimony on Moderatus's thought, which looks like a Neopythagorean anticipation of the Neoplatonic hierarchy of hypostases? In the Sextus passage, the monad and indefinite dyad are said to be the highest principles of all things (numbers, lines, surfaces, geometrical bodies, the four elements, and the cosmos). But the indefiniteness of the dyad is neither explained nor really employed in the generation of numbers and things, suggesting that we have a doxographical report that was not really understood philosophically. By contrast, Plato's *Parmenides* is philosophically thorough, but the indefinite dyad is never mentioned; yet in a thinker such as Plato, who does not care about terms so much as about what is really at stake, the intended point—that the cooperation of two components is necessary for anything to come into being—may nevertheless be legitimately recognized in the *Parmenides*.

In the history of scholarly criticism, hypotheses 4 and 7 have been related to the indefinite dyad (of the Unwritten Teachings), ontologically in 4 and epistemologically in 7. But hypothesis 3 is more revealing, since the nature of the "other than the one" reveals itself as unlimitedness, and in hypothesis 2 the doubling of the existent one has also been seen as referring to the indefinite dyad; the resultant doubling of every "part" yields an indefinite multiplicity (143a2) applicable to both intelligible and sensible realms, as Aristotle attests. And even in the first hypothesis, to deny the dissimilarity of the one would be akin to distinguishing between first and second principles. So the *Parmenides* shows us how we are to think of the initially puzzling idea of an indefinite dyad, but we need other dialogues such as the *Republic* and *Timaeus* to arrive at the concept. Sextus's report is Platonic and must be very old because of its explicit use of the term "indefinite dyad" and it is certainly complementary to the *Parmenides*. So this provides a necessary caution that the whole of Plato's philosophy cannot legitimately be deduced from a single dialogue, especially if that dialogue does not provide the key to its own decryption.

Very much in tune with Szlezák's view but in a different key, Zlatko Pleše gives a powerful sense of the different options available for Plato-interpretation in the first and second centuries C.E. from Plutarch's dialogue *The E at Delphi*, in which Ammonius, Plutarch's teacher, is given a major role in praise of the highest God. Is Ammonius a character expressing Plutarch's own views, or is he a historical personality reflecting the monistic tendencies of Alexandrian Platonism, such as the derivational monism and the one beyond being of Eudorus? Pleše rejects both of these possibilities as unwarranted by the text and argues instead that Ammonius's speech is a sophisticated treatment of Platonic dichotomies (Being/Becoming, thought/sense-perception, eternity/time) from the *Timaeus*, *Sophist*, *Philebus*, *Cratylus*, and *Republic*, within which earlier compatible Pre-Socratic theories are integrated and strong resemblances to the *Parmenides* can be detected (e.g., Ammonius's abrupt introduction of "otherness" in the light of *Parmenides* 143a4–b8 and in the very setting of Plutarch's dialogue, with its equation of Parmenides with Ammonius and Socrates with Plutarch). Ammonius's views are not out of step with those of Plutarch. The history of Platonism is marked by its cleavage into two different traditions: one dogmatic, reaching back to the Old Academy, and the other skeptical, initiated by Arcesilaus. What we find in Ammonius's speech is Plutarch's passionate homage to the continuing unity of those traditions and their common opposition to empiricism.

To conclude the first section of vol. 1, Noel Hubler casts serious doubt upon E. R. Dodds's famous claim that the first-century Neopythagorean philosopher, Moderatus, had anticipated Plotinus's supposedly unique theory of hypostases by developing a theory of emanation through a series of three Ones. Hubler argues that, in basing his claim upon a single passage in the sixth-century commentator, Simplicius, Dodds failed to take into account Simplicius's own stated preference to supplement, clarify, or apply descriptions designed to deny the application of physical attributes to the intelligible realm of Neoplatonic metaphysics. In his analysis of Simplicius's text, Hubler argues that Simplicius's Neoplatonist summary and Porphyry's own apparent version of Moderatus cited by Simplicius recount two different theories, Porphyry's version being consistent with other testimony he provides about Moderatus and with what we know from other sources about the Neopythagoreanism of Moderatus's time. In sum, a textual source long thought to be definitive for our reconstruction of the history of thought turns out to be a figment of Simplicius's Neoplatonic imagination.

We may add, however, that the problem of the origin of the supposed Neoplatonic hypostases very much remains at issue, for Plotinus himself makes no claim to originality for his thought and asserts that his only innovation was the theory of the undescended soul (5.1 [10], a theory rejected by Iamblichus and the later Neoplatonists anyway). So if not Plotinus, and if not Moderatus or other Neopythagoreans of the first century, then where did the theory of three Ones become mapped onto, or out of, the first three hypotheses of the Parmenides?

SECTION 2: MIDDLE PLATONIC AND GNOSTIC TEXTS

The second major section of vol. 1 brings us into direct contact with one of the major revolutions in recent times in our ways of analyzing and categorizing ancient thought. Scholars have typically tried to separate Platonism from Gnosticism just as they have also tried to distinguish rational philosophy from irrational religion. The picture that has recently emerged and that will appear clearly to the reader of both volumes is much more complex, for with the discovery of the Nag Hammadi texts, and especially, for our purposes, the Sethian Gnostic "Platonizing" texts (*Three Steles of Seth*, *Allogenes*, *Zostrianos*, and *Marsanes*), we are in the presence of a highly sophisticated religious, soteriological Platonism with complex triadic and even enneadic structures, a "Platonic" competitor of early Christianity with equally strong Jewish roots that antedates not only Iamblichus and Proclus but also Plotinus and Porphyry. In this "Gnostic" Platonism, as in other strands of a very complex overall Platonic tradition, religion and philosophy are interwoven. Moreover, as we will see below, there are no hermetic seals to compartmentalize strands of this complex tradition that we have hitherto regarded as separate. These different texts reflect upon, and speak sometimes to one another in unexpected ways.

In the first presentation of the second section of vol. 1, John Turner argues that with the Platonizing Sethian treatises we are at the cusp of a shift from what is known as Middle Platonism, for which the principal Platonic dialogue of reference is the *Timaeus*, towards the Neoplatonism of later times, for which the *Parmenides* and *Symposium* (and the three kings of Plato's *Second Letter*) assume greater importance. This shift can be seen already during the first and second centuries in Platonists like Moderatus and Numenius who were attracted by the Neopythagorean doctrines of Eudorus and Thrasyllus, aspects of which probably go back to Speusippus. As a result, various expositions and lemmatic commentaries like the Turin *Anonymous Commentary on the Parmenides* began to uncover the various metaphysical realities in the hypotheses of the second part of the *Parmenides*. In the case of the Sethian treatises, the Unknowable One, clearly beyond being, is described in negative terms derived from the first hypothesis, from which the Barbelo Aeon emanates as a divine Intellect in a sequence of Existence, Vitality/Life, and Mentality/Intellect roughly parallel to the unfolding of the second One from the first One of the *Anonymous Commentary*. In addition, the negative theologies of these texts in relation to the Unknowable One (variously characterized in different Sethian texts) are based upon common sources, probably Middle Platonic epitomes of or commentaries on the Parmenides, one of which is shared by *Allogenes* and the *Apocryphon of John*, and another by *Zostrianos* and Marius Victorinus (first detected by Michel Tardieu and Pierre Hadot in 1996), thus providing incontestable proof of a pre-Plotinian theological interpretation of the *Parmenides*' first hypothesis and suggesting an interpretation of the second hypothesis as the emergence of a second from a first One.

All of this suggests that expositions or commentaries on the Parmenides were available in the late-second or third centuries; that they were used by the authors of *Zostrianos* and *Allogenes*, works known to Plotinus and Porphyry; that they were Middle Platonic works; and that in this milieu the *Anonymous Commentary* may well be pre-Plotinian (as Bechtle and Corrigan have suggested), especially since the *Anonymous Commentary* appears to depend, in part, not only upon the apparently late-second-century *Chaldean Oracles* but also upon the source common to both Victorinus and *Zostrianos*.

This web of intertextual affiliations, therefore, provides an entirely new view of the history of thought, compelling the modification of Willy Theiler's long-standing hypothesis, namely, that every Neoplatonic, non-Plotinian doctrine simultaneously in Augustine and in a late Neoplatonist author must come from Porphyry. The Trinitarian theology of Marius Victorinus may come via Porphyry, but it is based not exclusively in Neoplatonism but in Middle Platonic thought such as that of the Platonizing Sethian treatises.

There follow two presentations that take a more cautious approach to some elements in this overall picture. Johanna Brankaer argues by means of a comparative analysis of the Sethian Platonizing texts that, while oneness is certainly applied to the supreme entities, there is no developed henology such as we find in Plotinus. The articulation of the one and the many is common to both the *Parmenides* and Sethian speculation, but oneness is often connected to Being rather than to a One "beyond being." What we see in the Gnostic texts, therefore, is a sophisticated adaptation that recalls Platonic and Neoplatonic texts, but is really transformed to the different purpose of a soteriological system.

Volker Drecoll next undertakes to analyze one of the common sources mentioned by Turner above, namely, the source common to *Zostrianos* and Victorinus (on the assumption that this must have been a Greek text) and argues, on the basis of comparison between the two texts, that there is a surprisingly small list of common expressions and even that these might simply reflect common currency of the day. He therefore suggests that the Tardieu-Hadot hypothesis should be reconsidered in the light of other possible hypotheses: 1) Abramowski's hypothesis that behind the parallel sections there was a common source produced by a crypto-Gnostic Nicene circle at Rome that Victorinus used without knowing its Barbelo-Gnostic origin. Drecoll rejects this, however—on the grounds that we have virtually no evidence for such a circle—in favor of the easier hypothesis, namely 2) that Victorinus read Gnostic texts but was perfectly capable of rejecting Gnosticism, and so presented us with a patchwork of different sources, including Gnostic sources, just as Plotinus read *Zostrianos* without becoming a

Gnostic. But 3) did Victorinus use the Greek *Zostrianos* or a text dependent on it, perhaps a Neoplatonic text with the Gnostic myths and images expurgated or a Coptic version that could have changed the Greek source? Drecoll concludes therefore that we know too little to assume an unknown common source (though it certainly looks like a plausible solution) or to use this assumption to infer a pre-Plotinian date for the *Anonymous Commentary*. There may have been a common source, but we cannot exclude other possible alternatives.

In the following presentations, we now move to detailed comparative analyses of some of the major texts in question, most of them definitely Middle Platonic, but at least one—the *Anonymous Commentary on the Parmenides*—whose attribution oscillates back and forth, as it were, between Middle Platonism and Neoplatonism according to the eye of the beholder. First, John Turner and Luc Brisson undertake comparative analyses of the *Chaldean Oracles*, Gnostic texts, and the *Anonymous Commentary on the Parmenides*. Turner highlights some striking structural similarities in these texts on several different levels: First, the six-level system of the *Chaldean Oracles* is similar to the schemes of Sethian texts. Second, the enneadic structure that Hadot discerns (on the basis of John Lydus) in Porphyry's interpretation of the *Oracles* is strongly reflected not only in Allogenes' portrayal of the Invisible Spirit's Triple Power, namely infinitival Existence, indeterminate Vitality, and determinate Mentality, as an enneadic sequence of three emanative phases in which each term of the triad sequentially predominates and contains the other two within each phase of its unfolding. Third, there are striking structural and functional resemblances between the Chaldean Hecate and the Sethian triple-powered One and also between the Sethian Aeon of Barbelo and the three phases of Hecate's existence as prefiguration, source, and place of the instantiation of ideal multiplicity. Turner concludes, therefore, first, that the Sethian authors seem familiar with Neopythagorean arithmological speculation, with the Being–Life–Mind triad perhaps derived from Plato's *Sophist*, and with the implied metaphysics of the *Oracles* and, second, that the Being–Life–Mind triad, despite differences in nomenclature, functions in very much the same emanational context in the *Anonymous Commentary on the Parmenides* as in the Sethian texts, with the major difference that the Sethians (except for the *Three Steles of Seth*) locate the triad at the level of the first One and see it as the origin rather than the result of the emanative process.

What was therefore thought to be much later in the history of thought, namely, the theory of emanation, and the development of progressive enneadic structures comprising triads, turns out to be earlier, at least as early as the late-second or early-third century. This provides a very different view of the development of Platonism in a more amorphous and cosmopolitan environment.

Luc Brisson undertakes a similar comparative study on the basis of folios 9 and 10 of the *Anonymous Commentary on the Parmenides* (in relation to the first hypothesis) which he argues reveal a Neoplatonist critique of the Chaldean positive claim that we can know God. Since God is not an object, only in unknowing does the soul experience something of God. Unlike the Gnostics, we cannot claim to know either God or the mode of procession. Such a critique (undertaken in part via a critique of the Stoic criterion of truth) might be taken as evidence of a pre-Plotinian date for the *Commentary*, but Brisson holds to a post-Plotinian authorship since this critique implies that the One of the first hypothesis is beyond being and because it presupposes knowledge of 6.1 [10].8. Brisson draws two conclusions: First, he locates the shared source of Victorinus and *Zostrianos* in the *Chaldean Oracles*' description of the Father (frg. 3, 4, 7), which in turn had been influenced by Plato's description of the One in the first hypothesis of the *Parmenides* (142a). Second, he proposes that an earlier commentary on the *Parmenides* must have existed at the end of the second century, one that turned the first God into an Intellect—that is, determinate Being that was somehow assimilated to the first One of the *Parmenides*—and claimed that God could be known, if only indirectly. For the possibility of this knowledge, the authority of the *Oracles* was invoked. This positive commentary was cited by *Zostrianos*, criticized by the *Anonymous Commentary* and available, directly or indirectly, to Marius Victorinus.

Gerald Bechtle opens up a different avenue of inquiry: the relation of Plato's *Parmenides* and Aristotle's *Categories*. Starting from Hadot's monumental work, *Porphyre et Victorinus* (1968), and his collection of Porphyrian texts in Victorinus in vol. 2, Bechtle focuses upon group IV of those texts and particularly Hadot's insight in pinpointing a relation between the extant fragments of the *Parmenides Commentary* and the exegetical tradition regarding Aristotle's *Categories*. He poses the broader questions, where do the surviving bits of the *Anonymous Commentary on the Parmenides* fit into the *Categories*-related tradition? and can the latter cast significant chronological light upon the former? But he focuses here upon the well-established intertwinement of the two exegetical traditions by the end of the second century C.E., so standard in fact as to be mentioned casually in Alcinous's *Handbook*. Is there evidence, then, for the metaphysical relevance of the categories before Plotinus? The already established metaphysical discussion of Aristotle's categories in Plotinus and Lucius and Nicostratus is confirmed by Simplicius and Porphyry, as well as by Plotinus himself. Indeed, nine of Aristotle's categories can be found in some form in Plato's *Parmenides*, and the five greatest genera of the *Sophist* even more so. Bechtle then goes on to uncover a tradition of reading Aristotle's categories into the *Parmenides* in different ways on the part of Clement, Alcinous, Atticus, and Proclus, a tendency, he notes, that goes back to Nicomachus of Gerasa. This is an important project that is part of the unfinished work of the *Parmenides* seminar that needs to be extended to a study of the Stoic categories (as Bechtle has outlined elsewhere) and of Porphyry's *Isagoge* as well as its appropriation by Patristic authors, particularly the Cappadocians.

The question of the date of the *Anonymous Commentary on the Parmenides* has been much debated, with Bechtle arguing for Middle Platonic authorship, Corrigan attributing it to a member of the school of Numenius (perhaps Cronius) and Brisson suggesting at one point that it may have been authored by Numenius himself. On the other side, there are many advocates of the Hadot thesis (that it is by Porphyry), among them Dillon and, for the most part, Brisson. Volume 1 ends on a slightly agnostic note, but one that tends to favor authorship either contemporary with or after Plotinus.

Alain Lernould focuses on the tension implicit in the *Anonymous Commentary* to preserve the One's transcendence and yet to make it an entity that knows and that is not nothing. In particular, he examines fragments 1 (folios I–II), 2 (folios III–IV), and 4 (folios IX–X together with the major contemporary translations). He concludes, against the views of Bechtle, Corrigan, and Turner, that the *Commentary* must be after Plotinus (since, for example, in fragment 1, philosophical prayer, as an ascent of the mind to God conditioning the possibility of scientific discourse about God, is a specific feature of post-Plotinian Platonism). It is instead closer to Damascius than to Proclus, for the author suggests, not that we should rely on our concepts before negating them, but that we should not rely on our concepts at all, no matter how elevated, since these necessarily relate to what is immediately after the One, that is, the Chaldean triad of Father, Power, Intellect—a position closer to that of Damascius.

Volume 1 concludes on a historical knife edge, as Luc Brisson continues what has become his own extended commentary on the *Anonymous Commentary* with an analysis of folios XI–XIV in terms of Numenius's First and Second Gods and the second hypothesis of Plato's *Parmenides*. The anonymous commentator distinguishes two moments in Intellect, the first a state of absolute simplicity in which it seems to be blended with the One itself and the second a state in which it emerges from itself to return to itself fully as Intellect. This is a view that recalls that of Numenius, which Plotinus once appeared to accept (3.9 [13].1.15–18), but later in his treatise against the Gnostics (2.9 [33]) rejects. While Brisson does not take this as evidence for Porphyry's authorship of the commentary, he sees the commentator trying to account for the procession of Intellect from the first One into the second, yet remaining in its cause; he thus aligns himself with Plotinus in the process.

VOLUME 2: PLATO'S *PARMENIDES*: ITS RECEPTION IN NEOPLATONIC, JEWISH, AND CHRISTIAN TEXTS

Volume 2 is divided into two sections: first, *Parmenides* interpretation from Plotinus to Damascius and, second, the hidden influence of the Parmenides in Philo, Origen, Clement, and later Patristic thought.

SECTION 1: *PARMENIDES* INTERPRETATION FROM PLOTINUS TO DAMASCIUS

Matthias Vorwerk opens the volume with an overview of the scholarly state of the question on the origin of the Plotinian One from Dodds (1928) to Charrue (1978). He argues that in the crucial and only text (5.1 [10].8) where Plotinus introduces, as a correction to Parmenides himself, the differentiation of three degrees of unity from Plato's *Parmenides* that corresponds to his own three hypostases, he mentions the *Parmenides* only last in a series of Platonic texts and does not present it as the key text for his three hypostases. In fact, 5.1 [10].8 shows instead that Plotinus developed his system of hypostases or "natures" from a series of other Platonic texts (*Letters* 2.312e and 6.323d; *Timaeus* 35a–b, 41d; *Republic* 509b), showing considerable skill in interpreting them as complementary, that is, by subordinating Demiurge and Paradigm to the Good in tune with most Middle Platonic philosophers. Why, then, was Plotinus reluctant about the *Parmenides*? This is probably because the first three hypotheses cannot be interpreted systematically to correspond exactly with the three hypostases. They are introduced therefore to provide additional support for his interpretation and also because they provide a powerful conceptual source for thinking about the one and the many.

On the basis of Proclus's *Commentary on the Parmenides*, Kevin Corrigan gives an overview of the interpretations of all (whether 8, 9, or 10) of the hypotheses of the second part by Amelius, Porphyry, Iamblichus, Theodorus of Asine, Plutarch of Athens, Syrianus, and Proclus, and then provides a reconstruction of what Plotinus's position might have been despite the absence of direct evidence that Plotinus held an interpretation of any hypothesis beyond the first three. By means of small linguistic hints scattered throughout the *Enneads* and of comparison between Amelius and Porphyry, Corrigan argues that while Plotinus clearly did not care to make any systematic correspondences between hypotheses and their supposed subjects, he probably held an 8–9 hypothesis view, in between the positions of Amelius and Porphyry, but perhaps more complex. That is, like Proclus, he would not have needed to take hypotheses 6–8 or 9 to refer to actual realities, since what appears to be at issue in them are the negative discourses of quantity, matter, and so on. He concludes by pointing out in comparison with Plotinus and Porphyry that Hegel's later treatments of this topic in different works allow for both a metaphysical interpretation and a logical schema of possibility: thus the negative hypotheses constitute vanishing fields of discourse in which self-identity is dissolved. In this respect, Plotinus, Proclus, and Hegel seem to bear comparison.

Luc Brisson next broadens the focus to give us an unusual look at the human circle of Plotinus's intimates and associates, the roots of this circle in Middle Platonism, and its later opposition to Iamblichean theurgy through the figure of Porphyry. The evidence tends to show, he argues, that Longinus and Origen the Platonist (who had studied with Plotinus under Ammonius) defended an ontological or "being" interpretation of the second part of the *Parmenides*. If the Firmus mentioned in the *Life of Isidore* is Castricius Firmus, this means that some in Plotinus's own school were opposed to his new transcendent interpretation of the first hypothesis. In 5.1 [10].8, for instance, Plotinus relies no longer on the *Timaeus* but finds the principles of his exegesis in the *Parmenides*. The six fragments of the *Anonymous Commentary* reflect a similar historical situation, namely, they are in between Numenius (and Neopythagorean inspiration) and Theodore of Asine who reuses the *Commentary*'s doctrines. The author could well be Porphyry or Amelius. But Iamblichus rejects its audacious affirmation of the absolute transcendence of the first One coupled with the immanence of relative things preeminently in the first. In his promotion of theurgy, Iamblichus subsequently elevated the entire hierarchy of gods by one rank and broke the limits of the Parmenides because his ineffable One beyond the One fell outside Plato's hypotheses and therefore outside the text of Plato. Armed with his edition of Plotinus's works in his final years, Porphyry was therefore led to oppose the spirit of Greek rationalism to Iamblichus's break with that spirit.

This is a plausible picture, but is it right? Vorwerk would not agree with its analysis of 5.1 [10].8, and there is much evidence in pre-Plotinian periods for a One that is beyond being in some sense or other, as we have seen.

Tuomas Rasimus provides a groundbreaking alternative view by arguing against Hadot's attribution to Porphyry of 89 fragments of clearly Platonic technical metaphysics found in Victorinus's trinitarian treatises and in the six fragments of the *Anonymous Commentary on the Parmenides* (taking full account of the earlier work of Bechtle, Corrigan, and Turner) and by suggesting instead something that has hitherto been unthinkable, namely, that the authorship of the latter is more likely to have been Sethian Gnostic. Many of the ideas contained in the fragments of the *Anonymous Commentary* are better attested in Sethian texts than in the undisputed Porphyrian material and many of the supposed Porphyrian features (e.g., intelligible triad identified with the highest One; distinction between infinitival and substantive being; juxtaposition of paronyms, etc.) are already found in pre-Plotinian Gnostic sources, that is, in the *Apocryphon of John* and the possibly common, likely Gnostic, source behind *Zostrianos* and Victorinus. Some evidence even suggests that Porphyry cannot be the author of the *Anonymous Commentary on the Parmenides*. Indeed, as Serge Cazelais (2005) has shown, the expression, ὁ ἐπὶ πᾶσιν θεός, which occurs three times in the Commentary and six times in the undisputed Porphyrian evidence—and which Hadot took to be a veritable signature of Porphyry—occurs at least eighty times in the writings of Origen of Alexandria. The Platonizing Sethian treatises show a good doctrinal match with the fragments of the *Commentary*. The *Apocryphon of John* shows similarities with the *Chaldean Oracles* and even betrays signs of the use of Stoic physics in the service of Platonic metaphysics similar to that Hadot has claimed for Porphyry.

At the very least, then, we have to reassess Hadot's theory and the role of the Sethian Gnostics in the development of Neoplatonism, since the evidence shows that it was the Sethian Gnostics rather than Porphyry who were the innovators.

Is such a thesis really defensible? Certainly, the preponderance of evidence supports it. Furthermore, if it is possible for Victorinus or Plotinus to read Gnostic texts and not become Gnostics, then it is even more plausible for a Gnostic of considerable sophistication, and perhaps with intimate knowledge of a school such as that of Plotinus, to write a commentary for a different "Platonic" audience on a work of crucial importance to both groups. If Mozart could write the *Magic Flute*, then a Sethian Gnostic could have written a lemmatic commentary on the *Parmenides*.

So also Volker Drecoll takes up the question of Hadot's attribution of these eighty-nine fragments in Victorinus to Porphry and provides a detailed analysis of Victorinus's use of sources in the *Ad Candidum*, *Adversus Arium* 1B, 3, and 4. He concludes that there is no evidence for a single source and therefore no warrant for supposing that Victorinus at every point must be dependent on Porphyry. Drecoll and Rasimus together therefore indicate the need for a complete rethinking of these issues (and see Edwards below).

But we leave the *Anonymous Commentary* still poised between Hadot's thesis and its revision, a fitting way of representing the state of the question in contemporary scholarship, for Luc Brisson goes on to unpack vestiges of a logical interpretation in folios 7–8 of the *Commentary* that he interprets (within the historical schema of Proclus's *Commentary*) as a training for dialectic by means of a logical exercise that must be seen, in the manner of Aristotle's *Sophistical Refutations*, as an exercise for escaping sophism. From Iamblichus on, this interpretation was opposed by what became in Proclus the dominant interpretation of the *Parmenides* as a treatise on theology. In Brisson's view, to write such a commentary as the *Anonymous Commentary* is impossible without a library, senior philosophers, and a deeper commitment to a theological reading; this is impossible outside a scholarly context similar to that of the school of Plotinus.

The concluding papers of section 1 of vol. 1 concern some of the fascinating developments in later Neoplatonism: in Iamblichus, Syrianus, Damascius, and Simplicius, with the presence of Proclus, of course, everywhere.

John Finamore reconstructs from fragments of Iamblichus in Damascius and Proclus Iamblichus's unique interpretation of the *Parmenides*' third hypothesis as concerning not souls, but superior classes of beings (angels, daemons, and heroes). He interprets this as resulting from Iamblichus's interpretation of elements in the Phaedrus myth and of Diotima-Socrates' representation of daemons as two-way messengers between heaven and earth in the *Symposium*; and he argues that it reflects Iamblichus's peculiar view that there is a class of purified souls that can descend and yet remain unharmed. This interpretation, rejected by the later Neoplatonists, nonetheless allowed Iamblichus both to follow Plato (perhaps disastrously in the view of Porphyry and others, as Brisson argued above in "The Reception of the Parmenides before Proclus") and to create a working doctrine of theurgy in which each class of soul played a different role.

John Dillon explores the startling exegesis of the *Parmenides*' second hypothesis by Syrianus, Proclus's teacher, and his insight that each of the fourteen distinct propositions constituting this hypothesis corresponds to a separate level of entity within the intelligible world: three triads of intelligible gods, three triads of intelligible-intellective gods, an intellectual hebdomad (two triads and a seventh entity, the "membrane"). If we count each triad as a single unit, this results in nine units. Syrianus therefore adds another five: hypercosmic gods; hypercosmic-encosmic gods; encosmic gods; universal souls; superior classes of beings (angels, daemons and heroes, not—like Iamblichus—to be ascribed to the third hypothesis). This gives a total of fourteen to correspond to the fourteen propositions of the second hypothesis. What possible justification could Syrianus have found in the text? In a fascinating analysis, Dillon articulates a plausible justification for the entire structure that reveals a blueprint for the structure of both the intelligible and sensible universes.

Sarah Abel-Rappe then goes on to show how Damascius's treatment of the third hypothesis correlates with the way the Neoplatonists see the soul and its multiple configurations as the foundation of a "way of seeming" that is the ultimate subject of Damascius's *Commentary on the Parmenides*. If soul is the entry to non-being and the last four hypotheses are way-stations on the path to complete unreality, then the entry into the dimensions of soul begins in the third hypothesis. Unlike Iamblichus, for whom the soul's helplessness necessitates divine assistance, the soul is instead a self-mover that is nonetheless capable of altering the quality of its essence and so of its very identity by the focus of its attention and its capacity to experience time in different ways (instant-time and now-time). On the one hand, the individual soul is a modality of intelligible seeing. On the other hand, it is the gateway to Plato's own "way of seeming."

Finally, to conclude section 1 of vol. 2, Gerald Bechtle explores what it means to metaphysicize the Aristotelian categories. If the categories link language and reality and if they imply not only the ten most general classes of being but also the movement from the physical to the metaphysical (a movement unsupported by Aristotle's *Categories* on its own), then their application to divine things is understandable. Moreover, in the tradition of *Categories* exegesis, this application paved the way for their application to properly Christian theological entities (*praedicatio in divinis*), not simply in Boethius but even earlier with the Cappadocians (as Radde-Gallwitz's *Basil of Caesarea, Gregory of Nyssa, and the Transformation of Divine Simplicity* [Oxford: Oxford University Press, forthcoming] also makes clear). What does this metaphysicizing in Simplicius mean? Simplicius chooses to comment on the Categories and not the Parmenides, thereby reversing an entire Platonic tradition. So Bechtle examines the only two passages where Simplicius refers to the Parmenides and shows that while Simplicius himself does not refer the categories to anything other than sensibles as they are signified by words, nonetheless, in relation to his source, probably Iamblichus, he sees the One of the Parmenides, running through the different hypotheses/hypostases, as everywhere expressive of the community and continuity of the categories, whether applying to all of them vertically or only to one horizontally. Simplicius, by means of Iamblichus, therefore, reinvigorates a pre-Plotinian tradition that goes back at least as far as Alcinous.

Section 2: The Hidden Influence of the *Parmenides* in Philo, Origen, and Later Patristic Thought

In the papers of section 2 of vol. 2, on the *Parmenides* in relation to Jewish and Christian thought, we move from Philo and Clement through Origen and the Cappadocians to Pseudo-Dionysius, an examination, as far as we know, never before undertaken in this form.

David Runia points out that Philo never mentions Plato's *Parmenides* and that the *Timaeus* trumps any possible influence from the *Parmenides* we might try to find in Philo. Whittaker and Dillon suppose the influence of the first hypothesis at work in Eudoran, Philonic, Clementine, and Hermetic texts, but it is difficult to confirm this in Philo's well-known negative theology and also in what may appear to be the dialectical categories of the *Parmenides* (e.g., whole-part, limit-unlimited, etc.) in Philo's doctrine of creation. Clement of Alexandria, however, is different, despite the absence of explicit references to the *Parmenides* (except implicitly in Stromateis 5.112.2). In two passages (Stromateis 5.81–82 and 4.156) he uses the dialectical argumentation of the first hypothesis to develop a negative theology of absolute transcendence and of both the first and second hypotheses to develop a positive theology focused on the Son. Thus, the problem of the one and many is given a new theological solution that does not involve a hierarchy of gods.

Mark Edwards, in a groundbreaking work very much in tune with that of Tuomas Rasimus above, examines two topics: the use of a formula ἄρρητος καὶ ἀκατονόμαστος and the provenance of the *Anonymous Commentary* which uses the phrase. In the case of the formula, only Philo and Origen juxtapose the terms, but Christians could make use of privative terms without being driven to the antinomian logic of the *Parmenides*. In the case of the latter, however, if we cannot accept that the Being–Life–Mind triad antedated orthodox Platonism, but must have been an invention of Porphyry somehow intuited from the *Chaldean Oracles* and Plato's *Sophist*, then the *Zostrianos* we possess must be a secondarily doctored text. On the other hand, if reflections on the first and second hypotheses can be found in *Allogenes*, then perhaps such reflection is more Christian than Platonist. Is there any trace of Christianity then in the *Anonymous Commentary*? The formula ἄρρητος καὶ ἀκατονόμαστος found in Origen and Philo appears only in the *Anonymous Commentary* and in no other pagan text—a little like the "god over all" formula that is more characteristic of Origen than of Porphyry. So the author of the Commentary was perhaps a Christian or someone who occupied an intellectual hinterland, unknown to Irenaeus, of free trade between paganism and Christianity. If we cannot accept that a Christian of the second century might comment on Plato, then we should read the puzzling version of a passage from the *Republic* in the Nag Hammadi collection (NHC VI.5) that no one quite knows how to classify.

Edwards's second contribution poses the broader question what "dependence" really means when we uncritically call someone like Origen a "Platonist" and he rejects many facile characterizations or caricatures of what such dependence might mean, making us more aware that apparent similarity of phrase, doctrine, text, or even quotation is no guarantee that we do not actually encounter radical difference. We include this essay in this volume as a necessary corrective to seeing Platonism or even anti-Platonism everywhere or to characterizing thinkers like Philo and Origen as Platonists and then, as is often the case, reducing unique forms of thought to adjectival denominationalisms. Even in cases where we can detect traces of the use of or meditations upon Platonic dialogues such as the *Parmenides* or *Timaeus*, these may be in the service of an entirely different universe of reference.

Jean Reynard then gives us a fascinating tour of the possible presence or significant lack of the *Parmenides* in Gregory of Nyssa and his older brother, Basil of Caesarea. We can suppose direct or indirect influence of the *Parmenides* in Gregory's discussions of participation, virtue, unity of God yet plurality of hypostases, Christology, Gregory's peculiar theory of humanity and individual human beings, negative theology, and view of motion. But we cannot say for certain whether or not this is the case. Basil seems more promising because of his early connection with Eustathius of Cappadocia, a pupil of Iamblichus, and because of his youthful, disputed work *De Spiritu*, which shares strong links with Plotinus. But why is there such complete silence about the *Parmenides*? Reynard argues cogently that this was not because Basil and Gregory did not have the dialogue in their manuals, but because Iamblichus's Neoplatonic interpretation influenced and shaped Neo-Arianism, Aetius and Eunomius in particular, and so Iamblichean Neoplatonism represented a hard-line form of Neoplatonism that had to be rejected.

Kevin Corrigan takes up the same issues in a different key and argues that the shadow of the Neoplatonic hypostases and the hypotheses of the *Parmenides* (as explicitly connected by Plotinus in *Enn.* 5.1 [10].8—a work certainly read by Basil and Gregory of Nyssa) can be seen generally in Basil's *De Spiritu Sancto*, more prominently in Athanasius's *Adv. Ar.* 1.18, and conspicuously in Gregory Nazianzus's *Third Theological Oration*, where we can clearly detect a complex meditation upon the second hypothesis of the *Parmenides* partly through the lens of language from *Resp.* 8.545c–d and the dispute of the one with itself. The Trinity, Gregory argues, cannot be split from itself or become perfect by addition. It is perfect already by virtue of something like the Plotinian principle of synneusis. Thus Athanasius and the Cappadocians are concerned 1) to distance themselves from the Neoplatonic hypostases in the concrete knowledge that they are derived, in part, from Plato's *Parmenides*; 2) to show that the Trinity cannot be conceived as functioning like some second hypothesis either by addition or by being qualitatively or quantitatively cut up into plurality; and, 3) to indicate (especially in the case of Gregory of Nyssa) that while the overall Neoplatonic worldview obviously has to be rejected, there is nonetheless a triadic causal procession of sameness and otherness in Plotinus and Porphyry that results in the hypostases or individual persons, as it were, being substantially included in divine substance rather than being severally distributed into a hierarchy of different substances. Corrigan therefore concludes that the fourth-century Fathers were well aware of the second part of the *Parmenides* and that, in fact, this text was an indispensable backdrop, however indirect, for the formulation of Trinitarian theology in this century.

The strength and persistence of this hidden tradition of *Parmenides* interpretation is taken up by Andrew Radde-Gallwitz in the closing contribution of vol. 2 on Pseudo-Dionysius (or Denys the Areopagite) and the problem of contradiction, a problem also to be found in the Buddhist tradition as Radde-Gallwitz illustrates in his epigraph, a tetralemma from the third century C.E. philosopher Nagarjuna, which seems, like the language of Denys about God, to undermine the laws of non-contradiction and excluded middle. As we have seen in the earlier Patristic tradition, the *Parmenides'* first hypothesis leads to negative, the second to positive, theology. Denys, of course, cannot divide levels of Divinity like the pagan Neoplatonists and so must apply the two hypotheses to one God, but in what sense? To different aspects or moments of God (abiding and procession) to avoid contradiction, that is, a causal interpretation? Or to God in the sense that such language is not subject to either law, that is, a transcendent interpretation? Both solutions have been adopted by modern scholarship, but which is right?

If the causal interpretation is right, does such language name intrinsic properties or not? Proclus says they do not; they only name the relation of other things to God. But Denys appears to hold that they do name intrinsic properties or a diversity unified in God that he illustrates by means of a sun image (*Republic* 7) similar to Socrates' day analogy in the *Parmenides*, which seems a red herring since it explains only the simultaneous participation of many things in Being, not a diversity of unified divine properties. Denys, however, seems to mean that God contains causes that appear merely relative. But how, since he also denies every predicate he affirms of God? Radde-Gallwitz's solution is that the causal interpretation, instead of contradicting the transcendent interpretation, actually implies it. The laws of non-contradiction and excluded middle do not apply in theology. So we have in Denys a kind of ouroboric maneuver by which positive and negative theologies live only by ending in their own destruction.

Conclusion

In conclusion, then, let us briefly sum up some of the major results of these two volumes:

1) The preponderance of evidence overthrows the standard view, proposed originally by Proclus, that there was no metaphysical interpretation of the second part of the *Parmenides* before Origen the Platonist. It is more reasonable to discern such an interpretation going back to Speusippus, Plato's nephew and heir, approximately five hundred years and more before Origen.

2) At some time before the end of the first century C.E., someone in the Platonic-Neopythagorean tradition also came to the conclusion that Plato was presenting in the *Parmenides* a blueprint for the structure of reality. Even if we cannot be certain that Simplicius's account of Porphyry's report of the doctrine of Moderatus on the three ones is not simply Simplicius's interpolation of his own Neoplatonic views, nonetheless, the notion of a one in some sense or other beyond being must be pre-Plotinian since it goes back 1) to Sextus Empiricus's very old, Platonic account of Plato's last lecture, 2) to Speusippus's view of the one as the smallest principle beyond being from which all the dimensions of beings can be deduced, 3) to Alexandrian Platonism, especially Eudorus, and 3) to the Unknowable One of the Sethian treatises—not to mention 4) to Plato's dialogues themselves, including both the letters associated with his name and the early accounts of the unwritten teachings.

3) The evidence suggests that expositions or commentaries on the *Parmenides* were available in the late-second or third centuries, that they were used by the authors of the Sethian treatises, *Zostrianos*, and *Allogenes*, works known to Plotinus and Porphyry, and that they were generally Middle Platonic works.

4) In the case of the Sethian treatises, the Unknowable One, clearly beyond being, is described in negative terms derived from the first hypothesis, from which the Barbelo Aeon emanates as an Intellect in a sequence of phases designated as Existence, Life, and Intellect in a way roughly parallel to the unfolding of the second One from the first One of the *Anonymous Commentary*. In addition, the negative theologies of these texts in relation to the Unknowable One are based upon common sources, probably Middle Platonic epitomes of or commentaries on the *Parmenides*, one of which is shared by *Allogenes* and the *Apocryphon of John*, and another by *Zostrianos* and Marius Victorinus, thus providing incontestable proof of a pre-Plotinian theological interpretation of the *Parmenides*'s first hypothesis and perhaps even an interpretation of the second hypothesis as the emergence of a second from a first One.

5) Analysis of Victorinus's use of sources shows that Victorinus does not use a single source, whether derived from Porphyry, as Pierre Hadot supposes, or from someone else.

6) Contemporary scholarship on the *Anonymous Commentary* remains divided as to its date and authorship, as the reader will see throughout. Luc Brisson argues powerfully and consistently for a Plotinian or post-Plotinian author, Amelius or Porphyry. Gerald Bechtle, Kevin Corrigan, and John Turner have argued (elsewhere) for Middle Platonic authorship. A serious alternative has been proposed for the first time in vol. 2 on the basis of what seems to be the best interpretation of the strongest evidence. Tuomas Rasimus proposes a Sethian Gnostic and Mark Edwards a Christian author (in what almost amounts to the same thing). Before now such views were virtually unthinkable, but, we suggest, this will be a benchmark for future scholarship and the case of note either to reject or to explore further.

7) Indeed, the Being–Life–Mind triad, one of the most characteristically Platonic-Neoplatonic triads in the history of thought, and a triad partly derived from Plato's *Sophist* and the *Chaldean Oracles*, was most probably developed in large measure by Sethian Gnostic thinkers.

8) Despite the undoubted importance of Plotinus, the traditional view of Plotinus as the "father" of Neoplatonism and the "originator" of the doctrine of the three "Ones," should be seriously rethought on the basis that both Gnostics and Platonists seem to be the joint inheritors of a tradition that may well go back to the early Academy.

9) *Parmenides* interpretation and the *Categories* exegetical tradition are in important ways intertwined and Gerald Bechtle has uncovered a tradition of reading Aristotle's categories into the *Parmenides*, in different ways, in Clement, Alcinous, Atticus, and Proclus, a tendency that goes back to Nicomachus of Gerasa and assumes a different nuance later in Simplicius. This interwoven tradition is of major importance for the development of Christian thought.

10) The shadow of *Parmenides* interpretation looms large over the early Christian developments of both negative and positive theologies and plays a crucial, if often unspoken role, in the later need to combat hard-line Iamblichean Neoplatonism, reflected in Neo-Arianism, as well as in the development and formulation of Athanasian-Cappadocian Trinitarian theology, where it proves to be decisive. The *Parmenides* emerges from the shadow with new heuristic clarity in Pseudo-Dionysius's rethinking of cataphatic and apophatic theology.

Finally, we thank all the participants of the seminar, including our hosts in Tübingen in 2007, Volker Drecoll and Luise Abramowski. We are grateful to Alexander Cooper, a doctoral student in Philosophy at Emory University, for his translation of Thomas Szlezák's contribution, to Michael Chase of CNRS-Paris for his translations of the contributions of Luc Brisson, to the editors of *Zeitschrift für Antikes Christentum* and to its publisher Walter de Gruyter for permission to reprint four papers from their edition of the Tübingen conference, and to Billie Jean Collins at SBL Publications for her encouragement and help. The Graduate Institute of the Liberal Arts and the Fox Center for Humanistic Inquiry at Emory University have provided much needed support, as has also the Research Council of the University of Nebraska-Lincoln. We thank them warmly.

John D. Turner and Kevin Corrigan
Lincoln and Atlanta
June 2009

Section 1
Parmenides Interpretation from Plotinus to Damascius

1
PLOTINUS AND THE *PARMENIDES*: PROBLEMS OF INTERPRETATION

Matthias Vorwerk

The second part of Plato's *Parmenides* with its dialectical exercises on the One has received remarkable attention in the history of Platonism.[1] Interestingly, the more-or-less systematic interpretation of the hypotheses seems to have begun only with Plotinus, who understood the hypotheses of the *Parmenides* ontologically and referred the first three of them to the three hypostases of his own metaphysical system, that is, the One (or Good), Intellect, and Soul.[2] While it is undisputed that Plotinus adapted the first three hypotheses and exploited them for the formulation of his version of Platonic metaphysics, it still remains a matter of discussion whether Plotinus depended on the first hypothesis of the *Parmenides* to invent, as it were, the absolutely simple One, transcending being and predication, or whether he merely used it as justification for his metaphysical innovation. I will argue that the answer lies in between: Plotinus was both inspired by the first hypothesis and needed it as evidence for his Platonic orthodoxy. In the following, I will first give a brief survey of the most relevant scholarship on Plotinus's interpretation of the *Parmenides*. Then, I will focus mainly on a close analysis of what could be called Plotinus's "apology," namely, chapter 8 of *Enn.* 6.1 [10]: *On the Three Primary Hypostases*, in which Plotinus explicitly introduces the *Parmenides* in support of his metaphysics.

---

1. Proclus, *In Parm.* 630,37–643,5 Cousin provides a survey of ancient interpretations of the *Parmenides*, however, without giving names; in *Theol. Plat.* 1.10 = 1:42,4–9 Saffrey-Westerink, Plotinus is named as one of the old, i.e., first, interpreters of the *Parmenides*. See Saffrey and Westerink 1968–1997, 1, lxxv–lxxxix; Brisson 1994, 285–91.

2. These three hypotheses of the *Parmenides* are I: 137c3–142a6; II: 142b1–155e2; and III: 155e3–157b4. III is actually a corollary to II, but Plotinus considers it to be a separate hypothesis; see Brisson 1994, 46 with n. 96.

1. The Origin of the Plotinian "One"—*Status Quaestionis*

In his famous article "The *Parmenides* of Plato and the Origin of the Neoplatonic 'One,'" E. R. Dodds argued against attempts popular at the beginning of the twentieth century to ascribe the origin of the Plotinian One to oriental religious influences. Contrary to this line of interpretation, Dodds pointed to the second part of Plato's *Parmenides*, namely the first hypothesis, as the main source for the notion of a One that is beyond being and, hence, incapable of admitting any positive predication. With the help of a list of parallels between the first and second hypotheses of the *Parmenides* and descriptions in the *Enneads* of the One and the One-Being, namely Intellect and the ideas, respectively, he showed that the Plotinian One had Platonic roots.[3] The question, of course, arises whether Plotinus was the first to interpret the second part of the *Parmenides* not merely logically but ontologically, or whether he had predecessors. Against Proclus, who, in a survey of interpretations of the *Parmenides*, names Plotinus as the first representative of the ontological interpretation,[4] Dodds referred to Neopythagorean sources, who had developed already a notion of two Ones, a transcendent One and a One that is opposed to the Indefinite Dyad, or, in the case of Moderatus, perhaps even of three Ones.[5] Ultimately, Dodds proposed, the origin of the Plotinian One should be sought in the metaphysics of Speusippus, which, according to some sources, included a transcendent One.[6]

J. M. Rist, building upon Dodds's observations, argued that Moderatus, not Speusippus, was the first to interpret the *Parmenides* ontologically, since Moderatus speaks of three Ones, which are related to the first three hypotheses of the *Parmenides*, while his predecessors knew only of two (Rist 1962, 389–91, 397). According to Rist, Moderatus did not develop the notion of the transcendent One from the *Parmenides*, since it could already be derived from the Idea of the Good of *Republic* 6 (509b); rather he regarded the first hypothesis as a confirmation of

---

3. Dodds 1928, 132–33. For a similar defense of Plotinus against the charge of mysticism see Gurtler 1992.

4. See n. 1 above.

5. Dodds 1928, 136–39. It is far from certain to what extent the report on Moderatus's three Ones that we find in Simplicius, *In Phys.* 9:230,34–231,24 Diels accurately represents Moderatus's text, since Simplicius is not quoting first hand but from a lost treastise περὶ ὕλης by Porphyry (frg. 236 Smith). Saffrey and Westerink (1968–1997, 2, xxvi–xxxv) have argued convincingly that in Simplicius's report the part that speaks of the three Ones is Porphyrian and that, hence, Dodds falsely believed that Moderatus interpreted the *Parmenides* ontologically; see in particular xxxii–xxxv. However, the question is not settled; see Tornau 2000, 204–5 with n. 26.

6. Dodds, 1928, 40; see also Halfwassen 1993; Dillon 2003, 57.

it and, "in doing so, he incidentally discovered the famous *three* Ones of the Neoplatonic interpretation,"[7] which Plotinus in turn adopted.

After this strong trend to establish Plotinus's dependence on Pythagoreanizing or other Middle Platonic sources, B. D. Jackson proposed to reclaim Plotinus's originality in interpreting the *Parmenides*.[8] Going beyond Dodds, he not only studied verbal allusions to the *Parmenides* in the *Enneads* but also conceptual similarities, and he added to the parallels between the first two hypotheses of the *Parmenides* and the first two hypostases of the *Enneads* also parallels between the third hypothesis and the third hypostasis, Soul. Although he did not insist that Plotinus was the first to interpret the *Parmenides* ontologically, he suggested that Plotinus was original in adopting the notion of the one and the many of the *Parmenides* to develop his ontological hierarchy, and that it was in this respect that he differed from Neopythagoreans and Middle Platonists.[9]

The most extensive analysis of Plotinus's reception of the *Parmenides* has been presented by J.-M. Charrue in his study on Plotinus's reading of Plato.[10] He surveyed carefully references in the *Enneads* to the first three hypotheses of the *Parmenides*, both quotations and allusions, as well as conceptual parallels. Supposing Moderatus as the source of the ontological interpretation, Charrue inferred that Plotinus exploited only the first three hypotheses for his metaphysics, because Moderatus had done so too and had derived three Ones from them (Charrue 1978, 56–58). In spite of the influence of Moderatus, Charrue argues that it was Plotinus's own reading of the *Parmenides* that led to the development of the Plotinian system and that his reading of the *Parmenides* in turn influenced his understanding of other Platonic texts.

According to these interpretations it is clear that

1. the first hypothesis of the *Parmenides* played an important role in particular in the conception of Plotinus's first hypostasis, the absolutely simple One;
2. that Plotinus may not have been the first to interpret the first hypothesis ontologically if, in fact, Moderatus had already developed three Ones from the first three hypotheses.

The question that still remains open is whether Plotinus depended on the first hypothesis to develop the notion of the absolutely simple One or whether he

---

7. Rist 1962, 398–99. Narbonne (2001) argues similarly that the *Republic* was sufficient for Platonists to conceive of a first principle transcending being but that Plotinus provided with his interpretation of the *Parmenides* "a structure that could support all this" (p. 190).

8. Jackson 1967, 315–16. Similarly, Szlezák (1979, 34–36) denies significant influence of Pythagoreans on Plotinus, as Plotinus barely mentions them at all, and points to Iamblichus as the one responsible for the "Pythagoreisierung des Neuplatonismus" (p. 35).

9. Jackson (1967, 327), based on a combination of 5.1 [10].8.25–26 with 4.2 [4].2.52–55: One/ἕν, Intellect/ἓν πολλά, Soul/ἓν καὶ πολλά, form in bodies/πολλὰ καὶ ἕν, bodies/πολλά.

10. Charrue 1978, 43–115 and 264–66 on the *Parmenides*.

merely welcomed the first hypothesis as evidence and justification from Plato himself that he was not introducing a new principle but observing faithfully the Platonic tradition. As representatives of both views the following two statements may suffice.[11] J.-M. Charrue asks with regard to Plotinus's use of negative predication of the One:

> Plotin l'aurait-il imaginée s'il n'en avait trouvé les traits précurseurs dans la première hypothèse du Parménide? (Charrue 1978, 84)

And he concludes at the end of his book:

> C'est la lecture du *Parménide* qui paraît faire faire à Plotin ses principales découvertes et lui fournir les thèmes majeurs de sa philosophie.... L'interprétation plotinienne du *Parménide* marquait donc bien le point de départ d'un système hiérarchisé qui ... et la caractéristique de l'interprétation plotinienne de Plato. (Charrue 1978, 264 and 265)

E. R. Dodds, on the other hand, writes:

> But these Platonic texts are not the true *starting-points* of his philosophy: he does not believe in the One because he has found it in the *Parmenides*; on the contrary, he finds it in the *Parmenides* because he already believes in it. Nor does his exposition normally start from Plato: ... he will cite for confirmation a text from Plato. (Dodds 1960, 2)

Dodds sees Plotinus defending himself against charges of unorthodoxy and compares his practice of quoting Plato to that of seventeenth century philosophers quoting Scripture. He bases his claim in particular on Plotinus's "apology" in 5.1 [10].8, which is the key passage to a proper understanding of Plotinus's interpretation of Plato and his self-conception as a Platonic philosopher.

2. Plotinus's "Apology"

In ch. 8 of *Enn.* 5.1 [10]: *On the Three Primary Hypostases*, Plotinus defends himself against possible allegations of introducing new doctrines, with the help of a doxographical account that starts with Plato. His main intention is to show that already Plato had conceived of three hypostases, if only implicitly:

---

11. For further references see Gatti 1996, 10–37.

Therefore also Plato's divine principles are three: "All things are around the King of all"—for he means the first things—and "the Second is around the secondary things and, and around the tertiary is the Third."[12]

In the text preceding the quote Plotinus had shown that Soul is an image of Intellect (3.7) and Intellect an image of the One (7.1). These three hypostases constitute the realm of divine principles (μέχρι τούτων τὰ θεῖα, 7.49). Now he sets out to identify these same three principles in Plato and refers to a passage from the *Second Letter*, which by modern scholarship is not considered to be authentic.[13] In 312d-e the author of the letter writes about the first principle (περὶ τῆς τοῦ πρώτου φύσεως), but only in the form of a riddle (δι' αἰνιγμῶν). Then follows the passage that Plotinus quotes: "All things are around the King of all and for his sake, and he is the cause of all noble things; the secondary things are around the Second and the tertiary around the Third."[14] The text speaks of three Kings, as it seems, and in particular of a first King, who is described as the final cause of all things (ἐκείνου ἕνεκα πάντα).[15] The term "King" appears in the *Republic* in connection with the Idea of the Good and its offspring, the sun, who are said "to reign the one over the intelligible kind and region, the other over the visible" (βασιλεύειν τὸ μὲν νοητοῦ γένους τε καὶ τόπου, τὸ δ' αὖ ὁρατοῦ, 509d2-3).[16] In this context there are only two kings, not three as in the *Second Letter*, but Plotinus may not have had this passage in mind, since the term "King" had become already a common predicate for the first principle in earlier Platonists.[17] It was Numenius who first conceived of three Gods—if we disregard the dubious case of Moderatus[18]—, but the fragmented state of his works does not allow us to determine with certainty whether he made reference to the Second Letter. This seems to be probable, however, because Numenius calls the first God "exempt

---

12. Καὶ διὰ τοῦτο καὶ τὰ Πλάτωνος τριττὰ τὰ "πάντα περὶ τὸν πάντων βασιλέα"—φησὶ γὰρ πρῶτα—καὶ "δεύτερον περὶ τὰ δεύτερα καὶ περὶ τὰ τρίτα τρίτον," *Enn*. 5.1 [10].8.1-4. All translations are mine.

13. See Brisson 1987b, 81–84, 127–28; also Saffrey and Westerink 1968-1997, 2, xx–xxvi, and Atkinson 1983, 188 with further references.

14. περὶ τὸν πάντων βασιλέα πάντ' ἐστὶ καὶ ἐκείνου ἕνεκα πάντα, καὶ ἐκεῖνο αἴτιον ἁπάντων τῶν καλῶν· δεύτερον δὲ πέρι τὰ δεύτερα, καὶ τρίτον πέρι τὰ τρίτα, 312e1-4. Plotinus quotes it also in 1.8 [51].2.27-32 and alludes to it more frequently; see Atkinson 1983, 188.

15. For the One as final cause in Plotinus see Bussanich 1996, 51–55.

16. Cf. 597e6-8: Τοῦτ' ἄρα ἔσται καὶ ὁ τραγῳδοποιός, εἴπερ μιμητής ἐστι, τρίτος τις ἀπὸ βασιλέως καὶ τῆς ἀληθείας πεφυκώς, καὶ πάντες οἱ ἄλλοι μιμηταί.

17. E.g., Apuleius, *Apol*. 64; Numenius, frg. 12,12–13 des Places. See Dörrie 1970, 217–35 repr. 1976, with O'Brien 1992. For a history of the exegesis of the *Second Letter* in antiquity see Saffrey-Westerink 1968-1997, 2, xx–lix, on Plotinus xliii–xlix. Whether Moderatus had used the *Second Letter*, as Saffrey and Westerink (ibid., xxxii–xxxv) propose, remains a matter of speculation.

18. See above n. 5.

of all works and king" (ἀργὸν ... ἔργων συμπάντων καὶ βασιλέα, fr. 12,13 des Places), which comes close to the description in the *Second Letter* of the King of all as final cause.[19] Since we know that Plotinus read Numenius's works in class and was even accused of plagiarizing him,[20] it may be legitimate to infer that Plotinus was following him in giving the *Second Letter* a prominent place in his "apology," especially as the Plotinian hypostases were prefigured by Numenius's three gods.[21]

Plotinus continues:

> He [sc. Plato] also says that there is "a Father of the Cause"—calling Intellect Cause, for he considers Intellect to be the Demiurge; he [sc. the Demiurge], he says, makes the Soul in that mixing-bowl. Intellect being the Cause, he means by Father the Good, i.e., that which is beyond Intellect and "beyond Being;" but often he calls Being and Intellect "Idea."[22]

The second reference Plotinus provides is a short quotation again from a pseudo-Platonic letter, this time the *Sixth Letter* (323d). In that passage the author mentions "the God and Ruler of all things, of those that are and those that will be, and the Father and Lord of the Ruler and Cause."[23] Plotinus identifies the Cause as Intellect and explains that Intellect corresponds with the Demiurge of Plato's *Timaeus*—not without reason, since the Demiurge is presented as "the best of all causes" and as "intellect."[24] Plotinus refers the causality of the Demiurge to the mixing of the world-soul, which is described in detail in the *Timaeus* (35a1–36b6). However, he introduces subtle distinctions. Since the *Timaeus* speaks of the mixing of the world-soul and later (41d4–7) of the mixing of individual souls in the mixing-bowl, Plotinus infers that three kinds of soul can be distinguished:

---

19. See Saffrey and Westerink 1968–1997, 2, xxxv–xxxvi.
20. Porphyry, *Vita Plot.* 14.12 and 17.1–6.
21. Cf. frg. 15,4–5 des Places: ὁ μὲν οὖν πρῶτος περὶ τὰ νοητά, ὁ δὲ δεύτερος περὶ τὰ νοητὰ καὶ αἰσθητά. There are, of course, two notable differences: Numenius first god is both a being and an intellect; his third god is either the world-soul or the ensouled cosmos, at least not an undescended soul. According to *Vita Plot.* 17.4–6 Amelius wrote a book *On the Dogmatic Differences between Plotinus and Numenius* (Περὶ τῆς κατὰ τὰ δόγματα τοῦ Πλωτίνου πρὸς τὸν Νουμήνιον διαφορᾶς).
22. λέγει δὲ καὶ "τοῦ αἰτίου" εἶναι "πατέρα" αἴτιον μὲν τὸν νοῦν λέγων· δημιουργὸς γὰρ ὁ νοῦς αὐτῷ· τοῦτον δέ φησι τὴν ψυχὴν ποιεῖν ἐν τῷ κρατῆρι ἐκείνῳ. τοῦ αἰτίου δὲ νοῦ ὄντος πατέρα φησὶ τἀγαθὸν καὶ τὸ ἐπέκεινα νοῦ καὶ "ἐπέκεινα οὐσίας." πολλαχοῦ δὲ τὸ ὂν καὶ τὸν νοῦν τὴν ἰδέαν λέγει, 5.1 [10].8.4–9.
23. τὸν τῶν πάντων θεὸν ἡγεμόνα τῶν τε ὄντων καὶ τῶν μελλόντων, τοῦ τε ἡγεμόνος καὶ αἰτίου πατέρα κύριον, 323d2–4.
24. *Tim.* 29a6 (ἄριστος τῶν αἰτίων), 39e7 (νοῦς); cf. the distinction between τὰ διὰ νοῦ δεδημιουργημένα and τὰ δι' ἀνάγκης γιγνόμενα, 47e4–5. For the identification of the Demiurge with the Plotinian Intellect see 5.9 [5].3.26; 5.20 with Vorwerk 2001, 91–94.

one that is in the mixing-bowl, which Plotinus equates with the undescended hypostasis Soul; one that is descended but pure, namely the world-soul; and one that is descended but somehow inferior to the world-soul, so that it descends deeper into matter and animates individual bodies.[25] Hence, with the help of the *Timaeus*, Plotinus extrapolates from the term "Cause," which is more fully characterized in the *Sixth Letter* as "Ruler of all things, of those that are and those that will be," two hypostases, Intellect as the paradigmatic cause of the cosmos and Soul as that by means of which Intellect orders the cosmos. The "Father of the Cause" is then easily identified with the first hypostasis, the Good. The Idea of the Good of the *Republic* is "beyond being" (509b), a phrase that Plotinus quotes, but extends: "beyond Intellect and 'beyond Being'" (ἐπέκεινα νοῦ καὶ "ἐπέκεινα οὐσίας").[26] The passage from the *Republic* provides support only for the generation of the ideas by the Idea of the Good, but it does not mention any Intellect.[27] That is why Plotinus adds that Plato equated Being, Intellect, and Idea. If the Idea of the Good is the cause of all other ideas and the ideas are identical with Intellect, then the Idea of the Good is the cause of Intellect, namely, its Father. Moreover, if the Idea of the Good is beyond Being and Being is identical with Intellect and the ideas, then the Idea of the Good is beyond Intellect and the ideas. There is no obvious passage in Plato that equates Intellect and ideas, but Plotinus interpreted the *Timaeus* in such a way that he located the paradigm of the *Timaeus* within the Demiurgic Intellect.[28] Thus Plotinus deduces from the *Sixth Letter* three hypostases: the Father of the Cause/the Good, the Cause/Intellect, and that which is caused/Soul, perhaps again following Numenius.[29]

Plotinus concludes:

> Consequently, Plato knew that Intellect derives from the Good and Soul from Intellect; and these teachings are not new, and they have not been formulated now but long ago, however not explicitly; my present teachings are merely interpretations of those earlier ones and they prove that these doctrines are old with the help of references to the writings of Plato himself.[30]

---

25. Cf. 4.3 [27].1-8, esp. 7.8-12; 4.8 [6].8; also 5.1 [10].1-2.
26. Cf. 1.6 [1].9.36-39; 6.8 [39].16.34; 1.7 [54].1.19-20, and Whittaker 1969, 91-104.
27. τὸ εἶναί τε καὶ τὴν οὐσίαν ὑπ᾽ ἐκείνου αὐτοῖς προσεῖναι, 509b7-8.
28. See 5.9 [5].8.1-7 with 6.7 [38].8.22-32; 39.28-34 and *Sophist* 248e-249d4; also 5.9 [5].9.1-8 with *Timaeus* 39e7-9 and Vorwerk 2001, 134.
29. Cf. frg. 12,2-3 des Places: τοῦ δημιουργοῦντος δὲ θεοῦ χρὴ εἶναι νομίζεσθαι πατέρα τὸν πρῶτον θεόν, and 13-14: τὸν δημιουργικὸν δὲ θεὸν ἡγεμονεῖν δι᾽ οὐρανοῦ ἰόντα.
30. ὥστε Πλάτωνα εἰδέναι ἐκ μὲν τἀγαθοῦ τὸν νοῦν, ἐκ δὲ τοῦ νοῦ τὴν ψυχήν. καὶ εἶναι τοὺς λόγους τούσδε μὴ καινοὺς μηδὲ νῦν, ἀλλὰ πάλαι μὲν εἰρῆσθαι μὴ ἀναπεπταμένως, τοὺς δὲ νῦν λόγους ἐξηγητὰς ἐκείνων γεγονέναι μαρτυρίοις πιστωσαμένους τὰς δόξας ταύτας παλαιὰς εἶναι τοῖς αὐτοῦ τοῦ Πλάτωνος γράμμασιν, 5.1 [10].8.9-14.

At this point Plotinus has concluded his "apology." He has presented the principal passages in Plato that support his metaphysical system and shown that he is no innovator but merely an interpreter of Plato.[31] One might wonder why it is that he has not introduced the *Parmenides* here if it is so fundamental for the development of the three hypostases? The answer may be that the *Parmenides* was not that fundamental after all, at least not for a justification of the three hypostases. Therefore it is only within the doxography which Plotinus provides in chaps. 8.14–9.32—reaching from Parmenides over Anaxagoras, Heraclitus, Empedocles, Aristotle to Pythagoras and Pherecydes—that he introduces the first three hypotheses of the *Parmenides* as a correction of Parmenides himself:

> Plato's Parmenides speaks more accurately when he distinguishes from each other the First One, which is the One more properly speaking, and a Second, which he calls One-Many, and a Third, the One-and-Many. Thus, he also is in agreement with the three natures.[32]

In the preceding passage (8.14–23) Plotinus criticized Parmenides, particularly for calling being one in spite of its multiplicity. It is with respect to the notion of unity that he considers Plato's Parmenides to be more accurate because of his differentiation of three degrees of unity: the absolutely simple One (ἕν, *Parm.* 137c4–142a7), the One-Many (ἓν πολλά, 144e5), and the One-and-Many (ἓν καὶ πολλά, 155e5). Only then does he add that this distinction corresponds with the three hypostases, the "three natures" (8.23).

The fact that the *Parmenides* is introduced by Plotinus last has been observed already by Saffrey-Westerink, who explain:

> Cela doit signifier qu'il procède du plus connue au moins connu, et que même c'est lui probablement qui introduit le *Parmenide* de Platon, dont il interprète les trois premières hypothèses par les trois hypostases, comme une autorité nouvelle dans cette question des principes premiers.[33]

---

31. Atkinson 1983, 191–92 remarks quite appropriately that Plotinus's exegetical method is reminiscent of allegorical interpretation of myths, in so far as it tries to uncover hidden doctrines.

32. ὁ δὲ παρὰ Πλάτωνι Παρμενίδης ἀκριβέστερον λέγων διαιρεῖ ἀπ' ἀλλήλων τὸ πρῶτον ἕν, ὃ κυριώτερον ἕν, καὶ δεύτερον "ἓν πολλά" λέγων, καὶ τρίτον "ἓν καὶ πολλά." καὶ σύμφωνος οὕτως καὶ αὐτός ἐστι ταῖς φύσεσι ταῖς τρισίν, 5.1 [10].8.23–27. Proclus, *In Parm.* 1240,32–37 Cousin distinguishes similarly between the historical and Plato's Parmenides: καὶ ταύτῃ διέστηκεν ὁ παρὰ Πλάτωνι Παρμενίδης τοῦ ἐν τοῖς ἔπεσιν, ὅτι ὁ μὲν εἰς τὸ ἓν ὂν βλέπει καὶ τοῦτό φησιν εἶναι πάντων αἴτιον, ὁ δὲ εἰς τὸ ἕν, ἀπὸ τοῦ ἑνὸς ὄντος εἰς τὸ μόνως ἓν καὶ πρὸ τοῦ ὄντος ἀναδραμών. He probably has our passage in mind.

33. Saffrey and Westerink 1968–1997, 2, xlv.

Saffrey-Westerink correctly see that Plotinus uses in his "apology" (8.1–8) well known Platonic passages, but I think they misinterpret the function of the *Parmenides* in 8.23–27: it is not introduced primarily as Platonic support for the three hypostases but as a criticism of the historical Parmenides; only then is it recognized as providing further evidence (σύμφωνος οὕτως καὶ αὐτός) for the three hypostases. The division of chapters devised by Ficino should not lead us to misunderstand the structure of the text. The section on Parmenides (8.14–27) is not an addition to the preceding section on Plato (8.1–14) but the opening of the doxography of philosophers other than Plato: Pre-Socratics, Aristotle, Pythagoreans (8.14–9.32). Hence, in 5.1 [10].8 Plotinus does not present the *Parmenides* as the Platonic key-text for the three hypostases or for the absolutely simple One beyond being.[34]

3. Conclusion

Plotinus developed the system of three hypostases not primarily from the *Parmenides* but from other Platonic texts, continuing a tradition that had culminated before him in Numenius. The Platonic passages to which Plotinus refers in 5.1 [10].8.1–9 are *Ep.* 2.312e and 6.323d in combination with *Tim.* 35ab, 41d and *Resp.* 509b. None of these allows Plotinus to say that Plato identified the first principle with the One; however, he infers from them that Plato did assume three principles (*Ep.* 2.312e, and implicitly 6.323d):
1. the Good: πάντων βασιλεύς, *Ep.* 2.312e; αἰτίου πατήρ, *Ep.* 6.323d; τἀγαθόν, *Resp.* 509b.
2. Intellect: δεύτερος, *Ep.* 2.312e; αἴτιον, *Ep.* 6.323d; Demiurge, *Tim.* 35ab, 41d; ἐπέκεινα οὐσίας, *Republic* 509b.
3. Soul: τρίτος, *Ep.* 2.312e; (the product of αἴτιον, *Ep.* 6.323d;) κρατήρ, *Tim.* 41d.

Obviously, Plotinus displays a fair amount of creativity in reconciling these passages, just as some of his Platonist predecessors had done before. He probably was

---

34. See above pp. 24–25 with n. 7. It is interesting to see that in 5.1 [10] there is only one allusion to the *Parmenides* outside ch. 8. In 5.2 Plotinus adapts the verb ἀποστατεῖν, which is used in the second hypothesis, and applies it to the soul: πολὺς οὖν οὗτος ὁ θεὸς ἐπὶ τῇ ψυχῇ·τῇ δὲ ὑπάρχει ἐν τούτοις εἶναι συναφθείσῃ, εἰ μὴ ἀποστατεῖν ἐθέλοι; cf. *Parm.* 144b1–2: ἐπὶ πάντα ἄρα πολλὰ ὄντα ἡ οὐσία νενέμηται καὶ οὐδενὸς ἀποστατεῖ τῶν ὄντων. This may, in fact, be an allusion to the *Parmenides* passage, as in both texts reference is made to the multiplicity of being; however, if Plotinus were consistent in his interpretation of the hypothesis, he should not have used a phrase from the second hypothesis to qualify soul. Moreover, according to Sleeman and Pollet (1980, s.v.), Plotinus uses the verb ἀποστατεῖν quite frequently in a variety of contexts. Therefore the passage is of little significance. What is significant, however, is the fact that Plotinus does not use in 5.1 [10] the terminology of the *Parmenides* to characterize the three hypostases although he refers to the *Parmenides* in 5.1 [10].8 as evidence for them.

not aware of the dubious authorship of the *Letters*; but even so, the philosophical context of the passages he quotes remains mysterious, and intentionally so (*Ep.* 2.312d). In Plato's dialogues, on the other hand, there seems to be a lack of consistency in the description of the first principles: The *Republic* proclaims the idea of the Good as the cause of all other ideas, without explaining in detail the relationship between ideas and intellect or ideas and cosmos; the *Timaeus* illustrates the latter, introducing a divine Demiurge who creates both the cosmos as a copy of an eternal Paradigm and the Soul, but is silent on the first principle itself, the Good. Rather than understanding these puzzling discrepancies as different versions of the same philosophical doctrine, for example, by identifying the idea of the Good with the Demiurge, Plotinus interprets them as complementary, that is, by subordinating Demiurge and Paradigm to the Good. Thus Plotinus accepts the identification of Paradigm and Demiurge current in most Middle Platonic philosophers,[35] but emphasizes the absolute transcendence of the Good beyond being, which is less clearly stated in the *Republic*, but logically necessary in view of the simplicity of the first principle (see 2.9 [33].1.1–16).

It is the inconclusive nature of evidence in prominent Platonic texts concerning the first principle that must have drawn Plotinus's attention—or the attention of those who might have taken a similar approach before him—to the *Parmenides*. There he found in the first hypothesis a description of a One that does not participate in being and could be equated to the Good beyond being described in the *Republic*. Furthermore, he referred the second and the third hypothesis to Intellect and Soul respectively, because he assumed that these hypotheses represented less unified versions of the One, the One-Many (*Parm.* 144e) and the One-and-Many (*Parm.* 155e). Plotinus concludes in 5.1 [10].8.23–27 that Plato's Parmenides agrees with his theory of the three hypostases, but nowhere else; it is only in this one passage that Plotinus explicitly points to the *Parmenides* in support of his system of three hypostases.

The reason for Plotinus's reluctance to present the *Parmenides* more openly as Platonic evidence for the three hypostases is probably the fact that the first three hypotheses cannot be interpreted systematically so as to correspond exactly with the three hypostases. Whereas the first hypothesis fits the nature of the Plotinian One well, because it negates all predicates that may be conferred on it, the second and especially the third pose greater difficulties.[36] Plotinus quotes from the second hypothesis frequently, but neglects the fact that it includes the attribution of time to the second One, which he identifies with Intellect (*Parm.* 151e–155d), and that it makes this One the object not just of knowledge, but also

---

35. For an account of Middle Platonic interpretations of the place of the ideas see Dörrie and Baltes 1999, no. 131 with the commentary pp. 312–36; on Plotinus no. 131.7 with pp. 329–36.

36. See Jackson 1967, 322–27; Charrue 1978, 85–114.

of opinion and sense-perception (155d). All these characteristics are irreconcilable with the Plotinian Intellect. To the third hypothesis Plotinus only refers for the term "One-and-Many," which he clearly links to the Soul in 5.1 [10].8.26, but he disregards all other attributions.[37]

The fact that Plotinus did not fully explore the second and particularly the third hypothesis and that he did not discuss problematic elements in them that contradicted the nature of Intellect and Soul, indicates that he did not intend to interpret the first three hypotheses of the *Parmenides* systematically.[38] Plotinus realized that the first hypothesis provided Platonic evidence that supported his doctrine of the absolutely simple One and allowed him to identify it with the Idea of the Good beyond being. Furthermore, the first and second hypothesis proved to be a fruitful conceptual source regarding the problem of the one and the many, as Jackson and Charrue have shown, and allowed him to explore the nature of the different Ones with the help of a rich set of terminology and phraseology. However, the hypotheses of the *Parmenides* were not suitable to derive the three hypostases from them.

---

37. See Charrue 1978, 104–14, esp. 109, n. 129.
38. Charrue 1978, 260 similarly concludes that Plotinus is eclectic in his interpretation of the hypotheses.

2
PLOTINUS AND THE HYPOTHESES OF THE SECOND PART OF PLATO'S *PARMENIDES*

Kevin Corrigan

1. THE PROBLEM

Plotinus identifies the first three hypotheses of the *Parmenides* with his own three natures or hypostases: the One, Intellect, and Soul (5.1 [10].8). Beyond this identification, however, we have no idea what he might have thought of the *Parmenides* as a whole or of the second part of the *Parmenides*, except for his statement that "Parmenides in Plato speaks more accurately" than Parmenides himself; he distinguishes from one another (διαιρεῖ ἀπ' ἀλλήλων) the first one from the second (ἓν πολλὰ) and the third ones (ἓν καὶ πολλά; see *Parm.* 137c–142a, 144e5, 155e5), and so avoids the problem of Parmenides having posited a unity that turns out to be a multiplicity. There are obvious problems with Plotinus's interpretation: the problem of time, for instance in relation to the second hypothesis. Where does time fit into the timeless picture of Intellect?[1] But some part of an answer may be that the second hypothesis, for Plotinus, represented intellect *latiori sensu* and, therefore, had to include time or, at least, that essential aspect of soul's movement between being and the distension of becoming that constitutes time in, for example, 3.7 [45].11. So maybe the problems are not inseparable.

All of this, however, seems to imply that Plotinus regarded the hypotheses of the *Parmenides* as divisions of reality or, perhaps, as divisions of three natures or hypostases, in the first case, followed by divisions of discourse about other things, entities, or non-entities (for example, bodies and matter), and in the second case, that did not for him possess intelligible hypostasis or *ousia* in the fullest sense. Perhaps too we may suppose that Plotinus was not interested in a systematic

---

1. See Armstrong's classic article (1971, 67–76).

metaphysical interpretation of the *Parmenides* or that he was only interested in lining up his own view of three hypostases with Platonic authority. I doubt the latter very much. But is there any way of finding out what Plotinus might have thought about the other hypotheses? No one, as far as I know, has ever tried to answer this question—or even pose the question seriously, since there appears to be no evidence.[2] And for my part, I don't think we can find anything for sure, but perhaps we can still make a few suggestions, suggestions rendered even more tentative by our ignorance of whether Plotinus held that the second part of the *Parmenides* contained eight or nine hypotheses—or perhaps, for him, only three. Can we say with any certainty that Plotinus believed even in a fourth hypothesis? I want to locate any suggestions, first, within the context of ancient interpretations.

My overall thesis might be summed up as follows: Plotinus, I believe, had an interpretation, however provisional, of the whole of the *Parmenides*, but he was not directly interested, in his own writings at least, either in spelling out every single detail of what would, in any case, have had to have remained provisional or in allocating a determinative rank to every hypothetical representation in the second part of the *Parmenides*. This is not to say that he did not take Plato seriously. He obviously did—however much he was also prepared to leave many details to individual interpretation. What is virtually unthinkable, in my view, is the argument from silence: that a dialogue that either overwhelmed thought or drove it totally crazy, but in either case compelled the reader to *think*, did not provoke *any* so-called metaphysical enquiry about its hypotheses for five hundred years or more. Such a failure would not be the tragic–comic outcome of the complex artistic/philosophic and always absent figure of Plato himself, but its entire contradiction. The survival of Plotinus's writings is one of the most unusual accidents of history, and yet his writings give no interpretation of the second part of the *Parmenides*. Plotinus is thus—at least for the most part—a paradigmatic example of the silence of the previous five hundred years. Yet it is absurd to suppose that he, like so many before and after him, was unaware of the importance of the trajectories of Platonic representative discourse as also of the potentially fatal ambiguities in any represented discourse, however well-intentioned such discourse may be.

2. Proclus: Ancient and Modern Views

Proclus provides a useful context for naming the history of metaphysical interpretations.[3] He gives six major variant interpretations:

---

[2]. For several hints, however, see Saffrey and Westerink's excellent introduction (1968, 1, lxxviii–lxxix).

[3]. See *In Parm.* 1052,31–1064, 17.

(I) Amelius (according to the identification of the scholiast[4]) held that there were eight hypotheses:

1) The One
2) Intellect
3) rational souls
4) irrational souls
5) matter, in so far as there is some suitability attached to it to participate in forms
6) matter, as ordered and as having actually received forms
7) matter, as altogether deprived of forms
8) forms-in-matter (ἐνύλα εἴδη)

(II) Porphyry held that there were nine hypotheses,[5] the first three agreeing with Plotinus:

1) The first God
2) The Intelligible level
3) Soul (all soul, not just the rational)
4) body as ordered in some way
5) body unordered
6) matter ordered
7) matter unordered
8) forms-in-matter (as conceived in their substratum)
9) forms-in-matter (taken by themselves apart from matter)

(III) Iamblichus (on the scholiast's identification)[6] held that there were nine hypostases:

1) The One and all divine henads
2) The Intellectual level
3) Angels, demons, and heroes (not soul)
4) rational souls
5) secondary souls woven onto rational souls
6) forms-in-matter and all seminal reasons (περὶ τῶν ἐνύλων εἰδῶν καὶ πάντων τῶν σπερματικῶν λόγων)
7) matter

---

4. On this see Saffrey and Westerink, 1968, lxxx; Morrow and Dillon 1987, 411.
5. *In Parm.* 1053,37–1054,37.
6. *In Parm.* 1054,37–1055,25.

8) body in the heavens
9) generated, sublunary body

Finally, (IV), (V), and (VI; *In Parm.* 1057,5–1064,17), the Philosopher from Rhodes (Theodorus of Asine, according to Saffrey [1984, 65–76] who held a total of ten hypotheses), Plutarch, and Syrianus (as well as Proclus himself, more or less), who held in different forms, first, five positive hypotheses:

1) The One;
2) Intellect—intelligible henads;
3) soul—the objects of discursive reason (τὰ διανοητά);
4) corporeal forms (περὶ τῶν σωματικῶν εἰδῶν);
5) the receptacle of bodies.

And these were followed by four negative hypotheses "as refutations of false arguments which thus negatively confirm the necessity of an absolute principle like the One" (Bechtle 1999a, 76).

Theodorus therefore pairs positive and negative hypotheses in the order: 2 and 7; 3 and 8; 4 and 9; 5 and 10; in each case, the former positive hypothesis confirms what is deduced, while the negative overturns what has been deduced; for example, in the case of the receptacle, the fifth hypothesis sees the receptacle as harmonized through the existence of the One, while the tenth excludes the receptacle from such harmony through the non-existence of the One.

So in Proclus's presentation we get a range of from eight to ten hypotheses. However, Amelius's eight hypotheses and Theodorus's ten hypotheses seem on the face of things problematic. Alcinous (*Didask.* 6, 10), as we have seen in vol. 1, seems to have thought that Plato introduced Aristotle's ten categories in the *Parmenides*, and the idea of a list of categories—even ten—is not implausible to some modern thinkers.[7] Many modern commentators, like Proclus himself, see only nine hypotheses and this seems to be supported by divisions in the text, as in the following schema:

I. Affirmative
1. *ei hen estin*   137c3
2. *hen ei estin*   142b3
3. *to hen ei estin*   155e4
4. *hen ei estin*   157b5
5. *hen ei estin*   159b2

---

7. Cf. Natorp 1903, 237; Scolnicov 2003, 29, n. 93.

II. Negative
6.	hen ei me estin	160b3
7.	hen ei me estin	163b7
8.	hen ei me estin	164b4
9.	hen ei me estin	165e2–3

Alternatively, other modern interpreters such as Scolnicov (2003, 26–29), find eight hypotheses on the basis of the following schema:

I. Affirmative: if the One is:
1.	consequences for the One in relation to itself	137c
2.	consequences for the One in relation to the others	142b
3.	consequences for the many in relation to the one	157b
4.	consequences for the many in relation to themselves	159b

II. Negative: if the One is not:
5.	consequences for the one in relation to the others	160b
6.	consequences for the one in relation to itself	163b
7.	consequences for the many in relation to the one	164b
8.	consequences for the many in relation to themselves	165c

In this context of significant divergent interpretation, it seems reasonable to try to situate any reconstruction of Plotinus's view against the background of Amelius and Porphyry's interpretations. Plotinus would probably have disagreed with both, yet Porphyry and Plotinus agree at least on the first three hypotheses and there are also some problems with and similarities between Amelius and Porphyry that should perhaps be noted. Let me take up the problems, as advanced by Proclus, first.

3. Proclus and Amelius

According to Proclus, Amelius's arrangement is correct in so far as it makes each hypothesis a principle or *arche* (although Proclus has difficulty in taking the irrational soul to be such an *arche*, which might suggest that Amelius was not thinking in terms of *archai*), but incorrect in so far as it telescopes the hypotheses, makes form posterior to matter, and ranks unordered matter (hypothesis 5) prior to ordered matter (hyp. 6), though Proclus admits that even its critics have at least in part supported this. What then did Amelius omit and why? Was Amelius thinking in terms of *archai* (metaphysical principles) or in terms of starting points in discourse that matched different levels of reality, whether these are "principles" in a technical sense or just "starting points"? And third, why is hypothesis no. 5 attributed to unordered matter? Plainly, Amelius must have omitted hypothesis 9 (165e2–3), either because he regarded it as part of hypothesis 8 or perhaps on the ground that it had no referent, since "the others" can be said to have no existence, neither as one nor as many, in relation only to themselves if the one does not exist. Hypothesis 9 on these terms, therefore, was not a starting point, but a vanishing point for Amelius. And the difference between no. 9 and no. 4 might just have been this: that there *are* irrational souls. Finally, might hypothesis no. 5 have been given priority over actually ordered matter because it was, in Amelius's view, dealing with some kind of *intelligible* or psychic matter? If all this is so, Amelius perhaps omitted no. 9 because it possessed no referent, accepted all eight hypotheses as in some sense providing "starting points," rather than "metaphysical principles," for exploring levels of reality, and considered hypothesis no. 5 to be related to the emergence of intelligible matter. All of which is admittedly highly speculative.

4. Proclus and Porphyry

Let us turn now to Porphyry. According to Proclus's criticism, while in some respects this schema follows a proper order and division, it fails in (at least) three respects: first, it takes the same things twice, hypotheses 4, 5, and 6 (body ordered, unordered, and ordered matter) being insufficiently distinguishable; second, it does not introduce the "principles of things"; "for how can some ordered body be a principle?" (*In Parm.* 1054, 17); third, if hypothesis 9 takes form without matter conceptually, then it cannot be a principle, since principles are not conceptual, but real. There follows a more telling argument: "In general, then, there are many objections clearly to this view, and especially the fact that the ninth hypothesis overturns all possibilities, and allows nothing to exist even conceptually, and argues specifically against this so-called conceptual form (τὸ κατ' ἐπίνοιαν λεγόμενον εἶδος)."

Unlike Amelius, then, Porphyry introduced body immediately after soul, leaving no room for any intelligible or psychic matter, and treated hypotheses 8 and 9 as referring in different ways to enmattered form, whereas Amelius either telescoped these two hypotheses into one or regarded hypothesis 9 as having no referent. Whereas Proclus treats the first five hypotheses as metaphysical principles (One, Intellect, Soul, form, matter) and the last four as negatively confirming the foundation for the first five, Amelius and Porphyry seem to have treated the hypotheses as both principles and starting points for dialectically unfolding or dividing different levels of diminishing reality. Amelius seems to have allowed for intelligible matter in some sense or other (hypothesis 5), whereas Porphyry substituted body in hypotheses 4 and 5, followed by matter and, finally, enmattered forms.

5. Plotinus: Hypotheses 9 and 8

How does Plotinus fit into this picture? Is it possible to uncover what Plotinus might have thought about hypotheses 4-9 from implicit remarks in the *Enneads*? Probably not, but I do believe we can make some likely suggestions about all the hypotheses 4-9. Here I will make only a few suggestions.

Hypothesis 9, first. This hypothesis from *Parmenides* 165e2-3 until the end of the dialogue, argues that if the one does not exist, the others neither are nor are conceived to be either one or many, or again to possess any of the attributes they appeared to possess under the previous hypotheses, including hypothesis no. 8. Plotinus does appear to be thinking of just such a hypothesis in his first, early treatment of matter, in 2.4 [12].13, when he argues that what is distinctive about matter consists in its relation to "the others" (τὰ ἄλλα), in its being "other" than they. He then naturally thinks, in my view, of the second part of the *Parmenides*, and so the sense of τὰ ἄλλα takes on a slightly different meaning:

> Other things (τὰ ἄλλα—the others) are not only other, but each is also something as form, but this (i.e., matter) would appropriately be called only other (μόνον ἄλλο); but perhaps others (ἄλλα) so as not to define it in a unitary way by the term "other" (ἵνα μὴ τῷ «ἄλλο» ἑνικῶς ὁρίσῃς), but to show the indefinite by "others" (ἀλλὰ τῷ «ἄλλα» τὸ ἀόριστον ἐνδείξῃ).

Of course, this is highly compressed and, by no means, a commentary directly on the *Parmenides*, but Plotinus envisages a role of indefinite multiplicity for matter such that matter is "others" in the sense that it is neither one in any sense nor many in any quasi-determinate sense, but only indefinite. Of course, this is not to assume that the one or unity does not exist but only to suppose that where privation of everything, including unity, holds sway, there is only pure indefiniteness. Even if this is not a principle or a starting-point, but the reverse rather, i.e., a vanishing point, it is nonetheless a vanishing point indicated by a trajectory of discourse, definition etc. The *logos* that grasps it is a peculiar compound of definiteness and indefiniteness, a kind of "bastard reasoning". This seems to indicate that hypothesis no. 9 might have been the subject of some level of interpretation in the Plotinian universe, i.e., a level of discourse that is compelled in some curious way to do without the help of intelligible, sensible, and conventional forms of unity.

Hypothesis 8. In the *Parmenides* this hypothesis runs from 164b 4 and seems to deal with the others as others of each other (and not as "others of nothing") in the case where one does not exist. This seems to refer to pure "bulk" (ὄγκος) considered as infinitely divisible: "so all being, which is grasped by any thought, must be broken up into minute fractions (θρύπτεσθαι δὴ οἶμαι κερματιζόμενον ἀνάγκη πᾶν τὸ ὄν, ὃ ἄν τις λάβῃ τῇ διανοίᾳ); for it would always be taken as a mass without one" (165b). Plotinus seems to envisage this notion of bulk as a possibility for infinitely discontinuous magnitudes in 6.9 [9].1.12, where he argues that continuous magnitudes, if the one was not with them, would not exist: "at any rate, if they are cut up they change their being in proportion as they lose their one. And again the bodies of plants and animals, each of which is one, if they escape the one *by being broken up into multiplicity* (εἰ φεύγοι τὸ ἓν εἰς πλῆθος θρυπτόμενα), *lose* the substance they had and are no longer what they were but have become *others* and are those in so far as each is one (τὴν οὐσίαν αὐτῶν, ἣν εἶχεν, ἀπώλεσεν οὐκέτι ὄντα ἃ ἦν, ἄλλα δὲ γενόμενα...)." In other words, Plotinus envisages a nihilating, corruptive state of escaping any unity in which "eaches" actually become "others" and can only be identified paradoxically with those others to the degree that any unity remains. Otherwise, whatever "definition" they might have is in relation to the mass of which they are somehow parts.

This is precisely the description of hypothesis 8 in the *Parmenides*: "eaches are others of one another in multiples, for they cannot be in accordance with a one if one does not exist. But the mass of them is unlimited in number, and even if you take what seems to be the smallest bit it suddenly changes, like something in a dream; that which seemed to be one is seen to be many, and instead of very small it is seen to be very great in comparison to the bits chopped up small out of it *(πρὸς τὰ κερματιζόμενα ἐξ αὐτοῦ)*" (164c–d). Again, a similar notion is clearly envisaged by Plotinus, even as he argues against its reality, that is, by virtue of the reality of the intelligible world, in 6.2 [43].12.10. Do numbers just exist in themselves without soul or real unity? How should we consider them?

> But if they were to enquire how the point partakes of the good, if they are going to assert that it exists by itself (καθ' αὐτὸ), then, if they assert that it is soulless (ἄψυχον), their enquiry is the same as in the case of other things of this kind; but if in others, in the circle for instance, this is the good of the point and its desire to directed to this, and it will strive as far as it can towards the transcendent through this circle. But how can the genera (the kinds of being) be these things? Can they really be each chopped up small (τὰ κερματιζόμενα ἕκαστα)?
>
> No, the one by genus is as a whole in many. (6.2 [43].12)

In other words, are apparently lifeless things (like mathematical entities and soulless or dead bodies, for instance) *really* indefinite, isolated multiplicities and are the genera of being like this too? Even with apparently soulless things, since soul and the intelligible world are not separated from them, this is not the case, Plotinus argues elsewhere in 6.7 [38].11, that is, *from the perspective of the intelligible world*. Nonetheless, from the perspective of the others without the intelligible or the one, if there *could* be such a perspective, things would be "defined" only in terms of each other and so even the "each" would be lost in the infinitely divisible trajectory of such bulk or mass. Therefore, Plotinus envisages here not a genuine perspective as such, but rather a possible trajectory of discourse in the vanishing multiplicities of the sensible world; and in this connection, I propose, he thinks clearly, if implicitly of hypothesis 8 of the *Parmenides*.

5.1 PLOTINUS, AMELIUS, AND PORPHYRY

How could Porphyry and Amelius have thought of hypothesis 8 as relating to forms-in-matter (as conceived in their substratum, for Porphyry) and how could Porphyry have considered hypothesis no. 9 to be again about ἐνύλα εἴδη but now taken in themselves apart from their matter? Possibly because these two hypotheses, even as Plotinus seems to have conceived them, deal with "the others" in relation to themselves; and enmattered forms precisely as enmattered, in the first instance (i.e., hypothesis 8), denote mass in the absence of conspicuous unity. Amelius seems to have rejected any other viewpoint beyond this and, therefore, either to have telescoped 8 and 9 or rejected 9 as a genuine hypothesis at all. Plotinus, however, may be regarded as in between Amelius and Porphyry on this issue, for, on the one hand, he points to "the others" as indefinite multiplicity *empty* of all real content and, on the other hand, his discussion at this level is about material indefiniteness that has fallen through or escaped entirely any positive notions of matter at all. Hence, we might suppose that Porphyry wants to give the hypothesis some real reference and function, viz., ἐνύλα εἴδη, but surely not forms as abstracted from matter, for these would not be ἐνύλα, but ἄϋλα εἴδη. He therefore refers to them as abstracted even from the positive matter that gives any sensible substantiality. Could this have been Porphyry's meaning? If so, he is—like Amelius—rather different but also quite close in a certain way, to what appears to have been the view of Plotinus.

Can we make anything more systematic of Plotinus's allusions—if such they are—to the second part of the *Parmenides*? Probably not, for two reasons. First Plotinus does not discuss hypotheses 4 and following. Second, when he does refer to 160b2, hypothesis 5 (on the 9 hypothesis schema), he seems to refer to it entirely out of context: "the one is all things and none of them" (in 5.2 [11].1.1 and 6.5 [23].1.27). On the other hand, it could also be argued that the closing words of hypothesis 5, relating all things—unities and the others—to the one and yet distinguishing them, might be considered appropriate to the beginning of a treatise like 5.2 [11], which does just that: relate to and yet distinguish all things from the one; or to 6.5 [23].1, which performs a similar task in relation to the spontaneous sense of unity in all souls and in all being.

5.2 HYPOTHESES 4–7

On the other side of the equation, however, Plotinus's implicit view does not appear to be entirely dissimilar to those of Amelius and Porphyry.

1. Unlike Amelius, but like Porphyry, hypothesis 4 most probably relates to body. Since the one that is whole, ὅλον ἓν ἐκ πολλῶν (157c), in Plato, resonates

with Plotinus's view of sensible substance, which is a compound "from many" (unlike *nous* which is not from many, but whole before and in the many) and an imitation of substance, a locus of continuity (as also in the *Parmenides*). Plotinus, it may therefore be supposed, might have held hypothesis 4 to refer to body.

2. Like Amelius, but unlike Porphyry, hypothesis 5 should really reflect Plotinus's view of matter: separate, utterly deprived of unity. For Plotinus, this is matter qua matter, perhaps with an appropriateness for participation, as *Enn.* 3.6 [26] argues in particular, and not unordered body as in Porphyry's apparent interpretation. At the same time, as Proclus points out in relation to the phrase, "that which does not exist," this can refer not only to matter but to the whole sense world and even to non-existence in souls; so too hypothesis 5 could be taken to have a broader reference, but at the same time the phrases Plato uses characterize Plotinus's theory of matter in so far as matter, in its own nature utterly deprived of the one, needs to participate in unity and being. So on this reading, hypothesis 4 refers to body, that is, perhaps organic body as opposed to "more mattered" bodies (a distinction Plotinus draws in 6.3 [44].9), and hypothesis 5 refers to matter as destitute and therefore in need of the One. Of the "separate" nature of matter and form, Plotinus explains in 1.8 [51].14 that this cannot be understood topically.

3. What then of hypotheses 6–9? Amelius sees only three hypotheses: 6) matter as ordered, 7) matter derived, and 8) form-in-matter; Porphyry holds to four: 6) matter ordered, 7) matter unordered, 8) forms in their substratum, and 9) forms-in-matter taken by themselves apart from matter. Proclus complains of Porphyry's view that Porphyry takes everything twice since body ordered and body unordered cannot be distinguished from matter ordered and matter unordered.

I want to suggest that Plotinus's view might well have been somewhat in-between Amelius and Porphyry. I don't think we can have any clear idea what Plotinus thought about hypotheses 6 and 7, since there is no evidence. But if, as we have argued above, hypotheses 8 and 9 appear for Plotinus to have permitted a reference to magnitudes and to ultimate matter respectively in so far as these refer to "the others" as infinitely divisible in relation to themselves (in hypothesis 8) and as neither one nor many, neither same nor different, in the disappearance of discourse altogether (in hypothesis 9), then perhaps hypotheses 6 and 7 also refer to magnitude and matter respectively not as many or as others but as *not one*: i.e., that is, perhaps, to continuous and discontinuous magnitudes to the degree that they do not have a *one*. If this were the case, then Plotinus's view might have been different from those of Porphyry and Amelius, dealing with body to the degree body is deprived of unity and then, ultimately, of matter as completely deprived of unity. One passage that might suggest an interpretation of this sort is the opening chapter of 6.6 [34] on numbers, as well as a stray remark in 6.7 [38].23.11–12 to the effect that evils are later than the nature of the Good "in those things that do not participate [in the Good] καθ' ἕν." Plotinus is thinking of both moral and physical evil in this instance; and he takes up a similar question in relation to magnitudes and the number of the infinite (ἄπειρος ἀριθμός; *Parm.* 144a; cf. 164d) at the beginning of 6.6 [34]: is multiplicity evil *qua* infinite outpouring of itself? And he answers:

> For a thing is multiple when, unable to tend to itself, it pours out and is extended in scattering; and when it is utterly deprived of the one in its outpouring it becomes multiplicity, since there is nothing to write one part of it to another; but if something comes to be which abides in its outpouring, it becomes a magnitude.

Magnitude therefore has a kind of halt in it that gives to it the stability of magnitude, but there is also—related to magnitude?—a kind of infinite deprivation of unity. Is this another perspective of magnitude such as we find with continuous magnitudes in 6.9 [9].1 or the distinction between continuous and discontinuous magnitudes later in the same chapter? In the first instance, Plotinus argues, continuous magnitudes would not exist, if the one was not with them: "at any rate, if they are cut up, in proportion as they lose their one they change their being": and in the second instance, "what has separate parts, like a chorus, is furthest from the one, and what is a continuous body is nearer." No, the position of 6.6 [34] seems to go beyond this. In 6.6 [34].1 Plotinus envisages a more radical distinction still between unified magnitude and magnitude that has no "one:"

> ... when a thing comes to exist in magnitude, if it is by separation of parts, it exists as each and every one of its parts, and they each of them exist, but not the original thing itself (ἀλλ' οὐκ αὐτὸ τὸ ἐξ ἀρχῆς); but if it is going to be itself, all its parts must tend to one; so that it is itself when it is one in some way, not large. So through magnitude and as far as depends on magnitude it loses itself; but as far as it possesses a one, it possesses itself.... (1.14–22)

Here Plotinus clearly envisages a perspective of reality and discourse in which there is magnitude and *the one does not exist* ("but not the original thing itself"). From this perspective of separation, only the individual parts exist as its "identity," but this identity is only a loss of identity, which is really only the existence of the the parts in terms of each other. Again, if hypotheses 6 and 8 are correlatives, this perspective would characterize these two hypotheses: that is, magnitude as not one and the others defined in terms of themselves. And if hypotheses 7 and 9 are also correlative, then perhaps 7 should rather be understood in terms of formless matter as privation (in Plotinus's understanding) and 9 as the total disappearance of both unity and multiplicity.

6. Conclusions

All of the above is speculative. Plotinus did not have an interpretation of all the hypotheses and we don't even know how many hypotheses he thought there were. However, this τολμηρὸς λόγος of mine might suggest that he could have thought there were nine hypotheses and that their referents were in the following order:

1) The One
2) Nous
3) Soul
4) Body
5) Matter with a suitability for form
6) Magnitude as not one
7) Formless matter
8) Magnitudes as individual forms of otherness defined in terms of themselves
9) Notional multiplicity as disappearing discourse susceptible of neither unity nor multiplicity, neither sameness nor difference.

If this interpretation is correct, then perhaps Proclus's refutation of the view (in relation to his treatment of hypothesis 1) that what is denied of the One are the two classes of quantity, the discrete and the continuous, hitherto imputed to unknown Middle Platonic sources, might also reflect at least part of the view of Plotinus (and Porphyry). Proclus rejects this view on the grounds that there are more than two classes of quantitative knowledge and it is not clear *in situ* (*In Parm.* 1083) whether Proclus restricts this view to the first hypothesis or extends it to the whole second part of the *Parmenides*, since he also mentions in the same breath "those who seek to ferret out the ten categories in this passage" (Alcinous—as above—*Didask*. 6.10 (159,43-44 Whittaker-Louis) as well as those who "allege that it is the five genera of being which are being made use of here."[8] Plotinus's apparent view, however, would have been more complex since, like Proclus, he would not have needed to take hypotheses 6–9 to refer to actual entities as such, since what appears to be in question are the negative discourses of quantity and matter, that is, quantity precisely as *not one*, and the passages we have seen in the *Enneads* are ambivalent in this regard.

7. Afterlife

What is perhaps worth pointing out is that Plotinus's and Porphyry's apparent interpretation is very like the one implicitly plotted by Hegel in his impression-

---

8. Dillon 1987, 433 n. 59 suggests Amelius and possibly Plotinus.

istic treatment of skepticism in the Self-consciousness section (Master-Slave: Stoicism, Skepticism, and the Unhappy Consciousness) of the *Phenomenology of Spirit*. Stoicism posits the world as its own unity, while skepticism lets that unity go. Skepticism "*makes* this 'other' which claims to be real, vanish" (sect. 204). The field of Skepticism, for Hegel, in other words is precisely the negative hypotheses of the second part of the Parmenides:

au: what is this a reference to?

> In Skepticism, now, the wholly unessential and non-independent character of this "other" becomes explicit *for consciousness*: the thought becomes the concrete thinking which annihilates the being of the world in all its manifold determinateness, and the negativity of free self-consciousness comes to know itself in the many and varied forms of life as a real negativity (sect. 202)

This nihilating character of free and infinite self-consciousness catches something of Porphyry's hypothesis 9 as well as of Plotinus's treatment of magnitudes as not-one. Skepticism's "polemical bearing towards the manifold independence of things" succeeds in negating "otherness, desire, and work." Why?

> ... because it turns against them as a free self-consciousness that is already complete in itself; more specifically, because it is *thinking*, or is in its own self infinite, and in this infinitude *the independent things in their difference from one another are for it only vanishing magnitudes* (*und hierin die Selfstandigkeiten nach ihrem Unterscheide ihr nur als verschwindende Grossen sind*, p. 160, Werke 3, Suhrkamp). The differences ... are only the abstraction of differences ... (section 202).

Thus, for Hegel, Skepticism becomes "the *absolute dialectic unrest*, this medley of sensuous and intellectual representations whose differences coincide, and whose identity is equally again dissolved ...." This consciousness, instead of being self-identical, is in fact nothing but a "purely casual, confused medley, the dizziness of a perpetually self-engendered disorder" (section 205), that is, as in the above passage from section 202, a vanishing point of non-unified magnitudes into the differences endlessly referring only to themselves until difference is annihilated into the endless movement of restless, non self-dependent thought: " the abstraction of differences". This is precisely, in my view, Plotinus's view of vanishing magnitudes and of Porphyry's ninth hypothesis: the *abstraction* of ἐνύλα εἴδη.

But how can this be reconciled with Hegel's view in the *Lectures on the History of Philosophy* (2:59–62) that the whole of the *Parmenides* was regarded by the Neoplatonists, especially Proclus, and apparently by Hegel himself "as the true revelation of all the mysteries of the divine essence. And it cannot be regarded as anything else, however little this may at first appear, and though Tiedemann (*Platon, Argumenta*, p. 340) speaks of these assertions as merely the wild extravagances of the Neoplatonists" (in Hegel 1955, 2:60). An answer to this question is that Hegel's view allows both for metaphysical interpretation and a logical schema of possibility for further interpretation. On the one hand, he holds the view that this dialogue "really contains the pure Platonic doctrine of Ideas" (2:59), a view that I think is essentially correct, but needs considerable unpacking. On the other hand, "the divine essence" contains many different moments: "the Idea in general as it is either for sensuous consciousness or for thought" (2:60), so what we have is not a "satisfying" negative theology: "as the negation of the negation, expressive of true affirmation" (2:60), but rather an inseparable whole of affirmations and negations, any particular moment of which, if taken separately, can be a cul-de-sac or vanishing-point for thought, especially the negative hypotheses (see 2:57–62, ch. 19). Hegel's view, therefore, as do those of Plotinus, Porphyry, and Amelius, allows for a holistic, metaphysical approach while taking seriously the deconstructive and constructive metaphysical traces in all forms of representational discourse, especially the vanishing fields of discourse and experience which open upon the disappearance, erasure, or simple non-appearance of unity or upon the nihilation of the others either into the others or into the empty "medley" of attempted representations in which the self-identity of consciousness is dissolved and yet its infinite self-engendering freedom is paradoxically, but forever only implicitly affirmed.

3
THE RECEPTION OF THE *PARMENIDES* BEFORE PROCLUS[1]

Luc Brisson

As far as the ontological interpretation of the *Parmenides* is concerned, the commentary by Proclus, only a part of which remains, but whose substance can be reconstituted from Damascius,[2] remains a monument that cannot be neglected. Through the intermediary of Marsilio Ficino, this interpretation was the only one known in Europe, practically until the twentieth century; even today, any reading of the *Parmenides* must take a stance with regard to it. Here, I will attempt to detach myself from this interpretation, and above all to keep my distance from the history of the exegesis of the *Parmenides* which, as part of an appropriative strategy, Proclus recounts at the beginning of the sixth book of his *Commentary* (col. 1051.34–1014.12 = 1051.26–1064.10).[3] My intention is to show that, at the beginning of the first half of the third century C.E., the dominant interpretation of this dialogue was an ontological one. It was then challenged by a different interpretation in which the One no longer plays the primary role, taken up and developed by Plotinus, which was in turn defended and utilized by all Neoplatonists up to Proclus and Damascius. With this goal in view, I will discuss the interpretations of Longinus and Origen the Platonist,[4] both of whom, like Plotinus, attended the School of Ammonius at Alexandria.

---

    1. Translated from the French by Michael Chase and reprinted by permission from *ZAC* 12 (2008), 99–113 (© Walter de Gruyter 2008).
    2. On Damascius, see Hoffmann 1994, 541–593.
    3. The text is analyzed by Saffrey and Westerink in their Introduction to Proclus (1968, 1:lxxix–lxxxix). References to Proclus, *In Parm.* are from Cousin[2] first, then by Steel.
    4. Beatrice (1992, 351–67) has attempted to show that Origen the pagan never existed. According to him, all ancient testimonies refer to Origen the Christian. Origen was master of Plotinus, then directed him to Ammonius; Longinus was both disciple of Origen and his co-disciple under Ammonius. Like the majority of scholars (particularly Goulet [1977, 483–84]), I believe the two Origens have nothing to do with one another. Here I will only be speaking of

1. Longinus

In two passages of his *Commentary* on Plato's *Parmenides*, Damascius cites the interpretation Longinus gave the expression τὰ ἄλλα, which occurs frequently in the second part of Plato's *Parmenides*. It is impossible to know whether Longinus had commented on Plato's *Parmenides*, or whether the opinion reported by Damascius was taken from another work, not necessarily a commentary. This latter hypothesis seems the most likely, for neither Damascius nor Proclus, whom Damascius follows systematically in his own *Commentary on the Parmenides*[5] (although he never stops criticizing him), attributes a *Commentary on the Parmenides* to Longinus. It should be noted, moreover, that no trace of this commentary is found in the *Anonymous Commentary on the Parmenides* attributed by Pierre Hadot to Porphyry, who was Longinus's disciple before becoming the student of Plotinus.[6]

In the first passage, Damascius (*In Parm.* §306, commenting on Plato, *Parm.* 146a9–147b8) seeks to answer the following question: "How can we define what 'the others' are, for this definition will be useful for the current reasoning and for all those who follow?"

> Moreover, "the others" are not simply different from the one; if this were so all the forms would be different from the one, and even from each other,[7] so that in that case the one would also be other than "the others."[8] But their proper meaning is as follows: not, like the different, to be divided with regard to the same, but to signify a kind of substance in an improper sense,[9] as substance in the proper sense[10] is signified by the Beautiful itself, the Good itself, and each of the "things themselves," as we say, which are beings in the proper sense of the

---

Origen the pagan, that is the Platonist. On Origen the Platonist, see my "Prosopographie," in Brisson 1982, 113–14.

5. Introduction to Damascius, *Le traité des premiers principes* (Westerink and Combès 1986–1991). This work is followed by Damascius, *Commentaire du Parménide de Platon* (Westerink and Combès 1997–2003).

6. Porphyry, *Vit. Plot.* 20.91, 21.14.

7. As is the case in the *Sophist*, where all that exists is different from all the rest by virtue of its identity. We find this opposition at every level of realities; in particular, each form is the Same as itself, and Different from all the other forms. The opposition between the One and the others, by contrast, involves two levels of realities. Intelligible form, whatever it is, which is one, is opposed to the other things which participate it and are situated at the level of the sensible.

8. This would make no sense, if we suppose that the One is on the side of the Intelligible, whereas the others are on the side of the sensible.

9. The term ἀκυρότης is a *hapax*.

10. The term κυριότης is found in Proclus (*In Alc.*, 129.5 and 260.10) and in Simplicius (*In cat.*, proemium = 8:9,22 Kalbfleisch).

term.[11] Therefore, just as these things are "themselves," so the things that are homonymous to them,[12] and are resemblances of them,[13] are other, but they are not those very things that are called beings.[14] And this is perhaps the way Longinus,[15] too, used to say that "the others" signify some substance and not difference,[16] < but > it is substance in an improper sense, just as we saw that "itself," when added to the forms, indicates substance in the proper sense. That the "others" must be conceived in this way is clear from the fact that the one is said to be identical to the others, whereas it could not be said to be identical to the different things in accordance with Difference.[17] Again, it is also obvious from the fact that in what follows, the "others" are shown to be identical to each other and to the one.[18] In brief, this is why Parmenides too devoted particular investigations to the "others" in addition to all the hypotheses on the subject of the one. (Damascius, *In Parm.* §452, III, p. 75.1–18)

In the second passage, Damascius (*In Parm.* 452, commenting on *Parmenides* 163b7–164b4), seeks to answer another question: "What is the nature of 'the others,' and why did Parmenides change 'the other things' into 'the different things'?" In the following paragraph, Damascius explains how Longinus, who maintains (see § 306 of *In Parm.*) that the "others" do not signify the "differents," is able to explain the change from "the other things" to "the different things."

Fourth, it was said before, and let us say it again now, that the "others" do not signify the "differents,"[19] nor subsistence in the absolute sense, but a mode of subsistence, as Longinus said.[20] And since the Beautiful-itself is a certain kind of subsistence of the beautiful, that is, the beautiful *qua* archetypal and veritable, then all else that is beautiful is the image of that one, for it is not the Beautiful, but something different similar to it. This is also why the "other," in so far as

---

11. This is the definition of the forms found almost everywhere in the Platonic corpus, especially *Phaedo* 65d4–8; see also 78c6–8.
12. See *Parm.* 133d, where sensible things receive their name from the intelligible forms.
13. See *Parm.* 130a–131a.
14. This is not a horizontal opposition between the Same and the Different, but a vertical opposition between realities in themselves, or the forms, and those that participate in them; that is, particular sensible things.
15. Here begins frg. 39 in Patillon and Brisson 2001. It is very difficult to tell where Longinus's intervention stops. It seems to me that it consists simply in the definition of "the others," not as alterity, but as a reality of a certain type, in the sense that the reality of the forms is not of the same type as that of sensible things.
16. In other words, τὰ ἄλλα cannot be identified with τὰ ἕτερα.
17. According to the principle that a thing can only be different from something different from itself; *Parm.* 146d.
18. For the identity of the other things among themselves, see *Parm.* 147a1–3; for the identity of the other things and the one, see 147b3–6.
19. Damascius is answering his own question; see *supra*.
20. Longinus, frg. 40 Patillon and Brisson 2001.

it has become different as a result of its abasement,[21] possesses, linked to its mode of substance, that difference with regard to which it is named.[22] Hence, it seemed to signify only one relation, like the different. In truth, however, it manifests beings of a certain kind, but along with this being of a certain kind comes also difference; and, since Parmenides has seized upon this difference to carry out his demonstration, he seemed to identify the "others" and the "differents."[23] (*In Parm.*, §452, IV, p. 125.1–14)

By assimilating the "other things" (τὰ ἄλλα) in the second part of Plato's *Parmenides* to sensible things, Longinus expresses a specific conception of the intelligible, whose two characteristic features, in the *Parmenides*, are unity and identity (see Brisson 1994, 37–39). Nevertheless, the "other things" are ontologically different from the intelligible forms in which they participate. Consequently, they can be said to be "different," as long as we specify that they are not on the same level of reality.

We can distribute in two columns the essential points of what, according to Damascius, Longinus says of the "other things" (τὰ ἄλλα), and of what is opposed to them:

in themselves (ταῦτα αὐτά)	imitations (ὁμοιώματα)
appropriate name (ἴδιον ὄνομα)	homonyms (ὁμώνυμα)
genuine reality (οὐσία)	mode of reality (τρόπος τῆς οὐσίας)
subsistence in the absolute (ἁπλῶς ὑπόστασις)	mode of subsistence (τρόπος τῆς ὑποστάσεως)
substance in the proper sense (κύριος)	substance in the improper sense (ἄκυρος)
form (εἶδος)	image (εἰκών)
model (ἀρχέτυπος)	image (εἰκών)

We can thus understand how a form is defined by the application of the characteristic of "identity," and how "... the *other*, in so far as it has become different as a result of its abasement, possesses, linked to its mode of substance, that otherness with regard to which it is said to be other" (*In Parm.* §452, IV, p. 125.7–9)

In other words, whereas an intelligible form is defined by its identity, for instance the Good-in-itself, that which is "other" features an alterity with regard to intelligible form, as a function of its difference with regard to that from which

---

21. The "other" associated with the sensible differs from the One associated with the intelligible, yet this difference is not situated on the same ontological level, but involves two such levels. Hence the allusion to abasement.

22. "Other things" are named after the intelligible form in which they participate; see the comments on homonymy, *supra*.

23. In the *Parmenides* we sometimes find an equivalence between τὰ ἄλλα and τὰ ἕτερα: see *Parm.* 148b2–3, 159c2, 164b6–c1.

it is different. The reasoning is subtle, but impeccable, and it leads to the conclusion that "the others," which designates the sensible, cannot be identified with "the Different," considered as one of the great intelligible genera of the *Sophist*. In this perspective, the form, characterized by unity and identity, represents genuine being, and can therefore be said to be such-and-such in the proper sense of the term; by contrast, sensible things, which are "other" than the intelligible form, are mere images thereof, in so far as they feature a difference with regard to the form in which they participate. They can therefore be said to be "such and such" only in a derivative sense.

How does this inform us about the interpretation of the *Parmenides* upheld by Longinus? That interpretation seems to have been based on the following positions:

1. The second part of the *Parmenides* takes up the hypothesis set forth by Parmenides and defended by Zeno.

2. The hypothesis set forth by Parmenides had to do with being (τὸ ὄν), as in Parmenides' poem; and the defence of Parmenides' thesis dealt with beings (τὰ ὄντα).

3. The being (τὸ ὄν) of which Parmenides spoke in his poem was interpreted, from a Platonic viewpoint, as genuine reality, that is, as the intelligible, implying the notion of form.

4. This genuine reality pertaining to all forms featured two fundamental characteristics: identity, which made each one a reality in itself, and unity,[24] which accounted for its immutability; it remains one and the same even as it is participated by many sensible particulars. All the criticisms Parmenides directs against the notion of participation attack one or the other of these characteristics. An intelligible form cannot be participated by sensible things without losing its identity and/or its unity (Plato, *Parm.* 130d3–133a9, see in particular 131a4–c11).

5. In this perspective, the other things (τὰ ἄλλα) had to be considered as the sensible things that participate in the forms, and which are the images thereof. These sensible things are multiple, and they do not cease changing.

6. The second part of the *Parmenides* thus had to be interpreted as a dialectical exercise having as its object being, that is, reality in itself, or the intelligible.

---

24. In his treatise Πρὸς ἀριθμητικούς (*Math.* 11–20), Sextus Empiricus mentions and then comments upon a passage from the first part of Plato's *Parmenides* (*Parm.* 129b–d). The opposition between intelligible form, considered as a monad—that is, a unity— and sensible things, which are necessarily multiple, appears in the form of the opposition between the One and the Many. This leads straight to paradox, for it is impossible to imagine a participation that would enable both the unity and identity of the monad to be preserved in the multiplicity of sensible things; either the monad, in which all intelligible forms consist, remains one and maintains its identity, in which case it cannot account for the multiplicity of sensible things; or else this monad in which intelligible form consists is indeed within the multiplicity of sensible things, but then it ceases to be one and loses its identity.

7. This genuine being can be considered in so far as it remains one, and in its relation with the sensible things that participate therein, which are the "others."

8. Being (τὸ ὄν) can be construed as the subject of ἐστι, and the first predicate of "one" (ἕν). But this hypothesis can be affirmed or denied. In each case, negative and positive consequences derive therefrom both for being, which is or is not one, and for the others. Hence, we have eight series of deductions.

The difference between this interpretation and mine (see Brisson 1994), which is very close to it, resides in the fact that I construe the subject as being (τὸ ὄν) understood not as the intelligible, but as the world, in so far as I believe it is anachronistic to consider that Parmenides' hypothesis could have to do with genuine being considered as the intelligible. By contrast, Longinus's interpretation agrees very well with the two subtitles of the *Parmenides*: "On the forms," "Logical genre." In addition, it features the considerable advantage of preserving the unity of the dialogue: both parts deal with the forms, and must confront the problem of participation.

2. Origen the Platonist

I would like to compare this interpretation with the position of Origen,[25] whom Longinus met at Ammonius's classes; Longinus followed both Origen and Ammonius's teaching.[26] This implies that Origen was Ammonius's assistant, just as Amelius, it seems, was the assistant of Plotinus.[27] According to Proclus, Origen considered that the notion of a One that is a pure One, rather than a one-that-is, like that associated with the second series of deductions of the *Parmenides*, was a mere empty name.

> Therefore, that the One is the first principle of all, and the first cause,[28] and that all the others are inferior to the One, I think that what precedes has made it utterly clear. For my part, I wonder at all these exegetes of Plato who have indeed conceded the intellective kingdom among beings, but who have not revered the unutterable transcendence of the One and its existence, which is transcendent of the entire universe, and above all Origen, who shared the same education with Plotinus.[29] Indeed, he too stops at the intellect and the very first being,[30] and he dismisses the One, which is beyond all intellect and all being. If this were because it is greater than all knowledge, all definition, and all intuition,[31] we

---

25. Weber 1962, 5, frg. 7. Above all, however, see now Saffrey and Westerink 1974, 2:x–xx as well as Narbonne 1999, 23–51.

26. See Porphyry, *Vit. Plot.* 20.36–37.

27. See Brisson 1987a:793–860.

28. On the One as αἰτία πρώτη or πρωτίστη, see Proclus, *Elem. Theol.* 11,29-34 Dodds.

29. See Porphyry, *Vit. Plot.* 3.10–12, 12.25–35; see also 20.36–38.

30. The typical Middle Platonic position.

31. A reference to Plato, 142a1–8..

would not say that he departs either from agreement with Plato or the nature of things;[32] but if it is on the grounds that the One is entirely non-existent and non-subsistent,[33] and that the intellect is what is best, and that primary being is identical with the primary One, then we cannot agree with him on these matters, and Plato would neither approve of him nor would he count him among his disciples. For such a doctrine is, I believe, very distant from Plato's philosophy, and is replete with Peripatetic innovations.[34] Well, if you wish, in a few words let us fight for Plato's view, not only against this man, but also against all the others who have become the champions of the same doctrine, and let us show that Plato says the very first cause is beyond the intellect and transcends all beings, as Plotinus, Porphyry, and all those who have inherited their philosophical tradition think he says.[35] (*Plat. Theol.* 2.4, p. 31.1–28)

This passage from the *Platonic Theology* is the only place where Proclus explicitly attributes a series of theses on the first principle to Origen. However, the same theses are set forth anonymously in Proclus's *Commentary on the Parmenides*, as we will see below.

Chapter 4 of Book Two of the *Platonic Theology* is explicitly presented as a refutation (ἀπάντησις) of those who refuse to consider the One as the first principle. This position had been mentioned by Plotinus in his treatise *On numbers* (*Enn.* 6.6 [34].11–13), and it comes up at least three times in what remains to us of the *Commentary on Plato's Parmenides* by Proclus. Origen denies the transcendence of the One with regard to the Intellect, and his argument involves three theses: 1) the One is entirely without existence or subsistence; 2) The intellect is the best thing there is; 3) absolute being and the absolute One are identical. These three theses, merely stated in the *Platonic Theology*, are found once again in three passages of the *Commentary on the Parmenides*, in which they are re-situated within their context and justified. The One is bereft of existence and subsistence (*In Parm.* 6.1064.21–1006.16 = 1064.17–1066.12); the One is a mere name (*In Parm.* 7.64.1–16 Cousin); absolute being and the absolute One are identical (*In Parm.* 7.36.8–31 Cousin).

1. This position concerning the One is situated within quite a broad doctrinal context, but it aims at an interpretation of Plato's *Parmenides*. How? In the passage we have just seen, the objection that the One that has the first rank is entirely without existence or subsistence implies that what is under discussion is

---

32. The expression "Plato or the nature of things" means "Plato or the truth." It is used by Iamblichus, following Proclus (*In Tim.* 1:152,28–30 Diehl). Iamblichus is here criticizing Porphyry's doctrine on demons, which could well originate with Origen.

33. This criticism comes straight from Plato's *Parm.* 141d6–142a1.

34. If the preeminence of the One is refused, we fall back on the notion of the Aristotelian Prime Mover.

35. For a review of all these interpretations, see Saffrey and Westerink's "Introduction" (1968, 1:lxxix–lxxxix).

the One spoken of in the first hypothesis, where it is explained that the One does not even participate in being (*Parm.* 141d6–142a1). But this negative interpretation is preceded by a positive interpretation, which holds that the One features an unspeakable transcendence because it is superior to all knowledge, all definition, and all intellectual grasp, which interpretation is also based on a passage from the end of the first hypothesis of the *Parmenides*. In short, the One of Plotinus and Proclus is what is described by the first hypothesis of Plato's *Parmenides*.

2. Origen thus maintained a typical Middle Platonic position. For the Middle Platonists, the dialogue of reference is the *Timaeus*, and reality is structured by three principles: God, the Model, and Matter. God was to be identified with the Good of the *Republic* and the Demiurge of the *Timaeus*. Since this Good is the very first God, nothing can be superior to him; and this supremacy determines the type of relation God maintains with the second principle, the Model. The Middle Platonists envisaged the problem by recalling the passage from the *Timaeus* (29a6–7) where the demiurge is said to "rest his eyes on what always remains identical." From this they derived the belief that, in a way, the intelligible forms were God's "thoughts," although this did not prevent the forms from having an existence in themselves, outside the divine intellect. The Model thus corresponded to the Intelligible, which, as the object of the thought of the first God, or the Intellect, was external and inferior to him.

3. Proclus cannot help remarking that this doctrine has its roots in the most classic theses of Aristotelianism. To decapitate Platonism of its first principle, the One or the Good, is to fall back on the Aristotelian prime mover. To proclaim that the intellect is best, and to say that the One is convertible with being, is to return to the great Aristotelian doctrines.

4. Other Platonists defended such an interpretation of the *Parmenides*. In his *Life of Isidore*, Damascius tells how Proclus's disciple Marinus had abandoned Proclus's theological interpretation in his own commentary. According to Marinus, the dialectical discussion did not deal with the divine henads, but with the intelligible forms. Isidore[36] supposed that Marinus had been influenced by the opinions of Galen[37] and of Firmus,[38] who was Porphyry's co-disciple under Plotinus. These testimonies show that in the circle of Ammonius, and perhaps even

---

36. According to Damascius *Vit. Isid.*, frg. 244 (= Photius, *Epit. Phot.* 275 = 200 Zintzen). For further information on Marinus, see Saffrey and Segonds 2001, ix–xxxix.

37. Galen had composed a treatise in eight books entitled *Synopsis of the Platonic dialogues*, the first book of which was devoted to the *Cratylus*, the *Sophist*, the *Statesman*, the *Parmenides*, and the *Euthydemus* (cf. Goulet 2003, 440–66). The compendium of the *Parmenides* is quoted in the *Fihrist*: for a summary see Tarrant 1993, 58–68.

38. Probably Castricius (surnamed Firmus), the disciple of Plotinus and friend of Porphyry (Porphyry, *Vit. Plot.* 7.24–29). It was to bring him back to the practice of vegetarianism, which Castricius had renounced, that Porphyry wrote the *De abstinentia* (cf. Brisson 2000, 425). In his Modern Greek translation of the *Life of Plotinus*, P. Kalligas wonders whether this Firmus

in that of Plotinus, some Platonists continued to defend the thesis that the *Parmenides* was a dialogue on the forms.

From a historical viewpoint, this information on Origen's position is of the greatest interest. We have here a proof that, like Plotinus, Origen practiced an in-depth analysis of the *Parmenides*, and we have every reason to believe that it was their master who had oriented them towards this Platonic text; moreover, Longinus's marked interest in the *Parmenides* seems to lend support to this supposition. An anecdote narrated in the *Life of Plotinus*[39] implies that Origen may have been closer to his master than Plotinus; this would allow us to suppose that Ammonius defended an ontological interpretation of the second part of the *Parmenides* rather like those of Longinus and Origen. Moreover, if the Firmus mentioned in the *Life of Isidore*[40] is Castricius Firmus, this would mean that within Plotinus's own School, some were opposed to the interpretation that saw a description of the transcendent One in the first hypothesis.

3. Plotinus

Reversing perspectives, we can say that at the beginning of the third century C.E., an interpretation of the *Parmenides* was developed in opposition to the ontological interpretation we find particularly in Longinus and Origen. This new interpretation implied the One beyond being, probably of Neo-Pythagorean inspiration, which relied on a reading of the *Second Letter* attributed to Plato, and on the doctrine of the Pythagorean Moderatus, who lived under the emperor Nero, and whose doctrine of the three "ones" was, according to Simplicius (*In phys.* 1.7 = 225,21–231,33 Diels), mentioned by Porphyry. Nevertheless, I agree with Saffrey-Westerink that in that part of this passage (p. 230,36–231,5) we find not an exposition of Moderatus's doctrine, but an attempt made by Porphyry to harmonize Moderatus's doctrine with his interpretation of the *Parmenides*, which is criticized by Proclus in his *Commentary on the Parmenides* (6:1053.38–1054.37 = 1053.27–1054.30). In summary, a new interpretation of the *Parmenides*, dealing not with being but with the One, became established in the time of Plotinus. It will have undergone its first elaborations in a circle of Neo-Pythagorean Pla-

---

could not be one of the *minusculi tyranni* mentioned by the *Historia Augusta* (Kalligas 1991, in a note to his translation of 7.24).

39. The anecdote in question is comprehensible only in the context in which Ammonius's students had sworn to reveal nothing of the their master's teachings (*Vit. Plot.* 3.29). See Porphyry, *Vit. Plot.* 14.20–25: "When Origen once came to a meeting of the school he (= Plotinus) was filled with embarrassment and wanted to stop lecturing, and when Origen urged him to continue he said. "It damps ones's enthusiasm for speaking when one sees that one's audience know already what one is going to say"; and after talking for a little while he brought the session to an end." (trans. Armstrong).

40. See Damascius, *Vit. Isid.* in Photius.

tonists that must have included some Gnostics, and took its inspiration from Numenius.[41]

In Treatise 10 *On the Three Hypostases That Have the Rank of Principles*, which was written around 260 C.E., Plotinus explains in a few lines (*Enn.* 5.1 [10].8.1–27) the way he himself conceived of his philosophical situation and project. Presenting himself as an exegete of Plato, he claims to be concerned to set forth a Platonic doctrine that the dialogues contain *implicitly*. In contrast to his predecessors, therefore, Plotinus no longer relies only on the *Timaeus*, but finds the principles of his exegesis in the *Parmenides*, as well as the ultimately adequate description of what is, in his view, the cause of all things: the One. With regard to the One, Plotinus follows the *Parmenides* (137c–142a), which develops all the consequences of the hypothesis that the One exists. If we wish to preserve the unity of the One, we cannot attribute anything to it: it is by definition nonpredicable. As soon as we affirm that the One is such-and-such a thing, or that it possesses such-and-such a quality, we add an attribute to it, and "multiply" it. We must therefore reach the disconcerting conclusion that we cannot even say that the One exists, since that would be equivalent to attributing being to it, or the predicate "existence." To speak about it (that is, to say anything other than "One"—but even this is already too much, since we are giving it a name) is always to add something to it. Thus, we must conclude "that of it there is no name or definition. Of it there is neither science nor sensation nor opinion" (142a). The One, then, as Plotinus often repeats, is ineffable simplicity; that of which we can say nothing and to which we can attribute nothing without adulterating it.

Out of what remained, in the Platonic *Parmenides*, a provisional and aporetic hypothesis (soon replaced by another hypothesis concerning the One that exists), Plotinus chose to make the very definition of the principle from which the whole of reality proceeds: despite its ineffable simplicity, the One is the cause of all things. In addition, if one takes an interest in the following Platonic hypotheses, this use of the *Parmenides* allows the naming of two modes of being, or rather, since "being" is one of these two realities, two other realities that possess existence. Three things exist: those three "first" realities corresponding to what Plotinus considers the object of the first three hypotheses of the *Parmenides*, and which exhaust the totality of the real. It is then up to the treatises to say what is covered by each of these three realities which have an existence or "hypostasis," and to understand how they are related to each other.

This is precisely Plotinus's goal in Treatise 10, and he certainly does not confine himself, by way of Platonic sources, to the *Parmenides* alone, but instead makes of this dialogue the new matrix from which it becomes possible to reread

---

41. See the conclusions of Brisson 1999a, 173–88.

the *Timaeus*, and also the *Republic*—that, too, is a re-casting of Middle Platonism. In fact, Plotinus finds his three hypostases in the first three hypotheses of the second part of the *Parmenides*. The One is described in the first hypothesis (*Parm.* 137c4–142a8), the Intellect and the Intelligible in the second (142c1–155e3), and the Soul in the third (155e4–157b5). With Plotinus, the history of Neoplatonism began, which was based on a new reading of the second part of the *Parmenides*, considered as the exposition of a theological doctrine that one tried to place in agreement first with the *Orphic Rhapsodies*, and then with the *Chaldaean Oracles*. The conceptual tools, language, and arguments he uses to achieve this end are not simply those of Plato, any more than they are exclusively Stoic. Plotinus forges his doctrine by drawing upon various scholarly sources, and in his treatise he combines Stoic questions or arguments with an extremely deft mastery of the categories and terminology of Aristotle.

"There are three things," says Plotinus, that are called "principles" and "genuine realities" because they alone have a real existence, or "hypostasis." The first principle is, simply, the One, then follows the Intellect (which is also being and life), and finally the Soul. It is from these three primordial realities that an explanation of all things is possible.

4. The *Anonymous Commentary*: Porphyry, Amelius, Theodore of Asine

In the *Anonymous Commentary on the Parmenides*, which P. Hadot has attributed to Porphyry,[42] the same type of ontological interpretation of the One is criticized from a post-Plotinian viewpoint. Unlike other such interpretations, however, the ontological interpretation criticized in the *Anonymous Commentary* is characterized by its religious dimension and its insistence on the exceptional unity of the first God, who is still assimilated to an intellect on the level of being. The six fragments of this commentary that were able to be reconstituted extend over fourteen columns, corresponding to fourteen folios, all of which corresponds to a commentary on the second part of Plato's *Parmenides*, from 137a–b to 143a. The commentary reveals itself to be a critique, carried out from a Neoplatonic viewpoint, of an interpretation situated within a Middle Platonic context.

In short, if the second one is being, intellect, and life, it is because it participates in the first one, which is associated with the act of being, intelligizing, and living. The triad of being, life, and thought is thus transmitted to the second one by the first, which possesses it in an absolute mode. Such a doctrine, which

---

42. Hadot (1968, vol. 2) and Linguiti (1995) attribute this commentary to Porphyry. Bechtle (1999a) attributes it to a Middle Platonic author.

represents an effort to obtain a subtle synthesis between Middle Platonism and Neoplatonism, has contradictory consequences.

On the one hand, the argument seems to lead to the affirmation of the absolute isolation of the first one. It is without relation to things, and we are nothing with regard to it, and there can only be reciprocal ignorance between mankind and god, considered as the first one. At the same time, however, it makes possible an entire affirmative theology, for all that is relative in what comes in the second can be conceived as existing in the absolute sense in the first. One could then say that prior to the determinate being, there is pure and absolute existence; before knowledge, there is a pure, absolute knowledge. Procession then appears as the movement by which something that exists in the first one in a pure modality determines itself and enters into relation, first with itself, and then with other determinate realities. Thus, intelligence moves from its state of rest and coincidence with the one to a movement of distinction and emergence, then of conversion and return to self, which enables it to enter into relation with itself. Pure thought becomes thought that thinks itself. In brief, the first is a pure act of being, thinking, and living, whereas the second is a determinate power that exhibits the following characteristics: substance, thought, and life. In this perspective, the first one possesses in an eminent mode all that defines the second one, which participates in it. Plotinus does not say this explicitly, yet since the first hypostasis produces the second, it must in any case contain, in one way or another, what is found in the second.

Can parallels be found for such a position? Going back in time, it seems we must refer to Numenius for the following two points, concerning the relations between the two intellects: the first intellect limits itself to thinking, whereas the second, the demiurge, works according to the thoughts of the first. The second one is good, because it participates in the Idea of the Good, with which the first intellect is identical.

Further on in time, if we do not take into consideration the testimony of Marius Victorinus, who, as Pierre Hadot has clearly shown, is quite obviously inspired by the *Anonymous Commentary*, we find in the *Commentary on the Timaeus* by Proclus (Proclus, *In Tim.* 3:274,11–12 Diehl) a highly interesting passage relative to Theodore of Asine,[43] which recapitulates the beginnings of his system as follows:

1. That which comes first is rightly celebrated by him as unspeakable, ineffable, the source of all things and the cause of goodness.
2. After this first one, which is also transcendent of all things, comes the triad which, for Theodore, determines the intelligible plane. He calls it

---

43. Theodore of Asine, see Deuse 1973.

ἕν, and it is made up (a) of the breath which, in some way, belongs to the word ἄρρητον, a breath of which the rough breathing of ἕν is an imitation, and (b) of the vault of the ε itself, taken by itself, without the following consonant, and (c) henceforth, of the letter ν.

3. After this triad comes another one, which delimits the intellective depth, and another which determines the demiurgic depth. One is the fact of being prior to being, the fact of intelligizing prior to the intellect, and the fact of living prior to life.
4. After it comes the demiurgic triad, which has being in the first place, the intellect in the second, and the source of souls in the third.
5. After this triad comes another: the soul in itself.

At the third level, therefore, we find the opposition pointed out by the author of the commentary.

Intellective depth	Intelligible depth
εἶναι πρὸ τοῦ ὄντος	τὸ ὄν
νοεῖν πρὸ τοῦ νοῦ	ὁ νοῦς
ζῆν πρὸ τῆς ζωῆς	πηγὴ τῶν ψυχῶν

The parallelism is striking. Ought we therefore to think that Theodore of Asine is the author of the commentary? It seems not, simply because everything concerning the intellective depth and the demiurgic depth is found at a much lower level than in the commentary. For the commentator, there is nothing prior to the first-ranking one, and above all there is no ineffable, which Iamblichus was the first to hypothesize. Nor do we find the phonetic and mathematical comments on the one, which is situated at the second rank in Theodore of Asine. In this perspective, what is found at the first and the second rank is found here at the third and fourth rank. We should note, moreover, the use of the term βάθος, which was used by the Gnostics.

It follows that the commentator is situated historically between Numenius (who inspired the Gnostics), from whom he takes his inspiration, and Theodore of Asine, who reuses his doctrines, but at a lower level in his system. Porphyry is an excellent candidate, but it could also be someone like Amelius.[44]

Yet this, in my view, is not the most important point. This point resides in the audacious synthesis between the affirmation of the absolute isolation of the first one, which is without relation to things, and the fact that everything that is relative in what comes second may be conceived as existing in the absolute sense in the first. On the one hand, there can only be reciprocal ignorance between

---

44. On Amelius, see Brisson 1987a: 793–860 and Corrigan 1987: 975–93.

mankind and god, considered as the first one, whereas on the other, an entire affirmative theology is possible concerning the second one. We thus find here an attempt at a synthesis between the Middle Platonic and the Neoplatonic interpretation: the former proposed an ontological interpretation of the *Parmenides* while rejecting the one of the first hypothesis into absolute nothingness, in order to begin with the second, while the latter associated the first two hypotheses respectively with the one and with intellect, which is indissociable from the intelligible.

5. IAMBLICHUS

As far as Plato is concerned, Iamblichus[45] defended a radically new position in the interpretation he proposed of the hypotheses of the *Parmenides*, in which the Neoplatonists read the organization of the first principles. In order to ensure a place high up in the hierarchy of the gods for the "superior beings" that play a fundamentally important part in theurgy, he was led to elevate the entire hierarchy of the gods by one rank, and to transcend the limits of the *Parmenides*, since he was obliged to posit an ineffable god, the One, outside the hypotheses of the *Parmenides*.

The interpretation of the second part of the *Parmenides*, which, on this interpretation, contains nine hypotheses, gives the following interpretation of the first three hypostases:

[the ineffable god]
first hypothesis: god and the gods
second hypothesis: the intellectives and the intelligibles
third hypothesis: the "superior beings"

According to that interpretation the human souls, associated with the fourth hypothesis, are dependent on the superior beings. In so far as philosophy comes to the gods through the superior beings, it is impossible to grasp it otherwise than by their intervention, and no human effort gives access to it, even progressively; so philosophy is placed on the same level as poetry, divination and initiation.

Thus, at least in the view of Proclus, Iamblichus rendered himself guilty of adopting two non-Platonic positions, for he did not the consider the *Parmenides* to contain all Plato's theology, and because he offered an interpretation of the hypotheses of the second part of that dialogue that could not be reconciled with the Platonic text. To refute Iamblichus's position, Porphyry had recourse to Plotinus. By producing a new edition of Plotinus's work, organized according to the

---

45. On Iamblichus, see Dillon 1973.

Plotinian and Porphyrian interpretation of the hypotheses of the *Parmenides*, Porphyry, at the very end of his life, tried to oppose the authority of the man who was his master at Rome to Iamblichus's system—that is, to theurgy. In so doing, he remained faithful to Greek rationalism, as represented in particular by Plotinus.

Translated by Michael Chase, CNRS, Paris (Villejuif)

4
Is Porphyry the Source Used by Marius Victorinus?

Volker Henning Drecoll

The questions raised by this paper have an impact on two main issues. The first concerns the knowledge of the philosophy of Porphyry. If Marius Victorinus extensively used Porphyry as a source, we would expect to find important pieces of otherwise unknown works of Porphyry hidden in the text of Victorinus, pieces that would be very important for the ontological thought of this philosopher.[1]

The second issue consists in the understanding of the most speculative trinitarian theology of Early Latin Christianity.[2] Thus, Victorinus, in using Porphyry, could be perhaps a very important "catalyst" by way of introducing a certain Neoplatonic profile—a Porphyrian one—into the history of Christian thought. Even if his successors, especially Ambrose and Augustine, did not accept Victorinus's theological solutions in detail (see Hadot 1962, 409–42), their own attention to Porphyry could have been provoked by Victorinus.

For these two issues, Pierre Hadot's book, *Porphyre et Victorinus*, is the cornerstone of every analysis (see Hadot 1968). The book was written more than forty years ago, so of course, everything that can be said today constitute only footnotes to the work of this great scholar. Indeed, it is very impressive to see Hadot at work in 1968. At that time he already recognized, for example, that the passages at the beginning of *Adv. Ar.* 1.49–50 are drawn from an external source, even if he didn't know the parallel passage in the Nag Hammadi treatise *Zostrianos* as we do today.[3] Even without knowledge of the parallel passages

---

1. For the earlier research on Porphyry, see the survey by Smith 1987. For the more recent research, see Saffrey 2000.

2. On Victorinus, see Madec 1989, 342–55; Drecoll in press. The earlier research is summed up in the groundbreaking work of Hadot (1971). Quite problematic is the systematization of Victorinus's thought by Baltes (2002), which lacks a detailed analysis of the sources of Victorinus's works.

3. See for this Tardieu 1996; Barry, Funk, Poirier, and Turner 2000.

in *Zostrianos*, NHC VIII.1, he identified certain passages that made extensive use of a Greek source. However, since we now know the parallels between *Adv. Ar.* 1.49–50 and *Zostrianos*, Hadot's identification of the source of these passages as Porphyry can no longer be maintained, even if we still have no certain result on the nature of the source that Victorinus used. In my opinion, we have four hypotheses:[4] a) Victorinus and *Zostrianos* used a common Greek, perhaps Middle Platonic source (Tardieu and followers); b) Victorinus used Christian material whose Gnostic character he did not recognize as such because in Rome such Gnostics were highly assimilated members of Christian circles (Abramowski 2005); and c) Victorinus perhaps used actual texts known in the school of Plotinus, perhaps even the Greek original of the *Zostrianos* directly; or d) a Neoplatonic text that was itself dependent on *Zostrianos* (these possibilities I would like to maintain in discussion). Anyway, it is clear that these passages of *Adversus Arium* that Hadot ascribed to Porphyry are not Porphyrian, but date back to another, perhaps even pre-Plotinian source. This also raises the question of the origin and provenance of the other passages recognized as Porphyrian by Hadot.

1. The Work of Hadot

First, Hadot summarizes what he calls the "plan des traités," distinguishing between the "theological" and the "philosophical parts." The latter have no explicit reference to the Christian Trinity or the trinitarian persons, but are generally Neoplatonic and philosophical in their contents (see Hadot 1968, 1:45–67, esp. 50–63). Hadot identifies three groups of texts "mal integrés":[5]

> Group 1: passages about the 4 levels of being and non-being in *Ad Candidum*.
>
> Group 2: several passages from *Adversus Arium* IA and (more often) IB (here, passages parallel to *Zostrianos* are included) and some passages from *Adversus Arium* III.
>
> Group 3: passages about the unity and difference between life and living in *Adversus Arium* IV (see Hadot 1968 1:68–74).

After delineating these passages, as a second step, Hadot states that all three groups belong to a single source. Even if he claims close doctrinal, lexicographi-

---

4. For the details and bibliography see Drecoll, "The Greek Text behind the Parallel Sections in *Zostrianos* and Marius Victorinus" in vol. 1:195–212 of the present work.

5. See Hadot 1968, 1:65–67, with 5 criteria: 1. „contenu seulement philosophique", 2. Neoplatonic character, 3. „mal intégrée", 4. „cohérence interne", 5. „beaucoup … de mots grecs philosophiques" (ibid. 67).

cal, and stylistic relations between these three groups, he mentions only three doctrinal points common to them,[6] as follows:

1. The hierarchy of being described in group 1 is the same in the other two groups. The highest level is the One, who is God, pure Being, then follows Intellect or the second One, then the Soul, and finally the material realm.
2. As the second One, the Intellect constitutes itself by autogeneration, going from inside to outside, as the actualization of a pure potentiality.
3. Being, Life, and Intelligence are the "structure conceptuelle fondamentale" of all three groups. Life and Intelligence are the active dyad opposed to the first principle, the One or pure being.

In the second chapter of his book, Hadot sketches the history of Platonism after Plotinus. His result: the reception of Plotinus in the West is quite often linked to Porphyry, while the reception of Plotinus in the East is mostly linked to Iamblichus. Therefore it is very probable, in his view, that in the West Porphyry would be a significant Neoplatonic source (see Hadot 1968, 1:86), which leads him to attribute the *Anonymous Commentary on the Parmenides*[7] to Porphyry.

In a first step, he lays out his arguments in favor of the attribution of the *Anonymous Commentary on the Parmenides* to Porphyry (see Hadot 1968, 1:107–13):

1. The *Commentary* is Porphyrian because it uses the *Chaldaean Oracles* not only for the ontology of the highest principles, but also in a manner that is similar to other works of Porphyry, which convey a certain diffidence toward the *Oracles*.
2. The *Commentary* uses the Stoic distinction between σύγχυσις and παράθεσις, as Porphyry does.
3. In the *Commentary*, the relation between soul and material world is opposed to the relation of the soul to the intelligible world: the more the soul approaches the intelligible world, the less she is linked to the material world. And this notion seems to be specifically Porphyrian in Hadot's view.
4. The *Commentary* presupposes a distinction between infinitival "To Be" and substantive "Being" (see Hadot 1968, 1:141), parallel to the distinction between the first One and the Intellect or Second One. This, in the opinion of Hadot, is Porphyrian, because Porphyry identifies the One

---

6. See Hadot 1968, 1:74–75. This very important point of his analysis consist only of two pages.

7. For the *editio princeps* see Kroll 1892, 599–627. The *Anonymous Commentary* is newly edited by Linguiti (1995, 63–202).

with the Father of the *Chaldaean Oracles* who has also the title Ὕπαρξις.[8] This leads to two further points: a) the first element of the intelligible triad is identified with the highest One (see Hadot 1968, 1:97–141); b) the Second One, the Intellect, is a kind of actualization of the pure "To Be" of the first One, so that one can even speak of two Intelligences, the first being pure, stable existence, while the second is the Intellect's activity of thinking, proceeding outwards and returning to itself.

5. In general, the *Commentary* presupposes the teaching of Plotinus, but at the same time it is very close to Middle Platonic doctrines, which fits very well the profile of Porphyrian Neoplatonism.

In Hadot's eyes, it is not absolutely clear whether Victorinus knew or used the *Anonymous Commentary on Parmenides*,[9] but he finds in Victorinus several points that are "typiquement porphyriennes." The three most important "Porphyrian" points in Victorinus that are shared with the *Anonymous Commentary* are:

1. There is an "intelligible triad" that is identified with the highest One, in which the infinitival "To Be" constitutes a first hypostasis (see Hadot 1968, 1:97–98.141).
2. There is a clear distinction between "Being" and "To Be" (Hadot 1968, 1:141).
3. There are two intelligences, of which the second is the actualization of the first (Hadot 1968, 1:141–42).

The seminar whose work is included in the present volumes has dealt with the reception of Plato's *Parmenides* in Late Antiquity, also taking into account Gnostic sources. The results of this seminar raise serious doubts about whether the observations of Hadot summarized above indeed point to Porphyry. With regard to the three elements mentioned above:

1. The notion that the first One, a pure and potential One, can be identified with the first element of the intelligible triad can be found even in *Zostrianos*, which also testifies to an identification of the Invisible Spirit/highest One with the intelligible Triad (called the Triple Power),

---

8. It should be kept in mind that in the fragments of the *Oracula Chaldaica* the term ὕπαρξις does not occur; cf. only the verb in frg. 84,3 according to Majercik 1989, 8, 82. Hadot 1968 1:96.112 refers to Damascius, *Dub. et sol.* 43–44, but without regarding possible interpretations or developments of later Neoplatonism.

9. This is often neglected in the reception of Hadot's work, but the result of his comparison is: "Ces coincidences ne nous permettent pas pourtant d'affirmer que Victorinus ait lu le commentaire de Porphyre Sur le Parménide" (Hadot 1968, 1:143); so Hadot takes into consideration that Victorinus could have found the main ideas in other works of Porphyry. The *Anonymous Commentary* is just the "missing link" to fulfill the lacunae of the tradition of Porphyry's work.

although in other places this Triad seems to exercise a second, intermediary function between the two highest principles.[10]
2. The distinction between infinitival "To Be" (εἶναι) and substantive Being (τὸ ὄν or τὰ ὄντα), as well as the classic juxtaposition of paronyms can be found also in *Allogenes* (XI.61.32–39; see Turner 2000a, 90–92; 2004, 67–72). Bechtle has remarked that there are also some passages in Plotinus that are very close to these thoughts, so this distinction need not be regarded as specifically Porphyrian (see Bechtle 1999a, 252–54).
3. The notion that the second One, Intellect, is constituted by a process of externalization and actualization of a hidden potentiality linked to the first One, can also be found in *Allogenes* as well as in *Zostrianos* (see Turner 2000a, 91).

So the points stressed by Hadot should be considered rather as evidence of a certain intellectual background for Victorinus rather than as compelling arguments for Victorinus's use of a Porphyrian source. We cannot even exclude the possibility that the Anonymous *Commentary* is earlier than the treatises of Plotinus.

In this paper, I will not attempt to deal with the authorship of the Anonymous *Commentary on the Parmenides*, or to mention all comparable parallels to *Adversus Arium* that can be found in the authentic fragments of Porphyry, comparing them with similar expressions from Plotinus and others. What I want to do instead, is to ask to what extent we can determine that the material Victorinus used belongs to a single author. If this is not true, the hypothesis of "Victorinus using Porphyry" collapses. This is why, in a second part, I would like to examine briefly the material described as "mal intégré" by Hadot, seeking for Victorinus's exact method of utilizing his sources.

2. Marius Victorinus's Use of Sources

Generally, Hadot is right in identifying some passages where Victorinus makes intensive use of sources in *Ad Candidum*, *Adversus Arium* 1B and 3, as well as in large sections of *Adversus Arium* 4. In spite of this, the analysis of the detailed argumentation seems to suggest a different picture of Victorinus's use of sources than Hadot has proposed.

A) *Ad Candidum*

The beginning of *Ad Candidum* directly addresses Candidus (*Cand.* 1.4: *o generose Candide*). There follows an introductory chapter that in Hadot's eyes is

---

10. See Turner 2000a, 88–90. Perhaps it is even noteworthy to observe the different position the Triple Powered One has in the Sethian texts, for this see Turner 2000a, 81–94; Turner 2004, 56–72.

Neoplatonic. And indeed, there are some words that seem to be Neoplatonic, for example, νοῦς πατρικὸς (with the *varia lectio*: *sensus paternus*, cf. the critical apparatus to *Cand.* 1.6), but if we carefully observe the first lines of the ch. as a whole, it actually constitutes a harmonized mixture of biblical and Neoplatonic expressions rather than a direct use of a strictly Neoplatonic source. Of course Victorinus presupposes *Timaeus* 28c when he writes: *difficile intellegere, edicere autem impossibile*, but he immediately continues by quoting Paul, Rom 11:33 (*Cand.* 1.11–14). So perhaps we should be careful in determining each non-biblical wording as an indication of a pagan source. For the second half of ch. 1, ch. 2, and the beginning of ch. 3, the wording is quite biblical, so we have no pagan source here. Of course even in ch. 2 there can be found philosophical terminology, stating that God is *supra omnia*, above All, beings and non-beings alike (*Cand.* 2.19–20). These sentences stem from a source, and indeed Hadot thought so (see 1968, 2:13), but here again, if we follow the argumentation, it seems more probable to me that Victorinus summarized some essential thoughts from a source he used later on in chs. 7–10 than that he was directly quoting (or perhaps translating) a source. This is confirmed by the fact that only five lines later one finds a distinction between *deus*, on the one hand and *Iesus* as *filius* and λόγος (referring clearly to John 1:1), on the other hand.[11] The main point raised at the beginning of the discussion is the question whether anything in God could belong to non-being. This is very clear from the beginning of ch. 3, where Victorinus says: "I would like to hear, dear Candidus, what, in your opinion, is non-being" (*Cand.* 3.1–2). The first answer recorded by Victorinus explains that God is the *causa* for all being, and as such, he cannot be the same thing as that of which it is the cause. This leads him to a general explanation of the modes of non-being. And here, indeed, I think Hadot rightly assumes a source used by Victorinus, although it rather resembles a kind of excerpt.[12] In ch. 4, Victorinus picks up a fourfold explanation of non-being (privation, difference by nature, not-yet-being, and being-beyond-all-being). Even here it is hard to determine whether or not the application *Appellabimus utique omnino* ὄν, *quoniam eorum quae sunt pater est* is inserted in the quotation of a source. The full application in chs. 5 and 6 beginning with *verum est igitur* seems to me to be Victorinus's own explanation of why he is using the source's theory of four kinds of non-being. In my view this is clear by the fact that he repeats these four kinds, explaining in each case what this would mean for God as *generator* (*Cand.* 6.2).[13]

---

11. Hadot 1968, 2:20 included these lines in brackets to group 1 of Porphyrian texts.

12. See Hadot 1960, 700: "exposé scolaire," and pp. 700–701 for notes on the background of the four kinds of non-Being.

13. Ibid., 702: Victorinus appends ch. 6 to an "exposé," including chs. 6–11. This could also be the case for *Cand.* 6.5–13, but perhaps the *audi* in *Cand.* 7.1 indicates the citation of a source, so previous lines would be Victorinus's summary.

The beginning of ch. 7, however, starts again with a new explanation. *Audi quemadmodum dico* (*Cand.* 7.1) marks clearly the beginning of a new unit. Then there follows for nearly seven pages of the CSEL-edition a fully abstract dissertation on the levels of being, ending with the words: *De his quae non sunt, nunc sic habeto* (*Cand.* 10.36) Within this section, there is a clear tripartition: chs. 7–8 concern the two highest levels of being; a single sentence then summarizes this and opens the following section (*Cand.* 8.19–21); ch. 9, then deals with the two levels of non-being; and finally it is explained in which sense the soul has existence in spite of her mutability (ch. 10). This whole section is a very clear unit, not depending on the main questions of *Ad Candidum*. If we had only these pages from Victorinus we would not recognize them as Christian discourse. There is no hint of Jesus or the Trinity or anything comparable to chs. 1 or 4. Moreover, these four levels of being or non-being are not linked to the four modes of non-being, explained in ch. 3, so there is no clear evidence for the assumption that both sources must belong to the same author.

Therefore I think we should differentiate between those chapters where Victorinus uses only single words and terms of Platonic origin, inserted in his mind and thinking, and those passages where a direct use of sources is very probable on the grounds of the text's internal argumentation as confirmed by linguistic hints. This leads me to the suggestion that even the following chs. 11–14[14] are also the Victorinus's own interpretation, utilizing and seeking to apply the doctrine of the source used by him in chs. 7–10. For the second half of the work, there is no question of pagan sources, due to the obvious preponderance of biblical material and the Christian nature of the terminology and the problems discussed.[15]

B) SOURCES IN *ADVERSUS ARIUM* 1B AND 3

Various texts from different books and contexts are assembled as group 2 by Hadot. They are the following:
1. An excursus about the soul in *Adv. Ar.* 1.32.
2. The text parallel to *Zostrianos*, dealing with a negative theology of the highest principle.
3. The continuation of this passage in *Adv. Ar.* 1B, namely chs. 51–52, 56–57, 60–64.
4. A short section from *Adv. Ar.* 3.2, about the connection between life and motion; a section from *Adv. Ar.* 3.4 about the connection between

---

14. It is unclear to me whether ch. 11, the explanation of the *conversio* (see Hadot 1960, 712) belongs to the source used in ch. 7–10 or is a consequence drawn by Victorinus according to the technique of inference used by philosophical schools.

15. This is in my opinion also the case for ch. 15, where the Christian terminology is quite strong (thus Hadot 1968, 2:19–20 included it with brackets).

life and thinking; and from *Adv. Ar.* 3. a comparison of the triad being, living, thinking with the elements of vision.

Beside these texts, Hadot mentions various minor texts, for example a short definition of *substantia* as distinct from *exsistentia* (*Adv. Ar.* 1.30.18–32). I leave aside the texts that Hadot enclosed in brackets to signify that Victorinus reformulated his source and thus, even according to Hadot, Victorinus is the actual (although not independent) author of these texts.

I begin by examining the continuation of the passage in *Adv. Ar.* 1.49–50 that parallels *Zostrianos*. Since its detection, no one has ever claimed that the source of this parallel to *Zostrianos* could be Porphyry (see Hadot 1996, 117–25, esp. 125). So the question now is: Does this continuation in chs. 51–64 using the same source, or did Victorinus change his source—or not use a source at all?

In ch. 51, Victorinus uses strange terminology indeed. Not only does he start with the term *unum unum*, defining it as motion and infinite life, but he also goes on to develop the concept of the Son's (*filius*) generation, starting with a *feminea potentia* that is made as man by reversion upon his his source; Victorinus considers this process to be the *typus*, the paradigm for Christ's generation, even his virginal birth. I acknowledge that Victorinus is using a source here, but the source used seems different than the one used in *Adv. Ar.* 1.49–50.[16] There he was almost quoting a text foreign to his personal piety, that—as we know from *Zostrianos*—was devoid of any specific Christian elements. But here in ch. 51, the application to Christ as the Son is very clear, not only mentioning the λόγος (already mentioned in ch. 50.16), but even including a quotation of holy scripture and an intentionally specific use of the term *filius*. The virgin birth is a problem explained in detail in the second half of ch. 51, and leads directly to the incarnation and birth of Christ, who becomes explicitly identified with the *filius* at the end of the chapter.

Here Victorinus has used a source, but has adapted it in a quite creative manner to his Christology. More precisely: he has used single elements of a source, mainly an identification of the second ontological level as *unum unum* and life, and then the concept of initial manifestation and subsequent reversion to represent female and male phases in the Son's generation. But even the use of this concept of female—male is intensively infiltrated by Victorinus's own terminology and Christology.

In ch. 52, Victorinus starts again with a principal explanation of God as *potentia*, a potentiality of three powers, existence, life, beatitude (earlier mentioned in 1.50.11). Then he explains how these three powers pervade one another. This explanation ends in ch. 53 with a treatment of the relation between Son and

---

16. Already for the use of the postulated common source of *Zostrianos* and Victorinus in chs. 49–50, it was noted that the second half is rather a kind of paraphrase than direct quotation, see Abramowski 2005, 513–66, esp. 535.

Father, described from a biblical point of view; here it is beyond question that Victorinus is the author.

Chapter 52 begins with a *ponamus* (1.52.2), and this sounds like the opening of a longer explanation. But in the following sentences the author sums up earlier chapters: two times he says: *sicuti demonstratum* (1.52.9–11), referring back to ch. 50 (one of the chapters that parallel in *Zostrianos*). This could mean that the source used previously in ch. 50 also had this reference, but it could also mean that Victorinus is now applying the contents of ch. 50 to his own theology. That this could be the case is perhaps confirmed by the strange verb *ministrari* used in reference to the λόγος as the giver of life. The verb *ministrari* is a Latin equivalent to the Greek διακονέω, but here not with the simple meaning "to serve," but in a special, transitive sense: to mediate something to somebody (see 1.52.18). Origen, for example, used this verb with this meaning, referring to the διακονίαι of the κύριος in 1 Cor 12:5 (see Origen, *Comm. Jo.* 2.10.78.3). The *ministrari* of life could be a Christian interpretation of the second person of the Trinity. This suggests that beginning only with *Adv. Ar.* 1.52.22 onwards Victorinus was using the same, non-Christian source as he did in ch. 50. But even here, only few lines later, the Spirit is mentioned, together with the terms *operatrix* and *manifestatio*, in a way reminiscent of 1 Cor 12:6–7, where *operationes* and *manifestatio* are related to the Holy Spirit; moreover, the verb *vivefacere* in *Adv. Ar.* 1.52.35–37 may reflect John 6:63. So here again, a Christian background is probable. The last lines of the chapter also sound quite Christian, prompting Hadot to include them in brackets, but perhaps it would be better to do this with the whole chapter.

Chapter 54 refers clearly to the beginning of *Adv. Ar.* 1B.48. Here it is significant that the parallel passage in *Zostrianos* only begins in ch. 49, so that the introductory remarks about the synonyms and the difference between the various Christian terms such as Spirit, λόγος, νοῦς, Holy Spirit, wisdom, and substance do not stem from the source used in chs. 49–50. The clear reference of ch. 54 to the ontological qualification *consubstantialis* suggests to me that Victorinus shaped this paragraph by himself. The same goes for ch. 55. Indeed, Hadot mentions only six lines of ch. 54 for his group 2, there also enclosing the term *consubstantialis* in brackets (see Hadot, 1968, 2:32).

For the following ch. 56 it is clear, even in the opinion of Hadot, that it is a mixture of biblical references or allusions and philosophical terminology. In detail only a few (and in the context of *Adversus Arium* not new) words remain for supposing a source used by Victorinus here, so the addition of this ch. to group 2 by Hadot seems to me unconvincing. In spite of this, the expressions (not assigned to group 2 by Hadot) *spiritus tripotens* and echo (ἠχώ) seem interesting, perhaps minor reflections of the use of a source such as *Zostrianos*.

Chapter 57 applies the interpretation of God as triad of existence, life, and beatitude to the Holy Spirit, combining this with the *intus–foris* terminology and various biblical references (Exod 33:23 and John 1:3). The same is the case for ch. 58, attributing one and the same motion (*motio*) to the λόγος and the Holy Spirit and going on to refer to various biblical texts in the second half of the chapter. But even in the first half there is a close relation to specific Christian concepts, for example, the name Jesus, the idea that the Holy Spirit is indeed the mother of Jesus,[17] and the use of the term *administratio* in combination with *vivefacere* for the function of the Holy Spirit. So perhaps it would be better not to include this section in the texts of group 2 (as Hadot does for ch. 57, but not for ch. 58; Hadot 1968, 2:33–34). Chapter 59 completes the biblical references.

An extrinsic source could be used again in chs. 60–61. Or perhaps there are two different sources. A first instance of extrinsic material used in ch. 60 is the concept of circular motion as a way of explaining the connection of the first principle as potential motion, corresponding to the point (σημεῖον) as the potentiality of active motion, symbolized by the γραμμή, the line, formed by a perfect—that is, circular, motion.[18] I wondered if perhaps the image of the sphere could have been added by Victorinus, because this is based on the concept that this motion is twofold, including life and intelligence, so the circular motion becomes a motion in two axes producing a sphere. And indeed this could be the case, because in 1.60.22–27 the sphere is mentioned only once, and the concept seems to be complete without the sphere. On the other hand, in the philosophical tradition from Aristotle onwards there is a close link between circular and spherical motion as perfect motions.[19] So one may even imagine that the concept of a sphere could be attributed to the source. Even Hadot remarked that Victorinus integrated various Christian elements in the source he used (not only in the last sentence, but even 1.60.6–8 with the father-son-terminology).

Chapter 61 begins with a reference to the circular motion of ch. 60, but immediately after this, the chapter uses Christian terminology, suggesting that the soul is the image of the Son, who is in turn the image of the father. The rest of the chapter does not presuppose the concept of circular motion or spheres, but simply develops a concept of the several levels of the soul's action. The distinction between *intellegibile* and *intellectualis* is alluded to,[20] as well as a kind of light-

---

17. See "Gospel of the Hebrews" according to Origen, *Comm. Jo.* 2.12.87 = 4:67,19–23 Preuschen.

18. Victorinus applied this immediately to the relation between Father and Son in *Adv. Ar.* 1.60.6–7; "aber es ist schwer zu sagen, wieviel vom Text um diese Zeile herum aus seiner eigenen Feder stammt" (Abramowski 2007, 145–68, esp. 147).

19. See, e.g., Plotinus, *Enn.* 2.2 περὶ τῆς κυκλοφορίας, esp. 2.2.10–15.

20. The soul is *potentia vitae intellectualis*, i.e., *intellegens, non iam ut intellegens et intellegibile* (1.61.8–12). This last expression can mean a) in its movement down from the intellect it is only *intellegens*, no longer *intellegens et intellegibile*, or b) as *intellegens* it is no longer even *intellegibile*. It is not clearly stated, how the expression *potentia vitae intellectualis* is related to the *intellegibile*, but it can be assumed that the *intellegibile* is the higher level, where there is no distinction between the object, the process and the subject of thinking, while *intellectualis* is the lower part of the soul. This can be compared with *Cand.* 9, where the *potentia dei* is *intellegibilis*

ontology (where the term *verum lumen*, φῶς ἀληθινόν could be considered as Christian as in John 1:9 and the Nicene Creed, cf. *Adv. Ar.* 4.29.20–21), but as a whole the argumentation could also stem from a pagan source. So in this case it seems to me Hadot is completely right to add these lines to group 2.

Then finally, from ch. 62 onwards, Victorinus comments on the phrase from Gen 1:26 *iuxta imaginem et similitudinem*; the entire text seems to me to be a quite coherent unit, so I am not convinced that there are any included passages from a source that was not originally concerned with Gen 1:26.[21]

To sum up this analysis of *Adversus Arium* 1B: there are various contexts in which Victorinus used a source or sources. This can be assumed sometimes only for few lines or even single terms, sometimes we cannot clearly recognize if Victorinus picks up terms from chs. 49–50 or uses a source similar to that used in chs. 49–50. Sometimes only a small piece of thirty to forty lines could be used (e.g., in the second half of ch. 61). But all these pieces don't compel us to assume a single and coherent source. The nature and genre of the sources used are not clear enough, so of course all this borrowed material could belong to a single source, but it is also possible that Victorinus used multiple and even disparate sources. Perhaps Victorinus developed his concept of the Trinity on the basis of such triads as *esse, vivere,* and *intellegere* or existence, motion (life), and beatitude derived from the source used in chs. 49–50, and while doing this, integrated even other material, not by direct quotation, but integrating it into his own argumentation.

This seems to me to fit perfectly the way in which material from a philosophical anthropology is used in *Adv. Ar.* 1.32.16–78, where Victorinus uses some kind of excerpt for demonstrating the hendiadic movement that consists of life and intelligence (*Adv. Ar.* 1.32). Neither the term ὁμοούσιος nor the goal of the excursus (the close relation between *vita et intellegentia* parallel to that between Jesus and the Holy Spirit) seems to me to stem from the source, but Victorinus integrated this material into his own thought. In a similar way, Victorinus seems to me to develop the triad drawn from the source used in *Adv. Ar.* 1B.49–50, be it the Greek *Zostrianos*, a Neo-Platonic text, or an already-Christianized source. Even the argumentation of *Adv. Ar.* 3.4.6–46 could be inspired by a source, but

---

et intellectualis and appears as an activity of the *intellegentia* with a *potentia intellectualis*, and this results in a *mundus intellectualis* in which the souls participate (*Cand.* 9.4–7.18.–19). In my opinion, the term *intellegibilis et intellectualis* indicates that the divine potentiality includes both levels, the higher level of the *intellegibile* et the lower one of the *mundus intellectualis*. Both texts are different, but fit quite well the twofold terminology of νοητός and νοερός that can be found in Plotinus (cf. *Enn.* 5.1 [10].3.13; 5.1 [10].4.7 etc.), so this is no indication for a specifically Porphyrian concept (as Hadot 1968, 1:100–101 argues).

21. This is even the case if we accept that *quomodo istud, audi* introduces another source, as Abramowski 2007, 148 argues. At least, Porphyry cannot be considered as author here.

shaped and formulated by Victorinus.[22] It also seems difficult to decide whether the comparison with the elements of vision in *Adv Ar.* 3.5 belongs to the material that inspired the argumentation of *Adv. Ar.* 3.4; perhaps this is merely an *exemplum* added by the rhetor Victorinus himself.[23]

Finally, one last observation: The material used in *Adv. Ar.* 1B (including also *Adv. Ar.* 1.32 and *Adv. Ar.* 4.2.4–5) is very different from the kind of source that Victorinus very likely used in Ad *Candidum*, which casts doubt on the assumption that the material stems from the same author,[24] be it Porphyry or someone else.

c) The Texts from *Adversus Arium* 4

For Hadot, nearly the whole substance of *Adversus Arium* 4 is inspired by long passages quoted from Porphyry (see Hadot 1968, 2:39–55). He assumes here a strictly organized method of paronyms used to explain the interrelationships between the members of the triad *esse–vivere–intellegere*. He recognizes its difference from the triad used in *Adversus Arium* 1B by virtue of its use of the method of paronyms, because in book 4 the ranking of *esse/existentia, vivere/vita, intellegere/intellegentia* is crucial (see Hadot 1968, 2:376,424–425). For Hadot, this difference is typical of the discrepancies that occur quite often in Porphyry's thought.[25]

An initial reading of *Adv. Ar.* 4 caused me to wonder about the beginning of the book, which deals only with the question of the difference between living and life, but not the distinction between either "To Be"/Being or the Understanding/ Intelligence. Almost all of the first three chapters seem to me to be drawn from a brief source that explained the method of paronyms on the basis of the Living and Life distinction.[26]

At the end of ch. 3, the author sums up this method, applying it to God as the source of life. The short apologetic phrase *scio hoc obscurum videri posse* suggests that these last lines constitute Victorinus's own application of the source's doctrine. In any case, the passage is a bridge to the clearly Christian and bibli-

---

22. In this text Victorinus sketches a reciprocal relation of each element of the triad *esse –vivere–intellegere*; cf. for the reciprocal structure of similar triads Turner 2008, 39–58.

23. Hadot 1960, 940–41 proposed that chs. 4–5 are "textuellement emprunté à une source néoplatonicienne."

24. Hadot 1996, 122 states: "Mais par ailleurs les textes qui forment le groupe I sont très différents, dans leur contenu et dans leur forme de ceux qui forment le groupe II."

25. See Hadot 1968, 372: "Porphyre lui-même ... n'hésite pas à juxtaposer sans les unifier, des réponses différentes à un même problème."

26. This is an important difference from the interesting comparable passage in Proclus, *In Parm.* 1106,1–1108,15 Cousin (= 3.85–89 Steel), to which Hadot refers (1968, 1:355–67, Greek text also in 2:117–20).

cal thought of ch. 4, and this seems to be the case even for the first half of ch. 5, because it follows the linking phrase *deus et spiritus* from John 4:24 that was used in ch. 4, together with other biblical terminology such as θρόνοι as a category of angels (cf. Col 1:16).

On the other hand, the second half of ch. 5 seems to be use a doxographical source, mentioning that in the beginning (here Victorinus cautions the reader that strictly speaking, God is not subject to time) God generates the universal substances of the whole world (the "ideas"), and within the ideas, he generates first the most general ones, such as the triad ὀντότης, ζωότης, νοότης or the dichotomy identity/alterity. This triad could have been mentioned in the source, even if it is unclear whether the cyclical predominance among its three terms—by which each one includes also the processes or results of the other two—was subsequently added or linked to the source here used by Victorinus.

That this could be Victorinus's own addition can perhaps be confirmed by chs. 6–7, where he uses the method of paronyms, intentionally linking them to biblical concepts. I suspect that Victorinus, again using the method of paronyms derived from the source of chs. 1–3, is here developing his own trinitarian thought. The same could be the case for ch. 8. Even here we find a mixture of triadic reflections, supplemented by biblical arguments, and at the beginning of ch. 9, Victorinus explicitly defends his own wording: *quot hic mysteria, quot genera quaestionum*. The whole reflection of chs. 9–10, based on the relation between *spirare* and spirit, is directly applied to the relation between Father and Son, and resembles traditional Christian theological doctrine, culminating in the ὁμοούσιος doctrine at the end of ch. 10. I am not convinced that Victorinus used a source here.[27]

However, a foreign source could have been used from the end of ch. 10 onwards (4.10.45) into chs. 11 and 12, including the initial 14 lines of ch. 13 (see Hadot 1960, 998–99). This would point to a source that dealt with the power of life and its action in the world. This source could either be directly Christian or at least an extrinsic source reread in a Christian sense, perhaps by Victorinus himself, because the biblical concept of the θρόνοι as angels recurs twice again (4.11.10 and 11.25) together with clear references to Jesus Christ and the Holy Spirit, and even to Gen 1:26. Despite this, the flow of these chapters is hardly interrupted by these small sentences. So here I think Hadot is right. This could indeed be a section about the role of motion and the power of life throughout the different levels of the world. But this section has nothing to do with the method of paronyms. So the only link between this section and the larger context is the reference to life and God as the origin of dynamic life pervading the world.

---

27. Hadot 1960, 996 came to the result: "Victorinus expose à nouveau le superior tractatus."

The difference between living and life is resumed only in the second half of ch. 13, nearly repeating the thoughts of earlier chapters and in ch. 14 continues— with biblical references—in a quite similar manner.

Victorinus introduces ch. 15 as an example, in the process summing up the results of earlier chapters (*dicimus* 4.15.3) and goes on to state that eternity is the potentiality of all present times, which can be compared with the relation between "living" as the potentiality of an individual's life and actual "life" as the manifestation of fully formed living, which is said to illustrate the relation between Father and Son. I am not convinced that Victorinus actually quotes an extrinsic source here, but does use a comparison he has recalled from a such a source and integrates it into his own argumentation.

The application to the Holy Spirit in ch. 17 is clearly not based on a supposed pagan source, and the greater part of ch. 18 is based on biblical arguments. In this context there appears a short paragraph (*Adv. Ar.* 4.18.45–59) that links the terminology of living and life to the triad *esse-vivere-intellegere*. This leads to the question whether Victorinus is here quoting a source. If not (and Hadot does not include this paragraph in his group 3), one could imagine that Victorinus himself links source material about Living/Life and the dynamic power of life/motion to the triad *esse-vivere-intellegere*.[28] Though not certain, this is a possibility that should be kept in mind.

If this is the case, then it seems probable to me that the majority of chs. 19–24 is also an argumentation developed by Victorinus dealing with an exact citation of Plotinus, *Enn.* 5.2 [11]. This assumption can be supported with the following arguments:

1. The beginning of ch. 19 distinguishes between two modes of *unum unum* in a strict sense whose absolute infinitival being (εἶναι) beyond being can be distinguished from the derived, determinate being of ὄν and λόγος. This argumentation repeats terms from the earlier books of *Adversus Arium* (adding nothing new) and leads directly to a theology of the λόγος, which is the principal aim of chs. 19–20, ending with the Johannine Prologue. Even this is only a step on the way to establish once more the ὁμοούσιος doctrine in ch. 21.
2. Then, with the words *haec omnia sic docemus*, Victorinus begins a new series of arguments. God as τριδύναμος repeats the *tripotens in unalitate* of *Adv. Ar.* 1.49,4, an important term in the passage parallel to *Zostrianos*. Therefore the wording at the end of ch. 21 using *singularitas* and *unalitas* is perhaps a reference back to this passage.

---

28. Tardieu 1996, 105 mentions "le grand commentaire qu'il donne de l'exposé dans le livre IV de l'Adversus Arium (21,19–29,38)" with "les tics du style rhétorique de Victorinus ... abondants."

3. Finally, after the opinions of certain *nonulli*[29] are mentioned, Plotinus is quoted, and the term *principium* is extensively explained. But even here in chs. 22–24, the most important terms can be regarded as references to the passage parallel to *Zostrianos* or to Plotinian terminology.

Since it is hard to find a passage that compels us to assume another source, I propose to take into account even the possibility that Victorinus was exploiting a theology that he knew from Plotinus and his school, but in a quite independent manner. Terms such as *omniintellegentia, omnicognoscentia,* and so on, could have been invented or formulated against the background of subsequent reflection on the theology contained in the passage parallel to *Zostrianos*. But I do not perceive here a specific Porphyrian flavor. Of course it is possible that Porphyry stood behind these arguments, but this is as uncertain as many other alternative hypotheses.

A final passage that I would like to discuss is ch. 25, where one finds an excursus about the transition between contraries. This could stem from a new source, but again, one not related directly to the triad *esse–vivere–intellegere*. Only as a second step, from line 44 onwards and mainly in ch. 26, does Victorinus link this to his theology, developing it again in chs. 26–33. Only small pieces of these chapters can be considered as derived from a pagan source. Whether the juxtaposition of the *duae intellegentiae*, briefly mentioned at the beginning of ch. 29, is a reason for assuming such a source, I doubt. It seems to me that schemes like "hidden" versus "manifest" and the like are very familiar to Victorinus, so it is not very surprising if he sums up his reflection with words like *haec* (namely the activity of thinking) *foris, haec filius* (*Adv. Ar.* 4.29.3). The proximity to biblical terminology in ch. 29 could be supporting evidence for the assumption that Victorinus is here developing his own thought.

The main difference between this analysis of *Adversus Arium* 4 and that of Hadot, consists in the value given to the method of paronyms. Hadot argues that there is a consistent system behind *Adv. Ar.* 4, but this may not be true. For the crucial point, the difference between "To Be" and Being, Hadot can only adduce the paragraphs linked to the theology of the λόγος, and even there by including certain sentences as later additions made by Victorinus. So the result of *Adv. Ar.* 4

---

29. Only the assumption that the opinion of these *nonnulli* points not only to the author of chs. 22–24, but to all texts Hadot assigns to group 3, leads to the assumption that the author of this text (and and accordingly also the author of groups 1–2) must be Post-Plotinian (see Hadot 1996, 119–20). But perhaps the discussion of the Plotinus quotation goes back to Victorinus himself, who knows an interpretation of Plotinus he disagrees with. The Plotinus quotation and the *nonnulli* are no argument against the hypothesis that we have no directly used source in *Adv. Ar.* 4.21.26–24.39, but instead a kind of explanation of the triad from Victorinus himself.

is quite ambiguous, especially given that the method of paronyms is almost never applied to the first principle.[30]

Conclusion

That Victorinus used material beyond merely the passage parallel to *Zostrianos* we can assert as certain. But I submit that there is no striking evidence for the assumption that the variety of extrinsic materials that appears in the different contexts in *Adversus Arium* belongs to one source or author. Perhaps we should better assume that Victorinus is puzzling over very different pieces of material, piecing them together in his own thought. The discovery of the *Zostrianos* parallels eliminates not only the hypothesis that Victorinus used Porphyry in *Adversus Arium* 1.49–50, but even calls into question the entire scenario delineated by Hadot. Perhaps the character of Victorinus as a creative and independent thinker who was inspired by several different philosophical and even Gnostic texts has to be reaffirmed. Of course we know only a small portion of the material he could have used, and perhaps even texts of Neoplatonic provenance belonged to such material. Further studies should reconsider the question whether the Neoplatonic material that can be found in Victorinus contains specific Porphyrian characteristics. But merely a few resemblances to single expressions that occur in the *Chaldaean Oracles*, or the distinction between νοητός and νοερός, or the difference between "To Be" and Being or the method of paronyms, or the intelligible triad *esse–vivere–intellegere* or the concept of a second, determinate One as the manifestation of an initially pure potentiality are insufficient arguments for this assumption. With the detection of the previously unknown parallels between *Zostrianos* and *Adv. Ar.* 1.49–50, it is only by luck that we have discovered one such source that points to an intellectual climate in which all these elements were common currency, even despite the considerable differences among the individual texts. But it is far from certain whether the different sources used by Victorinus belong to a single author. So one can only speculate about the number of treatises he was using aside from the text used in *Adv. Ar.* 1.49–50.[31] The assumption that at all these points Victorinus must be dependent on Porphyry is anything but necessary.

---

30. Hadot 1996, 123 takes into consideration that „Dans son ensemble, ce groupe III pourrait donc avoir une ou plusieurs sources assez proches de celle dont nous parlons, sinon identiques à elle."

31. I would assume two different texts for *Ad Candidum*, and at least eight texts for *Adversus Arium*.

5
Porphyry and the Gnostics: Reassessing Pierre Hadot's Thesis in Light of the Second- and Third-Century Sethian Treatises[1]

Tuomas Rasimus

Pierre Hadot published a series of magisterial studies in the 1950s and 1960s (Hadot 1957, 1960, 1961, 1966, 1968), where he attempted to reconstruct Porphyry's metaphysics, and argued that instead of being simply an editor and a popularizer of Plotinus (see Hadot 1968, 1:482), Porphyry was in fact a great Neoplatonic innovator. Hadot's thesis is based largely on two sets of anonymous fragments that he assigned to Porphyry: the some eighty-nine fragments embedded in Marius Victorinus's theological works;[2] and the six fragments of the *Anonymous Commentary on the Parmenides* of the now destroyed Turin palimpsest.[3] Recently, several scholars have raised doubts against Hadot's influential theory,[4] both in terms of his actual arguments, and in light of the subsequently

---

1. I wish to express my thanks to Zlatko Pleše and Margot Stout Whiting for their valuable comments concerning my arguments and my English.

2. These are collected in Hadot 1968, 2:13–55. Fragments 90–93 are treated separately (see Hadot 1968, 1:73). Some of the 89 fragments are further sub-divided into several units, e.g., §§36, 36a, 36b. For Hadot's methods for identifying the fragments from Victorinus's own text, see Hadot 1968, 1:67.

3. The fragments of the *Commentary* were presumably discovered in a northern Italian monastery in 1803. The first critical edition was published by Kroll in 1892, but the manuscript was subsequently destroyed in a fire in 1904. Other editions, based on the *editio princeps* and one surviving photograph of the manuscript, have been produced by Hadot (1968, 2:61–113) and Bechtle (1999a, 17–65). Several scholars have accepted Hadot's attribution of the *Commentary*'s fragments to Porphyry. See Abramowski 1983; M. Williams 1985, 50; Dillon 1992; Majercik 1992; King 1995, 26.

4. Smith 1987; Wire 1990; Tardieu 1996; Bechtle 1999a; Corrigan 2000b; Turner 2000b; Turner 2001; Cazelais 2005.

published Sethian Gnostic[5] evidence from the Nag Hammadi library. In fact, most of the suggested Porphyrian features that are found in Hadot's two sets of fragments—but not always in the undisputed Porphyrian evidence—are found in these Sethian texts. This is especially the case with the Coptic translations of *Zostrianos* and *Allogenes*,[6] whose Greek versions were read, though eventually refuted, in Plotinus's seminars, and which were also known to Porphyry.[7] What does this new Sethian evidence mean for Hadot's thesis, and for our understanding of the history of Neoplatonism? I will argue in this article that Hadot's thesis is in itself inconclusive—even problematic—and that Sethian Gnostics were probably the innovators of most of the "Porphyrian" concepts that we find in Hadot's fragments. This seems all the more likely as many of these "Porphyrian" features are already present—some implicitly, others explicitly—in a pre-Plotinian Sethian text, the *Apocryphon of John*.[8] It will be argued that advocates of Sethian Gnosticism brought with them innovative ideas, including the famous being–life–mind triad, to Plotinus's seminars; and that a fruitful exchange of ideas between the Gnostics, and Plotinus and his students, took place before (and perhaps even after) the somewhat exaggerated Gnostic controversy in the 260s.

Pierre Hadot's Thesis

Let me here first summarize Hadot's reconstruction of Porphyry's metaphysics itself before I enter into a discussion of the sources. According to Hadot, Porphyry combined Plotinian and Chaldean speculations on the first principles in an innovative manner (Hadot 1968, 1:92, 482–493). To his teacher Plotinus, Porphyry

---

5. Sethian Gnosticism is often thought to be the earliest and classic form of Gnosticism, whose roots may go back to the first century C.E., perhaps even earlier. See especially Schenke 1974, 1981; Pearson 1990; Turner 2001; and Rasimus 2009. Hadot (1960, 850) only had access to Till's (1955) edition of the Berlin Codex (BG 8502), which contains one version of the *Apocryphon of John*, but was unaware of the "Platonizing Sethian Treatises" (a term coined by John D. Turner), viz., *Zostrianos* (NHC VIII.1), *Allogenes* (NHC XI.3), *Steles Seth* (NHC VII.5), and *Marsanes* (NHC X).

6. The best edition of *Zostrianos* is Barry et al. 2000; and new textual evidence has been published by Tardieu (1996) and Kasser and Luisier (2007). For the editions of *Allogenes*, see Turner and Wintermute 1990; King 1995; Funk 2004.

7. *Vit. Plot.* 16; cf. also *Enn.* 2.9 [33] which contains numerous references to *Zostrianos*. For discussion, see below.

8. Although the four Coptic manuscripts of the *Ap. John* (NHC II.1; III.1; IV.1; BG 8502.2) come from the fourth and fifth centuries, their Greek *Vorlagen* are generally dated to the second or early-third century. See Tardieu 1984, 10, 37–39; Logan 1996, xx, 26–69, 191, 283; Turner 2001, 128–41, 257–301. Irenaeus (*Adv. Haer.* 1.29; ca. 180 C.E.) quotes from a version or a source of the *Apocryphon of John*. The *Ap. John* may even be connected to the Johannine schism (ca. 90–125 C.E.) as evinced in 1–2 John. See Tardieu 1984, 10, 37–39; Turner 2005; and Rasimus 2009. The standard edition of the *Ap. John* is Waldstein and Wisse 1995.

would owe the theory of the One and the Intellect. Plotinus's One is the transcendent first principle beyond being and intellect,[9] while the Intellect proper, the second principle (the "One-Being") comes to know itself in its procession out of and turning back towards the One.[10] Although Plotinus sometimes also attributes "life" to the Intellect, and speaks of being, life and mind as internal aspects of the Intellect,[11] he never clearly formulated the later famous being–life–mind triad, whose explicit formalization Hadot attributed to Porphyry.[12] In the *Chaldean Oracles*[13]—a Stoicizing Middle Platonic collection of oracular statements that Porphyry introduced to Neoplatonism—Porphyry then found a triad of first principles, Father-power-intellect (Hadot 1968, 1:260–72). In the actual surviving fragments of the *Oracles*, such a triad is never explicitly mentioned, but Porphyry would have deduced it from fragments 3 and 4 (Majercik), where the Father is said to have snatched himself away without sharing his fire with his intellectual power (3), and where it is stated that while the power is with the Father, the intellect is from him (4). A triadic structure of everything is also alluded to in several fragments (27; cf. 2, 23, 28, 29, 31). Guided by his understanding of fragment 27 ("For in every world shines a triad, ruled by a monad"), Porphyry would have arranged the first three principles in an ennead where each member of the triad implicitly contains and predominates the other two: (1) *Father*-Power-Intellect; (2) Father-*Power*-Intellect; (3) Father-Power-*Intellect* (Hadot 1968, 1:260–72). Porphyry would also have identified the Chaldean Father with ὕπαρξις, undetermined existence above determined being (Hadot 1968, 1:112, 267–72, 488–90). This term was supposedly attested in the Chaldean tradition itself, as suggested by Damascius,[14] although it is not found in the surviving fragments.[15] In any case, by identifying this Chaldean Father-existence with the Plotinian One, and by combining the two triads, Porphyry—according to Hadot—ended up with an ennead of first principles at the top of his metaphysical system: (1) *Existence*–Life–Mind; (2) Existence–*Life*–Mind; (3) Existence–Life–*Mind* (Hadot 1968, 1:262–67). This system leads to the unavoidable conclusion that the Plotin-

---

9. *Enn.* 5.4 [7]; 5.1 [10]; 5.6 [24]; 2.9 [33] 1; 6.7 [38] 37–42; 6.2 [43]; 5.3 [49] 10–17.
10. *Enn.* 5.1 [10]; 6.7 [38] 37.18–22.
11. For the occurrences, see below.
12. Hadot (1957) thought that because Plotinus nonetheless spoke of the formulaic triad without clearly explaining it, he must have received it as an established concept. For discussion, see below.
13. See the edition, translation and commentary by Majercik (1989).
14. *Princ.* 2.3.5–6 Westerink-Combès = §44 Ruelle; 2.36.5–6 Westerink-Combès = §54 Ruelle; 2.71.1–7 Westerink-Combès = §61 Ruelle.
15. The term, ὕπαρξις, occurs only in the frame material in Proclus (*Plat. Theol.* 4.21 = frg. 84). However, the verb, ὑπάρχω, does occur in the actual fragments 1, 20 and 84. Corrigan (2000b, 161) thinks that Hadot's suggestion that the word ὕπαρξις was already a substitute for the Father in the *Oracles*, is a "strong possibility."

ian One is not purely transcendent due to its characterization as existence, and due to its being the first member of the intellectual triad, implicitly even containing the other members. Such a deviation from Plotinus was in fact criticized by later Neoplatonists,[16] but supposedly Porphyry felt he could save enough of the One's transcendence by attributing to it a higher, undetermined and potential existence above determined being (see Dillon 1992). This kind of distinction between the undetermined and determined aspects for all the members of the intellectual triad would then also have been coined by Porphyry, partially using paronymic cognates for higher forms (e.g., "to live" for the transcendent undetermined "Life") existing potentially in the One; Porphyry was supposedly also fond of paronyms ending in -ότης.[17]

Such an innovative combination of Plotinian and Chaldean views would have caused Porphyry to come up with several characteristic and innovative ideas that include (many of the following items overlap as they represent various aspects of the same ideas): (1) the use of the being–life–mind triad (with variants, including existence–life–mind, and existence–life–blessedness; see below) to explain the generation (externalization) of the Intellect from the One;[18] (2) the concept of the prefiguration of the Intellect within the One;[19] (3) the distinction between undetermined and determined aspects of being, life, and mind;[20] (4) the use of ὕπαρξις (Latin: *exsistentia*) to denote the undetermined being or existence;[21] (5) the enneadic structuring of the being–life–mind triad (and/or Father–power–intellect);[22] (6) the use of the principles of mutual implication and relative predominance;[23] and (7) the method of paronyms.[24] Much of the following discussion will, in fact, revolve around these doctrinal concepts. It should be noted that, according to Hadot, Porphyry invented many of these ideas not only by interpreting the *Chaldean Oracles*, but also by transposing ideas from Stoic physics to Platonic metaphysics.[25]

---

16. Damascius, *Princ.* 2:1.4–2.10 Westerink-Combès = §43 Ruelle. Proclus's testimony (*In Parm.* 1070.15–30), which Hadot (1968, 1:258–59) and Majercik (1992, 479 n. 20) mention does not name Porphyry, although a doctrine similar to that in Damascius's passage is criticized.

17. Hadot 1968, 1:352–75. For paronyms, see below.

18. Victorinus: e.g., §§80–89 Hadot; *Anon. in Parm.* XIV.17–26. See Hadot 1968, 1:141–42.

19. Victorinus: e.g., §§41, 80–89 Hadot; *Anon. in Parm.* XIV.17–26. See also the preceding note. See Hadot 1968, 1:299.

20. Victorinus: e.g., §§65, 70, 78, 86a Hadot; *Anon. in Parm.* XII.29–35.

21. Victorinus: e.g., §§23, 23a; 86a–89 Hadot (*Adv. Ar.* 1.30,18–31; *Cand.* 1.2.14–23; *Adv. Ar.* 4.25.44–28.22); *Anon. in Parm.* XIV.6.15.17.18.23.25; cf. XII.29–35.

22. Victorinus: e.g., §§65, 76 Hadot.

23. Victorinus: e.g., §§30, 41, 56, 65, 76, 88 Hadot.

24. Victorinus: e.g., §§10, 65, 76 Hadot.

25. See Hadot 1968, 1:89–90 n. 5, 109–10, 225–34, 485–88.

While such a picture of Porphyry's metaphysics is alluded to in some later *testimonia* (especially Lydus, *Mens.* 4.122; Augustine, *Civ.* 10.23, 29; Damascius, *Princ.* 2:1.4–2.10 Westerink-Combès = §43 Ruelle; Proclus, *In Tim.* 3:64,8–9 Diehl), Hadot's reconstruction derives its force from the two sets of anonymous fragments he has assigned to Porphyry. These are the 6 fragments of the *Anonymous Commentary on the Parmenides*, and especially the 89 passages in Victorinus that Hadot considered to be borrowings from Porphyry's lost *Commentary on the Chaldean Oracles*. Due to later *testimonia* and fragments of surviving genuine works by Porphyry, we do know that he commented on both Plato's *Parmenides* and the *Chaldean Oracles*.[26] However, the little information we have on these works cannot alone corroborate the attribution of the fragments in question to Porphyry (see Bechtle 1999a, 90–91). Thus, Hadot built his case mainly on two general claims: (1) as the fragments show fidelity to Numenius (see below) and presuppose Plotinus's worldview, yet are at the same time relatively simple in their metaphysics, they must derive from early Neoplatonism, and therefore the only suitable candidate is Porphyry (Hadot 1961; Hadot 1968, 1:79–98, 102–7); (2) a comparison between the fragments and the undisputed Porphyrian evidence (i.e., surviving genuine works and later *testimonia*) in terms of their (a) doctrinal contents, (b) vocabulary, and (c) interpretative strategies (i.e., use of the *Chaldean Oracles* and Stoic physics), shows such a close correspondence that Porphyry must be the author of the fragments (Hadot 1968, e.g., 1:98–102, 107–43). It should be noted here that the *Anonymous Commentary on the Parmenides* lacks several doctrinal features that are found in Victorinus's fragments (e.g., the enneadic structuring of the being–life–mind triad with the principles of relative predominance and mutual implication), and thus presents a somewhat simpler metaphysical scheme. However, I do agree with Hadot in that the metaphysics of these two sets of fragments are very similar and may well derive from the same milieu.

Several scholars have reacted against Hadot's first general claim, especially against the assumption that the fragments presuppose Plotinus's worldview and must therefore be post-Plotinian. Bechtle, Corrigan, and Turner argue that since Plotinus's three hypostases (One–Intellect–Soul) are already attested in Moderatus,[27] and most of the main features of the *Anonymous Commentary on*

---

26. Damascius (*Dub. et sol.* §238 = 2:112–13 Ruelle) seems to indicate that Porphyry commented on *Parm.* 144c (Plato: ἀλλ' εἴπερ γε οἶμαι ἔστιν ἀνάγκη αὐτὸ ἀεί ἕωσπερ ἂν ᾖ ἕν γέ τι εἶναι μηδὲν δὲ ἀδύνατον; Porphyry *apud* Damascius:"Ἔνατον τί «τὸ ἕν γε τι» σημαίνει καὶ τὸ τί προσκείμενον; ἆρα ὅτι ἀντίκειται τῷ οὐδὲν τὸ τί ὡς Πορφύριος ἢ ὅτι τὸ τί δηλοῖ τὸ μεθεκτὸν ἕν). See Hadot 1968, 1:102–3. For Porphyry's interpretation of the *Chaldean Oracles*, see especially Lydus, *Mens.* 4.122; Augustine, *Civ.* 10.23, 29; and Damascius, *Princ.* 2:1.4–2.10 Westerink-Combès = §43 Ruelle.

27. In discussing his three hypostases, i.e., One–Intellect–Soul, Plotinus suggests that his ideas are not new (*Enn.* 5.1 [10].8). Indeed, Moderatus's description of the Three Ones

the Parmenides (the same would also apply to Victorinus's fragments) in Middle Platonic sources, there is no need to assume a post-Plotinian provenance for the *Anonymous Commentary*.[28] Cazelais has pointed out that the expression, ὁ ἐπὶ πᾶσιν θεός, which occurs three times in the *Anonymous Commentary on the Parmenides*, and six times in the undisputed Porphyrian evidence—and which Hadot took to be a veritable signature of Porphyry (Hadot 1968, 1:113)—occurs at least eighty times in the writings of Origen of Alexandria![29] This, together with the arguments of Bechtle, Corrigan, and Turner, would favor a non-Porphyrian and pre-Plotinian date for the *Anonymous Commentary*, according to Cazelais. Finally, Tardieu has shown convincingly that three of the eighty-nine fragments of Victorinus are paralleled almost word for word in *Zostrianos*.[30] From this, Tardieu drew the conclusion that Victorinus and the author of *Zostrianos* had access to a common source, which was Middle Platonic and possibly by Numenius.[31] Hadot himself, in his reply to Tardieu, admitted that these three fragments indeed cannot be by Porphyry, and may, in fact, well derive from a pre-Plotinian Gnosticized (originally perhaps Numenian) text, known to both Victorinus and the author of *Zostrianos* (Hadot 1996). Majercik, however, has suggested that the common source is none other than Porphyry, and that the parallels in *Zostrianos* are to be explained by the latter's dependence on Porphyry.[32] We will return to Majercik's suggestion below. Thus, the relationship of the fragments to Plotinus has remained vague, as cases for both pre- and post-Plotinian date can be made.

Hadot's first general claim also entails three further assumptions. First, the fragments cannot be post-Porphyrian due to their relatively simple (and different) metaphysics in comparison with later Neoplatonists. To my knowledge, no one has successfully disputed this assumption,[33] and I think it is valid. The same goes for the second assumption about the fragments' "fidelity to Numenius," as

---

(Simplicius, *In phys.* 9.230.34–231.27 Diels) seems to prefigure Plotinus's scheme. Despite the Porphyrian filter through which this passage has been transmitted, its description of the first principles appears to be essentially non-Porphyrian and is probably authentic. See Dillon 1996, 347–49; Turner 2001, 363–72.

28. Bechtle 1999a, e.g., 77–91; Corrigan 2000b; Turner 2001, 724–36.

29. Cazelais 2005, esp. 209–12. Hadot himself (1961, 434) had also noted the term's occurrence in Origen, but he attributed it to Celsus. However, as Cazelais has shown, the term's occurrence is not restricted to Celsus's passages in Origen, nor even to the work *Contra Celsum*.

30. The common material occurs in Victorinus, *Adv. Ar.* 1B 49.7–50.21 (§§36, 36b, 37, 41 Hadot) and is scattered in *Zost.* 64.11–68.26; 74.8–21; 75.6–24; 84.18–22; with additional parallels in 79.16–22; 17.1–3; 15.13–17; 3.8–13. Tardieu 1996, esp. 27–45.

31. Tardieu 1996, 112–13. Similarly Brisson 1999a.

32. Majercik 2001. See also Majercik 1992, esp. 486. Cf. Abramowski 1983.

33. Cf., however, Edwards (1990), who suggests a post-Porphyrian authorship for the *Commentary* due to some difficulties in Hadot's arguments, but who also dismisses the Gnostic evidence almost completely.

the Numenian theory of Two Intellects—where the first God thinks by using the second one, the Intellect proper; and where the second God participates in the Goodness of the first one (frgs. 17, 19–22 des Places)—can be seen, for example, behind the fragments' concept of prefiguration of the Intellect in the First One. In fact, Numenius has even been suggested to be the author of the common source behind Victorinus and *Zostrianos*;[34] and someone from the "school of Numenius and Cronius" has been treated as the possible author of the *Anonymous Commentary on the Parmenides* (Corrigan 2000b, 160–61). Plotinus, of course, lectured on Numenius (*Vit. Plot.* 3; 14), and the early *Enneads* show Numenian influence in describing two states of the Intellect (e.g., 5.4 [7]; 6.9 [9]; 3.9 [13]), so much so that Plotinus was even accused of plagiarizing Numenius (*Vit. Plot.* 17–18). Clearly, Numenius's influence was felt in late Middle- and early Neoplatonism.

However, the remaining third assumption is particularly problematic in light of the new Sethian evidence. According to Hadot, Porphyry is the only suitable candidate from the era of early Neoplatonism for being the author of the fragments. As will be shown in detail below, Sethian texts contain most of the "Porphyrian" features that are found in Hadot's fragments. This alone makes Sethian authors suitable candidates as well, perhaps even more suitable than Porphyry, because some of the innovative features of the fragments that *are* attested in the Sethian texts are *missing* from the undisputed Porphyrian evidence.

This brings us to Hadot's second general claim, according to which a comparison between the fragments and the undisputed Porphyrian evidence in terms of their doctrinal contents, vocabulary and interpretive strategies, shows such a close correspondence that Porphyry must be the author of the fragments in question. Let us first take a closer look at the Porphyrian evidence before we turn to investigating the Sethian texts themselves.

It must be admitted that many of the innovative doctrinal features (see the list above) that we find in the fragments of Victorinus and the *Commentary*, do find a parallel, or at least an echo, in the undisputed Porphyrian evidence. First, the being–life–mind triad is attested in Porphyry, although only in the so-called "non-canonical order" (being–mind–life), in Proclus (*In Tim.* 3:64,8–9 Diehl). Such a non-canonical triad also appears twice in the *Sententiae* (21 and 40), although Porphyry does not apply it there to the summit of his metaphysical system. However, the statement made in *Sent.* 12 that there is Life beyond Intellect may indeed suggest the canonical order in Porphyry. The Chaldean triad, Father-power-intellect, for its part, is hinted at in later *testimonia* (especially Lydus, *De mensibus* 4.122; Augustine, *Civ.* 10.23, 29; Damascius, *Princ.* 2:1.4–2.10 Westerink-Combès = §43 Ruelle). Furthermore, the self-constitutive

---

34. Tardieu 1996, 112–13. Similarly Brisson 1999a. Cf. Hadot 1996.

process of coexistence within, procession out of, and turning towards the source, is described in *Sententiae* 41, but apparently only as a more general principle.[35]

Second, the idea of the prefiguration of the Second One or the triad in the first principle, is clearly hinted at by Porphyry: Intellect is in God because God is everywhere and nowhere (*Sent.* 31); and Intellect has pre-eternally originated from the One (*Hist. Phil.* 18). Third, the concept of various forms of higher and undetermined being, life and mind that coincide with the One, is also found in Porphyry: things beyond intellect can be understood super-intellectually and super-essentially (*Sent.* 10; 25–26); and the eternal Intellect has something supra-eternal in it (Proclus, *Plat. Theol.* 1.11 p. 51.4–10 Saffrey-Westerink). Fourth, the term ὕπαρξις is attested of the "Father" (*Hist. Phil.* 18), and elsewhere the Father is identified as the first principle (Damascius, *Princ.* 2:1.4–2.10 Westerink-Combès = §43 Ruelle). Fifth, the enneadic structuring of the intelligible triad (whether the Plotinian or the Chaldean one) is also attested in later *testimonia* (Lydus, *Mens.* 4.122; Proclus, *In Tim.* 3:64,8–9 Diehl); and Porphyry's edition of Plotinus's *Enneads*, including *Vita Plotini*, testifies to Porphyry's general interest in enneads. Sixth, the same *testimonia* as in the previous case imply the use of the principles of mutual implication and relative predominance. Seventh, a general interest in the use of paronyms is attested for Porphyry (*Isag.* 69.14–70.24), as well as its application to the intelligible triad (Proclus, *In Tim.* 3:64,8–9 Diehl).[36]

However, some of the suggested "Porphyrian" concepts found in the fragments do not, in fact, occur in the undisputed Porphyrian evidence; and some concepts that do occur are problematic. First, the being–life–mind triad never explicitly occurs in its canonical order in the undisputed Porphyrian evidence, but always in a non-canonical order where mind precedes life. Such a non-canonical order is attested for Plotinus and the Sethians as well, and once for Victorinus, but the Sethians and especially Hadot's fragments generally favor the canonical order.[37] Porphyry, according to the undisputed evidence, never used it

---

35. Cf. Dodds 1963, 225; Hadot 1968, 1:322.

36. Cf. Lydus, *Mens.* 4.94, where ὀντότης alone occurs.

37. Canonical order: Victorinus: §§24, 29a, 30, 41, 44, 60, 65, 76, 77, 78, 79, 81, 86a, 88, 89 Hadot; *Anon. in Parm.*: XIV.15–26; *Allogenes*: 49.26–38; 59.10–20; 60.16–37; 61.36–37; 62.19–23; *Zostrianos* (*parallel to Victorinus): 20.22–24; *66.16–17; *66.23–67.2; *68.1–7; 73.8–11; 75.7–10; 79.10–15; 86.15–22; *Steles Seth*: 122.19–25; 125.28–32; Plotinus: *Enn.* 1.6 [1] 7.11–12; 5.4 [7] 2.17–18; 5.4 [7] 2.43–44; 6.9 [9] 2.24; 5.6 [24] 6.20–22; 3.6 [26] 6.10–17; 3.6 [26] 6.23–24; 5.5 [32] 1.38; 6.6 [34] 9.27–29; 6.7 [38] 23.22–25; 5.3 [49] 16.38–42; 1.8 [51] 2.5–7.

Non-canonical order: Victorinus: §22 Hadot (= *Cand.* 2.21); *Allogenes*: 49.26–38; *Zostrianos*: 14.13–14; 15.5–11; 15.13–17; Plotinus: *Enn* 1.6 [1] 7.12; 5.9 [5] 10; 6.9 [9] 9; 3.9 [13] 6.3–6; 6.4 [22] 3.31–35; 5.6 [24] 6.20–22; 3.6 [26] 6.23–24; 3.6 [26] 7.7–8; 3.8 [30] 8.8–12; 3.8 [30] 10.1–2; 5.5 [32] 10.12–14; 6.6 [34] 8.1–2; 6.6 [34] 8.9–10; 6.6 [34] 8.11–13; 6.6 [34] 8.15–17; 6.6 [34] 8.17–23; 6.6 [34] 9.29–32; 6.6 [34] 15.1–3; 6.6 [34] 18.35–36; 6.6 [34] 18.51–53; 6.7 [38] 13.42–43.

(unless *Sent.* 12 hints at such an order). The non-canonical order may be related to Plotinus's three hypostases of One–Intellect–Soul or its Middle Platonic precursors (exegesis of *Tim.* 39e)[38]—in which case Life would equal Soul—and in that case, the triad would not have the function of describing the Intellect's prefiguration in and self-generation out of the One, which is what we find in Hadot's fragments. Occasionally, Platonists seem to have used the non-canonical order verbally while the actual, logical order remains canonical: one may choose to list the items in the order of beginning–end–middle.[39] However, Proclus's testimony, which is the only clear indication that Porphyry used the being-mind-life triad in a metaphysical context, insists that Mind precedes Life. Thus, we do not have a clear indication that Porphyry used the being–life–mind triad either in its canonical order, or in connection with the Intellect's self-generation which is essential to Hadot's fragments and occurs *passim* in the Sethian texts; the description of such a process in *Sententiae* 41 appears only as a general principle.

Evidence for Porphyry's use of paronyms for the being–life–mind triad that end in -ότης is also weak. We hear only once that Hestia, existing within the Father as a source and cause of all being, equals ὀντότης (Lydus, *Mens.* 4.94).[40] On the other hand, such specific paronyms that end in -ότης, are very common in Victorinus's fragments and Sethian texts.[41]

In the three fragments of Victorinus (especially §41 Hadot) that share material with *Zostrianos*, we encounter a set of concepts that (a) find no parallel in the undisputed Porphyrian evidence, (b) were already considered problematic by Hadot in his 1968 book,[42] and (c) have since 1996 convinced Hadot that they cannot, after all, be Porphyrian (Hadot 1996). These concepts are: (1) God as πνεῦμα, (2) τριδύναμος, and (3) μακάριος. Of course, all these concepts—or very similar ones—occur individually in Stoic and Middle Platonic sources.[43]

---

38. See Hadot 1957, 118; Edwards 1990, 14–19; and Turner 2001, 407–24, 514.

39. Cf. the *Anon. in Parm.* XIV.15–26.

40. Cf. Majercik 1992, 482; Hadot 1968, 1:374. *Ad Gaurum*, where ζωότης occurs, is, according to the manuscript, a work by Galen, although the treatise is often (but not always, see Hadot 1968, 1:460 n. 2) attributed to Porphyry.

41. Victorinus: e.g., §§10, 65, 76 Hadot; *Allogenes*: 49.26–38; *Steles Seth*: 122.19–23; *Zostrianos* (a) ⲘⲚⲦⲀⲦⲞⲨⲤⲒⲀ: 75.16; (b) ⲘⲚⲦⲰⲚϨ: 15.4–5; *66.25; [75.8]; 85.22; (c) ⲘⲚⲦⲈⲒⲘⲈ: 23.26; 28.27; 67.3; 75.10; 75.14; 75.19 (ⲘⲚⲦⲀⲦⲈⲒⲘⲈ: 117.6); (d) ⲘⲚⲦⲘⲀⲔⲀⲢⲒⲞⲤ: 3.9; 14.13; 15.7; 15.14; 37.22; *66.17; 73.10; 75.11; 75.17; 76.13; 79.14; 80.23; 84.13; 86.21; 87.12; 97.4; 123.18; 124.9; (e) ⲘⲚⲦⲚⲞⲨⲦⲈ: 15.11; 75.15; 79.15; 85.14; 86.18; (f) ⲘⲚⲦⲀⲄⲀⲐⲞⲤ: 75.19. The Coptic ⲘⲚⲦ- often translates the Greek -ότης, although ⲘⲚⲦⲀⲦⲈⲒⲘⲈ can also translate ἄγνοια (I owe the latter observation to Zlatko Pleše).

42. Hadot (1968, 1:293–97) admitted that the term, τριδύναμος, has a "Gnostic flavor" to it, and that the denomination "Spirit" for the One may not derive from a Neoplatonic source.

43. God as πνεῦμα is a common Stoic notion; the *Chaldean Oracles* speak of τριγλῶχις and τριοῦχος (frgs. 2, 26); and the Pythagoreans described the Monad as "blessed." See Hadot 1968, 1:288–97.

However, the only other instances where such a *combination*—applied to the being-life-mind triad—occurs, are the Sethian texts. What is especially significant in this regard is that one of those Sethian texts is the pre-Plotinian, and most likely second-century *Apocryphon of John*. We will investigate this material and its implications for Tardieu's discovery of a Middle Platonic common source behind Victorinus and *Zostrianos*, in more detail presently.

Moreover, Hadot's two sets of fragments contain terminology and expressions that have been taken to be specifically Porphyrian. This, however, is also problematic, as most of the expressions are in fact better attested in pre-Plotinian sources, or do not find strong support in the undisputed Porphyrian evidence. (1) The expression, ὁ ἐπὶ πᾶσιν θεός, as noted above, occurs about thirteen times more often in Origen than Porphyry (eighty times vs. six times; Cazelais 2005). If anything, it seems to be a specifically Christian expression, as its roots can also be seen in Paul's letters.[44] (2) The expression διὰ σμικρότητός ... διαφευγούσης ("due to smallness ... escapes"), found in the *Anon. in Parm.* II.3, is, according to Hadot, also a sure sign of Porphyry's authorship (Hadot 1961, 436–38). It is here in the *Anonymous Commentary* used to mitigate the earlier criticism of Speusippus, by admitting that while the reason we cannot comprehend the power of the One is its great separation from us, perhaps the reason is *also* due to some smallness that escapes our understanding. A similar (but not identical) expression with the preposition ὑπό occurs twice in Porphyry's *In harmonica Ptolemaei* 17.20, stating that the intelligible escapes sensation due to its smallness; and a similar (but not identical) idea, that power increases with the decrease of corporeal mass, is found in *Sententiae* 35. These few parallels are not exact, and thus the related expression in the *Anonymous Commentary* is not, in my opinion, a sure sign of Porphyry's authorship.[45]

(3) The expressions, God as an "idea" of being (*Anon. in Parm.* XII.32; XIV.12), or an "idea" and logos of itself (Victorinus, *Adv. Ar.* 1.50.16), are not attested in the undisputed Porphyrian evidence at all. The latter variant, however, occurs in *Zostrianos* (66.21; 74,9); and similar expressions occur in Numenius,[46] Plotinus,[47] and implicitly in the *Apocryphon of John*. In the *Apocryphon of John* NHC III.21.23–24, the "Blessed One" (i.e., the Invisible Spirit) is said to have revealed his appearance (ἰδέα) to the evil archons. Of course, this is not exactly what we find in Hadot's fragments, but the term ἰδέα is, nonetheless, connected

---

44. The expression in the gen. pl., ὁ ἐπὶ πάντων θεός, occurs in Eph 4:6 and Rom 9:5. See Majercik 2001, 270.

45. Thus also Edwards 1990, 23.

46. Numenius (frg. 20 des Places) considered the first God as the "idea of Good" (ἀγαθοῦ ἰδέα).

47. Plotinus, as Corrigan (2000b, 152) has shown, considered the One as a "limit" (πέρας) of intellectual beauty (*Enn.* 6.7 [38].32.34), and identified the "limit of intellect" as an ἰδέα ἐν στάσει (6.2 [43].8.23–25).

with the first principle in the *Apocryphon of John*. In arguing for a Porphyrian background for these concepts, Majercik appeals to the post-Porphyrian Julian the Emperor, who also speaks of the first principle as an "idea of being," and who identifies "being" with "intelligible as a whole" (*Or.* IV 5 Lacombrade 132cd). Because Porphyry also identified the Intellect, that is, the One-Being, with "the intelligible plane" (Proclus, *In Parm.* 6:1053,37–1054,10 Cousin), Majercik thinks Julian is using a specifically Porphyrian concept, which would subsequently strengthen the attribution of the *Commentary* to Porphyry (Majercik 2001, 278). In my view, the material from Julian does not increase the likelihood of that attribution: the concept of God as an "idea of being" is not found in the undisputed Porphyrian evidence, and the identification of the second hypostasis with the whole of the intelligible is, it seems to me, what, for example, Plotinus (*Enn.* 5.9 [5]; 6.4–5 [22–23]; 5.5 [32]) and the Sethians (e.g., *Zost.* 21; 115–116) taught as well.

(4) God's "simplicity," combined with his being "single" and "alone," occur together with an apparent exegesis of *Chaldean Oracles* 3–4,[48] both in the *Anon. in Parm.* (IX.1–4: ἁπλότης; XII.4: ἓν μόνον) and a passage in Damascius (*Princ.* 3.145.10–18 Westerink-Combès = §119 Ruelle: Ὁ γὰρ εἷς οὗτος ὅλος πατὴρ ... πατὴρ μόνον ... ἁπλότητος). Since such expressions applied to God are also found in Porphyry's *Hist. phil.* 15 ("simplicity," ἁπλότης) and 18 ("single and alone," ὁ θεὸς ὁ πρῶτος καὶ μόνος), and because Porphyry is known to have speculated on the *Chaldean Oracles*, Majercik has proposed that the combination of the three expressions with the Chaldean exegesis in the *Anonymous Commentary* would strengthen its attribution to Porphyry (Majercik 2001, 272 n. 26). This proposal rests partially on the assumption that Damascius is quoting a Porphyrian teaching. However, Damascius does not here claim Porphyrian provenance, while he elsewhere says explicitly when he is quoting Porphyry (e.g., *Princ.* 2:1.4–2.10 Westerink-Combès = §43 Ruelle). In addition, the three expressions occur also in the material common to Victorinus (*unum simplex, Adv. Ar.* 1.49.12; *solus in solo*, 1.50.9; *soli*, 1.49.20; *simplicitate unus*, 1.50.10) and *Zostrianos* (ΟΥΑ ΠΕ Ν̄ϨΑΠΛΟΥΝ, 66.20; cf. 67.20; ΟΥΑ ΟΥⲰΤ, 64.14; ΜΑΥΑΑϤ, 64.22), where, importantly, they are connected with God's triple-power identified as the existence-life-blessedness triad. This speculation on the triple-power can be seen as an equivalent to the Chaldean exegesis in the *Anonymous Commentary* and Damascius, which sought to explain the relationships among the members of the triad of Father–power–intellect. Thus, the combination of the three expressions with a "Chaldean" exegesis is not confined to Porphyry, but is found in several

---

48. Damascius, *Princ.* 3.145.10–18 Westerink-Combès = §119 Ruelle: "The Father alone ... Power is brought into relation with him ... He is the Father of Intellect"; *Anon. in Parm.* IX.1–4: "He has snatched himself away from all things that are his.... Power and Intellect have been unified in his simplicity."

sources, some of which are anonymous and Gnostic. Tardieu has suggested that the author of the *Anonymous Commentary on the Parmenides* was here, in fact, dependent on the common source behind Victorinus and *Zostrianos* (Tardieu 1996, 100–101).

(5) The expression τὸ μὴ ὄν *super* τὸ ὄν ("the non-being above being"), used by Victorinus (*Cand.* 14.1 = §19 Hadot) to denote the transcendent first principle beyond being, is found twice in *Sent.* 26.3-6 in a practically identical form: τὸ ὑπὲρ τὸ ὄν μὴ ὄν. This alone, of course, is not enough to prove that we are dealing with a uniquely Porphyrian phrase. Indeed, *Allogenes* describes the Unknowable One as a "non-being" (ⲀⲦϢⲰⲠⲈ, 55.30; 62.23; 65.33; 66.27; ⲀⲦⲞⲨⲤⲒⲀ, 53.31), and as "not one of those things that exist, but another thing (ⲔⲈⲚⲔⲀ), superior to all superlatives" (63.17-20). Turner has speculated that the Coptic ⲔⲈⲚⲔⲀ could perhaps translate the Greek τι, thus bringing the concept into relation with the Stoic category of τι,[49] which, according to Hadot, underlies the suggested Porphyrian expression. Hadot argued that Porphyry replaced the supreme Stoic category of τι—which simultaneously contains and transcends both being and non-being—with his "non-being above being."[50] But it is perhaps even easier to see this logic in the passage from *Allogenes*, where the term τι possibly occurs, than in Porphyry's *Sent.* 26, where τι does not occur. Be that as it may, Porphyry's use of the expression is limited to one single paragraph in the *Sententiae*, and this alone does not make the expression specifically Porphyrian.

(6) The rest of the suggested Porphyrian expressions and specific terms in the fragments are too vague and common to prove anything.[51] In fact, the *Commentary* includes eleven words that even Hadot considered to be problematic for his theory.[52] Some of these, especially (ἀ)σύζυγος and πλήρωμα, would seem to be more at home in Gnostic speculations.[53] Likewise, Hadot's appeals to the

---

49. Turner 2004, 54. The parallel passage in the *Ap. John* ("he is not something (ⲞⲨⲖⲀⲀⲨ) among beings but he is far superior, not as being superior but himself"; NHC II.3.26-29 parr.) has ⲖⲀⲀⲨ, which indeed translates τι.

50. Hadot 1968, 1:159-78, 485-88.

51. According to Hadot (1961, 430-38), the *Commentary* contains (a) common philosophical words (ἀνεννόητος [1 undisputed Porphyrian occurrence cited by Hadot], ἀνεπινόητος [1], ἐξαλλάττειν [6], ἔχεσθαι [1], καταλαμβάνειν [1]); (b) words that are common to Porphyry (ἐξηγητικός [3], μηνύειν [17], οὐσιοῦσθαι [4], παράστασις [9], προσόντα [5]); and (c) certain expressions that are common to Porphyry (ἰδιότης [2]; ὅλος [4]; ποιεῖσθαι [5]; ὑπόστασις [3]). Hadot 1968, 1:89 n. 2, adds the following "common" Porphyrian terms: προσπάθεια [5], δίκην ἀποτίννυσθαι [2], σπᾶν, ἀποσπᾶν [7], ἀναπόσπαστος [1], ἀπερίσπαστος [2], ἐπισπάσθαι [1], παράσπασις [1], κατασπᾶν [2], σωτηρία τῆς ψυχῆς [2]. Cf. the criticism of Edwards 1990, 23-24.

52. The problematic words are: ἀκραιφνότης, ἀναγγελτικός, ἀσύζυγος, ἄσχετος, ἑνάς, ἐνούσιος, προούσιος, καθυπονοεῖν, παρέλλειψις, πλήρωμα, πληρωτικός. Hadot 1961, 431-34.

53. Πλήρωμα occurs, for example, in Irenaeus's description of the Valentinian "Great Account" (*Adv. Haer.* 1.1-8): 1.1.23, 48; 2.65, 72, 95, 100-101; 3.1, 57, 88; 4.1, 3, 6, 13, 87; 5.27,

Commentary's "Porphyrian theory of the knowledge of God,"[54] and the idea that "God may seem like nothing to us because we are nothing in relation to him,"[55] are not unique to Porphyry, nor do they necessarily find exact parallels in the undisputed Porphyrian evidence.[56]

We may finally consider the attitudes represented in the fragments towards the *Chaldean Oracles* and their use of Stoic physics; for, according to Hadot, Porphyry's innovative metaphysics stems from his interpretation of Plotinus in light of these Chaldaean and Stoic traditions. In Hadot's opinion, the somewhat critical attitude towards the *Chaldean Oracles* in the *Anonymous Commentary on the Parmenides* would be similar to that of Porphyry.[57] In the *Commentary*, the author seems to question the authority of both the *Oracles* themselves as well as

---

37, 58; 6.84; 7.3, 7, 9, 14, 24; 8.30, 31, 43, 89, 96, 102, 108–9,125, 173, 174 Rousseau-Doutreleau; in the *Ap. John* (NHC III.14.4; 21.8; 25.14; 27.20; 28.14,15; 30.20; 32.12,21 parr.); and in *Zostrianos* (77.8). Ἀσύζυγος occurs in the Valentinian "Great Account" (*Adv. Haer.* 1.2.57: *sine coniuge*; Epiphanius's Greek version in *Pan.* 31.12.5: ἀσύζυγον), and in Irenaeus's version or source of the *Ap. John* (*Adv. Haer.* 1.29.55–56: *sine coniugatione*; Theodoret's Greek fragment in *Haer. fab. comp.* 1.13 does not cover this section of Irenaeus's text). Σύ(ν)ζυγος, for its part, occurs in the Valentinian "Great Account" (*Adv. Haer.* 1.2.19, 59: *coniux*) and in the *Ap. John* (NHC III.14.18, 21, 23; 15.8; 21.1, 8; 30.11 parr.). See also *Corp. herm.* 6.

54. Hadot 1961, 426–27. Hadot identifies the following items as relevant: (a) the term "God" is much utilized; (b) God can be known only in learned ignorance; (c) one must become worthy of God to know him; (d) it is better to be silent than talk about God; (e) God knows everything; and (f) we must not attribute to God our own conditions because we are nothing. Such ideas of the *Commentary* occur in Porphyry's *Sent.* 25; *Marc.* 13; 15–16; *Antr. nymph.* 74.22; *Abst.* 2.34; *Epistula ad Anebonem*. However, I find it hard to see why these concepts would be specifically Porphyrian as they seem quite common, and can all be found in Gnostic sources as well. Cf. *Allogenes*, which speaks of "God" (e.g., 47.35–36; 56.20; 61.10–15), learned ignorance (59.26–60,12; 61.1–19), Allogenes' hundred-year preparation to become worthy of the vision of the One (56–58), the silence (52.18–28; 59.9–60.16; 61.21; 62.24–25; 63.35; 65.19; 68.32), God as "super-knowledge" (63.14–16; 64.10–23), who is surely beyond all human condition (cf. Plotinus, *Enn.* 6.7 [38].41; 3.8 [30].11) as he is described in terms of negative theology. Learned ignorance is found also in the *Chaldean Oracles* 1 and in Plotinus (*Enn.* 6.9 [9].3–4; 3.8 [30].9.29–32; 6.7 [38].36.15–16; 6.8 [39].21.25–33).

55. Hadot 1961, 426. The Porphyrian parallel (*Sent.* 27) here is not exact, as Porphyry speaks of the relationship between the sensible and the intelligible, and not of us and God. In addition, the author of the *Anonymous Commentary* adds that God has no relations to what follows, except that he knows the past and the future (IV.32–35). This, according to Corrigan (2000b, 153–54), tends to exclude Porphyry as the author, due to Plotinus's "detailed critique of a temporal, anthropomorphic paradigm for creative demiurgy" (*Enn.* 5.8 [31].7; 6.7 [38].1–13) that his star-student could not have ignored. Of course, Plotinus himself had already insisted that the One has no relations to what follows (*Enn.* 3.9 [13].9; 3.8 [30].10; 6.8 [39].8), and had spoken of the One's "nothingness": the One is not alive (3.9 [13].9); and nothing can be predicated of it (3.8 [39].10).

56. See the two previous footnotes.

57. Hadot 1968, 94, 107–8, 428. Cf., however, Edwards 1990, 22–24.

of those who have transmitted them, likely the *Juliani*, the traditional late-second century compilers of the oracles: "[*citing an exegesis of the Chaldean Oracles frgs. 3-4, i.e., the Father-power-intellect triad*] In a way, this is correctly and truly said, if gods, as those say who have passed on this tradition, really have proclaimed these things" (IX.8-10; trans. Bechtle). However, as far as we know, Porphyry never questioned the *Oracles* in quite this manner. We do have surviving fragments of two Porphyrian works that deal with the *Chaldean Oracles*. While in the *Philosophy of the Oracles*,[58] Porphyry seems to have accepted the saving power of theurgic rituals,[59] in his apparently later work, *De regressu animae*,[60] he is of the opinion that theurgy can only purify the lower part of one's soul (Augustine, *Civ.* 10.9, 23, 27, 28), and that true salvation requires philosophical contemplation (10.29). However, this reservation expresses a different kind of criticism of the *Chaldean Oracles* than what we find in the *Anonymous Commentary on the Parmenides*, as the latter questions the validity of (the transmission of) metaphysical speculations and not of theurgic rituals.

Hadot also sees Stoic concepts behind many of the suggested Porphyrian innovations.[61] These include: (a) the tensile ("tonique") movement of the divine πνεῦμα, where expansion produces quantities and qualities, and contraction unity and substance (Nemesius, *De natura hominis* 70.6-71.4), and which would explain Intellect's self-constituting process of stability/coexistence-procession-turning back;[62] (b) the *spermatikos logos* doctrine, where the seed already contains everything in itself potentially, and which would lie behind the idea of prefiguration (via Pythagorean speculations on the Monad);[63] (c) the idea that substance is determined by an active principle, expressed with the method of paronyms (e.g., νοῦς is determined by νοότης), which would explain Porphyry's use of the method of paronyms where cognates of the same root denote various degrees of being, life and mind;[64] (d) the concept of total blending, which would explain the idea of predominance in the triad;[65] (e) the designation of God

---

58. See the edition of Wolff (1983; reprint of 1856).

59. Nothing critical is recorded in the surviving fragments. See also Eunapius, *Vita Porphyrii*.

60. Preserved in Augustine's *De civitate Dei* (X.9-10, 16, 18, 21, 23, 26-30, 32; 12.21, 27; 13.19; 22.12, 27 Bidez). For the dating, see Bidez 1913, 15-16. See also Rasimus, forthcoming.

61. See Hadot 1968, 1:89-90 n. 5, 109-10, 225-34, 485-88.

62. Ibid., 225-37, 486. Hadot (1957, 135-36) also suggested that Numenius and Plotinus had already applied the tensile movement to the intelligible realm.

63. Hadot 1968, 1:311-12.

64. Ibid., 353, 364-66, 487-93.

65. Hadot 1968, 1:238-46, 486. See also Hadot 1957, 123-26, where he already argued that Philo's treatment of Abraham-Isaac-Jacob as representing three inseparable stages of παιδεία is not only based on the Stoic division of philosophy in three branches, but that it also anticipates Porphyry's enneadic intelligible triad. This suggestion has been criticized (see the discussion in Hadot 1957, 142-57).

as πνεῦμα (Hadot 1968, 1:295–97); (f) the concept of ὕπαρξις which would be elevated from its Stoic status as denoting incorporeal being to mean pure undetermined being above determined being (Hadot 1957, 487–93); and related to this, as previously noted, (g) the category of τι replaced, as it were, with the "non-being above being" (Hadot 1957, 159–78, 485–88).

The Stoic background of many of the suggested Porphyrian innovations is an attractive hypothesis. However, nothing proves that it was Porphyry who first came up with these Stoicisms. Using Stoic concepts in a Platonic framework was nothing new, as Hadot himself admits, but in his opinion, Porphyry was the most systematic thinker in this regard (Hadot 1957, 485). Yet, as we will see, many of these suggested innovative Stoicisms can be seen to be already at work in the pre-Plotinian *Apocryphon of John*. Moreover, an additional, specific example of the use of Stoic concepts may, in fact, disqualify Porphyry as the author of the *Anonymous Commentary*. We know that Porphyry used the Stoic theory of mixture in discussing the union of sensible and intelligible, using man's "animal" and "rational" natures as an example.[66] We also find such an example in the *Anonymous Commentary* 11–12 (see Hadot 1968, 1:109–13). But importantly, the author of the *Anonymous Commentary* uses it as an analogy to the theory of *intelligible* participation, which is specifically denied of Porphyry by later *testimonia* (Syrianus, *In Metaph.* 109, 12–16; Proclus, *In Tim.* 3:33,32–33 Diehl).[67]

Finally, and related to the question of the transposition of Stoic physics to Platonic metaphysics, we may observe that sometimes, in Hadot's fragments, attributes of lower realities are transposed to higher ones (regardless of whether the lower realities and their attributes occur in Stoic, Peripatetic or Platonic sources). This again would be characteristic of Porphyry (see Hadot 1961, 425; 1968, 1:487–93). In the *Anonymous Commentary* XIII.27–XIV.4, the author may have presupposed Aristotle's theory of common sense in describing the Intellect (Hadot 1961, 425); and in Victorinus's fragments, paralleled in *Zostrianos*, we find attributes of the One that Plato had used of matter and of the intelligible world in *Timaeus* and *Phaedrus*.[68] Even though we do find a similar technique of transposing concepts related to the sensible world to the higher realms in the undisputed Porphyrian material (cf. *Sent.* 44), we are simply dealing with a wider phenomenon, since Philo and Plotinus had already employed it.[69]

---

66. Hadot 1957, 89–90 n. 5 offers the following examples of Porphyry's Stoicizing speculations on the mixture of the sensible with the intelligible: *Symmikta Zetemata* 69 Dörrie 1959; *Gaur.* 10.5; *Sent.* 33.5.

67. Corrigan (2000b, 153, 165–67) points out that such a "Middle Platonic" doctrine of intellectual participation is, on the other hand, attested of Numenius, Amelius, and Plotinus. See Bechtle 1999a, 249–52.

68. Tardieu 1996, 65, 70–75.

69. Plotinus, in *Enn.* 6.8 [39].11.16 (χώραν καὶ τόπον, ὥσπερ τι χάος), appears to be thinking of Hesiod's Chaos (Armstrong 1966–1988, 7:262–63 n. 1) in describing incorrect notions

In summary, Hadot's case for the Porphyrian authorship of the *Anonymous Commentary on the Parmenides* and of the eighty-nine fragments embedded in Victorinus's theological works remains inconclusive at best. Porphyry cannot be demonstrated to be the only suitable candidate for being the author of the fragments, and the correspondence between the fragments and the undisputed Porphyrian evidence is not as close as Hadot assumed. Some evidence even suggests that Porphyry *cannot* be the author of the *Anonymous Commentary on the Parmenides*. On the other hand, it has already been stated that the Sethian evidence offers, in many instances, a better comparison with the fragments than does the undisputed Porphyrian material. Let us therefore take a closer look at the four Platonizing Sethian treatises, viz. *Zostrianos, Allogenes, Steles Seth*, and *Marsanes*, after which we will turn our attention to the *Apocryphon of John*.

The Platonizing Sethian Treatises

Most of the innovative "Porphyrian" doctrines that we encounter in Hadot's fragments are well attested in the Platonizing Sethian treatises. This is especially the case with the two texts that are known to have circulated in Plotinus's seminars, that is, *Zostrianos* and *Allogenes*. We will first take a closer look at Sethian metaphysical speculations in general before engaging in a more detailed comparison between them and Hadot's fragments.

The Platonizing Sethian treatises posit a triad of first principles at the summit of their system: Father/the Invisible Spirit; Mother/Barbelo; Son/Autogenes. This is the traditional Sethian triad, which is attested in several pre-Plotinian texts, e.g., the *Apocryphon of John, Trimorphic Protennoia* (NHC XIII.1) and the *Holy Book of the Great Invisible Spirit* (NHC III.2; IV.2). It is almost certainly based on Plato's Father–Mother–Child triad in *Timaeus* 48e–52d, and not on nascent Trinitarian speculations (Turner 2001, 252). In the *Apocryphon of John*, the Father's first thought externalizes itself as Barbelo, who in turn gives birth to the Son Autogenes (II.4.19–7.24 and parallels). But in the Platonizing Sethian treatises, the relations among the three supreme principles are expressed differently, in terms of deriving multiplicity from unity, as John Turner has shown (see especially Turner 2001, 512–47). The Invisible Spirit, using its triple-power (τριδύναμος)—identified as existence-life-blessedness/mind (see, e.g., *Zost.* 15.18–19)—externalizes the hidden (καλυπτός) potential multiplicity as the first-manifested (προτοφανής) aeon of Barbelo, whose final constituent is αὐτογενής, that is, self-constitution. The triple-power is the energy (ἐνέργεια; *Zost.* 79.21) by means of which this three-stage process takes place, perhaps simply a name given to the process itself. This new scheme, in all its variants, seems to have robbed

---

about the Good. Philo, in *Leg.* 3.36 (ὁ θεὸς … ὁ ἄποιος), speaks of God as unqualified, which is a Stoic notion of matter. See Tardieu 1996, 72–73.

the Son Autogenes of his previous independence and granted a quasi-independent status to the Triple-Powered One between the Invisible Spirit and Barbelo. It seems to me that this has resulted from various attempts to superimpose two new and related triads upon the traditional Sethian triad of Father-Barbelo-Autogenes: (1) existence-life-blessedness/mind, and (2) a specifically Sethian triad of καλυπτός-πρωτοφανής-αὐτογενής.[70] The latter triad describes the derivative process in functional terms, while the former identifies the three stages of the process itself. In *Zostrianos* 15.1–19, these two new triads are clearly combined with each other, resulting in the equation between existence (ὕπαρξις) and καλυπτός. Elsewhere ὕπαρξις is used of the first principle's undetermined existence (e.g., *Zost.* 66–68; 74). Because the Invisible Spirit's triple-power in turn somehow equals the triad of existence-life-blessedness/mind, we seem to have here an attempt at an "enneadic" structuring of the first Sethian principles: (1) Invisible Spirit-ὕπαρξις-καλυπτός, (2) Barbelo-life-πρωτοφανής, (3) Son-intellect-αὐτογενής. Depending on the viewpoint, the Triple-Power—if it is taken as describing the whole triadic process—can then be seen as a mediating entity between the principles,[71] or as belonging to the Invisible Spirit,[72] or Barbelo.[73] Similarly, depending again on the viewpoint, the members of the καλυπτός-πρωτοφανής-αὐτογενής triad can all be said to belong to Barbelo, but its first and third members can also be seen to coincide with the Father/Invisible Spirit and the Son/Autogenes, respectively.[74]

---

70. *Zost.* 15.6–12; 18.5–19; 19.5–21; 20.4–9; 22.9–23.5; 24.3–6; 41; 44.26–31; 58.14–16; 124.18–125.20; *Allogenes* 45.30–46.23; 51.17–26; 58.12–19. See the scattered references in *Steles Seth* 119.16; 122.14; 123.1–5; 126.5; and possibly in *Marsanes* 3.26–4.10 (Turner 2001, 540). Plotinus (*Enn.* 5.5 [32].7.31–34) and Victorinus (*Cand.* 14.11–25 = §20 Hadot: *occultum/absconditum-manifestatio-generatio*) may refer to this Sethian triad (Corrigan 2000a, 50–51; Tardieu 1996, 14), which occurs explicitly only in the Platonizing Sethian treatises, but whose seeds have been sown already in the earlier Sethian tradition (*Ap. John*, e.g., II.7.11–33 [αὐτογενής]; II.8.32 [ⲠϢⲞⲢⲠ ⲞⲨⲰⲚϨ < πρωτοφανής]; *Holy Book* NHC IV.55.25 [ϢⲞⲢⲠ ⲈⲦⲀϤⲞⲨⲰⲚϨ < πρωτοφανής]; 57.16 [καλυπτός]; e.g., 60.2 [αὐτογενής]. See Turner 2001, 540 n. 37). See also the later Codex Bruce, *Untitled* 6.12–13.

71. See, e.g., *Allogenes* 45.9–46.35 (the Invisible Spirit becomes the aeon of Barbelo by self-extension through his Triple-Powered One); *Marsanes* 4.10–22 (the tenth "seal" concerns Barbelo, the eleventh and the twelfth speak of the Invisible One who possesses three powers, and of the Spirit without being belonging to the first Unbegotten one, and the thirteenth seal speaks of the Silent One).

72. See, e.g., *Zost.* 20.15–18 (the Invisible Triple-Powered One); *Allogenes* 51.8–9; 66.33–35 (the Invisible Triple-Powered Spirit).

73. See, e.g., *Steles Seth* 121.31–32 (You [Barbelo] are a Triple-Power).

74. Cf. Turner 2001, 531–47. The tripartite division of the aeon of Barbelo into καλυπτός-πρωτοφανής-αὐτογενής can further be seen as an equivalent to a Middle Platonic (see Numenius frgs. 11, 13, 15, 16 des Places; Amelius *apud* Proclus, *In Tim.* 1:306,1–14 Diehl; Plotinus, *Enn.* 3.9 [13].1) tripartitioning of the Intellect into the contemplated, contemplating and discursive/demiurgic minds (Turner 2001, 696–97). This may explain the fact that πρωτοφανής—as the contemplating Intellect—is often identified as νοῦς (e.g., *Zost.* 18.5–7;

Let us now examine how the suggested "Porphyrian" features occur in the Platonizing Sethian treatises. First, the being–life–mind triad is attested in *passim*, especially in the canonical order, but also in the non-canonical order; we find both orders frequently in Plotinus, too (see above, esp. n. 37). The second principle's coexistence with, procession out of and turning back to the One, is also described both in terms of the Triple Powered One and Invisible Spirit,[75] and also with the help of the specifically Sethian triad of καλυπτός-προτοφανής-αὐτογενής. Second, the prefiguration of the Second One or the triad in the First One, is attested abundantly.[76] Third, the distinction between the transcendent undetermined, and lower determined forms of being, life and mind, are also frequently attested in the Sethian texts.[77] Fourth, the Sethian texts use the term ὕπαρξις for a higher and undetermined, even "non-being," existence, and attribute it to the first member of the intelligible triad and/or the first principle.[78] Finally, the enneadic structuring of the triad, including the use of the principles

---

38.17–18; 44.27–29; 54.19–20; 124.21–22; 129.4–6; *Allogenes* 45.33–35; 51.19–20; 58.16–18; *Steles Seth* 123.5–6).

75. *Zost.* 79.10–81.20; *Allogenes* 49.7–14; 53.10–18.

76. *Allogenes*, e.g., 47.10–14 (he contained them beforehand); 48.36–38 (the One truly exists); 49.26–38 (That-Which-Is contains Vitality and Mentality); 59.22–26 (the One embraces all these silently and inactively); 61.32–62.2 (he exists, acts, know and lives incomprehensibly); 66.28–30 (he contains them all, being at rest); *Zostrianos*, e.g., 20.2–15 (Barbelo as Kalyptos preexists in the Invisible Spirit); 20.18–19 (Invisible Spirit is [the source of them all]); *65.6–7 (the One is a preprinciple); *65.23–66.3 (the One is the totality of the truly existent ones); *66.14–67.4; *67.24–68.1; 77.20–21 (Barbelo has prepotency); 81.7–20 (Barbelo proceeded from the preexisting One); 82.5–13 (Barbelo foreknows the One and, as Kalyptos, is a reduplication of the One's knowledge); 84.12–22 (Barbelo is the Blessedness of the Invisible Spirit and knowledge of the primal Existence within the simplicity of the Invisible Spirit); 118.9–16 (Barbelo is the knowledge of the One, and the One as a triad is alive with life); *Steles Seth* 121.25–32 (Barbelo has preexisted from and through him); 125.28–32 (the One is the existence, life, and mind of them all).

77. *Allogenes* 48.17–19 (the One thinks himself); 48.36–38 (the One truly exists); 49.26–38 (That-Which-Is—Vitality—Mentality; Vitality possesses non-Being and Mentality); 61.32–62.2 (the One exists, acts, know and lives incomprehensibly; 65.32–36 (the One has a non-being [ὕπαρξις]); *Zost.* 20.18–19 (the Invisible Spirit is an [insubstantial Existence]); 58.16–20 (the Invisible Spirit is a knower and foreknower); *64.14–16 (the One preexists); *65.6–7 (the One is a preprinciple); *67.13–15 (Idea of an idea); 74.4–25 (the One truly preexists from himself); 77.20–21 (Barbelo has prepotency); 82.5–13 (Barbelo foreknows the One and, as Kalyptos, is a reduplication of the One's knowledge); 84.12–22 (Barbelo is the knowledge of the primal Existence within the simplicity of the Invisible Spirit); *Steles Seth* 124.18–20 (the One is a preexistent one); 126.14–15 (the One exists within himself).

78. *Zost.* 2.21–30; 3.8–11; 14.13; 15.10–16; 16.1, 11–12; 17.2; 20.21–22; 23.27; 30.18; 34.1, 5; 36.2; 40.10–11; *66.16–19; *68.16–17; 73.1, 8; 74.8–9; 75.7; 78.4, 11; 79.5–20; 84.16; 86.15–16; 95.5, 16; 98.5; 99.2; 107.3; 124.16; *Allogenes* 46.7–12; 47.25; 48.16; 53.31; 55.28–30; 57.6; 59.20; 60.31; 61.37–38; 62.23; 65.29–33; *Steles Seth* 124.26–27; 125.28.

of mutual implication and relative predominance, and of the method of paronyms, including those ending in -ότης, are found in Sethian texts,[79] most clearly in *Allogenes* 49.26–38:

> He is Vitality (ⲦⲘⲚⲦⲰⲚϨ < ζωότης), and Mentality (ⲦⲘⲚⲦⲈⲒⲘⲈ < νοήτης) and That-Which-Is (ⲠⲈⲦϢⲞⲞⲠ < ὀντότης/οὐσιότης). For then That-Which-Is constantly possesses its Vitality and Mentality (νοήτης), and <...> Vitality possesses non-Being and Mentality. Mentality possesses Life and That-Which-Is. And the three are one, although individually they are three.[80]

As noted above, the concepts τριδύναμος (the usual Coptic expression is ϢⲘⲚⲦϬⲞⲘ),[81] μακάριος,[82] and God as πνεῦμα,[83] that occur in the material common to Victorinus and *Zostrianos*, also occur *passim* in the Platonizing Sethian treatises. As in Victorinus, μακάριος has replaced the third ("intellect") aspect of the being–life–mind triad. Especially significant is the term τριδύναμος, which occurs in some later Neoplatonic authors,[84] and which is generally considered to be a Gnostic innovation.[85] This Triple-Power is, as noted above, a

---

79. *Zost.* 15.1–12 (Life–Blessedness–Existence; Vitality–Knowledge–Divinity; αὐτογενής-προτοφανής-καλυπτός); *66.14–20; *Steles Seth*: 125.25–33 (Father is One, and ὕπαρξις–life–mind of them all); *Allogenes* 49.26–38.
80. The Coptic text is emended slightly by both Turner (1990, 200–201, 252–53) and Funk (2004, 198, 246–47). But while both editors prefer to drop the extraneous word ⲠⲰⲚϨ at 49.31 (Turner drops also the following ⲈⲞⲨⲚⲦⲈ; Funk keeps it but drops the preceding ⲀⲨⲰ), Funk conserves the ⲚⲦⲘⲚⲦⲀⲦⲞⲨⲤⲒⲀ at 49.32–33 ("non-Being") *pace* Turner who had emended it to ⲚⲦⲞⲨⲤⲒⲀ ("Being"). According to Funk and Poirier, the "non-Being" could be taken as an equivalent of ϮϨⲨⲠⲀⲢⲜⲒⲤ ⲚⲚⲀⲦⲞⲨⲤⲒⲀ ("non-substantial existence") occurring later at 53.31–32. Thus, the passage at *Allogenes* 49.26–38 would be perfectly in line with the *locus classicus* in Proclus, *Elem. Theol.* 103 (Funk and Poirier 2004, 247). For the underlying Greek terms, see Turner 1990, 252–53; and Majercik 1992, 481–82. Νοήτης (possibly a corruption—or "strange neologism," as Turner puts it—of νοότης) occurs as such in the Coptic (*Allogenes* 49.30–31, 34).
81. The Triple-Powered One is spoken of in *Allogenes* 45.13, 21; 47.7–11; 51.8–9; 52.19, 30–35; 53.30–31; 58.24–26; 61.6, 19–20; 64.34–35; 66.33–35; *Zost.* 15.18–19; 17.6–8; 20.16–19; 24.12–13; 63.7–8; *66.14–18; 79.16–25; 80.18; 87.10–14; 93.7; 97.2–3; 118.9–12; 123.18–19; 124.3–4; 128.1–22; *Steles Seth* 120.21–22; 121.31–32; 123.23; and *Marsanes* 4.13–19; 6.19; 7.16–29; 8.5–20; 9.7–25; 10.8–11; 14.22–23; 15.1–3.
82. *Allogenes* 54.16; 59.9–20; 60.17–31; *Zostrianos*, e.g., 14.13; *66.17; 73.11; 75.17; *Steles Seth* 122.23.
83. See the common Sethian designation, the "Invisible Spirit," for the first principle, e.g., in the *Ap. John* NHC II.2.33; 5.12; 5.28; 7.14 parr.; *Zostrianos* 17.12–13; 20.17–18; 24.9–10; 118.11–12; 122.4; 129.11–12; *Allogenes* 49.9–10; 51.35; 64.36.
84. Proclus, *In Tim.* 2:41, 20 Diehl; *In Parm.* 1215.10–11; Hierocles, *In aur. carm.* 20; and, of course, Victorinus, *Adv. Ar.* 1.56.4–5 (§41 Hadot); 4.21.26–27 (§76 Hadot); Majercik 1992, 480.
85. Abramowski 1983, 111–12; Majercik 1992, 479–80; Pearson 1990, 157–58; Turner 2001, 153.

metaphysical tool used to describe the derivation of multiplicity from unity in three phases. Similar expressions, τριγλώχις and τριοῦχος, are found in the *Chaldean Oracles* (frgs. 2, 26), but the term τριδύναμος itself is already found in the second-century Sethian *Ap. John*, denoting the second principle, Barbelo.[86]

As noted above, the expressions "God's simplicity" and God as an "idea," are both found in *Zostrianos*, and the latter implicitly also in the *Ap. John*; and a variant of the "non-being above being," given especially its possible Stoic connection (τι), can be seen in *Allogenes* and the *Apocryphon of John*.

The *Chaldean Oracles*, as far as I know, are never explicitly referred to in the Sethian texts. However, several possible allusions can be pointed out. The attribution of the treatise *Zostrianos* to the eponymous "Chaldean" character can be taken as an indication of an appeal to that very Chaldean tradition. The same applies, of course, to the figure of Zoroaster, mentioned in the long recension of the *Ap. John* (NHC II.19.10 and and parallels), in the colophon of *Zostrianos*, and in Porphyry's reference to Gnostic apocalypses (*Vit. Plot.* 16).[87] In addition, the *Apocryphon of John* identifies the first two members of its supreme triad as Father and Power, the latter being the feminine triple-powered Barbelo (NHC II.5.8 parr.; see below). As for the use of Stoic concepts, it can be noted that the suggested Stoicisms in the material common to Victorinus and *Zostrianos* naturally occur in the latter. However, the author of the *Apocryphon of John* seems to already have utilized several Stoic notions in his representation of the Invisible Spirit, as Pleše (2006) has argued, and these would apply to the Platonizing Sethian treatises as well. A detailed discussion of the Stoicisms and Chaldeanisms in the *Apocryphon of John* will follow presently.

In terms of comparison of doctrines, terminology and interpretative strategies, the match between Hadot's fragments and the Sethian texts seems to be at least as good—if not better—than that between the fragments and the undisputed Porphyrian evidence. This fact cannot be explained away quite so easily as Majercik has attempted to do. She suggests that the Greek *Vorlagen* of our Coptic versions of *Zostrianos* and *Allogenes* are thorough revisions of the versions read in Plotinus's seminars, revised in light of Porphyry's criticism (Majercik 1992, 486). This is, of course, theoretically possible (see Tardieu 1996, 112; Brisson 1999a, 179), but it rests on the assumption that Porphyry *is* the author of the fragments in question, which needs to be proven first. And if Majercik were right, we would not expect to find the innovative "Porphyrian" ideas in the second-century *Apocryphon of John*. In fact, the occurrence of many of these ideas and terms in the pre-Plotinian *Ap. John* also increases the likelihood that Tardieu's common

---

86. NHC III.8.2–3: [ⲦⲰⲞ]ⲘⲚⲦ ⲚⲆⲨⲚ[ⲀⲘⲒⲤ]; *BG* 27.21–28.1: ⲦⲰⲞ[Ⲙ]ⲚⲦⲈ ⲚϬⲞⲘ; II.5.8: ⲦⲰⲞⲘⲦⲈ ⲚϬⲞⲘ.

87. The colophon is, in fact, a cryptogram, whose decipherment requires that one change the letters according to a key. On the deciphering of the cryptogram, see Turner 2000a, 661.

source behind Victorinus and *Zostrianos* really is Middle Platonic, and likely even a Gnostic(izing) source, as Hadot himself later suggested. Let us then investigate the *Apocryphon of John* in more detail.

The *Apocryphon of John*

The *Apocryphon of John* describes the first principle in terms of both negative and positive theologies. As Turner has pointed out, the author uses the *via negativa* and *via eminentiae* in a combination similar to that of the author of *Allogenes*: the first principle is in both texts said to be something superior to what is negated of him (Turner 2000b, 185–86). For example, "He is neither perfection, nor blessedness nor divinity, but rather something superior to them" (*Ap. John BG* 24.6–25.7; cf. *Allogenes* 62.28–36). Turner has shown that the *Apocryphon of John* and *Allogenes* contain several word-for-word parallels in engaging in this strategy of negation of all alternatives in order to launch the mind towards a higher level (Turner 2000b, 185). This, according to Turner, indicates a common source, likely a commentary on Plato's *Parmenides* (Turner 2000b, 185). The *Apocryphon of John* and *Allogenes* alike deny the One both infinity and unlimitedness, corporeality and incorporeality, greatness and smallness, quantity and quality, as well as participation in eternity and time (*Ap. John BG* 24.13–25.3; *Allogenes* 63.1–24). At the same time, the affirmative theology in the *Ap. John* describes the One as Spirit and Father, for example. Interestingly, the first principle is described as always existing (*BG* 24.2) yet his "being" is described as superior to that of others (24.20–25.1); he is also said to be life that gives life, and blessedness that bestows blessedness (25.15–16). Here we seem to have implicitly not only the being/existence-life-blessedness triad, but also the idea of the prefiguration of the triad in the One, as apparently higher aspects of being, life and blessedness coincide with the One. What is more, the second principle—Barbelo—who comes into existence out of the First One through the mediating "living" (ⲚⲰⲚϨ) water (26.18), is called τριδύναμος,[88] and her tripleness is stressed several times (27.21–28.2 parr.). Finally, the third principle, the self-generated (αὐτογενής) Son, who came from the Father, is also identified as blessed (μακάριος)[89] like the Father; and whereas the Son receives νοῦς (31.5–9 parr.),[90] the Father is said to contemplate

---

[88.] NHC III.8.2–3: [ⲦⲰⲞ]ⲘⲚⲦ ⲚⲀⲨⲚ[ⲀⲘⲒⲤ]; *BG* 27.21–28.1: ⲦⲰⲞ[Ⲙ]ⲚⲦⲈ Ⲛ̄ϬⲞⲘ; NHC II.5.8: ⲦⲰⲞⲘⲦⲈ Ⲛ̄ϬⲞⲘ.

[89.] NHC III.9.13–17: αὐτογενής is a spark of light resembling the blessed (ⲚⲀⲈⲒⲀⲦϤ̄) light, who came from the Father; BG 30.1–8: The self-generated (αὐτογένητος) μονογενής is a spark of blessed (μακάριον) light, who came from the Father; NHC II.6.13–18: the Only-begotten (ⲚⲈⲞⲨⲰⲢⲞⲨⲰⲦ) is a spark of light who came forth with a light resembling blessedness (ⲘⲚⲦⲘⲀⲔⲀⲢⲒⲞⲤ).

[90.] According to the *Ap. John*, the Son requests that the Father give him νοῦς. Although expressed in mythological terms, the idea that the self-constitution of the third member of the (νοεῖν) himself (26.15 parr.). Thus, the seeds of the being–life–*mind* triad—together with a variant of the two-Intellect theory—may be seen here as well.[91] Moreover, the peculiar expressions from Victorinus's fragment, God as πνεῦμα, μακάριος, and τριδύναμος, are not only found here in the *Apocryphon of John*, but they also occur in connection with an implicit form of the being/existence–life–blessedness/mind triad. In later Sethian texts, including *Zostrianos* and *Allogenes*, these speculations become explicit, and in them, Barbelo retains her intimate connection to the concept of τριδύναμος.

It is also interesting to note a certain correspondence between the *Ap. John* and the *Chaldean Oracles*. Both seem to assume a triad of supreme principles, of whom the first is the Father and the middle a feminine power. The triad in the *Apocryphon of John* is, of course, the usual Sethian one of Father-Mother-Son, but the tripleness and the power-nature of the middle member of the triad are stressed. We do not find such a specific stress on the triple-nature of the median power in the surviving fragments of the *Chaldean Oracles*. Since the *Apocryphon of John* connects the implicit being–life–blessedness triad with this triple-power, it would seem that the later enneadic structuring of the triad in *Allogenes* can be explained by Sethian material alone, without having to assume a dependence on Porphyry, as Majercik has argued. Hadot, of course, suggested that Porphyry invented the enneadic structure of the supreme intelligible triad, having innovatively derived it from the *Chaldean Oracles* (Hadot 1968, 1:262–67) that *imply* that there is a supreme triad of Father-power-intellect; that the Father gives birth to power and intellect; that the Father somehow coincides with the power; and that there is a general triadic structure in reality. In my view, however, the earlier Sethian speculations on the supreme triad and its Triple-Powered One explain the background for such an enneadic innovation at least as well as Porphyry's exegesis of the *Chaldean Oracles*.

Furthermore, Pleše has argued that the author of the *Ap. John* makes an extensive use of Stoic concepts in describing the Invisible Spirit and his relation to what follows from him. Interestingly, many of these descriptions are similar to the Stoicizing innovations that Hadot attributed to Porphyry! Pleše's observations include the following corollaries: (a) the first principle is described as πνεῦμα (Pleše 2006, 112–39); (b) the Invisible Spirit's *seeing* his own image in

---

divine triad is completed by his reception of νοῦς, is found here. This is reminiscent of the self-constitution of the Intellect in Hadot's fragments, where the Intellect becomes truly Intellect by turning back towards and contemplating the One.

91. The *Ap. John* may also allude to a Three Intellect theory, as Barbelo is also identified as the "First (actualized) Thought" of the Father. See Plotinus's criticism of three Intellects at *Enn.* 2.9 [33].1.6. Plotinus's criticism here may, of course, be aimed at Numenius (and Amelius!) as well, or generally at such interpretations of *Tim.* 39e that posited two or more Intellects, including Plotinus's own earlier view, as in *Enn.* 5.4 [7]; 6.9 [9]; 3.9 [13]. See Armstrong 1966–1988, 2:226–27 n. 1.

the luminous waters actualizes his first thought (Barbelo) and this points to Stoic influence, since the passage assigns priority to perception, "'to seeing one's own image,' as an essential prerequisite for concept-formation" (Pleše 2006, 97); (c) the Invisible Spirit's expansion from unity into multiplicity seems to be partially articulated with the help of the Stoic concept of the tensile movement of the πνεῦμα (Pleše 2006, 112–39), and this expansion all the way to the material realm seems further to be an articulation of the movement from tension (εὐτονία) to slackness (ἀτονία) of the divine breath permeating all levels of reality (Pleše 2006, 12); finally (d) the Stoic concept of the cosmic cycle—according to which, at the beginning of the cosmic cycle, the world is coextensive with the state of pure fire/πνεῦμα—seems to lie behind the notion of the Invisible Spirit's being the source of everything (Pleše 2006, 199). In addition, other Stoic concepts are applied to Ialdabaoth's fiery realm, to the demonic nature of the body created by the archons, and other aspects of the created cosmos, as both Pleše and Onuki have shown (see Pleše 2006, 122; Onuki 1989).

It seems to me that the easiest way of explaining the occurrence of many of the suggested "Porphyrian" features in the Platonizing Sethian treatises is to assume that the implicit speculations of the earlier Sethian tradition, as attested in the *Apocryphon of John*, have been taken over and made explicit by later Sethian authors. Such a move from implicit to explicit speculations within the same Sethian tradition is, in my view, the most natural explanation of the evidence. This then would also tend to exclude the possibility raised by Corrigan that the Sethian authors depended on the *Anonymous Commentary on the Parmenides* (Corrigan 2000b, 156–61) since the explicit speculations in the *Commentary* can be argued to be dependent on the developing Sethian tradition. The next and crucial question, then, is how internal to Sethianism was this development? Did the Sethians borrow from Plotinus and his students in formalizing their implicit ideas? And did Plotinus and Porphyry borrow some of their ideas from the Sethians, as the evidence seems to suggest?

Sethians in Plotinus's Seminars

When we first hear of *Zostrianos* and *Allogenes*—where the innovative "Porphyrian" concepts appear explicitly—we are in the middle of a Gnostic controversy in Plotinus's seminars. It seems to me that the implications of this controversy have been greatly exaggerated. A closer look at the available evidence rather suggests that the controversy was quite limited, and that it had little to do with philosophical doctrines.

According to Porphyry's *Vita Plotini* 16, the seminars were attended by certain *hairetikoi*, who had "abandoned the old philosophy." Porphyry identified them as "Gnostics," and apparently at least some of them as Christians.[92] These Gnostic *hairetikoi* claimed that Plato had not understood things perfectly, and appealed instead to the "apocalypses" of Zoroaster, Zostrianos, Nikotheos, Allogenes, Messos, and others. While Amelius refuted *Zostrianos* in forty books,[93] Porphyry himself showed that the book of *Zoroaster* was recent and pseudepigraphical, and therefore could not derive from the ancient figure of Zoroaster. Plotinus, for his part, in *Enn.* 2.9 [33], complains that it is impossible to argue in a proper philosophical manner with the Gnostics, because they insist, without careful argumentation, that they alone are right and that Plato and the other philosophers were wrong (especially 2.9.6, 9, 10). Plotinus also singles out some specific Gnostic doctrines that he finds unacceptable:[94] (a) unnecessary multiplication and naming of hypostases (2.9.1, 6); (b) strong partitioning of the Intellect, based on an erroneous exegesis of *Timaeus* 39e (2.9.1, 6); (c) erroneous stress on the evil nature of the cosmos, its maker, and the human body (2.9.4, 6, 8, 10); (d) the myth of the fallen Soul or Sophia, who causes souls to fall and take on human bodies, and who, in addition, illumines darkness and produces an image of an image (2.9.4, 10);[95] and (e) magical incantations, hissing sounds, and exorcisms (2.9.14). In so doing, Plotinus refers to a set of unique expressions and ideas that are found concentrated in *Zostrianos* 8-10: παροίκησις, ἀντίτυποι, μετάνοια, "image of an image," and Sophia's connection with "darkness" (*Enn.* 2.9.6.1-3, 10.19-33). It therefore seems likely that Plotinus is here quoting from a version of *Zostrianos*. Yet despite his occasionally harsh criticism of the Gnostics, Plotinus still continues to consider some of them his personal friends (*Enn.* 2.9.10).

From all this, we can make the following four observations: (1) Not all of the Gnostics were under attack by Plotinus and his students, but only the hardliners who arrogantly insisted they were right; these probably did not include those whom Plotinus continued to consider his friends (see Corrigan 2000a, 24-25). (2) Of all the Gnostic "apocalypses" mentioned by Porphyry, only two are singled out for criticism, namely, *Zostrianos* and *Zoroaster*. These may even be two editions of one and the same text, as the NHC *Zostrianos* mentions both Zoroaster and Zostrianos in its colophon. On the other hand, we do hear of a *Book of Zoroaster* in the long recension of the *Apocryphon of John*, so *Zostrianos* and *Zoroaster* may be two completely different writings. Be that as it may,

---

92. As the Christian character of the Platonizing Sethian treatises is not very clear—as opposed to many other Sethian texts, such as the *Ap. John*—then perhaps some of the Sethian Gnostics who attended Plotinus's seminars did not consider themselves Christian.

93. Brisson (1987a, 824, 842; 1999a, 180) thinks that Amelius's response to *Zostrianos* contained also his commentary on the Prologue of the Fourth Gospel, fragments of which survive in Eusebius, *Praep. Ev.* 11.18.26-19.1.

94. See also Turner 2001, 711-12. Cf. Corrigan 2000a, 43-44 n. 77.

95. This may be already echoed in *Enn.* 5.8 [31].5. Cf. Corrigan 2000a; Turner 2001, 711-12.

the other "apocalypses" do not receive any attention in Porphyry's description of the controversy. (3) Plotinus's criticism of Gnosticism, and of *Zostrianos* specifically, only singles out a few items, half of which are related to the mythological and ritual framework in which the philosophical speculations are couched. Much of the philosophical contents of *Zostrianos*, in fact, would have been acceptable to Plotinus and Porphyry (see below). (4) The greatest problem, however, seems to have been the erroneous appeal to authority. Both Porphyry and Plotinus say that these Gnostics bypassed Plato's authority, and Porphyry then specifies that the Gnostics instead appealed to their apocalypses and especially to the figures of Zostrianos and Zoroaster. This, together with the uncompromising, unphilosophical, and arrogant attitude on the part of some of the hard-line Gnostics is likely to have caused the controversy to escalate.

We can sketch the following scenario, based on what we know of Plotinus's seminars, the Gnostic controversy and the Sethian Gnostic tradition. Some of the philosophical ideas that Plotinus later singles out in his criticism (i.e., multiplication of hypostases and partitioning of the Intellect) came under discussion. This was normal practice in the seminars,[96] and the Gnostic positions were not extremely problematic either. After all, Porphyry and Plotinus himself could have been accused of similar ideas![97] As Plotinus himself indicates, the question of how the Gnostic ideas related to Plato's teaching was asked (*Enn.* 2.9 [33].6.42–62). This again was important for Plotinus himself, who attempted to show how his own ideas were compatible with Plato (e.g., *Enn.* 5.1 [10].8). Moreover, the fact that Porphyry was able to show that the Gnostic book of Zoroaster was a recent text (*Vit. Plot.* 16), was likely due to the occurrence of recently invented doctrines therein. However, some hard-line Gnostics were not willing to discuss, compromise or change their minds, as Porphyry had done concerning the Intellect containing the intelligibles (*Vit. Plot.* 18). The hard-liners felt they were in possession of an ancient religious truth transmitted by their savior Seth, and that was enough for them, but, of course, an appeal to Seth made no sense to Plotinus

---

96. Cf. Porphyry's own testimonies as to his own prolonged debate on the Intellect and the intelligibles with Amelius and Plotinus (*Vit. Plot.* 18), and on his three-day-long questioning of Plotinus on the relationship between the soul and the body (*Vit. Plot.* 13). Cf. also Amelius's complaint that there was a "great deal of disorderliness and futile talk" in the seminars (*Vit. Plot.* 3.37).

97. Multiplication of hypostases and the partitioning of the Intellect would seem to apply to Porphry's enneadic structuring of the first principles (Lydus, *Mens.* 4.122; Augustine, *Civ.* 10.23, 29; Damascius, *Princ.* 2:1.4–2.10 Westerink-Combès = §43 Ruelle; Proclus, *In Tim.* 3:64,8–65,1 Diehl). Porphyry also seems to have accepted exorcisms, at least in his youth (Eunapius, *Vita Porphyrii*; Eusebius, *Praep. Ev.* 4.23). A Numenian-like Two Intellect theory is hinted at in Plotinus's *Enn.* 5.4 [7]; 6.9 [9]; 3.9 [13]; and Plotinus, too, could speak of the evil nature of matter and the body (*Enn.* 4.8 [6].5; 1.2 [19].3; 1.8 [51]; cf. *Vit. Plot.* 1.1–2). Cf. *Enn.* 3.9 [13].3, and its relation to *Zostrianos* 8–10.

and his non-Gnostic students, who were asking for a connection to Plato. It is probably in such a context that the appeal to the Chaldean figures of Zoroaster and Zostrianos was made, or at least strengthened.[98] According to a contemporary tradition, Plato himself had learned secrets from them. Plato, in the tenth book of his *Republic*, relates the so-called vision of Er, concerning the judgment of souls after death as well as the geography of the world beyond (*Resp.* 10.13–16 [614a–621d]). By the early third century C.E., this Er was assimilated with Zoroaster, who in turn was identified as Zostrianus's great-grandson (Clement, *Strom.* 5.14.103.2–4; Arnobius, *Adv. nat.* 1.52).[99] The NHC *Zostrianos* may even identify both as one figure, as the names appear in the colophon side by side. Be that as it may, such an appeal effectively bypassed the authority of Plato, which—together with Porphyry's evidence for the recent and pseudepigraphical nature of the book of Zoroaster—was too much for Plotinus and his students, and this finally heated up the controversy.

As stressed above, the controversy was caused mostly by the uncompromising attitude of only some of the Sethians. Most of the philosophical contents of *Zostrianos* and the other Platonizing Sethian treatises would have been acceptable at least to Porphyry, in whose undisputed works we find many of the same innovative ideas. Plotinus also did not accuse the Sethians of harboring more than a few specific, erroneous philosophical concepts, some of them similar to those Porphyry is known to have entertained.

---

98. There are signs in *Zostrianos* that an earlier version of the text circulated under the name of Seth. Towards the end of the tractate, Zostrianos writes three tablets of knowledge for the future elect, and goes on to preach to the "seed of Seth" (130.1–17). This seems to be an allusion to the tradition of the pillars of Seth containing secret knowledge of primordial events reserved for the elect, i.e., the offspring of Seth. Such a tradition was known to Josephus (*Ant.* 1.68–72) and the author of the *Life of Adam and Eve* (*L.A.E.* 50.1–51.3). It also seems to have formed the basis of the strategy of Genesis rewriting in the *Apocalypse of Adam* (NHC V.5) and the *Holy Book*; the tradition is likewise alluded to in *Steles Seth*. In fact, the allusion to the three tablets in *Zostrianos* may be specifically to the three tablets as presented in *Steles Seth*. As I have argued elsewhere (Rasimus 2009), the tradition of Seth's pillars forms the basis of the Gnostic interest in and appeal to Seth: facing Jewish accusations of forgery due to their Genesis rewritings (such as found in Irenaeus, *Adv. Haer.* 1.30), the Gnostics needed to bypass the authority and antiquity of Moses in favor of someone who could have demonstrably transmitted a "hidden truth" concerning the primordial events. The known tradition of the pillars of Seth was picked up and elaborated for this very reason. One may also point out that, of the Platonizing Sethian treatises, *Allogenes* also seems to go under the name of Seth, as "Allogenes" was not only a title ultimately based on a statement of Seth's birth in LXX Gen 4:25 (σπέρμα ἕτερον), but was also attested as a name of Seth in Gnostic circles according to Epiphanius (*Pan.* 40.7.1–2).

99. Turner (2001, 294–95 n. 29) states that in the MS of Arnobius's *Adversus nationes*, the name "Zostrianos" would be written as "Osthanes." However, in Le Bonniec's edition (1982, 178–79), the Latin text has "Zostrianus," and the critical apparatus does not mention alternate readings.

In fact, Plotinus seems to have been open to Sethian ideas, especially during the period of his early works.[100] Hadot supposed that because Plotinus simply used the being–life–mind triad without ever clearly explaining it from his first *Ennead* onwards, he must have received it from earlier Platonic tradition (Hadot 1957). Hadot speculated that the source was a piece of (unattested) school-Platonic exegesis on *Timaeus* 39e,[101] and especially *Sophist* 248e–249a,[102] as Plotinus himself sometimes connects the triad with these passages.[103]

However, the same triad is implicitly present in the pre-Plotinian *Ap. John*, and explicitly attested in the later Platonizing Sethian treatises. It thus seems that it was the Sethians who brought the triad to Plotinus's attention. It also seems to me that the *Sophist* passage is rather used as a later proof-text for the triad, and cannot have served as its source, as it is hard to explain why only and specifically being, life and mind would have been picked out from that passage (thus leaving out, for example, motion and soul). The variant form, existence-life-blessedness that occurs frequently in Sethian texts and is already implicit in the *Ap. John*, does not seem to derive from the *Sophist* passage either. Furthermore, unlike Plotinus, the Sethian authors never seem to clearly connect the triad to *Sophist* 248–249, and this also suggests that its connection to the *Sophist* passage is secondary. Quite possibly, the formalization of the implicit Sethian triad took place in Plotinus's seminars, and it may have been Plotinus himself who first connected the triad to the *Sophist* and *Timaeus*, to justify his own use of it.[104]

Plotinus and the Sethian Gnostics of course shared much that is common to Platonists of the third century, but they also shared more specific ideas and

---

100. Cf. Sinnige 1984. Corrigan (2000a, 36) suggests that Plotinus continued his dialogue with the Gnostics until the end of his life, or at least until the time he wrote *Enn.* 1.8 [51]. This *Ennead* discusses the evil nature of matter and the body.

101. *Timaeus* [39e]: "So this part of the work which was still undone He completed by molding it after the nature of the Model. According, then, as Reason (νοῦς) perceives Forms existing in the Absolute Living Creature, such and so many as exist therein did He deem that this World also should possess" (trans. Lamb).

102. *Sophist* [248e]: "But for heaven's sake, shall we let ourselves easily be persuaded that motion and life and soul and mind are really not present to absolute being, that it neither lives nor thinks, [249a] but awful and holy, devoid of mind, is fixed and immovable?" (trans. Fowler).

103. E.g., *Enn.* 5.9 [5].10 (real being is life, intelligence, motion, rest …); 6.9 [9].9 (soul sees the spring of life and of intellect, the principle of being, the cause of good, the root of soul); 6.6 [34].8 (the "absolute living being" is being, intellect, life); 6.2 [43].6 (the being of soul is both being and life, and it makes itself many by contemplation and movement); 1.8 [51].2 (the Good gives from itself intellect, real being, soul and life).

104. Plotinus does accuse the Gnostics of an erroneous exegesis of *Timaeus* 39e (*Enn.* 2.9 [33].6) but not in connection with the being–life–mind triad. Based on the Nag Hammadi evidence, the Sethian authors never clearly connected the being–life–mind triad to *Sophist* 248–249 or *Timaeus* 39e.

concepts, such as the being–life–mind triad; the related idea of the traversal of Life from the One into the Intellect (*Enn.* 3.8 [30].11; *Allogenes* 49.5–21); the doctrine of the Intellect containing the intelligibles (*Enn.* 5.5 [32]; cf. *Vit. Plot.* 18; *Zostrianos* 21; 115–116); and the notion of learned ignorance (*Enn.* 6.9 [9].3–4; 3.8 [30].9.29–32; 6.7 [38].36.15–16; 6.8 [39].21.25–33; *Allogenes* 59.26–60.12; 61.1–19).[105] In addition, many of the supposed "Porphyrian" innovations that we find in the Sethian texts are also found implicitly in Plotinus: the prefiguration of the Intellect in the One (or the Two Intellect theory; *Enn.* 5.4 [7].2; 5.3 [49].15.26–35); the description of a procession out of the source and turning back towards it (*Enn.* 5.2 [11].1.1–18; 6.7 [38].37.18–22); and the idea of relative predominance and mutual implication (*Enn.* 5.8 [31].4). Furthermore, we can also detect specifically Gnostic-like ideas in Plotinus's works.[106] These include the audacity (τόλμα),[107] sin (ἁμαρτία), or stupidity (ἄφρων) of the soul that leads to its fall (*Enn.* 4.8 [6].5; 5.1 [10].1; 5.2 [11].2); and the concept of the evil matter (1.8 [51]).

All this suggests that, despite the limited Gnostic controversy, Plotinus and Porphyry could have accepted, and probably did accept, innovative Sethian ideas and made them their own. Noteworthy in this regard is that while Porphyry reported that Plotinus was accused of plagiarizing Numenius, he never accused the Gnostics of plagiarism, only of pseudepigraphy (which possibly was provable based on his knowledge of their own recent innovations!).[108] This could be taken as an additional indication that the Sethian Gnostics did not borrow extensively from Plotinus or Porphyry.

CONCLUSION

What does all this mean for Pierre Hadot's thesis that Porphyry is the author of the fragments of Victorinus and of the *Anonymous Commentary on the Parmenides*? It seems to me that in light of the new Sethian evidence, one can assign the fragments to Porphyry only by accepting that he borrowed extensively from the Sethians—which in itself does not seem impossible. Hadot's arguments in favor of the Porphyrian authorship of the fragments all apply to the Sethian Gnostics attending Plotinus's seminars: the Platonizing Sethian treatises show a good doctrinal match with the fragments; the *Apocryphon of John* especially

---

105. Turner 2000a, 532; Turner 2001, 711–12. Cf. Corrigan 2000a, 43–44 n. 77.

106. Cf. Sinnige 1984; and Jonas 1993, 251–327.

107. Neopythagoreans, of course, had already described the dyad's desire for a separation from the monad as τόλμα. See Iamblichus, *Theol. Arith.* 9.4–6 de Falco. See also Henry and Schwyzer 1977, 185 n. 1.

108. Falsifying Plato, of which Plotinus does accuse the Gnostics, is not the same thing as plagiarizing Numenius, Plotinus, or Porphyry; faithfully reproducing Plato was, in fact, expected of a Plotinian philosopher.

shows similarities with the *Chaldean Oracles*, and even betrays signs of the use of Stoic physics in the service of Platonic metaphysics (by extension this is true of the Platonizing Sethian treatises as well); Plotinian and Numenian influence is only to be expected from someone attending Plotinus's seminars; and some of the special terminology of the fragments is better attested in Christian (Gnostic) than pagan (Porphyry) sources.

Does the Sethian evidence then force us to assume a Gnostic authorship of these fragments? While the match between the fragments and the Sethian evidence seems to be better than in the case of Porphyry, the mythological and even extravagant tone of the Sethian texts is quite different from that of the fragments. One could ask: How could a Sethian Gnostic write a cool-headed lemmatic commentary on Plato's *Parmenides*? Or, how could Victorinus use "heretical" Gnostic sources in his fight against Arianism (see Brisson 1999a, 179)? First, the difference in tone/genre can be explained by the targeting of different kinds of audiences. The Platonizing Sethian treatises—full of traditional Sethian mythology, jargon, communal hymns and baptismal speculations—seem to have been written for the author's Sethian circle only. These texts may have never been intended for circulation in Plotinus's seminars, although they did end up circulating there for reasons that are not clear.[109] But if a Sethian attendant of the seminars wanted to gain access to Plotinus's inner circle by proving his worth, as Porphyry once did (see *Vit. Plot.* 4; 13; 18), such a Sethian author could well have written a lemmatic *Parmenides* commentary (to use the previous example). We know that the Sethians were interested in *Parmenides*, and that some of them were able philosophers.

As for Victorinus's use of "heretical" Gnostic material, we may ask alternatively, how could he have been attracted to one of the greatest known enemies of Christianity, Porphyry,[110] either? It seems to me that Victorinus—if he even knew the identity of his source(s)—was ready to accept any argument that strengthened his own position against the Arians, no matter where it ultimately originated. We may also point out, along with Tardieu, that some Gnostics also quarreled with Arian teachers, and hence had utilized anti-Arian arguments themselves, which could in theory make them acceptable to Victorinus.[111]

---

109. We may compare this situation to Christian heresy hunters getting their hands on original Gnostic works; cf. Irenaeus's refutations of Gnostics (*Adv. Haer.* 1.29–31) and Valentinians (e.g., 1.1–8) in Lyon. See also Tertullian's claim that Valentinians were willing to expose their proper doctrine only after they were sure of the discussion partner; until then, they only spoke in terms acceptable to the emerging church (*Val.* 1).

110. Porphyry's writings against Christianity were still being refuted centuries afterwards. Porphyry was feared due to the sharpness of his critique, based partially on his knowledge of the Christian Scriptures. Cf. Augustine, *Civ.* 19.22. See also Berchman 2005, 114.

111. Philostorgius (*Hist. Eccl.* 3.15) describes a quarrel between the Arian Aetius and "Borborians," who are likely the same "Borborians" or "libertine Gnostics" (classified as Sethian today) Epiphanius describes in his *Pan.* 26. See Tardieu 1987.

In the end, we may not be able to prove beyond reasonable doubt either a Porphyrian or a Sethian authorship of Victorinus's sources or of the *Anonymous Commentary on the Parmenides*. However, we have seen that many of the ideas contained in these fragments are better attested in Sethian texts than in the undisputed Porphyrian material. We have also seen that many of the suggested "Porphyrian" features are already found, albeit sometimes only implicitly, in pre-Plotinian Gnostic sources, that is, the *Apocryphon of John* and the possibly common Gnostic source behind *Zostrianos* and Victorinus. Hence, in light of the Sethian evidence, we must reassess Pierre Hadot's theory and conclude that it was the Sethian Gnostics rather than Porphyry who were the innovators, and that the role of the Sethian Gnostics in the development of Neoplatonism has been greatly underestimated in previous scholarship.

6
COLUMNS VII–VIII OF THE *ANONYMOUS COMMENTARY ON THE PARMENIDES*: VESTIGES OF A LOGICAL INTERPRETATION

Luc Brisson

The third fragment, dealing with the One in time, may inform us about the form that the interpretation of the *Parmenides* may have assumed before Plotinus. The tenth deduction of the first series is first cited in its entirety (141a5–d6) in column VII. The logical structure of the argumentation is then analyzed (column VIII, 1–21), and the commentary ends with objections to the proposed interpretation (column VIII, 21–35). Columns VII and VIII follow one another, since they are written on the *recto* and *verso* of the same *folio*.

1. Translation:
[VII]...

PARMENIDES —. So if it is like that; the one could not even be in time at all; could it? Or isn't it necessary, if something is in time, that it always comes to be older than itself?

YOUNG ARISTOTLE —. To be sure.

PARMENIDES —. Therefore, that which comes to be older than itself comes to be, at the same time, younger than itself, if in fact it is to have something it comes to be older than.

YOUNG ARISTOTLE —. What do you mean?

PARMENIDES —. I mean this: there is no need for a thing to come to be different from a thing that is already different; it must, rather, already be different from what is already different, have come to be different from what has come to be different, and be going to be different from what is going to be different; but it must not have come to be, be going to be, or be different from what comes to be different: it must come to be different, and nothing else.

YOUNG ARISTOTLE —. Yes that's necessary.

PARMENIDES —. But surely older is a difference from younger and from nothing else.

YOUNG ARISTOTLE —. Yes it is.

PARMENIDES —. So that which comes to be older than itself must also, at the same time, come to be younger than itself.
YOUNG ARISTOTLE —. So it seems.
PARMENIDES —. But it must also not come to be for more or less time than itself; it must come to be and be and have come to be and be going to be for a time equal to itself.
YOUNG ARISTOTLE —. Yes, that too is necessary.
PARMENIDES —. Therefore, it is necessary, as it seems, that each thing that is in time and partakes of time be the same age as itself and, at the same time, come to be both older and younger than itself.
YOUNG ARISTOTLE —. It looks that way.
PARMENIDES —. But the one surely had no share of any of that.
YOUNG ARISTOTLE —. No, it didn't
PARMENIDES —. Therefore, it has no share of time; nor is it in any time.
YOUNG ARISTOTLE —. It certainly isn't, [VIII] as the argument proves.[1]

We must say first of all that Plato carries out the following syllogism:[2] "If the One was neither older nor younger nor the same age as itself, such a One could by no means be [5] in time, either." He posits as an antecedent:[3] "If the One were neither older nor younger nor of the same age as itself," from which he draws this consequence: "it could by no means be in time" [10], and he converts what has just been said into this formula: "Is it not necessary, if a thing is in time, for it always to become older than itself?" Taking this conclusion as a premise, he deduces from it that what is older is always older than something younger. But "older" is said of what is [15] older in itself, that is, an old man, for the old man is called "old" in an absolute sense. But whenever we say "older," indicating also[4] by this word a relation to someone younger, as when one says "more wealthy," indicating that he was born previously [20], with the age of the younger one being supposed in the notion of "older"[5] Yet how can that which becomes older than itself become at the same time younger than itself? For to become younger than oneself means that the time [25] of one's own life is greater than it is. And to be the same age even while becoming younger than oneself, is completely impossible. For time does not become smaller, as if the past did not exist, to make it become younger. It is certainly not in the domain of bodies either [30] that its age decreases, to make it become younger. To this, some have replied that it is a sophistical reasoning, carried out in the manner of an exercise.[6] For a person does not become younger by becoming older, [35], but he ceases to be. So that when it is said that... (my translation).

---

1. Plato, *Parm.* 141a5–d6, translation by Mary Louise Gill and Paul Ryan.
2. The term ἀκολουθία is often used to designate a causal or logical implication. For the latter case, see in particular *Enn.*, 5.8 [31].7.41–42; and 1.8 [51].2.13.
3. For a similar use of the term ἀναφορά, see *Enn.* 2.3 [53].17.10.
4. The verb προσσημαίνειν is a technical term Aristotle (see especially *Int.* 3.16b5–25).
5. This is the logical interpretation; see Steel 2002, section 3.1.1.
6. This is Proclus's position; see Steel 2002, section 3.1.2.

These two columns are not philosophically interesting, but they are an invaluable testimony to the logical interpretation of the *Parmenides* before Porphyry and therefore before Plotinus (see Steel 2002, 31). The structure of the argument is as follows, according to the commentator, who begins by citing the tenth deduction of the first series in its entirety. Plato constructs a syllogism that he then converts, and it is this conversion that enables us to understand that it is necessary, if a thing is in time, for it always to become older than itself. This conclusion can be admitted without discussion, but Plato will draw an absurd consequence from it. He begins with a proposition that is acceptable to all: what is older is always older than something younger. Yet in a very particular context, this proposition entails an absurdity: what is older than itself[7] will be of the same age or younger than itself. This proposition is still absurd, whether one takes "older" in one or the other of these senses, absolutely or relatively, for "older" always implies a relation to something "younger." 1) If we take "older" in an absolute sense, the absurdity consists in the fact that the length of time is what it is, and it cannot be prolonged or shortened. To save Plato, it was claimed that since the consequence he draws is absurd, he wants to train the reader to refute a sophistical argumentation. 2) The author of the commentary must also have evoked the case in which "older" is taken in a relative sense, but no trace remains of his exposition, although, it seems to me, the commentator may be alluding to this case in the following phrase "It is certainly not in the domain of bodies either that its age decreases, to make him become younger." When one is within the process of becoming, one may compare the past to the future or the present: for instance, from a strictly mathematical viewpoint, x minutes in the past = x minutes in the present = x minutes in the future.

We find a trace of these two positions in Proclus's *Commentary on the Parmenides*. Proclus first evokes the position 1) that takes "older" in an absolute sense:

> His (Plato's) purpose in this and the following passage is to establish that everything that partakes in time is older than, and of equal age with, itself: and since he wishes this, he necessarily begins by demonstrating that something is older than itself; and in so far it is older than itself, it is plain that it is also younger than itself; for it is in relation to itself that it is called both younger and older. Now this argument might seem to be problematic at the extreme, one might even say sophistic; for how could something be simultaneously older and younger than itself? Surely the Socrates who has become older than himself is not also younger than himself; at any rate being older is present to him, while being young is gone from him. So some commentators have given up in face of this argument, and have not scrupled even to say that here Plato seems to indulge in sophistry, all too readily transferring their own ignorance to the argu-

---

7. Parmenides in himself, and relative to others.

ment. Others again, in trying to stand up to these critics, have championed the truth rather too weakly, for they say the same thing is at the same time younger and older; in respect to future time it is younger, for it has not attained yet to that; in respect to past time, on the other hand, it is older, since it has already lived through. But this is not what it is to become both simultaneously younger and older than oneself, but rather younger than one thing and older than another; so that the argument of these commentators is quickly revealed to us as being weak. (*In Parm.* 7.1225.30–1226.15 = 1225.24–1226.12)

He then moves on to the second position 2) that takes "older" in a relative sense.

Again, another set of commentators declared that everything is both older and younger than itself, what is now existing being older, and what was before younger, and that which is now older can be said to be older than what was formerly younger; but they too fail to understand the sense of Plato's statement (141b3–c1), which sets what is against what is, what will be against what will be, and what has been against what has been, these in all cases being relative expressions; so then, it is not possible to say that what now is older has become older than what had become younger; for this is to mix up times and not to preserve the rule which he himself laid down regarding all relative expressions. (*In Parm.* 7.1226.15–26 = 1226.12–21)

These two positions can be associated with the first type of interpretation proposed in the history of Plato's *Parmenides*, according to which the *Parmenides* is a dialogue on dialectic.

The first commentators who became interested in the *Parmenides*, who date from the beginning of the first century of our era, thus in the time of Thrasyllus, distinguished three chapters in Plato's dialogue (Steel, 2002, section 3.1; 1997, 67–92).

1) *Aporiai* against the theory of the forms;
2) An exposition of the method necessary for achieving the truth;
3) Training for this method.

In fact, the three parts have in reality only one goal in view: training for dialectical argument. The first section shows the necessity of dialectic, the second indicates the method to be followed, and the third provides training for this method. Despite this fundamental agreement, two divergent viewpoints were adopted, probably in the same School and at the same time.

A Reply to Zeno

Some considered the *Parmenides* as a reply to Zeno, in the sense that Socrates suggests to Parmenides' disciple that he apply his method no longer to the domain of sensible things, but to that of the intelligible.[8] Through this dialogue, Plato supposedly shows that he can do much better than Zeno. As Carlos Steel points out, the reply (ἀντιγραφή) is a well-known literary genre in antiquity. More than a simple critique, its goal was to propose a position contrary to that of the adversary, while imitating or even parodying him. Proclus reports that according to some interpreters, one may distinguish three types of reply (ἀντιγραφή) in Plato (*In Parm.* 1.631.21–632.27 = 631.12–632.20). Sometimes, Plato replies to an adversary by imitating what he has written, not without improving or adding what was lacking. The *Menexenus* is a good example, in which Plato rivals with Thucydides over the funeral oration. Another kind of reply (Hermias, *In Phaedr.* 8.14–20) proceeds by imitation and refutation, as in the *Phaedrus*, where Socrates begins by entering into competition with Lysias before contradicting his position. The *Parmenides* would be an example of a reply by contradiction (see *In Parm.* 1.631.36–632.6 = 631.25–632.6). In fact, however, the young Socrates does not criticize Zeno, but simply seeks to complete his position, by moving from the intelligible to the sensible. It is no doubt to this type of interpretation that the commentator alludes when he says: "It is certainly not in the domain of bodies either that its age decreases, to make it become younger" (col. VIII, 29–30).

An Exercise in Logic

Other commentators considered the *Parmenides* as a dialogue that provides instruction in logic. In the classification transmitted by Albinus and Diogenes Laertius, it is ranged among the logical (λογικοί) dialogues, together with the *Sophist*, the *Statesman*, and the *Cratylus*, which constitute sub-species of the dialogues that provide instruction (ὑφηγηματικοί). For these interpreters, the *Parmenides* gives an exposition on the dialectical method and the hypothetical syllogism, which, according to them, was not invented by the Stoics, but by Plato. Proclus evokes this kind of interpretation at the beginning of his commentary: "Some of our contemporaries and predecessors have referred the purpose of this dialogue to logical exercise" (Proclus, *In Parm.* 1.630.37–631.1 = 630.26–631.1, trans. Morrow and Dillon) and "Although discounting, then, the interpretation of the dialogue as polemic, some say that its purpose is logical exercise" (Proclus, *In Parm.* 1.634.6). Finally, at the very end: "But since Parmenides denies and asserts different propositions in the different hypotheses, and often denies and asserts the same things at different stages on different subjects, and is in general clearly indulging in a "serious game" and working his way through the whole nature of things, and is not, as some have absurdly held, simply pursuing a soulless and empty logical exercise ..." (*In Parm.* 6. 1051.35–1052.1 = 1051.25–1052.2). Let's give a historical example. At the beginning of the Imperial period, when the Pla-

---

8. On this subject, see Brisson 1994, 9–73; Gourinat 2001, 233–61.

tonists rediscovered the doctrinal character of Plato's philosophy after a long period during which an aporetic reading had prevailed, they began by classifying Plato's dialogues following the division of the Stoics. Since the *Parmenides* provided no positive teaching, even on the Forms, one sought to find in it a teaching on dialectics, superior even to Aristotle, since it appealed to the conditional syllogism. Alcinous used the *Parmenides* to illustrate the logical part of Plato's doctrine: "We shall find hypothetical syllogisms used by him when propounding arguments in many of his works, and most of all in the *Parmenides* ..." (Alcinous, *Didask.* 159.7–8, trans. Dillon). Let us take up Alcinous's exposition.

Alcinous defines the syllogism as follows: "A syllogism is a form of words in which, when certain assumptions are made, something other than what has been assumed necessarily follows from those very assumptions" (*Didask.* 158.20–22). Those of which both the premises and the conclusions are simple propositions are categorical, while those composed of hypothetical premises are hypothetical, and those which comprise both sorts are mixed (*Didask.* 158.23–27).

There are three kinds of categorical syllogisms. In the first, "the middle term is an attribute in one of the propositions, and subject in the other" (*Didask.* 158.32–33), for instance in the *First Alcibiades* 115a1–116a11, in which this reasoning is found: "(All) just things are fine; (all) fine things are good; therefore (all) just things are good" (*Didask.* 158.40–41). In the second, "the common term is predicated of both" (*Didask.* 158.34–35), for instance at *Parm.* 137d4–138a1 (see 145a2–b5) where, from the fact that that which has no parts is neither straight nor round and from the fact that that which has no figure is neither straight nor round, it is concluded that that which has no part has no figure either. In the third kind, the middle term is the "subject of both propositions" (*Didask.* 158.35–36), for instance also at *Parm.* 137d4–138a1 (see 145a2–b5) where it is demonstrated that that which has a figure pertains to quality, that what has a figure is finite and therefore that that which has a figure is finite.

There are also three kinds of hypothetical syllogisms, which, according to Alcinous are particularly numerous in the *Parmenides*. In addition to the simple hypothetical syllogism (*Didask.* 159.7–9), there is a second kind, in which "the common term follows the two extremes" (*Didask.* 159.15–16), and of which he finds an example in the *Parmenides* 137d4–138a1 and 145a2–b5. And there is a third kind, in which "the second term precedes the two extremes" (*Didask.* 159.20–21), and of which he finds an example at *Phaedo* 74a9–75e7. Last come the mixed syllogisms by consecution, in which "if the premise is true, the consequence is also true" (*Didask.* 159.27–28), as at *Parmenides* 144e8–145b5. There are also "mixed" syllogisms that refute by consecution. It seems that in this context, we find in the passage cited in col. VII a mixed syllogism that refutes by consecution. Since this passage from the *Parmenides* results in an absurdity, one may wonder what Plato's goal was that ended up with such a negative result. The commentator echoes this critique, and answers it as follows: "To this, some have replied that it is a sophistical reasoning carried out by way of an exercise" (col. VIII, 30–31).

If we adopt this line of defense, the *Parmenides* must be considered in the manner of Aristotle's *Sophistical Refutations*, as an exercise for escaping sophism. Aristotle himself, moreover, seems to have considered the *Parmenides* under this angle, particularly in the *Topics*.[9] Proclus makes fun of this type of interpretation, which according to him is ridiculous, because it reduces the *Parmenides* to the level of the sensible and of childhood: "How can an old man like Parmenides waste his time playing with words? How could this "lover of the spectacle offered by the truth" (*Resp.* 5.475e4) of what exists, devote so much energy to acquiring the 'mastery' (*Parm.* 135a2) of this method, whereas he pays not the slightest attention to the existence of all the rest, he who has succeeded in the ascension of that sublime observatory of the one-that-is? Unless, quite simply, that, doing something like that, Plato is ridiculing Parmenides, by making him descend from the level of the most properly intellectual visions of the soul, to exercises suitable to young boys."[10] Proclus could oppose this type of interpretation to the one which, from Iamblichus on, made the second part of the *Parmenides* a treatise on theology.

As seems to be indicated by an analysis of the following developments, to write such a commentary (the *Anonymous Commentary on the Parmenides*), requires a library, senior philosophers, and deep convictions that the second part of *Parmenides* should be read not as logical, but as a metaphysical or a theological treatise. It seems to me impossible to make all these references outside a scholarly context similar to that of the School of Plotinus when Plotinus, helped by Amelius and Porphyry, was refuting Gnostic treatises (see Porphyry, *Vit. Plot.* 16).

Translated by Michael Chase, CNRS, Paris (Villejuif)

---

9. Aristotle, *Top.* 1.2.101a29–31 et 36–37 (see *Parm.* 136a–c); 7.4.163a37–a13.
10. Proclus, *Theol Plat.* 1.9.34,17–35,7.

7
IAMBLICHUS'S INTERPRETATION OF *PARMENIDES*' THIRD HYPOTHESIS

John F. Finamore

In Iamblichus's commentary on the *Parmenides* frg. 2 the philosopher adopts an interpretation of the third hypothesis that no other Platonic philosopher before or after him has done. According to Iamblichus the hypothesis concerned not soul but the so-called superior classes, that is, angels, daemons, and heroes. As Dillon has suggested (Dillon 1973, 389), the reason for this unusual interpretation surely has to do with the importance of these intermediary divinities in Iamblichus's religious system. I wish to examine this Iamblichean doctrine and consider the reasons behind it.

We of course do not possess Iamblichus's commentary to Plato's *Parmenides*. Syrianus (*In Metaph.* 38.36–39.6 = Iamblichus, *In Parm.* frg. 1) informs us that Iamblichus did write such a commentary, and Damascius refers often to Iamblichus in his own commentary to the *Parmenides*.[1] We can be certain therefore that Iamblichus did write a commentary, and it seems likely that we can find hints of its contents throughout Proclus's and Damascius's commentaries to Plato's work.

In this paper I wish to concentrate on Iamblichus's interpretation of the third hypothesis. Proclus relates Iamblichus's unusual view in his own commentary on the *Parmenides* in a longer passage in which he discusses the history of Neoplatonic interpretation of the hypotheses (1051.34–1064.17).[2] Here is the text concerning the third hypothesis (*In Parm.* frg. 2.7–11):

---

1. See Dillon 1987, xxx–xxxi, where he says that "we have about ten references to" Iamblichus's commentary in Damascius's *In Parm.* See frgs. 3–14. Cf. Dillon 1973, 22–23.
2. On this passage, see Saffrey and Westerink 1968, lxxix–lxxxxix; Dillon 1973, 387–88; Westerink and Combès 2003, 138 n. 8.

The third [hypothesis, the commentators around Iamblichus say³] does not yet concern Soul, as those before them [had said], but concerns the classes superior to us—angels, daemons, and heroes—for these classes are immediately dependent upon the gods and are superior to universal souls. This is the most astonishing thing they say, and they therefore place this rank before souls in the hypotheses.

τὴν δὲ τρίτην οὐκ ἔτι περὶ ψυχῆς, ὡς οἱ πρὸ αὐτῶν, ἀλλὰ περὶ τῶν κρειττόνων ἡμῶν γενῶν, ἀγγέλων, δαιμόνων, ἡρώων (ταῦτα γὰρ τὰ γένη προσεχῶς ἐξηρτῆσθαι τῶν θεῶν καὶ εἶναι καὶ αὐτῶν κρείττονα τῶν ὅλων ψυχῶν· τοῦτο δὴ τὸ παραδοξότατόν φασι, καὶ διὰ τοῦτο τὴν πρὸ τῶν ψυχῶν ἐν ταῖς ὑποθέσεσι τάξιν λαβεῖν

This remarkable view is confirmed in frg. 12, taken from Damascius's commentary on the *Parmenides* 4.3.15–4.1:

There remains the great Iamblichus's doctrine that the hypothesis concerns those always following the gods. For this is the most persuasive of all the ancient interpretations and has many inducements for belief from the conclusions regarding daemons⁴ in the *Symposium*.

λείπεται δὴ ἡ περὶ τῶν ἀεὶ θεοῖς ἑπομένων εἶνναι τὴν ὑπόθεσιν, κατὰ τὸν μέγαν Ἰάμβλιχον· ἔστιν γὰρ αὕτη πιθανωτάτη πασῶν τῶν παλαιῶν ἐξηγήσεων καὶ πολλὰς ἔχουσα πρὸς πίστιν ἀφορμὰς ἐκ τῶν ἐν Συμποσίῳ δαιμονίων συμπερασμάτων.

Damascius is respectful of Iamblichus's doctrine, but he goes on to disagree with it. For Damascius, as for Syrianus and Proclus, the third hypothesis concerned human souls, not divine ones.

To see what is at issue, let's turn to the third hypothesis in the *Parmenides* 155e4–156a4:

"Let's speak again the third time. The one, if it is as we have recounted, isn't it necessary for it—being one and many, and not one and not many, and partaking of time—because it is one sometimes to partake of being and because it is not [one] sometimes not to partake of being?"

"It is necessary."

---

3. Proclus does not name Iamblichus in this fragment, but his name is supplied by a scholiast. See Saffrey and Westerink 1968, lxxxii n. 1; Westerink and Combès 2003, 138 n. 8; Dillon 1987, 387, 412; 1973, 387.

4. I agree with Steel 1982, 85 n. 22 against Dillon 1973, 223 that the adjective δαιμονίων refers the class of daemons and should not be translated "remarkable." Westerink and Combès 2003, 4 concur; see also their note on p. 139.

"So, when it is partaking, will it be able at that time not to partake, or when it is not partaking, to partake?"

"It will not be possible."

"Therefore it participates at one time but does not participate at another, for in this way alone it might partake and not partake of the same thing."

"Correct."

"Is there a time when it lays hold of being and [another] when it releases it? Or how will it be able to have the same thing at one time and not have it at another, if it does not lay hold of it and let it go at some time?"

"It cannot."

ἔτι δὴ τὸ τρίτον λέγωμεν. τὸ ἓν εἰ ἔστιν οἷον διεληλύθαμεν, ἆρ' οὐκ ἀνάγκη αὐτό, ἕν τε ὂν καὶ πολλὰ καὶ μήτε ἓν μήτε πολλὰ καὶ μετέχον χρόνου, ὅτι μὲν ἔστιν ἕν, οὐσίας μετέχειν ποτέ, ὅτι δ᾽ οὐκ ἔστι, μὴ μετέχειν αὖ ποτε οὐσίας; ἀνάγκη. ἆρ' οὖν, ὅτε μετέχει, οἷόν τε ἔσται τότε μὴ μετέχειν, ἢ ὅτε μὴ μετέχει, μετέχειν; οὐχ οἷόν τε. ἐν ἄλλῳ ἄρα χρόνῳ μετέχει καὶ ἐν ἄλλῳ οὐ μετέχει· οὕτω γὰρ ἂν μόνως τοῦ αὐτοῦ μετέχοι τε καὶ οὐ μετέχοι. ὀρθῶς. οὐκοῦν ἔστι καὶ οὗτος χρόνος, ὅτε μεταλαμβάνει τοῦ εἶναι καὶ ὅτε ἀπαλλάττεται αὐτοῦ; ἢ πῶς οἷόν τε ἔσται τοτὲ μὲν ἔχειν τὸ αὐτό, τοτὲ δὲ μὴ ἔχειν, ἐὰν μή ποτε καὶ λαμβάνῃ αὐτὸ καὶ ἀφίῃ; οὐδαμῶς.

From this passage, the Neoplatonists drew some important conclusions. The "one" in question exists in time (and thus is below the realm of Intellect) but partakes of Being in the realm of Intellect. However, since it both does and does not partake of being and since it exists in time, this "one" is intermediary between Intellect and Nature, partaking of one of these at one time and the other at another. When it "releases" being, the Neoplatonists infer that it descends to Nature, and alternately ascends again. Thus, this "one" is closely associated with souls, since their nature is intermediary and they do make such descents and ascents. But which sub-group of souls might be concerned here?

Damascius, in the section of his *Parmenides* commentary in which he gives Iamblichus's interpretation (3.7–4.19), is discussing the *skopos* of the third hypothesis (1.23).[5] He says that he can easily establish that this is the ascent and descent of souls into and out of the world of generation (3.8–10). He (agreeing with Proclus) rules out the possibility that the "one" in question refers to the forms existing in a substrate, which belong in the fourth hypothesis (3.10–13),

---

5. On this passage, see Steel 1982, 84–87 and the notes of Westerink and Combès 2003, *ad loc.*

or to divine essence, whether psychic or corporeal, which belongs to the second hypothesis (3.13–15). There remains, he says, only Iamblichus's interpretation (3.15–4.1). Damascius criticizes this theory in three parts, arguing that the daemons and other superior classes are always with the gods and do not descend (4.1–7), that the definition of time involved in the third hypothesis refers to entities like souls that are submerged in it and not like gods that are above it (4.7–13), and that the beings in this hypothesis are beneath the visible, generative gods but that it is the human soul and not daemonic ones that are so placed (4.13–19).

Of these arguments, it is the first that most concerns us (4.1–7):

> Nevertheless those who in their rank receive from these gods their characters in accordance with the conclusions about the gods [in the *Parmenides*][6] are eternal consorts. For, the superior classes are also the perfection of the allotments subject to the gods, inasmuch as they are in no way separated from the divine [i.e., from the gods in the second hypothesis]. The argument in the *Parmenides*, therefore, must concern not the essence which always follows the gods but that which is sometimes also separated.
>
> ἀλλ' ὅμως ὀπαδοὶ καὶ ἀΐδιοί εἰσιν οἱ παρὰ τούτων τὰς ἰδιότητας ἐν τάξει ὑποδεχόμενοι τῶν θείων συμπερασμάτων· τῶν γὰρ δὴ τοῖς θεοῖς κλήρων ὑπεστρωμένων πληρώματα καὶ τὰ κρείττω γένη, ἅτε οὐδὲ ὁπωστιοῦν ἀφιστάμενα τῶν θείων. ἀνάγκη ἄρα περὶ τῆς οὐκ ἀεὶ θεοῖς ἑπομένης οὐσίας, ἀλλά ποτε καὶ ἀφισταμένης εἶναι τῷ Παρμενίδῃ τὸν λόγον.

Damascius's point is that the subject of the third hypothesis is not the superior classes, which are always with the gods and hence do not descend, but human souls.

Damascius calls the superior classes "eternal consorts" (ὀπαδοὶ ἀΐδιοί, 4.1). The term ὀπαδός comes from Plato's *Phaedrus*, in the great myth in which the soul is compared to a charioteer driving two horses (246a3–256e2). At 252c3, Plato uses the term for lovers (clearly human souls) who follow Zeus and can thus endure Cupid more easily than those who follow other gods. At 248c3, how-

---

6. A difficult phrase: ἐν τάξει ... τῶν θείων συμπερασμάτων. Steel (1982, 85–86) paraphrases: "according to their rank, the properties that have been deduced in the hypotheses concerning their respective gods." Steel takes συμπερασμάτων as elliptical for "conclusions from the hypotheses of the *Parmenides*" and makes the genitive dependent on ἰδιότητας. Combès (4) translates "dans l'ordre des conclusions relatives aux dieux," making the genitive dependent on τάξει. It seems to me that Steel must be correct that the "conclusions" are those drawn from the second hypothesis of the *Parmenides* (cf. lines 7–8, below, where τὰ συναγόμενα συμπεράσματα are the conclusions drawn from the *Parmenides*) and that Combès is correct that the genitive depends upon τάξει. So, the superior classes receive their characters from the gods themselves (those described in the second hypothesis) and are therefore "in rank" beneath the gods, just as the second hypothesis had also shown.

ever, he uses the compound συνοπαδός of the soul that follows its leader-god and sees the Forms; as a result of this following and vision, that soul is "without pain" (ἀπήμονα, c4) for the next one-thousand-year cycle and, if it can continue to follow its leader-god and see the Forms successfully, it is "always free from harm" (ἀεὶ ἀβλαβῆ, c5). The Platonic context makes clear that these are human souls, but Damascius's discussion of "eternal consorts" shows that the Neoplatonists expanded their interpretation to differentiate souls that always accompany the gods (and hence are always without harm) and those that do not. For Damascius the former category concerns the superior classes and not human souls. How did Iamblichus understand this classification?[7]

As Steel and Combès both point out,[8] Iamblichus himself uses the phrase "eternal consorts" in the *De Mysteriis*. In 1.10, Iamblichus sets out to answer Porphyry's inquiry concerning distinguishing the various superior classes (daemons, heroes, and purified souls) from one another in accordance with their degree of passibility and impassibility (33.12–15). As usual, poor Porphyry has grasped the wrong end of the stick, and Iamblichus criticizes him for trying to make such a distinction at all. The superior classes are *tout court* impassible, even the lowest of them, the purified human souls. Iamblichus concludes (36.6–10):

> Since we have shown that it is impossible for the lowest of the superior classes, viz. soul, to have a share of passivity, why is it necessary to attribute it to daemons and heroes, since they are eternal and always consorts of the gods (ἀίδιοί τέ εἰσι καὶ συναποδοὶ τῶν θεῶν διὰ παντός)?[9]

But how could eternal consorts undergo occasional descents? Surely either they are constantly in attendance or they descend, as Damascius says.

The answer has to do with Iamblichus's interpretation of the *Phaedrus* passage. Plato, it should be noted, does not use the phrase "eternal consorts." Instead, he talks about the consorts who are "without pain" (ἀπήμονα, c4) "always free from harm" (ἀεὶ ἀβλαβῆ, c5). There can be little doubt that Damascius, following Proclus, took Plato to mean "free from the harm that comes from descending into generation."[10] Proclus, in fact, in *Institutio Theologica* prop. 185 made a three-

---

7. For Iamblichus's interpretation in the *De Anima*, see Finamore and Dillon 2003, 160–63.

8. Steel 1982, 86 n. 25; Combès 2003, 139 n. 2. The Greek word ὀπαδοί does not occur in the MS (Marcianus gr. 246, s. IX); the MS reading is οἴλοιοί, which holds no obvious meaning. It was Steel who suggested ὀπαδόι. which is rightly adopted by Combès.

9. The phrase also appears in 1.3.9.10–11: Ἐοικέτω δὴ οὖν τοῖς ἀιδίοις τῶν θεῶν συνοπαδοῖς καὶ ἡ σύμφυτος αὐτῶν κατανόησις.

10. This is how Hermeias, *In Platonis Phaedrum Scholia* (162.29–163.19) interprets the words. Following Syrianus, he says "Whichever soul, he [i.e., Plato] says, following its own god is able to see something of the Intelligible [objects] remains unharmed for all that cycle, that is it does not fall into generation, for this is suffering harm, to fall into generation" (ἥτις ἂν,

fold division of (1) gods, (2) their consorts who always participate in the gods, and (3) the consorts who sometimes participate in them.[11] The last group would include the very human souls that he would have wished to include in the third hypothesis.

Proclus makes further distinctions in his *Timaeus* commentary.[12] At 1.110.22–114.21, Proclus offers a "more sublime" (ὑψηλότερον, 110.23) reading of the myth of Phaethon. The myth of the fall of Phaethon in his chariot alludes to the souls that have their origin from the Demiurge but gain a cosmic post, each under a particular divine leader (i.e., planet). In a passage redolent with Neoplatonic astrological theory, Proclus divides these souls into not two but three classes (111.14–19)

> Of these souls, some remain pure always attached to their appropriate gods and govern the universe with them; others descend into generation, perform great deeds, and remain untouched by evils; others descend and are filled with the evils of generation and receive something from what they govern, for this is the last form of life.

> τούτων δὴ τῶν ψυχῶν αἳ μὲν ἄχραντοι μένουσιν ἀεὶ τῶν οἰκείων ἐξημμέναι θεῶν καὶ συνδιοικοῦσαι τὸ πᾶν αὐτοῖς, αἳ δὲ κατίασιν μὲν εἰς γένεσιν, μεγαλουργοὶ δέ εἰσι καὶ ἀκάκωτοι διαμένουσιν· αἳ δὲ κατίασι καὶ κακίας ἀναπίμπλανται γενεσιουργοῦ, καὶ εἰσδέχονταί τι παρὰ τῶν διοικουμένων τοῦτο ἔσχατον εἶδος ζωῆς.

We have, then, a similar division to that we saw in the *Elements*, but without the gods (because Proclus is talking only about souls) and with a bifurcation of the category of the consorts who sometimes follow the gods and sometimes not. There are such souls who descend but are still pure and those who descend and succumb to the evil inherent in Nature. Now, the souls that always follow the gods are clearly the superior classes, while those who succumb to evil are certainly human souls. But what of the middle category?

Proclus refers to this same triple division more elaborately at 1.131.27–132.5, dividing the divine and psychic essences into various categories.[13]

> Of souls [the division is] into the divine and their followers; of the divine, into the heavenly and those who care for generation; and of those following the gods,

---

φησὶ, ψυχὴ ἀκολουθήσασα τῷ οἰκείῳ θεῷ κατιδεῖν τι δυνηθῇ τῶν νοητῶν, ἀβλαβὴς μένει πᾶσαν ἐκείνην τὴν περίοδον, τουτέστιν οὐ πίπτει εἰς γένεσιν· τοῦτο γάρ ἐστι τὸ πημανθῆναι, τὸ εἰς γένεσιν πεσεῖν, 162.30–163.3).

11. See Dodds' note in Dodds 1963, 296 and Combès 1963, 139 n. 2.

12. See, with Combés 2003, 139 n. 2, Segonds 2003, 1.204 n. 4 for these and further texts from Proclus.

13. See Festugière 1966–1968, 1.179–180 note 1 for a chart of the divisions.

into those always co-ranked with them and those often separated from them; and those separated, into those that are set over generation in an undefiled way and those who are corrupted. For the descent is as far as these.

τῶν δέ γε ψυχῶν εἴς τε τὰς θείας καὶ τὰς ὀπαδοὺς ἐκείνων, καὶ τῶν θείων εἴς τε οὐρανίας καὶ τὰς τῆς γενέσεως προμηθουμένας, καὶ τῶν θεοῖς συνεπομένων εἴς τε τὰς ἀιδίως αὐτοῖς συντεταγμένας καὶ τὰς ἀφισταμένας πολλάκις, καὶ τὰς ἀφισταμένας εἴς τε τὰς ἀχράντως προϊσταμένας τῆς γενέσεως καὶ τὰς κακυνομένας· μέχρι γὰρ τούτων ἡ κάθοδος.

According to this schema, there are gods who function at two levels: in the heavens alone and in generation (the heavenly and sublunar gods). These gods in turn have at their disposal souls divided into three camps: those who always exist at their rank (τὰς ἀιδίως αὐτοῖς συντεταγμένας), those who descend but remain pure, and those who descend and are corrupted. Again, the first of these is the class of superior kinds who always remain with the gods and the last is the class of human souls.

Proclus helps clarify the last two classes of this tripartite scheme at 3.262.6–26. Here Proclus explains that various souls of different ranks attach to different leader-gods and receive their form of life and their character from them (262.7–8). He then elaborates using the Iamblichean schema of superior classes (262.14–26). Around each of the several leader-gods are other gods, angels, daemons, heroes, and pure souls. About human souls, Proclus makes these divisions, saying that there is (262.21–26):

... a chorus of pure souls shining in their purity and a number of other souls who sometimes raise the head of the charioteer into the Intelligible and sometimes are ranked with the encosmic powers of the gods. Of these latter, some accompany their god in accordance with one power and another with another.

καὶ ψυχῶν ἀχράντων χορὸς καθαρότητι διαλάμπων ἄλλων τε ψυχῶν πλῆθος ποτὲ μὲν αἱρουσῶν τὴν τοῦ ἡνιόχου κεφαλὴν εἰς τὸ νοητόν, ποτὲ δὲ ταῖς περικοσμίοις δυνάμεσι τῶν θεῶν συνταττομένων, καὶ τούτων αἵ μὲν κατ' ἄλλην, αἵ δὲ κατ' ἄλλην συνέπονται τοῦ θεοῦ δύναμιν.

We have here, with a clear reference to the *Phaedrus* myth, a division of pure souls. Some always accompany the gods and some do so only at times. This is, of course, the same distinction we saw drawn in *Elements of Theology* 185, but now with the added understanding that it is human souls alone who are in the class of souls that sometimes intellegize and sometimes are involved with generation. The other superior classes always accompany the gods. Thus, too, for Proclus, it is only human souls that descend to generation and only some subset of them that become corrupted there. Thus, in the triple division of 1.110.22–114.21 and 131.27–132.5, the middle group, the one that makes a pure descent, must include human souls only, for the superior classes can make no descent at all.

We find this schema echoed in Damascius's *Phaedo* commentary 1.477, where he says that daemons fill the space between gods and generation. These daemons differ from human beings precisely in that they always intelligize and thus "they especially are called 'consorts of the gods'" (ἐξαιρέτως αὐτοὶ ὀπαδοὶ λέγονται τῶν θεῶν, 1.477.2). So too at 2.94, Damascius emphasizes that the daemons differ from human souls by

> ... not being differently disposed at different times with regard to the better and to the worse but always perfect and not separated from their own virtue, without change, but not attached to what is superessential. This whole is the class of daemons.
>
> οὔτε ἄλλοτε ἄλλως ἔχον κατὰ τὸ χεῖρον καὶ τὸ κρεῖττον, ἀλλὰ τέλειον ἀεὶ καὶ τῆς οἰκείας ἀρετῆς οὐκ ἀφιστάμενον, ἀμετάβλητον μέν, οὐ συνημμένον δὲ τῷ ὑπερουσίῳ· τοῦτο δὲ ὅλον τὸ γένος δαιμόνιον (2.94.3–5)

Thus, Proclus and Damascius hold a firm, united view about the superior classes. All angels, daemons, and heroes are in constant attendance on the gods. Only human souls, in their interpretation of the *Phaedrus*, sometimes were consorts and sometimes were not. The other classes were intermediaries between the gods and generation, but they remained aloof from generation and attached to the gods as they controlled lower realms.

There is, however, reason to believe that Iamblichus interpreted Plato's words differently. In the *De Mysteriis*, Iamblichus distinguishes the various superior classes from the gods and from one another. We have already seen that he uses the term "eternal consorts" of the superior classes in this work. While Iamblichus is concerned to show that, as a group, angels, daemons, and heroes are superior to even pure human souls, he is equally concerned about the differences they possess among one another. In 1.20, Iamblichus deals with the difference between daemons and both the invisible and visible gods. One key difference concerns the kind of governance employed by the two groups (63.5–64.12). The gods rule the whole of the universe, while daemons have a more partial rule over specific regions within the whole. Indeed daemons are "in some manner cognate with and inseparable from the things they govern" (καὶ ἔτι συμφυεῖς πώς εἰσι καὶ ἀχώριστοι τῶν ὑφ' ἑαυτῶν διοικουμένων, 63.12–13). Further, Iamblichus says (64.7–9):

> Therefore the gods have been freed from the powers that incline[14] toward generation, but daemons are not completely purified from them.

---

14. For the verb ῥέπειν, see Des Places 1966, 76 n. 1; Finamore 1985, 56 n. 26; and Clarke, Dillon, and Hershbell 2003, 79 n. 110.

τοιγαροῦν οἱ θεοὶ τῶν ῥεπουσῶν εἰς τὴν γένεσιν δυναμεών εἰσιν ἀπηλλαγμένοι· δαίνομες δὲ τούτων οὐ πάντῃ καθαρεύουσιν.

For Iamblichus, it seems, there was a greater need to separate and distinguish the lower superior classes from higher entities. He was willing, indeed, to have the daemon's involvement with their material domain have an effect on their purity. This, of course, brings daemons closer to human souls and therefore subject to the same kind of contamination in their descent.

Book 2 of the *De Mysteriis* is dedicated to the differences among the superior classes. Iamblichus makes clear that daemons and heroes are lower than gods and angels in rank to such a degree that they are the superior classes that descend and are affected in a negative way by matter. In 2.1, Iamblichus associates daemons with encosmic natures (περικοσμίων φύσεων, 68.12–13) and with the realm of nature itself; heroes with human beings in the realm of generation.[15] In 2.5, the power to purify souls is perfect in the gods (τό γε ἀποκαθαρτικὸν τῶν ψυχῶν τέλεον μέν ἐστιν ἐν τοῖς θεοῖς, 79.7), but in the demons drags us down toward nature (δαίμονες δ' εἰς τὴν φύσιν καθέλκουσιν, 79.10) and in heroes draws us downward toward the concern for perceptible works (ἥρωες δὲ κατάγουσιν εἰς τὴν ἐπιμέλειαν τῶν αἰσθητῶν ἔργων, 79.10–11). Further, with regard to the consumption of matter in the presence of these divinities, the higher entities (gods and angels) consume it with speed whereas the daemons and heroes do not but manage it, presumably in its presence (80.15–81.4). Finally, in 2.6, the higher entities provide gifts that free us from our bodies and lead us to Intellect, whereas the daemons and heroes drag the soul down into nature (καθέλκει δὲ καὶ τὴν ψυχὴν ἐπὶ τὴν φύσιν, 82.10–11) and hold us down here in generation as we strive to reach the Intelligible fire (τοὺς δ' ἐπὶ τὸ πῦρ σπεύδοντας κατέχει περὶ τὸν τῇδε τόπον, 82.13–14).

It is clear, then, that whatever Iamblichus meant by the superior classes who were "always following" the gods, he did not mean that they did not descend into generation and have contact with matter. How did Iamblichus manage this?

Returning to Damascius's citation of Iamblichus in his *Parmenides* commentary, we recall that Damascius had some praise for Iamblichus's interpretation (4. 3.17–4.1):

> For this is the most persuasive of all the ancient interpretations and has many inducements for belief from the conclusions regarding daemons in the Symposium.

---

15. Cf. *Mys.* 2.2, where the activities of daemons are also encosmic (περικοσμίους, 68.4) and those of the heroes occupy an even narrower area (ἐπ' ἔλαττον μὲν διηκούσας, 68.6–7). Note that in 2.4, 77.19–78.2, the fire that accompanies the epiphanies of the gods is specifically described as filling the depths of the cosmos in a manner that is not encosmic (οὐ περικοσμίως, 78.2). In 2.5, daemons have an admixture of "encosmic vapors" (ἀτμοὶ περικόσμιοι, 80.5–6).

Indeed later at 4.19.9–18, when Damascius again considers Iamblichus's position, he argues that any change in the superior classes would not involve a shift from virtue to vice nor from their essential nature to a nature consistent with generation, for it is only the human soul that undergoes that sort of change. Then he turns to Iamblichus (Damascius, *In Parm.* 4.19.14–18; Iamblichus, *In Parm.* frg. 13):

> But if any of the superior classes undergoes a descent or ascent in some way or another (for indeed some such Iamblichus supposes among these classes), nevertheless the affection is most appropriate in our souls. For this reason the third hypothesis concerns these souls.

Although Damascius disagrees with Iamblichus, he makes two admissions that will help us reconstruct Iamblichus's reasoning. First, Iamblichus relied on the *Symposium* and its discussion of the intermediate nature of daemons. Second, he associated that intermediate nature with an actual descent into and ascent out of the realm of generation.

In the *Symposium*, Socrates takes Agathon to task for claiming that Eros was a god who possessed beauty and goodness. Rather, Socrates argues, Eros is a desire for these things and so must lack them, for no one desires what one already has (*Symp.* 199c5–201c9). Socrates then introduces Diotima, the learned woman from Mantineia who had an uncanny knowledge of Socratic elenchus. Diotima shows Socrates that Eros is neither good nor bad, neither beautiful nor ugly, but something in between, neither god nor human (201d1–202d9). When Diotima says that Eros is in between mortal and immortal, Socrates asks her what that might be (202d10–13). She replies that he is "a great daemon, for everything that is daemonic is between god and mortal" (δαίμων μέγας, ὦ Σώκρατες· καὶ γὰρ πᾶν τὸ δαιμόνιον μεταξύ ἐστι θεοῦ τε καὶ θνητοῦ, 202d13–202e1). Socrates asks for such a being's function (202e2), and Diotima replies (202e3–203a4):

> Interpreting and carrying matters human to the gods (prayers and sacrifices) and matters divine to humanity (commands and repayments for the sacrifices). Since it is in the middle, it completes both, so that everything is bound itself to itself. Through it, all the mantic art proceeds, the art of priests concerning sacrifices, rites, spells, and every mode of divination and magic. God does not mix with humanity, but through it is every communion and exchange between gods and human beings, for those who are awake and asleep.

> ἑρμηνεῦον καὶ διαπορθμεῦον θεοῖς τὰ παρ/ ἀνθρώπων καὶ ἀνθρώποις τὰ παρὰ θεῶν, τῶν μὲν τὰς δεήσεις καὶ θυσίας, τῶν δὲ τὰς ἐπιτάξεις τε καὶ ἀμοιβὰς τῶν θυσιῶν, ἐν μέσῳ δὲ ὂν ἀμφοτέρων συμπληροῖ, ὥστε τὸ πᾶν αὐτὸ αὑτῷ συνδεδέσθαι. διὰ τούτου καὶ ἡ μαντικὴ πᾶσα χωρεῖ καὶ ἡ τῶν ἱερέων τέχνη τῶν τε περὶ τὰς θυσίας καὶ τελετὰς καὶ τὰς ἐπῳδὰς καὶ τὴν μαντείαν πᾶσαν καὶ γοητείαν. θεὸς δὲ ἀνθρώπῳ οὐ μείγνυται, ἀλλὰ διὰ τούτου πᾶσά ἐστιν ἡ ὁμιλία καὶ ἡ διάλεκτος θεοῖς πρὸς ἀνθρώπους, καὶ ἐγρηγορόσι καὶ καθεύδουσι.

Now it should be clear that this passage is critical for Iamblichean religious philosophy. It presents *in nuce* what Iamblichus expanded into his own metaphysical schema. For the purposes of the third hypothesis of the *Parmenides*, it presented an opening for these intermediary beings (and indeed all the superior classes: angels, daemons, heroes, and purified human souls) in the Platonic universe. Clearly, Iamblichus saw from this passage that daemons ascended and descended, carrying messages to and from the gods and human beings. Iamblichus's interpretation of this passage in the light of contemporary religious practice is subtle. As we have seen, in his *De Mysteriis* he carefully constructed a hierarchy of souls superior to embodied human ones. Rather than drawing the line of active descent between gods and human souls, as Proclus and Damascius later chose to do, he drew the line within the superior classes themselves. As we have seen, the visible gods and angels[16] do not make the descent while daemons, heroes, and purified souls do.

Dillon (1973, 401) in his commentary to Iamblichus, *In Parm.* frg. 13, suggests (rightly, I believe) that Iamblichus imagined a special sort of descent for the lower ranks of the superior classes. Dillon adduces a passage from Proclus's *Timaeus* commentary in support of his view. The passage is at best only suggestive since it concerns not superior classes but rather the gods that show themselves at will, that is, the sublunar gods. Dillon argues wrongly that these gods are no different from the superior classes they rule in their chain, but the whole argument of *De mysteriis* books 1 and 2 militates against that view.[17] Gods, even lower gods, differ from the superior classes in several important respects, perhaps the most important of which is that gods (at any rank) do not descend into generation. Nevertheless, in the course of the discussion in the *Timaeus* commentary, Proclus does touch on the superior classes and in so doing helps us to see what Iamblichus's position would have been.

Proclus (196.11–16) argues first against the Stoic view and denies that gods mingle with matter. Next (196.16–24), he argues against Numenius and asserts that in their very essence gods are unmixed with matter (and not simply in their powers and energies). Proclus then asserts his general principle (196.24–27, partially quoted by Dillon).

> In every way those gods are unmixed with matter, ordering in an unmixed fashion things that are mixed and conjoining in an ungenerated fashion things that are generated and in an undivided fashion things that are divided.

---

16. Iamblichus later adds archangels and cosmic archons to the list of non-descending souls and hylic archons to the list of souls that make the descent to generation in *De mysteriis* 2.3.

17. See also Proclus's discussion at *In Tim.* 1.195.15–25.

πάντη ἄρα ἀμιγεῖς ἐκεῖνοι οἱ θεοὶ πρὸς τὴν ὕλην, ἀμιγῶς μὲν τὰ μεμιγμένα διακοσμοῦντες, ἀγενήτως δὲ τὰ γενητὰ καὶ ἀμερίστως τὰ μεριστὰ συνέχοντες.

Note that Proclus does not (indeed cannot, on Iamblichean principles) write that the gods descend. He instead separates them completely from all things material. These sublunary gods are, Proclus continues (196.30–197.1):

> ... leaders of angels, rulers of daemons, superintendents of heroes, each in its rank, directing all generation through this triple-natured army.

> ἀγγέλων ἡγούμενοι, δαιμόνων ἄρχοντες, ἡρώων προϊστάμενοι κατὰ τάξιν καὶ διὰ τῆς τριφυοῦς ταύτης σταρτιᾶς πᾶσαν κατευθύνοντες τὴν γένεσιν.

Thus, the sublunary gods are unmixed with the matter in generation, leaving the closer contact to the superior classes. Now, Proclus does not go on to say that it is the descents of these classes that bring the will of the gods to us, for as we have seen he would want to deny that doctrine. Iamblichus, however, would have argued otherwise.

Dillon argued that Iamblichus believed that the superior classes make a descent that was unmixed with matter (401). I believe that this is the correct view, and it is easy to bring evidence from Iamblichus's arguments about pure human souls to bear on the matter.[18] Iamblichus encountered difficulties concerning the descent of the lowest rank of the superior classes, the pure human soul. In *In Phaedonem* frg. 5, Damascius writes that Iamblichus had written both that these souls did not descend (frg. 5.1–2) and in his *Epistles* that (lines 8–11) they did descend into generation but in such a way that is "transcending of generation" (ἀγένητον)[19] and "not broken off from the things in the Intelligible" (πρὸς τὰ ἐκεῖ ἀδιάκοπον). Iamblichus is concerned with *Phaedo* 114c26, where philosophical souls are said to live without bodies forever more. Plato seems to be in contradiction with his own *Phaedrus*, and such moments bring out the resourcefulness in Neoplatonists. Here Iamblichus tries to have his cake and eat it too by arguing that these pure human souls in a sense both do and do not descend since their descent is such that the souls keep contact with the Intelligible while living their daily lives down here. Iamblichus has in mind souls such as Plato and Pythagoras, who would seem to be in the world but not of it, living pure lives and producing

---

18. On this topic, see Iamblichus, *An.* 58.1–8 with the notes of Finamore and Dillon 2002, 160–63. See also Finamore 1997, 168–71 and 173–76. The crucial passages from the *De anima* and *De mysteriis*, as well as *In Phaedr.* frg. 7, and *In Phaed.* frg. 5, are all discussed in these two works. Cf. Westerink and Combès 2003, 158–60 n. 2.

19. On the meaning of ἀγενήτως in Proclus, see Festugiere 1967, 2:44 n. 1, where he isolates two meanings: "not generated" and "transcending generation." The latter is more common and certainly the meaning Iamblichus intends here, as the phrase πρὸς τὰ ἐκεῖ ἀδιάκοπον shows. For further passages containing the adverb, see Westerink and Combès 2003, 158 n. 1.

benefits for all human beings. Damascius refers to Iamblichus's position again at *In Parm.* 4.24.1–7, where he reports that Iamblichus wrote in his *On the Migration of the Soul from the Body* that this class of pure souls, unlike other human souls,

> ... since it descends and ascends in a fashion that transcends generation, simply participates in and does not participate in Being; simply associates with and does not associate with the Intelligible. The descent of such souls simply introduces their presence to the things here.
>
> τοῦτο οὖν ἀγενήτως κατιὸν καὶ ἀνιόν, μετέχει μόνον οὐσίας καὶ οὐ μετέχει/ σύνεστιν γὰρ τῷ νοητῷ μόνον ἢ οὐ σύνεστιν, καὶ ἡ κάθοδος τῶν τοιούτων ψυχῶν παρουσίαν μόνον ἐμποιεῖ πρὸς τὰ τῇδε (4–7).

The repetition of "does ... does not" and of "simply" confirms that these souls are in a special position. Their descents occur in such a way as not to interfere with their connection to the Intelligible sphere. They are present to the body and to matter but do not become mixed with it. Note that this kind of interaction with the realm of generation differs from that of the gods, who do not descend and are not in contact with this realm directly.

If the lowest of the superior classes descend in this pure way, then the descents of the other classes must be even more pure. This is what we discovered in the *De Mysteriis*. Each class is somewhat purer in their interactions with the realm of generation. Thus, their descents are thereby different as well. The descents of daemons and heroes must be κατὰ τάξιν purer than those of pure souls; angels do not descend at all. Thus, there is a definite hierarchy in descents that mirrors the individual ranks of each class.

This would have been Iamblichus's solution, harmonizing the *Phaedo* and the *Phaedrus* by using the *Symposium*. The *Symposium* shows that daemons descend, he would argue. If they descend, then heroes and pure human souls must descend too. The *Phaedo*, however, suggests that some pure human souls do not descend. This idea, however, contradicts both the *Symposium* and the *Phaedrus*, where every ten thousand years all human souls (pure or not) descend. Thus, this doctrine must be explained by the notion of a special kind of descent that is, in one sense, no descent at all.[20]

---

20. A reader of an earlier version of this paper objected that Iamblichus did not include pure human souls among the superior classes in the third hypothesis. It is true that Proclus had mentioned only angels, demons, and heroes in his description in the *Parmenides* commentary, but (as I have argued above) Proclus and Iamblichus differed on this matter. Evidence from the *De Mysteriis* shows that Iamblichus wished to include pure human souls among those in the third hypothesis.

We can now reconstruct the sequence of thought. At the time Iamblichus was writing, there either was already existing or he himself created an interpretation of Plato's *Phaedrus* myth whereby the daemons mentioned therein were considered as perpetual followers of the gods. I consider it most likely that this interpretation preceded Iamblichus's writings and that he at first embraced the idea. A problem arose over the categorization of purified human souls. In what sense did they descend? And once that problem arose, there was a corollary concerning the superior classes generally. The *Symposium* taught that the gods did not descend here but that daemons carried messages back and forth. Did purified human souls and daemons make a real descent? Since heroes ranked just below daemons in Iamblichus's hierarchy, their descent became problematic as well. Certainly it would seem that pure human souls and heroes lived among other human beings. If daemons truly carried messages to and from the gods, they would seem to have descended as well. If these classes did descend, however, in what way did they differ from the ordinary run of human souls? And what of the *Phaedrus* myth's souls that always followed the gods? (And, too, there was the problem passage in the *Phaedo*, where some human souls seemed to escape this world forever.) Clearly, Iamblichus was faced with a dilemma that the neat bifurcation of "descending" and "not descending" souls was incapable of solving. I suggest that Iamblichus found the solution in the *Phaedrus* myth's claim that souls that successfully followed the gods were "unharmed" and that souls that were unsuccessful "fell." Here was a neat distinction among the first half of the bifurcation. Some souls descended and were unharmed and others were harmed by the forces of generation. It is this distinction that Iamblichus promulgated in his letter to which Damascius refers. Iamblichus meant it as a corrective to his and probably earlier claims about the *Phaedrus*. Thus, the three-tier structure became part of his philosophy, and those souls that always accompany the gods may or may not always do so, for they may descend but in a pure way. After Iamblichus, Proclus rejected Iamblichus's interpretation. For him, as well as for Damascius, all of the superior classes remained above. For these philosophers, the *Phaedrus* myth did not allow the Iamblichean bifurcation of superior classes. We have, then, another Iamblichean theory that later Neoplatonists rejected. For Iamblichus, however, his interpretation allowed him to follow Plato and create a working doctrine of theurgy in which each class of soul played a different role.

8
Syrianus's Exegesis of the Second Hypothesis of the *Parmenides*: The Architecture of the Intelligible Universe Revealed

John M. Dillon

Both the origins and the validity of the ontological interpretation of the second half of Plato's *Parmenides* are obscure, and issues on which I have had a certain amount to say myself in recent times.[1] As regards its origins, the thesis that I am prepared, albeit tentatively, to defend is that this interpretation, in some form, can be discerned as going back all the way to Plato's nephew Speusippus in the Old Academy, but if so, such a version would obviously not involve the whole panoply of the Neoplatonic metaphysical system, but simply an account of how the One, when combined with the Indefinite Dyad (under the guise of "Being") produces, first the whole set of natural numbers, and then, progressively, the various lower levels of reality, Soul, Nature (or the physical world, animate and inanimate), and ultimately Matter.

As to the *validity* of such an interpretation of the latter part of the dialogue, I would be rather more hesitant, but, of course, if it can be established that Speusippus did in fact view it in this way, that constitutes some sort of a presumption as to what his uncle had intended by it. All we can be sure of, however, is that, at some time at least before the end of the first century C.E. (when we find Moderatus of Gades adopting this interpretation) someone in the Platonic (within which we include the Neopythagorean) tradition came to the conclusion that Plato was here presenting us with a sort of blueprint of the structure of reality.

This basic issue is not, however, what I am concerned with on this occasion, but something a good deal more exotic. It is a doctrine, indeed, that arises out of

---

Reprinted, with permission, from *Syrianus et la métaphysique de l'antiquité tardive*. Edited by Angela Longo. Naples: Bibliopolis (© Istituto per il Lessico Intellettuale Europeo e la Storia delle Idee-CNR, 2009.

1. E.g., 2003, 56–59, à propos Speusippus.

the initial insight that the second hypothesis (142B–155D) provides an account of the generation of the cosmos, or at least of the intelligible level of reality, but it is one that develops this insight in a truly remarkable way.

It may be noted—and was duly noted by ancient commentators—that the first and second hypotheses are divided into a sequence of propositions, denied of the One in the first, asserted of it in the second, which could be seen to follow a certain logical order. A fuller version of the sequence occurs in the second, with fourteen distinct propositions (beginning with "If the One exists, it must be both one and being," at 142b3, and ending with 'If the One exists, it must be both older and younger than, and the same age as, itself," at 153b8),[2] while the first exhibits a slightly truncated version, comprising only eleven.

It is this second, fuller version that came to be seen as providing some kind of key to the structure of the intelligible world. However, although the second hypothesis had been taken at least since the time of Plotinus as representing the hypostasis of Intellect, no one until Syrianus, at the beginning of the fifth century, seems to have attained to the insight that each distinct proposition of which the second hypothesis is made up corresponds to a separate level of entity within the intelligible world. Proclus describes the rationale of his Master's procedure as follows, in book 6 of his *Parmenides Commentary* (1061,31–1062,17):

> His (sc. Syrianus's) position is that the first hypothesis contains the absolutely primal God, and the Second the intelligible realm. But because there is within the intelligible realm a plan, and the classes of gods are many, each of these divine classes receives from Plato a symbolic name, and all are presented by means of philosophical terms, and are not celebrated either by the names habitually employed by the authors of theogonies,[3] or by the names which reveal their natures, as in the case with the titles of the divine classes transmitted by the gods (sc. the Chaldaean Oracles), but rather, as I have just said, these classes of gods are presented by means of names familiar to the philosophers, such as "Totality," "Multiplicity," "Unlimitedness," and "Limit," names which are appropriate because they exhibit a suitable order; and all the divine processions are set out without exception, from the intelligible to the intellective to the hypercosmic, and for this reason all the conclusions are taken to be so many symbols of divine levels of being.
>
> It is also his position that everything which is stated affirmatively in the Second Hypothesis finds its denial in the First, and that shows that the Primal Cause transcends all the levels of gods, while these levels proceed each in accordance with a definite order which is proper to it.

---

2. What we in modern times take to be a sort of corollary to *Hyp.* 2.155e4—157b5, was more or less universally regarded in ancient times as a separate hypothesis, the third, portraying the generation of Soul.

3. Such as, in particular, Hesiod and the Orphic Poems.

He goes on to specify that the "one" of the Second Hypothesis, according to Syrianus, is neither (of course) the primal One, nor on the other hand is it a One that is inseparable from Being. It is in fact a divine henad, presiding transcendently over the multiplicity of the noetic realm, which on the one hand contains within itself the totality of henads, from which all other levels of being, beginning with the Forms, depend, and on the other hand generates all these other levels in due order. The way Syrianus sees it, as we learn from Proclus in a somewhat earlier passage of the *Parmenides Commentary* (1049,37–1050, 24 Cousin), the uniform premiss, "If there is a One," symbolizes the henad at the head of each order of gods, while the conclusion, which varies in each case, represents the particularity (ἰδιότης) of the class of gods (or superior beings) envisaged in each case. We will look at this rather confusing scenario in more detail in a moment.

Proclus's most eloquent acknowledgment, perhaps, of his indebtedness to Syrianus for this whole scheme occurs in book 3 of the *Platonic Theology*, where, at the end of ch. 23, following on a criticism of Iamblichus's identification of the subject-matter of the first hypothesis,[4] we find the following (83,10–18 Saffrey-Westerink):

> This, then, will be my procedure. I will take each of the conclusions separately, and will endeavour to refer it to the corresponding class of gods, following closely in this case also the inspired insights (ἐνθεασμοί) of my Master, that divine man with whom we have entered into the ecstasy of the study of the *Parmenides*,[5] as he revealed to us these sacred paths, which has truly roused us up from our sleep to the ineffable initiation into its mysteries.[6]

Proclus, then, makes it as clear as he can that for the basic insight that the Second Hypothesis presents an ordered blueprint of the whole realm of *Nous* he is more or less entirely indebted to his revered Master. Such an insight, however, on the part of Syrianus could not impose itself out of nothing. There was required first the considerable elaboration of the realm of *Nous* developed by Iamblichus about a century earlier, which postulated, not just a noetic triad of Being, Life, and

---

4. Iamblichus had actually identified this as "God and the gods," by "gods" meaning the henads, a class of entity that he seems to have been the first to propound. The totally negative nature of the conclusions does not seem to have bothered him, since, on Proclus's evidence (82,10–14 Saffrey-Westerink), he took this merely as an indication of the extreme degree of simplicity and unitariness (ἁπλότης καὶ ἕνωσις) of the henads (which he also, however, viewed as "objects of intellection"). Proclus dismisses this theory as quite inappropriate; as we will see, he, following Syrianus, would place them rather at the summit of the intelligible realm.

5. Indulging here in a creative borrowing of Socrates' (ironic) salutation of Phaedrus at *Phaedr.* 234d5–6: καὶ ἑπόμενος συνεβάκχευσα μετὰ σοῦ᾽ τῆς θείας κεφαλῆς.

6. Again, a creative use of a Platonic phrase, this time from the *Clitophon* 408c3–4. We find another, similarly hyperbolic, acknowledgement of dependence in the *Anon. in Parm.* Proclus, *In Parm.* 6.1061,20–31 Cousin.

Intellect, such as had been propounded by Porphyry[7] (and even recognized, non-systematically, by Plotinus himself[8]), but a system of three triads of intelligible gods, followed by three triads of intelligible-intellective gods, followed in turn by an intellective hebdomad—two triads and a seventh entity, termed the "membrane" (ὑπεζωκώς).[9] These, taken together (each triad being taken as a unit for the purpose), produce a total of nine levels of being, but even that only gets us to the segment 147c1–148d4, "both like and unlike both to itself and to the others." We still have five segments left, all in need of explanation.

Here Syrianus is able to adduce five further levels of divine entity below the "membrane": (1) hypercosmic gods; (2) hypercosmic-encosmic gods—these latter, like the intelligible-and-intellective triad, exhibiting the constant concern of later Neoplatonists to postulate intermediates between almost every level of entity, in order to foster what Dodds has termed the "law of continuity" (see *Proclus, Elem. Theol.*, prop. 216 Dodds); (3) the encosmic gods; (4) universal souls—these being still regarded as part of the intelligible realm, as will be explained further below; and lastly (5) the so-called "superior classes of being" (τὰ κρείττονα γένη), comprising the angels, daemons and heroes (which Iamblichus had actually made the subject of the third hypothesis, rather than Soul, as did all other Neoplatonic exegetes). This now gets us, at the cost of some degree of implausibility, down to 155d1, which is where we need to be.[10]

Having set that out thus succinctly, let us try to explore, in at least a selection of cases, what possible justification Syrianus could find in the text before him for his grand conception.

We may begin with an examination of the intelligible triads, the exposition of which extends, in three stages, from 142b5 to143a3. It should be specified at the outset that each divine triad is structured on the same model as is the fundamental triad into which the realm of *Nous* is divided in every Neoplatonist system beginning with that of Porphyry, that is to say, Being–Life–Intellect (though this manifests itself in this case rather as Unity–Potency–Being, ἕν, δύναμις, ὄν);[11] so it is, therefore, with this primary triad. For the details of the doctrine, we must

---

7. Observable in a passage of his *Timaeus Commentary,* preserved by Proclus (= frg. LXXIX Sodano), but also in the *Anon. in Parm.* frg. 6, which I accept as the work of Porphyry.

8. E.g., *Enn.* 6.7 [38].13; 6.2 [43].8. See Hadot 1957, 105–57.

9. Iamblichus, according to Proclus (*In Tim.* 1:308,18–23 Diehl), propounded this system in its full elaboration, not in his *Timaeus Commentary,* but rather in a special monograph entitled "On the Speech of Zeus in the *Timaeus*." Nonetheless, propound it he did.

10. There is then a short bridge passage, summarizing the findings arrived at since 142b5, from 155d1–e3, before the start of what the ancients took to be the third hypothesis.

11. This may indeed seem odd, but it is conditioned by the nature of the text; and in fact Unity can be regarded as the essence of the Intelligible, while Being can be taken as its intellect, inasmuch as the articulation which it presides over can be seen as a sort of self-consciousness. At any rate, it is essentially the same triad.

turn primarily to the exegesis of Proclus in the *Platonic Theology* (3.24–26), but Proclus has made it clear in the *Parmenides Commentary* (quoted above) whence he has derived his theory, and in the case of the first segment of the exegesis, we have welcome confirmation from Damascius in his *De principiis* (§48, 2.17, 14–17 Westerink-Combès) that the doctrine is to be attributed to Syrianus as well as Proclus.

We begin, as you recall, with the proposition (142b5–6), "If one exists, is it possible for it to exist, and not to partake in existence (οὐσίας δὲ μὴ μετέχειν)?" In the formulation of this thesis, Syrianus discerns not just two entities, One and Being, but a third, connecting the two, the relationship of μέθεξις or σχέσις. It is this relational entity that creates the first triad, and constitutes the element of δύναμις, making possible the outflow (πρόοδος) of One into Being, and the reversion (ἐπιστροφή) of Being towards the One.

This first triad represents the summit of the intelligible realm, and its link with the henadic realm. It is, in fact, as we have seen, the true home of the divine henads. At this stage, all the multiplicity characteristic of the intelligible, in particular the multitude of Forms, are still at a unitary, "hidden" stage. "The first triad," says Proclus,[12] "is called 'One-Being,' since its potency is in this case present only in a hidden mode (κρυφίως); for the triad does not proceed out of itself, but subsists in an undivided and unitary mode, because it receives its primary determination from unity proper to the gods (θεία ἕνωσις—i.e., the henadic realm)."

This, then, is the essence of the first triad of the intelligible gods. For the second, we turn to the concept of "one" as a whole with parts (142c7–d9). This produces a triad characterized primarily by potency and "procession," in which a measure of distinction between the components is first manifested. "For," says Proclus, "whereas everything at that level (sc. in the first triad) was unified and undistinguished, distinction becomes manifest in the second; Being and Potency are distinguished to a greater degree the one from the other, and what results from them is no longer just One-Being, but a Whole, containing within itself One and Being as parts."[13]

At this level, then, δύναμις, the middle term, no longer *unites* One and Being, but simply *links* them (συνάπτει, καὶ οὐχ ἑνοῖ, 87,10–11). This "moment" Proclus (and no doubt Syrianus before him) identifies with Eternity (*aión*) in the *Timaeus* (37d6), which, as we recall, "remains in One" (μένοντος αἰῶνος ἐν ἑνί),[14] while

---

12. *Plat. Theol.* 3.24 = 85,27–86,3 Saffrey-Westerink.
13. *Plat. Theol.* 25 = 87,1–5 Saffrey-Westerink.
14. Plato, of course, meant only that Eternity remains always in the one *state;* the Neoplatonists, from Plotinus on, chose to take this to mean that Eternity remains *in the One*, thus constituting a link between the realms of the One and of Intellect.

its image, the physical universe, proceeds into temporality. On this triad, Proclus has this to say:[15]

> The second triad, then, is called "intelligible totality" (ὁλότης νοητή), and its parts are One and Being—by which I mean its extremities—while its Potency, being median, here links, but does not unite, One and Being, as is the case in the triad prior to it. And since it is median between the two, by virtue of its communion (κοινωνία) with Being it makes the One appear as "One-Being," while by virtue of its communion with the One, it renders Being one. And so One-Being is composed of two parts, One-Being and Being-One, even as Parmenides tells us.

This second triad, then, introduces, in an archetypal mode, the feature of articulation, or partibility, which is characteristic of the lower levels of the realm of *Nous*. The third carries this process a stage further. The text, as you recall, at 142d9, continues the preceding argument by proposing that, of each of the two parts of One-Being, "oneness" can never be lacking to the part "being," nor "being" to the part "oneness." Thus each of the two parts, in its turn, will possess both oneness and being, and so each of these parts must be indefinitely divisible, and we arrive thus at the conclusion (143a2–3) that the One-Being must be unlimited in multiplicity (οὐκοῦν ἄπειρον ἂν τὸ πλῆθος οὕτω τὸ ἓν ὂν εἴη...).

For Syrianus, this signifies that this third intelligible triad is responsible, again in an archetypal mode, for the articulation of the "infinite multiplicity" that is unleashed by the second—infinite, he is at pains to point out, not numerically, but in power: "for," he says,[16]

> following on the hidden unitariness (ἕνωσις) of the first triad, and the dyadic distinguishing power (διάκρισις) of the second, there arises the processive nature (πρόοδος) of the third, having its substance constituted of parts, but of more numerous parts (sc. than the second), forming the multiplicity with which the triad prior to it was pregnant. For there is inherent in this triad a unity, a potency, and a being, but in this case the unity and the being and the potency are pluralized; and thus this triad as a whole is a totality (ὁλότης), each of its extremes, by which I mean unity and being, constituting a multiplicity which, while being linked together by the agency of a cohering potency, is in turn divided and pluralized.

This third triad, then, is the archetype of the distinction of the world of Forms into genera and species, and of their projection onto the physical world. Proclus (and, again, probably Syrianus) equates it with the Essential Living Being (αὐτοζῷον) of the *Timaeus* (37D), which comprehends within itself all the intel-

---

15. *Plat. Theol.* 3.25 = 87,8–16 Saffrey-Westerink.
16. *Plat. Theol.* 3.26 = 89,7–16 Saffrey-Westerink.

ligible living things "individually and by genera" (καθ ' ἕν καὶ κατὰ γένη, *Tim*. 30c6).[17]

This identification with entities in the *Timaeus* serves to clarify what Syrianus has in mind for the three intelligible triads. Between them, they constitute the governing mechanisms for the creation of, first, the world of Forms, and then, secondarily of the world of physical individuals. The first provides unity, the second distinction and multiplicity, and the third, the structure and articulation of genera and species.

To turn next to the intelligible-intellectual gods, we find the three elements of the triad at this level linked to those of the intelligible level by a system of analogies. The first, and most significant, element of this triad is Number, the generation of which is set out at 143a3–144e7—an exceptionally extensive stretch of text, but commensurate with the importance of this stage in the unfolding of Plato's scheme.[18] Proclus accords this a corresponding prominence in his exegesis, devoting fully seven substantial chapters of the *Platonic Theology* to it (4.28–34), and expounding therein, I have no doubt, what are substantially the views of Syrianus.

Proclus begins by making a distinction between the high degree of unity exhibited at the intelligible level, where the relation of σχέσις links together One and Being, keeping their distinction virtual, or "hidden" (κρύφιος), and the greater degree of distinction manifested at the intelligible-intellectual level, where the relation of otherness (ἑτερότης) makes their distinction actual and explicit, thus generating the multiplicity of numbers.[19] He then launches into a protracted celebration of the powers of Divine Number (θεῖος ἀριθμός), a concept made much use of by Syrianus in the *Metaphysics* commentary[20] (though Syrianus there speaks chiefly of θεῖοι ἀριθμοί in the plural, denoting the whole sequence of archetypal numbers, as opposed to the lower, "unitary" ones, which are all that Aristotle recognizes). Divine Number serves as the mediating force between the undistinguished unitariness of the intelligible level and the fully actualized multiplicity of the intellectual level.[21] The activity of otherness (which Proclus, and

---

17. *Plat. Theol.* 3.27 = 95,11 Saffrey-Westerink.
18. Especially if, as I would maintain, Speusippus is right in discerning here an ontological aspect to this exposition, to wit, the generation of number from the interaction of Monad and Dyad.
19. *Plat. Theol.* 4.27 = 79,15–80,6 and 28 = 81,3–82,11 Saffrey-Westerink.
20. Cf., e.g., *In Metaph.* 124.24–125.8; 130.24–131.8; 132.4–8; 146.5, 9.
21. Μέσος γὰρ ἱδρυθεὶς τῶν τε νοητῶν θεῶν καὶ τῶν νοερῶν καὶ τὸν ἕνα συνδεσμον αὐτῶν συμπληρῶν, 84,12–14.

I suspect Syrianus,[22] characterizes as predominantly "feminine")[23] serves, as he says (p. 89,10–13), "to divide 'one' from 'being', splitting the one into many units, and being into many beings"; and this process, once begun, continues down through the various levels of being, all the way to the material realm, to provide the essential degree of articulation of entities that makes the world an ordered cosmos. Number is thus of central importance in the economy of the universe.

The other two moments of the intelligible-intellectual triad may be dealt with more briefly, even as Proclus treats them. To the "whole" of the intelligible triad there corresponds on this level, as the median triad, "whole and part" (covered in 144e8–145a4). The three "moments" of the triad are identified, following Plato, as "one and many," "whole and parts," and "limited and unlimited in multiplicity." This triad is characterized (in *Theol. Plat.* 4.36), as was the corresponding one at the intelligible level, as συνεκτική, or "cohesive"—and indeed is identified, on the theological level, with a Chaldaean class of gods, the συνοχεῖς. Its purpose, in Syrianus's scheme, is presumably to give further cohesion and articulation to the activities of Number.

As for the third triad (covered in 145a4–b5), it is characterized as τελεσιουργός, or "perfective." As Plato argues, if "the one" is a whole, it must necessarily have end-points (ἔσχατα), and so a beginning, a middle, and an end; and so, shape (σχῆμα), and these correspond it the three "moments" of the third triad. This, in Syrianus's view (as expounded by Proclus in 4.37–78), allows it to bestow the qualities of reversion (ἐπιστροφή), perfection and intellectual shape on the lowest sector of the realm of Intellect, the intellectual order, and so keep in check any tendency to excessive fragmentation that it might otherwise have exhibited. This triad may be identified, in Chaldaean terms, with the τελετάρχαι, or "perfective gods."

One could continue at great length to work out his rationale for the identification of the various members of the intellective (demiurgic) hebdomad, and then of the various lower levels of god, but enough has been said here, I hope, to give some indication of how the great project was worked out, derived as it is from a close study of the details of the text. Whether this scheme dawned gradually on Syrianus over a number of years, or came to him suddenly one morning in his bath, we have no idea, but either way it deserves some degree of celebration, as constituting a sort of culmination of the initial insight that the second half of

---

22. The term θηλυπρεπής, which Proclus uses here, also occurs in Syrianus, *In Metaph.* 131.36, though as an epithet of the Dyad (as opposed to ἀρρενωπός, used of the Monad); but in fact the role of the Dyad is very much that of *heterotês*, so there is no great contradiction there. Proclus also recognizes both a "male" and a "female" function of number at 90,6, related respectively to the inherent characteristics of Limit and Unlimitedness.

23. In 4.30 = 89,6–91, 26 Saffrey-Westerink.

the *Parmenides* is not simply a logical exercise of some sort, but in fact a blueprint of the structure of the intelligible, and indeed of the physical, universe.

9
Damascius on the Third Hypothesis of the *Parmenides*

Sara Ahbel-Rappe

Damascius's *Commentary on the Parmenides* is found together with the *Problems and Solutions Concerning First Principles* on a single manuscript, Marcianus Graecus 246, separated by a lacuna.[1] This manuscript belonged to a celebrated philosophical library from the last quarter of the ninth century, whose contents included works of Plato, Proclus, Olympiodorus, Maximus of Tyre, Alexander of Aphrodisias, Simplicius, John Philoponus, and of course, Damascius. According to the conjecture of Westerink, this collection is a copy made shortly after the philosophical library at Alexandria was transferred to Byzantium, perhaps in the seventh or ninth centuries. In what follows, I will be discussing how Damascius's treatment of the third hypothesis of the *Parmenides* correlates to the Neoplatonic interpretation of the *Parmenides* as accounting for the devolution of reality: the soul and its multiply realized configurations are the foundation of a "way of seeming" that is the ultimate subject of Damascius's *Commentary on the Parmenides*.

In order to discuss the development of the commentary tradition on Plato's *Parmenides*, it will be helpful to have in view a sketch of the hypotheses recognized by the Neoplatonists in the second half of the dialogue, on which they based their exegeses:

(Table 1) The Hypotheses or Deductions of Plato's *Parmenides*

First Hypothesis: If the One is, what are the consequences for it? 137c4–142a8
Negative conclusions

Second Hypothesis: If the One is, what are the consequences for it? 142b1–155e3
Positive conclusions

---

1. I would like to thank Professors Corrigan and Turner for their work in editing this volume and for leading the entire *Parmenides* Seminar.

Third Hypothesis: If the One is and is not simultaneously, what are the consequences for it? 155e4–156b5 Negative and positive conclusions

Fourth Hypothesis: If the One is, what are the consequences for the Others? 156b6–159b: Positive conclusions

Fifth Hypothesis: If the One is, what are the consequences for the Others? 159b–1604: Negative conclusions

Sixth Hypothesis: If the One is not, what are the consequences for it? 160b–163b: Positive conclusions

Seventh Hypothesis: If the One is not, what are the consequences for it? 163b–164b: Negative conclusions

Eighth Hypothesis: If the One is not, what are the consequences for the Others? 164b5–165e1: Positive conclusions

Ninth Hypothesis: If the One is not, what are the consequences for the Others? 165e2–166c5: Negative conclusions

The Neoplatonists held that Plato's *Parmenides* was a theological disquisition that charted not only the fundamental principles of reality, but also the emergence of any possible form of being from One transcendent source (Saffrey 1987). It is in this tradition of exegesis upon Plato's *Parmenides* that the *Problems and Solutions* and the *Commentary on the Parmenides* find their place. Perhaps the most famous example of this traditional claim to orthodoxy is found in *Enn.* 5.1 [10].8, Plotinus's doxography concerning his doctrine of the three primary hypostases, Soul, Intellect, and the One: "our present doctrines are an exegesis of those [ancient teachings], and so the writings of Plato himself provide evidence that our doctrines are of ancient origin" (5.1 [10].8.11–15).[2] If the One is beyond Being (a premise that Plotinus took directly from Plato's *Republic*) then Being only emerges as a subsequent stage of reality, at the level of Intellect, while transitory Being, or becoming, originates in the third hypostasis, or Soul. Plotinus left it for his followers to iron out the details of precisely how the entire dialogue mapped onto the universe as a whole. Proclus, the fifth-century Athenian Neoplatonist, left a catalog of these attempts in book 6 of his commentary on Plato's *Parmenides* (6.1052,31–1053.9). There he set forth in astonishing detail the evolution of this exegetical tradition, beginning with Plotinus's disciples, Amelius and Porphyry, and ending with the interpretation of his own teacher Syrianus.[3]

---

2. On this passage, see the commentary of Atkinson 1983, 192.
3. Morrow and Dillon 1987, Introduction, section B. Saffrey-Westerink 1968–1997.

In fact, it has now become clearer that the metaphysical interpretation of the latter half of the *Parmenides* actually began at least as early as the Neopythaogrean, Moderatus, perhaps alluded to at *In Parm.* 1.640.17, when Proclus speaks of the "ancients."[4] Tarrant, starting from a suggestion made by E. R. Dodds in 1928, has shown that Moderatus recognized eight levels of reality in the hypotheses of the Parmenides. Tarrant quotes the following fragment from Porphyry's *On Matter* that purports to give a testimony on the theory of Moderatus:

> Following the Pythagoreans, this man [Moderatus] declares the first One to be above Being and all substance, while the second One, namely, true Being and the intelligible (he says it is the Forms) while the third, which is that of Soul... participates in the One and the Forms. (Simplicius, *In phys.* 9:230,36–40 Diels, trans. Tarrant 2000, 157)

Proclus's own elaboration of the Parmenidean hypotheses is very intricate, since he followed Syrianus in holding that:

> The First Hypothesis is about the primal god, and the Second is about the intelligible world. But since there is a wide range in the intelligible world and there are many orders of gods, his view is that each of these divine orders has been named symbolically by Plato ... all having their proper rank, and portraying without omission all the divine stages of procession, whether intelligible, intellectual, or supracosmic, and that thus all things are presented in logical order, as being symbols of the divine orders of being; (*In Parm.* 6.1061.21 trans. Dillon, with omissions)

In other words, as Dillon has succinctly said in his introduction to the translation of book 6, "the First and Second Hypotheses actually run through the whole extent and variety of the divine world from the intelligible monad down to the ... daemons, heroes and angels dependent on the divine Soul" (Dillon 1987, 388). From Syrianus, Proclus adapted two principles in his exegesis of the Parmenidean hypotheses; as Saffrey explains,

> there are as many negations in the first hypothesis as there are affirmations in the second and what is denied in the first hypothesis of the first god, the One, is precisely what is affirmed in the second hypothesis and which constitutes the essential characteristics of the gods subordinated to the One. (Saffrey 1965, 1: 58)

---

4. More controversially, John Dillon has published a paper in which Speusippus, Plato's immediate successor at the Academy, was already engaged in an ontological interpretation of the second part of the first hypothesis, which alludes to the Pythagorean derivation of all reality from the generation of numbers.

Saffrey then goes on to summarize the consequences of these discoveries as follows:

> In following carefully the series of negations of the first hypotheses or that of the affirmations in the second, one can immediately obtain the rigorous order of the classes of the gods in the divine hierarchy. (translated from the original French)

Most of Proclus's commentary is now missing, but some of it can be reconstructed from Damascius, and also from Proclus's *Platonic Theology*, books 3–6. The second hypothesis corresponds to the intelligible world, or *kosmos noetos*. However, in late Neoplatonism this order of reality itself is understood as containing three diacosms: the intelligible proper (νοητός) the intelligible-intellective (νοητός-νοερός) and the intellective (νοερός). These three intelligible diacosms are followed by three orders of gods: hypercosmic, hypercosmic-encosmic, and encosmic. The expansive triads beginning with the Second Hypostasis, or Nous, represent a complex synthesis of theological and philosophical traditions. Each diacosm capable of description under a Neoplatonic rubric corresponds to parallel metaphysical systems that derive from Orphic or Chaldean theologies.

After surveying the interpretations of the *Parmenides*[5] offered by Amelius Proclus, *In Parm*. 1052–1053), Porphyry (1053–1056) and Iamblichus (1054–1055), Proclus insists that all of these exegetes fail to take into account what he considers the major division among the hypotheses, namely that the first five hypotheses represent five levels of reality—in fact all the levels of reality that there are—as consequences of the One. Following upon this provision, Proclus goes on to interpret the next four hypotheses as showing the consequences, per absurdum, of denying the One's existence. As we will see in greater detail, Damascius parts with Proclus on the question of how the hypotheses reference the stations of the real. For now, however, it is important to note that, like Proclus who uses the interpretation of Syrianus, Damascius interprets the third hypothesis as a reference to Soul, which then becomes, in a sense, the gateway to Non-Being. Each of the subsequent hypotheses, then, delineates further stages in the total devolution of reality. For our author, Damascius, it seems that Plutarch's exegesis of the Parmenidean hypotheses comes very close to an acceptable interpretation. In fact, we know that Damascius was familiar with such an interpretation from his own *Commentary on the Parmenides*, as evinced at § 434 (84,5–9) Westerink-Combès. In Plutarch's scheme, we have the following correspondences:

---

[5]. On Proclus's catalog of the Parmenidean interpretive traditions, see especially the Introduction to vol. 1 of the Saffrey-Westerink (1965) edition of the Platonic Theology, section 7, L'exegèse des hypothèses du Parménide; as well as the introduction to book 6 in Morrow-Dillon 1987.

first hypothesis: God
second hypothesis: Intellect
third hypothesis: Soul
fourth hypothesis: Forms united with matter
fifth hypothesis: Matter
sixth hypothesis: Sensible existents
seventh hypothesis: All objects of knowledge
eighth hypothesis: Dreams and shadows
ninth hypothesis: All images below the level of dream life.

As Proclus in explaining Plutarch's schema comments (Proclus, *In Parm.* 1060–1061), the levels of unreality that correspond to the lower hypotheses are derivable from Platonic doctrine in the *Timaeus*, with its distinction between Forms and Forms in matter (*Tim.* 28a2); and also in the *Resp.* 6.509d5 and following, with its distinctions between the components of *eikasia*.

Just as Proclus's own commentary on Plato's *Parmenides* is mined for the history of Parmenidean exegesis, so Damascius's Commentary is a source for the reconstruction of the mostly missing books of Proclus's prior Commentary.[6] To delve into the intricacies of the individual gods named in Damascius's treatment of the Parmenidean hypotheses, including the Chaldean and Orphic correspondences, goes well beyond the scope of this introduction. But as Saffrey and Westerink have demonstrated in their edition of Proclus's *Platonic Theology*, Damascius was a very close reader of Proclus's text, and his exposition of, for example, the hebdomadal structure of the intellectual gods, reveals that he understood the system of Parmenidean exegesis as framed by Proclus, as well as its religious associations in the very baroque world of Neoplatonic triadic correspondences.

Damascius's *Commentary on the Parmenides* proceeds from the noetic triad (equivalent to the intelligible or Unified of the first principles) but then descends into the least real and most outward expression of Being, referenced by the Ninth Hypothesis. The Third Hypothesis refers to the one of the soul, since it includes negative language (If the One both is and is not). Hence Soul is the first order of reality to introduce Non-Being, or genesis. Soul is the entryway to Non-Being, and the last four hypotheses, for Damascius, represent various stations along the path to complete unreality. Although Damascius refers to this portion of the text as the third hypothesis, modern commentators sometimes treat it as an appendix (Gill and Ryan 1996, 119) or corollary (Sayre 1996: 240) of the Second Hypoth-

---

6. For the use of Damascius in reconstructing Proclus's commentary, see the Introduction to Platonic Theology in Saffrey and Westerink (1965, vol. 5). Saffrey and Westerink focus on the so-called hebdomadic structure of the intellectual gods and Proclus's reasons for adopting this arrangement in his exposition of the second hypothesis.

esis, "If the One is." However, in Damascius's construal, Plato is asking about a "third one," distinct in its degree of reality from the previous two deductions, respectively, the One and Intellect. This third one is the embodied soul, since here Plato introduces a one that exists in time, capable of undergoing generation and dissolution, and therefore birth and death (Damascius, *In Parm.* 4.1–50 Westerink-Combès). Of course, Plotinus had already referred *Parmenides* 155e5, to the One-Many (*Enn.* 5.1 [10].8.30) of Soul, his third hypostasis. And yet in discussing Soul as a hypostasis, Plotinus was more concerned with an examination of Soul in light of his theory of emanation from the One, as a fundamental constituent of reality. The individual soul was just one aspect of the hypostasis as such.

We will return to the question of the embodied soul's career shortly, but first a brief survey of the remaining hypotheses, four through nine, will orient the reader to Damascius's overall approach to the *Parmenides*. At *In Parm.* 85.15 Steel, Damascius summarizes his treatment of hypotheses four, five, and six: hypothesis four treats of Forms not yet entangled in matter; Five, of informed matter; and Six, of the entire class of sublunar individuals and composite entities, or as Damascius puts it, the "phenomenal one" (83.16 Steel). Hypothesis four describes a world in which matter does not yet play a part; the Forms are copies of the real beings of the second hypothesis (or Intellect). This function belongs to them by virtue of the activity of Soul, which then projects the Forms into matter. Continuing through the sequence of hypotheses, Damascius equates the Not-One of hypothesis seven with a Not-Being that is rooted in the imagination and as such retains the faintest trace of Being. The Not-One (or Others) of hypothesis eight express Being at its most individuated level—for Damascius the site of quantitative Being; and the Not-One of the final hypothesis, Nine, represents the complete negation of just this individuated existence. In other words, as Damascius descends down the series of hypotheses he sees the activities of individual souls as tending toward isolation from their universal source, and narrows in on the imaginary isolated productions of the embodied individual, and increasingly, on the physical aspects of individual things.

Whereas the *Problems and Solutions* (*Dubitationes et solutiones*) treats the topic of reality and its fullness, as well as the topic of whether and how this reality can be known by the human intellect, the commentary on the *Parmenides* actually treats the topic of unreality—of how the phenomenal world arises as a result of the activities of the individual soul. By far the most important issue in the commentary on the *Parmenides* concerns the question of whether or not the soul descends completely into the order of birth and death. This issue, as we will see, had a long history among the Neoplatonists and it is in this section of the work that we glimpse something of how Damascius responded to his predecessors on doctrinal matters. More importantly, though, it is in the commentary on the *Parmenides* that we are able to gain an understanding of Damascius's psychology.

After delineating the *skopos* of the third hypothesis (a discussion of the souls that descend or become embodied) Damascius launches directly into a doxographical controversy that starts even before Plotinus, as we learn from this sentence at *Ennead* 4.8 [6].8:

> If I am to be bold enough to express more clearly my own opinion against that of others, our soul does not descend in its entirety, but part of its always remains in the intelligible world.

Iamblichus famously argued against the position Plotinus expresses here. Although Iamblichus is aware that he is simplifying when he says that the latter wrongly equates Soul with Intellect, he distinguishes and even separates the Soul from Intellect, treating it as a lower hypostasis:

> There are some who ...place even in the individual soul the intelligible world... According to this doctrine the soul differs in no way from Intellect. The doctrine opposed to this separates the Soul off, inasmuch as it has come about as following upon Intellect. (*De Anima*, extracted from fragments 6–7 Finamore and Dillon 2002)

By contrast, Plotinus allows that one can find within the essence of the soul its source in the intellectual, and that "these alone [are] activities of the soul, all it does intellectually" (5.1 [10].3.18). Although his own commentary on the *De anima* is lost, evidently Iamblichus used Aristotle to critique the view of Plotinus, who characterized the lower aspects of the soul—those directly involved in bodily perceptions—as an illumination from the higher soul. From what can be reconstructed in the texts of pseudo-Simplicius, it seems that Iamblichus held that the entire soul descends into genesis. Once the soul is incarnate, its essence weakens; it is no longer able to re-ascend into the intelligible world without the aid of the gods. This whole doctrine is a theoretical justification for Iamblichus's endorsement of theurgy as the preferred means of spiritual ascent. And yet there is also a constraint on the definition of the soul in the philosophy of Iamblichus, since, as mediator between the gods and the mortal realm, the soul functions to extend the procession as far as possible and to reunite the cosmos with its causes.

When discussing his own doctrine of incarnation, Damascius employs his usual methodology, in which Iamblichus is a springboard for the criticism of what Damascius considers to be the improper innovations of Proclus as in the following passage (Damascius, *In Parm.* 15.1–5 Steel = 254.3–19 Ruelle):

> In addition to these considerations, if an essence is either eternal or generally free from change, it does not descend into birth and death at one time, and then ascend from birth and death at another. Rather, it is always above. If it is always above, then it will also have an activity that is always above. And so on this assumption, Plotinus' account is true, viz., that the soul does not descend as a whole. But [Proclus] does not allow this argument. For how could it be, when one part of the soul is in the intelligible, that the other part is in the worst evil?

Therefore the essence of the soul descends, becoming more divisible instead of more uniform, and instead of substantial, becoming more ephemeral.

In the last part of this citation, Damascius argues against the position that Proclus presents in virtually all of his writings on the soul, as for example in the *Institutio Theologica*:

> Every participated soul has an eternal substance but a temporal activity. (191.166–167 Dodds)

In Proclus's world of hierarchical entities, beings are strictly ranked into the categories of eternal, temporal, and something whose activity is temporal, while its substance is eternal. So soul is eternal but its activities are expressed in time. Proposition 29 of the *Institutio Theologica* clearly expresses this doctrine:

> Intermediate between wholly eternal beings and wholly created beings there is necessarily a class of beings which are in one respect eternal but in another measured by time i.e. they both exist always and come to be.

Returning to the text of Damascius we find that earlier on he refutes the position of Proclus and aligns himself with Iamblichus by arguing that an eternal essence will likewise have an eternal activity, but a changing essence will have a changing activity. And so Damascius reluctantly spells out his own position, one that accords with Iamblichus yet sounds, on the whole, somewhat unorthodox:

> Perhaps we must dare to express the doctrine with which we have long been in labor: there is some change with respect to our essence. For that this essence is not eternal even the *Timaeus* teaches us clearly, and that it has not gathered together all of the time as has the superior Soul, is what the lowering into the last part of the psychic essence, when the soul has descended, shows. (Damascius, *In Parm.* 13.1–5 Steel)

And just a little later on:

> Proclus envisions that the changes implied by the conclusions are connected to the activities and also the powers of the soul. For [he says that] its essence is eternal, but its coming to be is connected to its projections of the various lives and thoughts, which in turn are connected to time, while its essence is a temporal, which he understands as eternal. We on the other hand have already shown in our *Commentary on the Timaeus* that the soul as a whole is simultaneously subject to birth and death and also not subject to birth and death. Moreover now too we understand the conclusions [of Proclus concerning the Third Hypothesis] to apply to [the soul's] essence. (Damascius, *In Parm.* 252, 7–15 Ruelle)

According to Iamblichus, the soul suffers a break, a dispersal of its essence, during the process of embodiment. Since the human soul was "inclined toward the body that it governs" when it projected its lower lives, its οὐσία was broken apart and intertwined with mortal lives.[7] Here Iamblichus describes the descent of the soul as a "breaking apart," a metaphor employed by Plato in the *Phaedrus* when depicting the fallen horses that lose their wings in the cosmic procession. Again, citing what is in all likelihood a lost portion of Iamblichus, Priscianus says:

> It is reasonable then, or rather, necessary that not the soul's activity alone but also its essence and the highest part of itself—of our soul, I mean—is somehow dissipated and slackened and as it were sinks down in the inclination toward what is secondary. (Priscianus <ps-Simplicius>, *In de anima* 241.7–10 = Finamore and Dillon, Appendix D)

By contrast, Damascius does not so much emphasize the breaking up of the soul's essence. At times, indeed, he speaks of the vehicle of the soul as undergoing changes, yet he elucidates such changes more along the lines of ἀλλοίωσις, or alteration, rather than substantial change, as in the following passage from his commentary on the *Parmenides*:

> Or like the vehicle of the soul, which remains immortal and the same in number, but sometimes is more a sphere, and at other times is less a sphere, and sometimes is more filled with divine light, and sometimes it shuts down and is more like the ephemeral, and the living being suffers something essentially, so too the soul itself remains what it is but changes around itself and by itself, just in the way that is natural for incorporeal things to change, since for example sight remaining what it is, is perfected by light, and it is blocked under the darkness, and yet it does not perish unless the light or the darkness overwhelms it. (255.8–15)

In the *Problems and Solutions*, Damascius makes clear that the human soul, the rational soul, is fully able to maintain its essential nature through attention and self-awareness:

> Our own soul stands guard over its native activity and corrects itself. It could not be this kind of thing, unless it reverted onto itself. (12.3–5 Westerink-Combès)

This doctrine of self-motion, or the soul as the agent of its own change, is also a feature of Damascius's account in his *Commentary on the Parmenides*, as we read in the following passage:

---

7. Carlos Steel 1978, 59, n. 4, Priscianus or Ps.-Simplicius, *In de anima* 11.220.2–15.. Steel remarks on the verb παραθραύω, to describe the destruction of the soul's essence through embodiment. Shaw 1995, 100, n. 7, also comments on this passage.

> Of course our own soul, since it changes and is itself changed, is also in this way under its own agency changed from up to down. (253.19-20 Ruelle)

So, far from emphasizing the soul's helplessness in the face of embodiment, and hence its need for the assistance of the gods, Damascius espouses the exercise of philosophy as precisely the remedy for the suffering of the soul's essence—that is, as the proper method to affect the return of the soul to its essential nature. Damascius elaborates on this self-correcting or guardian capacity of the soul over its own status, again in the same commentary:

> And thus when it descends into genesis it projects countless lives and clearly it projects the substantial lives before the activity lives, and when it ascends it dispatches these and gathers itself together, and disappears, and it balances itself in the Unified and indivisible as much as possible. For by itself it leads itself up and down from within from the stern, and therefore from its very nature it moves itself. (253.23-27 Ruelle)

To review, then, we have seen that in his discussion of the third hypothesis in the *Commentary on the Parmenides*, Damascius suggests that the human soul should be defined as a self-mover, an entity capable, not of altering its nature or εἶδος, but rather, as he says on p. 18, of changing the quality of its essence. Perhaps this is a unique solution to the dilemma posed by Plotinus and criticized by Iamblichus. The soul is an eternal entity and so should not lose its nature. Nevertheless, it just so happens to be an indelible feature of the soul's very nature to alter its own qualities, depending on the objects of its contemplation. How it undertakes this alteration is also of interest.

What we have been calling the third hypothesis, or the Corollary on Temporal Change in Plato's *Parmenides*, is most famous for its sudden and somewhat dubious introduction of the term ἐξαίφνης, the instant, as that which escapes the law of the excluded middle, failing qualification by one of two opposite predicates during the transition between changes of state. In the commentary on the *Parmenides*, Damascius seizes on this new terminology to promote an important distinction between two different aspects of the soul's conceptual activity, which he calls the "instant" and the "now."

> This instant is partless by its character and therefore atemporal, but that was a measure and an interval of time as we showed, and that is what he [sc. Parmenides] called "now" in order to designate the present time, whereas he called this the instant because it came from unseen and detached causes into the soul. If we understood the "now" there as partless, then it would itself be a somatic instant, that is psychic. And so this is an instant, because it is in a way eternal, whereas that is now, since it is the limit of time that measures corporeal coming to be. (33.10-15 Steel).

For Damascius, the center of human consciousness, the activity of the soul, can be understood in one way as a temporally defined moment, what we might call a thought-moment, that is, a measure of time's super-ordinate flux that is artificially discriminated into successive "nows." At the same time, this center is also known, following the *Parmenides* of Plato, as an "instant," and as such acts as the doorway into atemporality. Expounding the method of passage, Damascius, again under the influence of Iamblichus, distinguishes three kinds of reversion: substantial, vital, and intellectual. The last describes the reversion of the soul towards its center, to take its place among the ranks of the intelligible domain. Damascius describes intellectual reversion in the *Problems and Solutions*, noting that it is a form of return to the realm of Being that nevertheless is still bound up with the world of the soul, the world of becoming:

> Now intellect returns both by means of substantial and vital reversion but in the third rank and as it were distantly, by means of cognitive intellection, and because intellect is gnostic, and so it returns by means of actuality or in actuality, but not substantially nor by means of the vital power. And that is why this kind of intellection is something that is involved more with becoming, and this is also more apparent to us, because it is especially distinct. (181.7–11 Ruelle)

In all of this, Damascius innovates wildly on the language of Plato's *Parmenides*. Readers of Plato will recall that in the Third Deduction, the instant is introduced in order to accommodate the conclusions of the First and Second Hypothesis. As the moment between motion and rest, the instant makes possible temporal change itself. For Damascius, this instant has become the inner life of the soul, its nature prior to the activity of thinking a particular thought, and hence, the ground of the soul's reversion to the realm of Being.

Here is another and even more unique solution to the puzzles that Damascius grapples with concerning the soul's dual membership in the intelligible and temporal orders of being. According to the way that the soul actualizes its essence, it admits of differing identities, as Steel (1978) has shown in his monograph, *The Changing Self*. In this sense, the various degrees of unreality that are detailed in the subsequent hypotheses of the *Parmenides* in Damascius's explication, inasmuch as he designates them as One, Not-One, Not-Being, Not-One, are also configurations of the soul itself:

> If the soul is divisible and indivisible in its totality, always its summit is more indivisible, its lowest degree more divisible…Therefore according to Parmenides as well, the summit of the soul is sometimes One, sometimes Being, sometimes all the degrees between [One and many], just as its lowest degree is sometimes in a similar way not-One, not-many (*In Parm*. 11.11–15 Steel).

Hence the crucial place of the third hypothesis in Damascius's exposition of the Parmenides is in showing how the life of the soul moves up and down the scale of being. Therefore Damascius understood this dialogue to be an illustration of the complete career of the soul, from the summit to the lowest degree of being. All the while, however, Damascius insists that the soul retains its fundamental reality and its εἶδος: it never irrevocably forfeits its place within the highest realms of being, however clouded its upward gaze may become. This text should be of great interest to students of the late-Neoplatonist school, for in it we glimpse Damascius's methods of exegesis, as he negotiates between Iamblichus and Proclus in coming to formulate his own very unique and subtle solution to a traditional philosophical problem. Damascius suggests that although the essence of the soul can incline toward the world of becoming or, in turn, toward the eternal world, there is something even within the human soul that is not subject to transformation. He calls this faculty or center of the soul "the immediate" but also "the faculty of awareness" (τὸ προσεκτικόν), which can also be understood as the capacity for attention. In the commentary on the *Phaedo*, Damascius discusses the προσεκτικόν, suggesting that it always underlies particular states of mind or consciousness.

> What is that which recollects that it is recollecting? This is a faculty that is different from all the others and is always attached to some of them as a kind of witness: as conscious of the appetitive faculties, as attentive to the cognitive ones.[8] (*In Phaed.* 1.271.1-4)

This capacity for attention is exactly the center of conscious activity, the psychic faculty that makes possible the amphibious life of the soul, now traversing the intelligible realm, now entering into sympathy with embodied life. Thus Damascius consistently speaks of an attentive faculty that operates throughout all psychic states, standing guard over its own activity and being in fact the One of the soul. This faculty can also be expressed as the capacity of the soul to engage in self-motion; and indeed, it is this very self-motion that allows the soul to identify at so many disparate stations of being.

Furthermore the attentive faculty functions as the gateway to reversion, and thereby initiates, from the point of view of the soul caught up in the temporal flow of discursive thinking, a return to the higher lives it remains capable of projecting. Although the flow of discursive thought takes up a measure of time, in a sense the central awareness is the instrument of self-reversion, or return to the soul's identity as an eternal being, free from the limitations of temporality. Damascius discusses this temporal aspect of the soul's capacity in another philosophical work, the *Corollaries on Space and Time*.

---

8. This translation was distributed by Lautner at the Boston Institute of Classical Studies 1997 Summer Institute: "Therefore to perceive that One perceives does not belong to every faculty of perception, but rather to the rational faculty alone" (Ps.-Simplicius, *In Phaed.* 11.290.6–8).

In the *Corollaries on Space and Time* Damascius explains that the ceaseless flow of mental states means that time is at root a condition of impermanence that precludes its own measurement. However, for convenience, our mind adopts the habit of breaking time up into units that are apparently more stable, as the years, months, days, and hours of ordinary time language. Even events that presupposed duration throughout a given period of time such as "battle" form part of this attempt to freeze time into semi-permanent units that seem to enjoy a more stable identity (*Corollary on Time* 798,30–35 trans. Urmson 1992: 21).[9] Nevertheless, the mind's attempt to orient itself in measurable time is destined to be a work of fiction. As a result of this fiction, the mind also clings to a sense of what is occurring now. But this "now" is itself an unreal boundary between a past that cannot be fixed and a future that cannot be fixed. In reality, the now is equally a fiction that nevertheless mirrors the true center of human consciousness, which Damascius calls ἐξαίφνης or the instant.

So far, we have seen that Damascius's psychology in his *Commentary on the Parmenides*, in the *Problems and Solutions*, and elsewhere accords with his general view of the priority of the contemplative life and the function of knowledge: the restoration of the individual to the realm of real being. Adopting such a stance, the descent into birth and death can be checked by knowledge alone. Later Neoplatonists who embraced theurgy while still maintaining a contemplative orientation to the topic of ascent sometimes spoke of *doxastic* purification (see Baltzly 2006). Self-knowledge itself becomes a form of catharsis, and is itself one of the ways by which obstacles toward ascent can be ameliorated. Ultimately knowledge is the last obstacle to reversion, even though it is itself a form of reversion. For Damascius, descent does not so much begin at the moment of embodiment, as we saw. Nor does ascent pertain to the actions of the gods on the human soul. Toward the end of the *Problems and Solutions*, Damascius clarifies the relationship between individual and cause, reframing the event of individuation or embodiment in a way that deemphasizes its temporal aspect:

> Now this multitude of beings, and to put it more clearly, the individuals that ever arise, it has anticipated as a single cause, not particular to me or you, but yet the cause of both me and you and those individuals that have ever been prior [to me or you] and those that will ever be. The way the individuals are contained in that nature and the way they are differentiated from it is like the light of the sun, which forever remains both in its own commonality and also is distributed individually to each being, because the sun contains a single illuminating cause of all the individual eyes. (§ 96 Westerink Combès)

---

9. The fragments of Damascius's purported work are from Simplicius's Corollaries on Space and Time, a text found in *Simplicii in Aristotelis Physicorum Libros Quatour Priores Commentaria*, vol. 9 of the *Commentaria in Aristotelem Graeca* (Diels 1882).

Again, Damascius offers this solution to the problem of embodiment by suggesting that the individual soul is best understood as a function of the intelligible domain, as a modality of its seeing. But in the *Commentary on the Parmenides*, Damascius is much more concerned with the devolution of reality from the realm of Being into the realm of Non-Being. In this respect of course, he relies on the central Neoplatonic interpretation of the hypotheses of the *Parmenides*, since the Neoplatonists essentially took this to be Plato's explanation for Non-Being, or Plato's own "way of seeing."

10
Metaphysicizing the Aristotelian Categories: Two References to the *Parmenides* in Simplicius's Commentary on the *Categories* (75,6 and 291,2 Kalbfleisch)[1]

Gerald Bechtle

I.

From a systematic point of view, this paper is situated in the wider context of the metaphysization of the Aristotelian categories. What does it mean to metaphysicize the Aristotelian categories? To cut a very long story short, the treatise Κατηγορίαι—an ancient title that may well not be its original title—commonly ascribed to the authorship of Aristotle, covers a complex thematic context between language and reality. The categories are attributions of a predicate to a subject; such predications are for Aristotle attributions of reality (of being/τὸ ὄν) to a subject: being is thus attributed to or predicated of a subject in many different ways. But they can be reduced to ten general modes. These are the ten categories. Often they simply correspond to the ten most general classes of being, the *genera generalissima*. That the theory of categories also implies an ontological classification—a classification of beings—is supported by the realist context of the *Categories*. For Aristotle's reflections start from things/realities, and all else seems secondary.

This being so, there would be certain tendencies, unsupported by the actual text of the *Categories*, to transfer the Aristotelian categories from the realm of "ordinary" ontological, that is, physical reality to that of metaphysical or theological reality. The reasons for this transfer lie in the history of the ancient interpretation of Aristotelian philosophy; but it would be too complex to enu-

---

1. Reprinted with permission from *ZAC* 12 (2008), 150–65 (© Walter de Gruyter 2008).

merate these points here.² At any rate, the possibility of an analogous transfer from physical to metaphysical (first) philosophy (= theology) means that the Aristotelian categories can be utilized to classify not only the realm of physical but also that of metaphysical being. Thus they can become crucial to a theology understood as a scientific discourse on the divine. The application of Aristotelian categories to divine realities used to be designated, in the Latin Western world, by the term *praedicatio in divinis* (which could be retranslated as τὸ κατηγορεῖσθαι ἐν τοῖς θείοις). The common wisdom is that this "predicating in the divine" goes back to and was initiated by Boethius. This is correct in so far as the medieval thinkers who practiced *praedicatio in divinis* took their cue from Boethius. But Boethius was hardly original. For *praedicatio in divinis* had already been developed in a Greek Platonist context, particularly in the Platonist commentaries on the *Categories*, forming an important "ancient" prefiguration of a concept habitually considered as exclusively "medieval."

The sixth-century philosopher Simplicius, who in his impressive commentary on the *Categories* synthesizes most of the relevant Greek exegetical tradition, emphasizes the wide-ranging importance of his subject matter right from the very first lines of his commentary (*In cat.* 1,3–7 Kalbfleisch): πολλοὶ πολλὰς κατεβάλοντο φροντίδας εἰς τὸ τῶν Κατηγοριῶν τοῦ Ἀριστοτέλους βιβλίον, οὐ μόνον ὅτι προοίμιόν ἐστι τῆς ὅλης φιλοσοφίας ..., ἀλλὰ καὶ ὅτι τρόπον τινὰ περὶ ἀρχῶν ἐστι (*sc.* the *Categories*) τῶν πρώτων.... Simplicius says that Aristotle's book *Categories* has been written about and commented on extensively because it is (1) an introduction to the whole of philosophy, and (2) *somehow about the first principles*. The latter point confirms that the Aristotelian treatise is seen by the tradition as being relevant to the theological level up to even its highest point, the ultimate principles (i.e., as somehow referring to both the noetic and even the transnoetic realm).³ To be sure, the *Categories*, unlike the Platonic *Parmenides*,

---

2. One important fact to be kept in mind is that Aristotle's ancient interpreters, even if concerned with one text at a time, are, as interpreters, aware of the whole Aristotelian (and Platonic etc.) corpus; thus in discussing, e.g., the *Categories*, other texts such as the *Metaphysics* always lurk in the background (cf., e.g., the striking parallel between the list of categories in the *Categories* and *Metaphysics* Δ respectively, or the treatment in either text of the concept of οὐσία—parallels that both link and separate these two works and that did of course not escape the ancient exegetes' attention, who needed a consistent and systematic picture of Aristotelian thought).

3. Simplicius is of course part of this tradition, even though, as we will see, he repeatedly distances himself from it in that he does not seem to endorse intelligible categories. But the statement here is a very general one about the treatise's relevance to first principles (ὅτι τρόπον τινὰ περὶ ἀρχῶν ἐστι τῶν πρώτων), and in so far as the *Categories* is the introduction to the whole of philosophy it must also be supposed to prepare for or somehow foreshadow, however vaguely, its first principles. *In cat.* 1,7 Kalbfleisch: ὡς ἐν τοῖς περὶ τοῦ σκοποῦ μαθησόμεθα λόγοις constitutes a reference to 9,4–13,26, where the σκοπός is treated. By unveiling the σκοπός the *Categories*' key purpose or goal is laid out, and Simplicius may imply that thereby

cannot be assumed to be a proper scientific account of the divine realm, but that does not mean that it is not τρόπον τινὰ relevant to it. This also explains why it would, *stricto sensu*, not be correct to speak of metaphysical or theological categories (for there cannot be multiple sets of categories); instead they somehow take on metaphysical importance as they are metaphysicized, i.e., applied or transferred to the metaphysical realm.

In what follows I wish to take a closer look at two passages from Simplicius's commentary on the *Categories*. As we will see, Simplicius summarizes, paraphrases, and also criticizes some already traditional aspects and problems in relation to the theme of noetic categories. Thus these passages give an impression of the manifestations of the metaphysicizing process that the theory of categories was susceptible to from at least the second century CE on (Simplicius cites Lucius and Nicostratus, amongst others). Of course, and although the phenomenon of using categories for divine beings is identical in both cases, the Christian context traditionally associated with *praedicatio in divinis* plays no role for Simplicius or for the authorities he cites. Also the Christian thinkers in Boethius' wake make their own selection of doctrinal points and thus entirely change the emphasis of the metaphysization of the Aristotelian categories (one crucial difference is that their focus is God, whereas the Platonists' focus is the theory of categories; to the former *praedicatio in divinis* is a tool, to the latter it is something that has to be figured out for its own sake in connection with the interpretation of the *Categories*). But the Christian *praedicatio in divinis* would undoubtedly not have existed had the Greek exegetical tradition of the *Categories* not paved the way. The two passages under consideration in this paper have been chosen because we find there the only two explicit references to the Platonic *Parmenides* in the whole of Simplicius's immense commentary. But apart from thus forming part of the history of the reception of the *Parmenides*, these references are highly significant in that they provide a link from the *Categories* tradition to the most theological text of all within the combined Aristotle and Plato canon of later Platonism (in this canon the *Parmenides*' position mirrors that of the Aristotelian *Metaphysics*).[4]

---

somehow a hint at the first principles (or at least at the noetic realm) is also given. This is confirmed by the famous section at 12,13–13,11 (within the treatment of the σκοπός), where Simplicius gives a unique account of the metaphysical foundation for the constituent elements of the σκοπός, i.e., words, concepts, and realities. Ph. Hoffmann thinks that this account can be attributed to Simplicius's teacher Damascius (cf. Hoffmann 1994, 574–75: "écho d'un cours oral de Damascius sur les *Catégories* d'Aristote").

4. The historian of late-ancient Platonist thought is accustomed to the idea that Plato's dialogue *Parmenides* could be considered as a text with metaphysical content. And the *Parmenides* was not just any metaphysical text, it used to be *the* metaphysical/theological text, i.e., the highest and final text in the Iamblichean canon of Platonic dialogues, providing a detailed account of late Platonist theology. At the opposite point of the spectrum we find the *Categories*, the actual starting point of the Aristotle reading list, and therefore situated close to, though not

Through the reference to the *Parmenides* these passages reinforce and lend further credibility to the context of the metaphysization of the categories implemented therein. Furthermore, regarding the history of the joint reception of the first text of the Aristotle canon (the *Categories*) and the last one of the Plato canon (the *Parmenides*), we are not simply in the presence of one among many instances of reading the *Categories* into the *Parmenides*; instead Simplicius, by choosing not to comment on the *Parmenides*, and focusing instead on the *Categories*, turns things around: the *Parmenides* is subsidiary to the reading and interpretation of the *Categories*.

II.

In Simplicius's *Categories* commentary there are two explicit references to Plato's *Parmenides*, namely at *In cat.* 75,6 and 291,2.

SIMPLICIUS, IN CAT. 75,3-8

Simplicius, *In cat.* 75,3-8, a passage towards the end of the commentary on *Categories* 1b25-2a10,[5] reads as follows:

> τὴν αὐτὴν κοινωνίαν καὶ συνέχειαν τῶν γενῶν διατείνει (i.e., continuity, συνέχεια), πάντα τοῖς ἀλύτοις δεσμοῖς τῆς ὁμοιότητος τὰ ὅλα συμπεραίνουσα. διὰ τοῦτο καὶ Πλάτων ἐν Παρμενίδῃ τὸ ἓν διὰ πασῶν μὲν διατείνει τῶν ὑποθέσεων, εἴτε περὶ θεοῦ εἴτε περὶ νοῦ εἴτε περὶ ψυχῆς ἢ σώματος ὁ λόγος γένοιτο, κατὰ τὴν ἐπὶ πάντα προϊοῦσαν διαφορουμένην κοινότητα.

The relevant context, clearly distinguished from what precedes by a transitional formula, and being no longer περὶ τῆς λέξεως (73,13—λέξις often signifies the

---

exactly, at the beginning of the entire curriculum (other preliminary texts must be accounted for, but then there are texts after the *Parmenides* as well). No one disputes that the *Categories* is a logical text—after all it is part of the *Organon*—and therefore an appropriate opening of a scholastic curriculum. By the time the *Parmenides* had become the highest authoritative text on theological questions, its logical character, asserted by Thrasyllus in the first century C.E., had been relegated to a secondary role—a change of emphasis brought about not least by a succession of influential *Parmenides* commentaries (some extant, some not) in late Antiquity. Since the *Categories*, as a predominantly logical text, was also heavily metaphysicized in later times—most visibly but to my mind (cf. the Simplicius passages cited) not only and not originally in the Latin medieval context—we have a structural parallel between the two texts that are, so to speak, the Alpha and the Omega of the later Platonic school tradition: as their real or perceived logical character shifts in a metaphysical direction, an important layer of meaning is added in the case of the *Categories*, and a henological theology can be read in the *Parmenides*.

5. Τῶν κατὰ μηδεμίαν συμπλοκὴν λεγομένων ἕκαστον ἕως τοῦ οἷον ἄνθρωπος, λευκόν, τρέχει, νικᾷ (Simplicius's lemma).

detailed literal explanation, in contrast to the discussion of the general meaning), starts at 73,15 and continues to the end of the commentary on that lemma at 75,22. Lines 73,15-28 are about kinds of problems raised by Plotinus and (the followers of) Lucius and Nicostratus (οἱ περὶ τὸν Λούκιον καὶ Νικόστρατον). These problems concern, e.g., the ontological status of Aristotle's categories, the difference and/or identity (related to homonymy/synonymy) of sensible and intelligible categories, and difficulties arising from the intelligibility of some of the categories.[6]

At 73,29-74,3 Simplicius criticizes those raising these problems because they assume that Aristotle's teaching is (or should be) about real beings *qua* beings, whereas it is at most about beings in so far as they are signified by words—and those things are above all τὰ τῇδε, and not τὰ νοητὰ ἀθέατα. Nevertheless it is possible for ὁ τῶν ὄντων φιλοθεάμων (Pythagoreans?) to "tran-scend" the sensibles towards the ineffable intelligibles τῇ ἀναλογίᾳ προσχρώμενος.

In the following passage (74,3-17) Simplicius continues to insist on the fact that Aristotle speaks about sensibles, just like ὁ πολὺς ἄνθρωπος. This is obvious, according to Simplicius, because Aristotle deals with the substance that everybody calls substance, and because in examining the (interrelated) sensible and discursive substances (beyond which he did not go) he considers the sensible to be the more important (as being decisive when considering sensibles). The primacy of sensibles (and particulars) over discursives (and universals) furthermore applies not only to substance but also to the other categories. In this context the close relation between words that signify (i.e., things—σημαντικαὶ φωναί) and sensibles is emphasized again. These words are common to everybody.

This consideration causes Simplicius to report (74,18-19) the *Metaphysics*' doctrine of the threefold substance, τὴν μὲν κατὰ τὴν ὕλην, τὴν δὲ κατὰ τὸ εἶδος, τὴν δὲ κατὰ τὸ συναμφότερον.[7] Having earlier posited matter and form as princi-

---

6. Plotinus, *Enn*. 6.1 [42].1.19-30 gives us a clearer and more focused idea of the exact nature of these problems than the Simplician passage (probably because Simplicius makes an attempt at conveying summarily various interconnected philosophical problems from a somewhat doxographical perspective, whereas Plotinus makes a straightforward philosophical argument and proposes a clear solution): μᾶλλον δὲ ἐκεῖνο πρῶτον ἐρωτητέον, πότερα ὁμοίως ἔν τε τοῖς νοητοῖς ἔν τε τοῖς αἰσθητοῖς τὰ δέκα, ἢ ἐν μὲν τοῖς αἰσθητοῖς ἅπαντα, ἐν δὲ τοῖς νοητοῖς τὰ μὲν εἶναι, τὰ δὲ μὴ εἶναι· οὐ γὰρ δὴ ἀνάπαλιν. Οὗ δὴ ἐξεταστέον, τίνα κἀκεῖ τῶν δέκα, καὶ εἰ τὰ ἐκεῖ ὄντα ὑφ' ἓν γένος ὑπακτέον τοῖς ἐνταῦθα, ἢ ὁμωνύμως ἥ τε ἐκεῖ οὐσία ἥ τε ἐνταῦθα· ἀλλ' εἰ τοῦτο, πλείω τὰ γένη. Εἰ δὲ συνωνύμως, ἄτοπον τὸ αὐτὸ σημαίνειν τὴν οὐσίαν ἐπί τε τῶν πρώτως ὄντων καὶ τῶν ὑστέρων οὐκ ὄντος γένους κοινοῦ, ἐν οἷς τὸ πρότερον καὶ ὕστερον. Ἀλλὰ περὶ τῶν νοητῶν κατὰ τὴν διαίρεσιν οὐ λέγουσιν· οὐ πάντα ἄρα τὰ ὄντα διαιρεῖσθαι ἐβουλήθησαν, ἀλλὰ τὰ μάλιστα ὄντα παραλελοίπασι.

7. Given the weight of the tradition, it was impossible for any of the major Platonists not to adduce the *Metaphysics* in this context (Simplicius, *In cat*. 78,5-8 gives a reference from as early as the first century B.C.E. [Boethus of Sidon]: μᾶλλον δὲ ἔδει, φησίν [*sc*. Βόηθος], προσαπορεῖν ὅτι ἐν ἄλλοις [*Metaphysics*] τὴν οὐσίαν διελόμενος εἰς τρεῖς ἄλλως μὲν τὴν ὕλην, ἄλλως δὲ τὸ

ples in both the sensibles and the intelligibles, Aristotle, according to Simplicius, shows them on the one hand to be the same (sc. principles) by analogy, and on the other hand to be different, that is, differing τῷ τρόπῳ τῆς ὑποστάσεως. Therefore, Simplicius says, this transition by analogy from the sensibles to the intelligibles is appropriate for Aristotle. And thus arises the question of what prevents, in the case of the ten categories, identity by analogy from being maintained, together with difference, in the case both of sensibles and intelligibles. In other words, why can there not be two analogous sets of ten categories, a sensible one, and an intelligible one?

If it holds that (see 74,28–75,3) there are ten genera/categories in this world, and the same ten in the noetic realm, is the community between τὰ τῇδε and

εἶδος, ἄλλως δὲ τὸ συναμφότερον οὐσίαν λέγεσθαι εἶπεν, ἐνταῦθα [Categories] δὲ μίαν τίθεται κατηγορίαν τὴν οὐσίαν). As is well known, Plotinus himself incorporated Aristotle's *Metaphysics* to a large extent not only into his "*Categories* treatise" Περὶ τῶν γενῶν τοῦ ὄντος, generally translated as *On the Genera of Being* (= *Enn*. 6.1–3 [42–44]; Plotinus makes use of *Metaphysics* Z in particular), but also into his writings in general, as already remarked by Porphyry: ἐμμέμικται δ' ἐν τοῖς συγγράμμασι καὶ τὰ Στωικὰ λανθάνοντα δόγματα καὶ τὰ Περιπατητικά· καταπεπύκνωται δὲ καὶ ἡ «Μετὰ τὰ φυσικὰ» τοῦ Ἀριστοτέλους πραγματεία (Porphyry, *Vit. Plot.* 14.4–7). The crucial passage *Metaph*. Z 10.1035a1–2 (εἰ οὖν ἐστὶ τὸ μὲν ὕλη τὸ δ' εἶδος τὸ δ' ἐκ τούτων, καὶ οὐσία ἥ τε ὕλη καὶ τὸ εἶδος καὶ τὸ ἐκ τούτων), referred to here at Simplicius 74,18–19, summarizes *Metaph*. Z's view of substance. Hence it almost automatically raises the old question—Plotinus can already be considered as responding to it—of the reconcilability of the notion of substance in the *Categories* and in the *Metaphysics*, a question that concerns nothing less than the coherence of Aristotelian philosophy in general. As our passage in Simplicius proves, this complex question had long ago (at least as far back as Plotinus) stopped posing a threat to Aristotle's coherence and credibility. For the *Metaphysics* passage had become complementary to the interpretation and commentary of the *Categories*, the Platonists having adopted a compatibilist stance on this matter. See also the allusion to the same passage from *Metaph*. Z in Porphyry, *In cat.* 88,13–15 Busse: {E.} ποσαχῶς ἐν ἄλλοις τὴν οὐσίαν λέγει; {Ἀ.} τριχῶς· καὶ γὰρ τὴν ὕλην καὶ τὸ εἶδος καὶ τὸ συναμφότερον λέγει οὐσίαν. John Philoponus's interesting discussion at *In cat.* 49,23–50,3 Busse limits the *Categories* to the οὐσία σύνθετος, making simple substance the object of either theology or physiology (this is vaguely reminiscent of Simplicius's limiting of the *Categories* to the sensible realm): ταύτης δὲ τῆς οὐσίας ἡ μέν ἐστιν ἁπλῆ ἡ δὲ σύνθετος, τῆς δὲ ἁπλῆς ἡ μὲν χείρων τῆς συνθέτου ἡ δὲ κρείττων· ἔστι δὲ σύνθετος μὲν οὐσία ἄνθρωπος καὶ τὰ τοιαῦτα, ἁπλῆ δὲ καὶ κρείττων τῆς συνθέτου ἡ ἀγγελικὴ καὶ ἡ ψυχικὴ καὶ αἱ τοιαῦται, ἁπλῆ δὲ καὶ χείρων τῆς συνθέτου ἡ ὕλη ἡ πρώτη καὶ τὸ εἶδος. διαλέγεται δὲ ἐνταῦθα ὁ Ἀριστοτέλης οὔτε περὶ τῆς ἁπλῆς καὶ κρείττονος τῆς συνθέτου (οὐ γὰρ πρόκειται αὐτῷ θεολογεῖν) οὔτε περὶ τῆς ἁπλῆς καὶ χείρονος τῆς συνθέτου (οὐ γὰρ φυσιολογεῖν αὐτῷ πρόκειται), ἀλλὰ περὶ τῆς συνθέτου μόνης. καὶ ταύτης φησὶ τὴν μὲν εἶναι πρώτην τὴν δὲ δευτέραν, πρώτην μὲν τὴν μερικὴν καλῶν δευτέραν δὲ τὴν καθόλου τὴν κατὰ τὰ εἴδη καὶ τὰ γένη. Notwithstanding the ancient tendency to integrate the two Aristotelian accounts of substance in the *Metaphysics* and in the *Categories*, the issue has continued to be a favorite of the scholarly discussion up to this day (cf., e.g., the idea of Aristotle's "two systems," containing two radically different and incompatible conceptions—in the *Categories* substances would be simple individuals, whereas they would be complexes of form and matter in the more mature work).

τὰ νοητά homonymous or synonymous? The answer is that it is neither homonymous nor synonymous, but ὡς ἀφ' ἑνὸς καὶ πρὸς ἕν, and thus obeying the law of analogy. The explanation for this is that there is *one* continuity of the primary and ultimate genera (συνέχεια μία τῶν πρώτων τε καὶ τελευταίων γενῶν), but one that neither confuses nor splits apart the two realms. Instead—and here commences our passage as quoted above—"it (*sc.* this continuity) extends the same community and continuity of the genera, accomplishing all things with the unbreakable bonds of similarity. This is why Plato, too, in the *Parmenides*, extends the One throughout all the hypotheses, whether the account is about God or the intellect, or the soul, or the body, in accordance with that differing commonality that proceeds as far as all things" (trans. Chase 2003, 90). This means that the One of the *Parmenides*, in its applicability to the different hypotheses/hypostases, in being everywhere the One, is brought into a direct parallel with the community and continuity of the genera/categories. As the One provides—is—continuity throughout the different levels of reality, so there is a continuity of the ten categories in their analogous presence in the physical (enmattered) and metaphysical (immaterial) worlds. The mode of this continuity is a "differing commonality," διαφορουμένη κοινότης, an expression that takes up and summarizes ἥτις (i.e., συνέχεια μία τῶν πρώτων τε καὶ τελευταίων γενῶν) οὔτε συγχεῖ τὰ ἔνυλα τοῖς ἀύλοις, πεπέρασται γὰρ ἐν τοῖς ἰδίοις ὅροις ἑκάτερα, οὔτε διασχίσει αὐτὰ ἀπ' ἀλλήλων διὰ τὸ κοινοῖς συνδέσμοις συνέχεσθαι καὶ ἐξηρτῆσθαι ἀεὶ τῶν κρειττόνων τὰ καταδεέστερα (74,32–75,3). In the light of Simplicius's text, it is certainly no exaggeration to say that the Aristotelian categories, which are also the highest genera, are ultimately held together or, as it were, "continuified," by the One of Plato's *Parmenides*.

This difficult but intriguing passage of Simplicius, taken together with the others, is sufficient for us to make our point about the relatedness and parallel treatment of the two texts, the Aristotelian *Categories* and the Platonic *Parmenides*, both of them certainly logical texts, but both of them becoming or having become metaphysical as well. Intersections have become interrelations. The common element in the passages cited so far is that the categories/categorial language appear relevant with respect to God, the Good, or the One, a fact that is of course to be expected if one deals with the intersections of the *Categories* and the *Parmenides* in the history of their Platonist reception.

To be sure, Simplicius himself (i.e., when speaking on his own behalf) clearly and repeatedly rejects the notion, held by other philosophers, that the *Categories* can be considered as concerning anything other than sensibles as they are signified by words. But of course he takes the problems raised by thinkers like Plotinus or Lucius and Nicostratus seriously enough to make (or report) arguments that tackle these problems, adducing what has traditionally been considered a pivotal passage in the *Metaphysics* in this context and taking into account the hypothesis of analogous sensible and intelligible categories. He even gives a detailed description of the relation between these two, objecting to homonymy and synonymy in this context, and preferring to work with the notion of continuity that is inspired by the One of Plato's *Parmenides*. Simplicius himself makes it very clear, in this passage (73,29–74,17) and elsewhere,[8] that he adheres to a view of Aristotle (in the *Categories*) as οὐ περὶ τῶν ὄντων ᾗ ὄντα ποιούμενος τὸν λόγον, ἀλλ' εἴπερ ἄρα, ᾗ ὑπὸ τοιῶνδε σημαίνεται φωνῶν, which is why Aristotle προηγουμένως μὲν περὶ τῶν τῇδε διαλέγεται (see also 74,3–5: ἐπεὶ ὅτι περὶ τῶν αἰσθητῶν διαλέγεται, περὶ ὧν καὶ ὁ πολὺς ἄνθρωπος τὴν ἐπίσκεψιν ποιεῖται)· ταῦτα γάρ ἐστιν τὰ προσεχῶς ὑπὸ τῶν φωνῶν σημαινόμενα. Thus Simplicius is not in favor of any metaphysization of Aristotle's *Categories* (in the sense that noetic categories could really be categories properly speaking). Therefore it is quite likely that he reports or summarizes here (possibly already from 74,18 up to 75,22) the opinion of someone who has tried to come to grips with the problems raised by Plotinus or Lucius and Nicostratus. And since the drift of the argument does not resemble what we know of Porphyry's reaction to Plotinus's treatment of the *Categories* in

---

8. Simplicius *In cat.* 76,18–19 (ὅτι περὶ τῆς αἰσθητῆς καὶ φυσικῆς οὐσίας ὁ λόγος καὶ τῆς ἐν ταύτῃ διανοητῆς) and 22–23 (οὐκ ἦν οὖν τοῦ παρόντος λόγου περὶ τῆς κοινῆς οὐσίας τῶν τε νοητῶν καὶ τῶν αἰσθητῶν ἀπορεῖν). See also 90,19–20 (ἡ γὰρ αἰσθητὴ οὐσία ἡ μάλιστά ἐστιν οὐσία). *In cat.* 205,22–35, in particular 22–24: ἰστέον δὲ ὅτι πολλὰ τῶν γενῶν ἐν τοῖς αἰσθητοῖς ἐστιν κυρίως, οὐκέτι δὲ ἐν τοῖς νοητοῖς, εἰ μή τις κατ' ἄλλον τρόπον αὐτὰ μεταφέρειν ἐπ' ἐκείνων βιάζοιτο, ὥσπερ τὸ κεῖσθαι καὶ τὸ πάσχειν. *In cat.* 277,5–11, in particular 7: οὐδὲ γὰρ αἱ κατηγορίαι περὶ τῶν νοητῶν εἰσιν, ἀλλὰ περὶ τῶν λεγομένων ... (which is not to say that there cannot exist such things as νοηταὶ ποιότητες—but they are not actual qualities, i.e., genuine categories). *In cat.* 290,9–10 (ἀλλ' ὅλως οὐ περὶ τῶν νοητῶν ἐστιν ὁ προκείμενος λόγος [after quoting Iamblichus on Porphyry on νοηταὶ ποιότητες]). *In cat.* 300,25–28 (τῇ γὰρ αἰσθητῇ καὶ φυσικῇ οὐσίᾳ τὰ μὲν συνεισῆλθεν ὡς ποιότης καὶ πρός τι, τὰ δὲ ἐπεισῆλθεν ὡς τὸ ποιεῖν καὶ πάσχειν, κινηθείσης ἤδη πρὸς ἃ ἠδύνατο, τούτοις δὲ ἐπηκολούθησαν τὸ ἐν χρόνῳ καὶ ἐν τόπῳ καὶ τὸ κεῖσθαι καὶ τὸ ἔχειν). *In cat.* 340,12–13 (τοσαῦτα καὶ περὶ τοῦ κεῖσθαι εἰρήσθω, ἐννοούντων ἡμῶν ὡς ἐπὶ σωμάτων εἴρηται κυρίως τὸ κεῖσθαι—this succinct Simplician commentary on an immediately preceding literal quotation from Iamblichus is directly comparable to 290,9–10). Simplicius is habitually considered to follow Iamblichus's νοερὰ θεωρία; on the basis of the evidence cited, I think he himself is actually much closer to Porphyry, at least as far as the restriction of the categories proper to the sensible realm is concerned. In this context it should of course not be forgotten that Simplicius (78,4–5) attributes this view already to Boethus of Sidon (ca. second half of the first century B.C.E.): ὁ μέντοι Βόηθος ... μὴ γὰρ εἶναι περὶ τῆς νοητῆς οὐσίας τὸν λόγον. See also Ps.-Archytas (perhaps also to be dated to the first century B.C.E., or else a bit a later) at Simplicius, *In cat.* 76,20–22: πᾶσα ὦν ὠσία φυσικά τε καὶ αἰσθητὰ ἤτοι ἐν τούτοις ἢ διὰ τούτων ἢ οὐκ ἄνευ τούτων πέφυκεν τᾷ διανοίᾳ τῶν ἀνθρώπων ὑποπίπτειν.

his *On the Genera of Being* (= *Enn.* 6.1-3 [42-44], it may well be that Simplicius's source is Iamblichus's commentary on the *Categories*.⁹

---

9. Luna in Hoffmann et al. 2001, 779-82, commenting on Simplicius, *In cat.* 75,5-8, comes to the conclusion that "on peut affirmer avec une certaine vraisemblance que la remarque sur le *Parménide*, par laquelle Simplicius confirme la thèse de l'analogie des genres sensibles et des genres intelligibles, est un élément porphyrien. Or, si le témoignage du *Parménide* invoqué pour étayer la thèse de l'analogie des genres est porphyrien, on peut croire que la thèse de l'analogie a, elle aussi, une origine porphyrienne" (p. 782). I think that Simplicius's source of inspiration here is Iamblichus, rather than Porphyry (generally speaking, one would expect Simplicius to draw more heavily on Iamblichus than on Porphyry if it were true, as it may well be, that Simplicius often used Porphyry's commentary via Iamblichus's commentary). Other possible sources, apart from Porphyry or Iamblichus, are unlikely (Concetta Luna seems to agree: "La mention du Corps chez Simplicius nous renvoie donc à une phase pré-proclienne de l'exégèse du *Parménide* et, en particulier, ou bien à Porphyre ou bien à Jamblique" [p. 782]). Luna's argument in favor of a Porphyrian origin of "la remarque sur le *Parménide*" and "la thèse de l'analogie" is based solely on 75,6-7, i.e., on εἴτε περὶ θεοῦ εἴτε περὶ νοῦ εἴτε περὶ ψυχῆς ἢ σώματος ὁ λόγος γένοιτο. She analyzes this passage in the light of Proclus's account (in his *In Parmenidem*) of the history of the Platonist interpretation of the *Parmenides*. According to her analysis of Proclus's account, the only philosopher who assigns all four hypostases mentioned (God, intellect, soul, and body) to the first four or five hypotheses of the *Parmenides* is Porphyry. But at least one other philosopher springs to mind, Plotinus himself. For at *Enn.* 6.2 [4].2.53-54 Plotinus may well hint at his interpretation of the fourth (τὰ δὲ ἐν τοῖς σώμασιν εἴδη πολλὰ καὶ ἕν) and the fifth (τὰ δὲ σώματα πολλὰ μόνον) hypotheses; see also Charrue 1987, 56 and n. 24. As to Luna's only concrete argument against Iamblichus, that is, his interpretation of the third hypothesis (κρείττονα γένη ≠ souls): would one really expect this uniquely Iamblichean tenet (or any other "most paradoxical" doctrines adduced by Proclus as "events" in the history of the interpretation) to crop up in a passing remark by Simplicius—let us not forget that Simplicius is the author of this text, and also of 75,6-7—meant to remind the reader in a few words of the archetypical Platonist *Parmenides* interpretation? But let us grant that Simplicius's parenthetical explanation εἴτε περὶ θεοῦ εἴτε περὶ νοῦ εἴτε περὶ ψυχῆς ἢ σώματος ὁ λόγος γένοιτο reflects in and by itself the typical early Plotino-Porphyrian exegesis of the *Parmenides*, serving to recall a landmark and, by Simplicius's time, classical *Parmenides* interpretation. From this it does not, of course, follow that the *context* of this phrase, i.e., the *Parmenides* citation and the analogy doctrine, is influenced by Plotinus, or by Porphyry, or, inversely, that it cannot be ascribed to Iamblichus's authorship. The remark p. 75,6-7 is embedded between διὰ τοῦτο καὶ Πλάτων ἐν Παρμενίδῃ τὸ ἓν διὰ πασῶν μὲν διατείνει τῶν ὑποθέσεων and κατὰ τὴν ἐπὶ πάντα προϊοῦσαν διαφορουμένην κοινότητα, and should therefore be read as what it is, i.e., as an exemplification/illustration, to be put in actual or virtual brackets. The context makes clear that the four hypostases are mentioned only so as to exemplify and be clear about the precise meaning of "extends the One throughout *all* the hypotheses," a remark that is itself adduced as a parallel for the continuity of the primary and ultimate genera that "extends the same community and continuity of the genera." God, intellect, soul, and body, then, are not meant to represent the complete picture of the precise correspondences between levels of reality and hypotheses. Nor should we make any inferences on the source of the *context* on the basis of a specific (e.g., Plotino-Porphyrian) *Parmenides* interpretation that the mention of these four levels may be seen as suggesting. Also, Simplicius's parenthetical remark is just a passing reference, and it is of a

This is a very important point and requires further elaboration. It seems to be confirmed by a comparison between what follows after the *Parmenides* citation up to the end of the commentary on the lemma (p. 75,8–22), as well as by a much later passage. At 75,8–9 the question is asked how τὸ πάσχειν and τὰ πρός τι and τὸ κεῖσθαι and the like can be in the intelligible world. The answer is, by analogy. The remainder of the text is dedicated to showing that the assumption of intelligible categories does not invalidate ὁ καθόλου λόγος τῶν κατηγοριῶν. Considering (and justifying) Aristotelian categories as part of the noetic realm, counter-intuitive though this may seem, is something that Iamblichus may well have done.

For at a later point, at 290,1–9, about one page before the occurrence of the second quotation from the *Parmenides*, Iamblichus is reported as correcting a doctrine[10] according to which only enmattered qualities, not intelligible ones, partake of "intension" (ἐπίτασις) and "remission" (ἄνεσις), that is, of more and less. Iamblichus, however, does not seem to find problematic the assumption of some kind of "more and less" at the level of intelligible quality, as his argument here and just before (289,13–33) in his refutation of Plotinus suggests[11] (and this

---

fairly general nature—just as Proclus's account, though very detailed, is still general in the sense that his priority, and even more so Simplicius's, lies with the relative consensus of the Platonist exegetical tradition: see Bechtle 1999b, 139 n. 10 (in this context we should also realize that Simplicius, as opposed to Proclus, does not interpret the *Parmenides*, but the *Categories*). Thus I find Luna's argument in favor of a Porphyrian origin of the *Parmenides* citation and its doctrinal context unconvincing. Further to that, I think the strongest reason against Porphyry is that the drift of the argument does not resemble what we know of Porphyry's reaction to Plotinus's treatment of the *Categories* in his *On the Genera of Being*. In particular the key concept of a συνέχεια μία τῶν πρώτων τε καὶ τελευταίων γενῶν that extends τὴν αὐτὴν κοινωνίαν καὶ συνέχειαν τῶν γενῶν, πάντα τοῖς ἀλύτοις δεσμοῖς τῆς ὁμοιότητος τὰ ὅλα συμπεραίνουσα would go well with Iamblichus, but would be odd if it were Porphyry's.

10. See also the original formulation of this doctrine at 285,1–3: τετάρτη δέ ἐστιν δόξα, ἥτις τὰς μὲν ἀύλους καὶ καθ᾽ αὑτὰς ποιότητας ἔλεγεν μὴ ἐπιδέχεσθαι τὸ μᾶλλον καὶ τὸ ἧττον, τὰς δὲ ἐνύλους καὶ τοὺς κατ᾽ αὐτὰς ποιοὺς ἐπιδέχεσθαι. This formulation apparently prompted Porphyry's qualification that the reason why immaterial qualities do not admit intension and remission is that they are substances—and *not*, presumably, that they are immaterial and by themselves (285,5–8). As the lines 290,1–3 make clear, Iamblichus—whose commentary on the *Categories* is, in this passage at least, Simplicius's source on Porphyry (ὁ Ἰάμβλιχος ... ἐκεῖνο τὸ τοῦ Πορφυρίου φησίν, ὅτι ...)—has no quarrel with the fact that all things exist substantially in the intelligible realm, but he objects to the claim (and Porphyry's qualified endorsement of it) that immaterial quality is incompatible with "more and less." For Iamblichus seems to think that even gradual variations, intension and remission, can be (substantially) inherent in immaterial quality—thanks to its λόγος. It is from the intelligible that material qualities and qualifieds derive their "more and less"—certainly not the other way round.

11. Iamblichus's own (positive) opinion is reported in the following difficult passage: ταῦτα δὲ πρὸς τὸν Πλωτῖνον εἰπὼν τὴν ἀληθεστάτην ἐπάγει θεωρίαν τοῦ δόγματος. "οὖσα γάρ τις, φησί, τῶν λόγων ἀσώματος οὐσία δίδωσιν (*sc.* ποιότης) ἑαυτὴν τοῖς δεχομένοις καὶ ποιοῦσα

is to say that a typically categorial feature manifestly unsuitable for the noetic realm nevertheless applies to an intelligible category). Iamblichus rejects Porphyry's view that all intelligibles and beings (and therefore immaterial qualities, too) are substances, οὐσίαι, and *therefore*—and *not* primarily because they are immaterial and by themselves, or for any other reason—do not admit more and less (see also Porphyry's opinion at 285,6-8: ἐκεῖναι γὰρ οὐσίαι εἰσίν, φησίν, καὶ διὰ τοῦτο οὔτε ἄνεσιν οὔτε ἐπίτασιν ἐπιδέχονται, ὥσπερ οὐδὲ αἱ ἄλλαι οὐσίαι).[12] It should be noted that Iamblichus only rejects the latter part of Porphyry's argument, that is, that the reason why intelligibles such as immaterial qualitites are prevented from admitting more and less is that they are substances. It is of course clear and unproblematic for Iamblichus that they are substances, i.e., that

---

τὸ ποιὸν περὶ τῷ σώματι οὐδὲν ἧττον μένει καθ' ἑαυτὴν ἀσώματος ἐν τῷ σώματι, τὸ εἶναι καθ' ἑαυτὴν ἔχουσα καὶ τῆς ὑποστάσεως αὐτῷ μεταδιδοῦσα μετὰ τοῦ μὴ ἀπολλύναι τὴν οἰκείαν φύσιν. ὅθεν δὴ ἔστι μὲν τὸ ἀπ' αὐτῆς ἀποτυπούμενον μόρφωμα οἷον ἐπίτασιν ἐπιδέχεσθαι, ἔστιν δὲ καὶ ἡ ἀσώματος οὐσία τῆς ποιότητος οἷα ἑστάναι ἐν τῷ αὐτῷ εἴδει, καὶ οὐ γίνεται διὰ τοῦτο ἄυλος, ἀλλ' ἔνυλος, οὐ μέντοι ὅλη τῆς ὕλης γίνεται, διότι καὶ ἑαυτῶν ἐστιν τὰ εἴδη καὶ κατὰ τὸ ἓν καὶ ταὐτὸ κυρίως ὥρισται καὶ διὰ τοῦτο οὐδὲ ἐν τῷ τῆς ὕλης γίνεσθαι ἀφίσταται πάντῃ τῆς ὅλης ἑαυτῶν φύσεως, μένοντα δὲ ἐν αὐτοῖς τρόπον γέ τινα ἀναπίμπλαται τῆς ἐναντίας πρὸς αὐτὰ ἐκστάσεώς τε καὶ ἀοριστίας" (Simplicius, *In cat.* 289,21-33).

12. See Porphyry, *In cat.* 138,24-29 Busse: {Α.} ἦν γάρ τις (*sc.* δόξα) ἣ τὰς μὲν ἀύλους καὶ καθ' αὑτὰς ποιότητας μὴ ἐπιδέχεσθαι τὸ μᾶλλον καὶ τὸ ἧττον ἔλεγεν, τὰς δὲ ἐνύλους πάσας καὶ τοὺς κατ' αὐτὰς ποιοὺς ἐπιδέχεσθαι. {Ε.} καὶ ὀρθῶς γέ σοι ἐδόκουν οὗτοι λέγειν; {Α.} οὐδαμῶς. {Ε.} διὰ τί; Porphyry answers this question at 138,30-32 Busse thus: {Α.} ὅτι αἱ ἄυλοι ποιότητες καὶ καθ' αὑτὰς ὑφεστηκυῖαι οὐκ εἰσὶ ποιότητες ἀλλ' οὐσίαι, καὶ διὰ τοῦτο ἐπίτασιν οὐκ ἐπιδέχονται, διότι οὐδὲ αἱ ἄλλαι οὐσίαι. This answer implies that according to the holders of the opinion with which Porphyry disagrees (and which is the same as Simplicius's fourth doctrine reported at 285,1-3 and 290,1-3) immaterial and καθ' αὑτὰς qualities really are *qualities*, which Porphyry denies (see also *Enn.* 6.1 [42].12.44-45: ζητητέον δὲ καὶ ἐνταῦθα καὶ εἰ αἱ τῇδε ποιότητες καὶ αἱ ἐκεῖ ὑφ' ἕν· τοῦτο δὲ πρὸς τοὺς τιθεμένους κἀκεῖ—the latter thinkers are probably the same as those criticized by Porphyry). This is of course consistent with the image we have of Porphyry as establishing the orthodox account that limits the categories to the sensible realm—even though Plotinus had of course already reached the same conclusion (but only after an unfruitful effort to have the categories bear upon both the sensible and intelligible realms—a failure that can be read as a Plotinian critique of Aristotle, whereas Porphyry makes the best out of this situation): ἀλλὰ περὶ τῶν νοητῶν κατὰ τὴν διαίρεσιν οὐ λέγουσιν· οὐ πάντα ἄρα τὰ ὄντα διαιρεῖσθαι ἐβουλήθησαν, ἀλλὰ τὰ μάλιστα ὄντα παραλελοίπασι (*Enn.* 6.1 [42].1.28-30). On the fact that "Plotinus—not Porphyry—was primarily responsible for the important role the *Categories* was able to play in Western philosophical thought" I find myself in agreement with the important article by De Haas (2001, 492-526). To be sure, Plotinus had at his disposal a vast array of traditional materials on the *Categories* that already contain some important arguments and theses we find in the *Enneads* (see also De Haas 2001, 505 n. 37). Strange (1992, 153 n. 488) notes that immaterial and καθ' αὑτὰς qualities are "the Platonic Forms corresponding to qualities."

κατ' οὐσίαν ἐκεῖ (*sc.* in the noetic realm) πάντα ὑπάρχει (290,6).[13] In this passage (290,5-9) we can get a glimpse of Iamblichus's νοερὰ θεωρία as applied to the theory of categories. Iamblichus, probably building on the argument of οἱ τιθέμενοι (*sc.* ποιότητας) κἀκεῖ (*sc.* in the intelligible realm) cited by Plotinus (*Enn.* 6.1 [42].12.45), does not think that intelligibles and real beings such as immaterial qualities (or other appropriate "noetic" categories) are exempt from some sort of (ordinary) variation of degree. He is quoted as saying (290,5-6) that καὶ ἐν τοῖς νοητοῖς διασῴζεται ἡ τάξις τοῦ λόγου τῆς ποιότητος, that is, even amongst intelligibles the position/rank of the principle of quality is maintained. I take this to mean that even on the noetic level quality basically remains quality if it is to produce the corporeal qualified—or, to use Porphyry's terms (in his *Categories* commentary at 138,30-31 [Busse]), even ἄϋλοι ποιότητες καὶ καθ' αὑτὰς ὑφεστηκυῖαι are indeed ποιότητες (which would of course be the exact opposite from what Porphyry actually says here). And even on the intelligible level quality admits typical common features such as more and less. This also means that even in the intelligible realm there can be variation of degree (at least in principle), even if everything in the intelligible realm exists substantially. Iamblichus's reason for claiming this is the parallel with intelligible rest and motion; they, as substances, also preserve τὸν λόγον τῆς ἐνυπαρχούσης ἐν ἑτέρῳ καὶ περὶ ἕτερον ἐνεργείας, that is, maintain their "energetic" character even in the noetic realm. Hence Iamblichus probably held that the categories *as such* could exist analogically on the noetic level as well, presumably because of the (position/rank of the) *logos* of each category which allows them to retain their specific place/order and character. Typical common features such as the admission of more and less (e.g., in the case of quality) are inherent in the λόγος (probably: principle) of each category. This is also confirmed by Simplicius's comment on the Archytas citation (290,12-15) which immediately follows (and in which there is, by the way, no trace of any metaphysization or νοερὰ θεωρία, which is curious—though maybe typical—given that Iamblichus probably relied on Archytas for his own position). For Simplicius, who also does not metaphysicize, says: καὶ οὕτως *κατὰ τὸν ἑαυτοῦ λόγον*, ὁ ποιότης, τὸ μᾶλλον ἕξει καὶ τὸ ἧττον καὶ οὐκ ἀπὸ τῶν μετεχόντων (290,16-17). More and less (e.g., whiter and less white) are not to be derived, then, from the participating qualifieds, but are lodged in the (participated) λόγος of quality itself (ἐν τοῖς μετεχομένοις λόγοις, 290,21).[14]

What has been said suggests that Iamblichus is in favor of intelligible categories; we thus have to imagine, for example, ποιὸν, πρός τι, κεῖσθαι and πάσχειν as existing in the noetic realm as well. By postulating categories above

---

13. See also Iamblichus's expression ἀσώματος οὐσία (used twice with reference to ποιότης) in the passage cited in the last but one footnote (Simplicius, *In cat.* 289,23, 28).

14. See also ἐπὶ δὲ τῶν συμφύτων χρωμάτων, οἷον τοῦ ἐν γάλακτι καὶ χιόνι λευκοῦ, φανερά ἐστιν ἡ *κατ' αὐτὸν τὸν φυσικὸν λόγον* κατὰ τὸ μᾶλλον ὑπεροχή (Simplicius, *In cat.* 290,24-25).

all as *categories*—rather than as substances—also on the noetic level Iamblichus presumably elaborates on a doctrine held by thinkers already criticized by both Plotinus and Porphyry. The information Simplicius provides us with in the passages adduced confirms Iamblichus's critical stance on his two great predecessors and the subtlety of his own position when dealing with the traditional arguments concerning sensibility/intelligibility issues in the Aristotelian theory of categories. As opposed to Porphyry,[15] Iamblichus does not simply cut the discussion short by denying typical "categorial features" such as more and less of substantial (intelligible) categories (thus suppressing the latter as *categories*); instead, he places the categorial features in the λόγοι of the categories themselves (i.e., in the participated rather than the participating), and is thus able to discuss intelligible categories as *categories*. In view of this, it is likely that the passage in Simplicius's commentary on the *Categories* from 74,18 (or so) up to 75,22, and thus also the *Parmenides* citation (with its most remarkable parallel between the One and the ten categories with respect to their relevance throughout the levels of reality), is essentially by Iamblichus.

SIMPLICIUS, IN CATEGORIAS 291,1-2

Thus the lines preceding the second reference to the *Parmenides* (Simplicius, *In cat.* 291,1-2) are closely linked to the context of the first *Parmenides* reference, despite a totally different lemma and more than two hundred edited pages between the two passages. Both contexts have in common that they allow deeper insights into what the assumption of the analogous presence of the categories in both the physical and metaphysical worlds can actually translate into, in terms of philosophical debate, commentary, and further doctrinal development. If I am correct, they are also both strongly influenced by Iamblichus's philosophical

---

15. That Iamblichus's opinion can differ significantly from that of Porphyry (and from Plotinus) will astonish only those who follow the beaten path of handbooks for which passages like Simplicius's account of the history of the interpretation of the *Categories* (from Plotinus to Dexippus) at *In cat.* 2,3-29 are overly important. But even this account, that is usually adduced to prove the direct line of dependence from Porphyry to Simplicius, is not without important qualifications. For Simplicius says: μετὰ τοῦτον δὲ ὁ θεῖος Ἰάμβλιχος πολύστιχον καὶ αὐτὸς πραγματείαν εἰς τοῦτο τὸ βιβλίον κατεβάλετο, τὰ μὲν πολλὰ (*not*: πάντα) τοῖς Πορφυρίου καὶ ἐπ' αὐτῆς τῆς λέξεως κατακολουθῶν, τινὰ δὲ ἐπικρίνων ἐκείνων καὶ διαρθρῶν ἀκριβέστερον μετὰ τοῦ συστέλλειν τὴν ὡς ἐν σχολαῖς πρὸς τὰς ἐνστάσεις μακρολογίαν, *πανταχοῦ δὲ τὴν νοερὰν θεωρίαν ἑκάστῳ σχεδὸν τῶν κεφαλαίων ἐπιτιθείς*... (2,9-14). De Haas (2001, 494-95) rightly insists on the fact that "the relation between Plotinus and Porphyry is not equivalent to the relation between Plotinus and all philosophers after Plotinus" and that later Neoplatonists "disagreed with both him [i.e., Porphyry] and Plotinus in their attempts to apply the ten categories to *both* the sensible and intelligible realms." De Haas mentions Iamblichus, Dexippus, and Simplicius, whereas I think that Simplicius does not at all himself endorse the Iamblichean νοερὰ θεωρία, on which see Dillon 1997, 65-77.

viewpoint. And both the physical/metaphysical doctrinal background and Iamblichus's influence are probably related in the sense that Iamblichus, correcting earlier views on the question, insists on the analogy between physical and metaphysical realms (Iamblichus has a predilection for strong analogies and makes use of them in other philosophical contexts). There are many passages in Simplicius where this physical/metaphysical background plays out fully and, more often than not, Iamblichus's influence is probably close at hand. The fact that the two sole *Parmenides* quotations (with their larger contexts) in Simplicius's work concern such questions of analogy, and probably reflect Iamblichean influence, must therefore be significant. Hence one may speculate, even though one may never be able to assert it, that Iamblichus played a vital role in bringing the *Parmenides* to bear on the *Categories* and/or *vice versa*, thereby reinvigorating an established pre-Plotinian tradition of which authors like Alcinous are indicative.

The lemma commented on in the larger context of the second reference to the *Parmenides* is Aristotle, *Cat.* 10b26–11a19,[16] covered by Simplicius, *In cat.* 283,29–291,18. At the beginning of the commentary on the lemma (283,29–284,11) Simplicius contextualizes, clarifies, and rephrases the lemma. Thus he sets the stage for the long discussion that follows in the text, up to 290,25, of "more" and "less" (μᾶλλον καὶ ἧττον) in the case of quality. The terminological pair "more" and "less" is equated with the more abstract and originally Stoic "intension" (ἐπίτασις) and "remission" (ἄνεσις). Then, four doctrines of intension and remission of qualities and qualifieds are discussed (*In cat.* 284,12–13: τέσσαρες δὲ εἰσὶν αἱρέσεις περὶ τῆς ἐπιτάσεως καὶ ἀνέσεως τῶν τε ποιοτήτων καὶ τῶν ποιῶν). The first is presented at 284,13–17 (Plotinus and other Platonists), the second at 284,17–32 (unidentified, but Aristotle's *Categories* itself is quoted as being representative of it, though with qualifications), the third at 284,32–285,1 (Stoics), the fourth at 285,1–8 (Porphyry is reported as objecting to this doctrine,[17] and Iamblichus objects in turn to Porphyry's critique). From 285,9–286,4 we have a piece of Aristotle λέξις.[18] The lines from 286,5–15 report a question by Iamblichus, and the passage at 286,16–34 deals with the phenomenon of the variety of views concerning intension and remission in qualities; the latter naturally leads to a more detailed discussion of the four schools of thought (286,35–290,10), starting with the Stoics. The passage from 290,1, containing first (up to line 10) Iamblichus's critique of the fourth doctrine and of Porphyry's objections to it, and

---

16. ἐπιδέχεται δὲ καὶ τὸ μᾶλλον καὶ τὸ ἧττον τὰ ποιά ἕως τοῦ ὥστε ἴδιον ἂν εἴη ποιότητος τὸ ὅμοιον ἢ ἀνόμοιον λέγεσθαι κατὰ ταύτην (Simplicius's lemma).

17. Cf. also note 12. Since the passage Porphyry, *In cat.* 138,30–32 Busse is different in wording (though identical in meaning) from the literal quotation Simplicius gives, Simplicius must here be quoting the Porphyrian commentary *Ad Gedalium*.

18. See οὕτω μὲν οὖν ἡ λέξις τοῦ Ἀριστοτέλους αὐτάρκους ἔτυχεν διαρθρώσεως (Simplicius, *In cat.* 286,4).

then (up to line 25) Archytas's testimony with Simplicius's (partially influenced by Iamblichus?) commentary, has already been discussed earlier in the context of the first *Parmenides* reference. The passage immediately before 290,1 stretches from 289,13-33 and contains Iamblichus's correction of the first, that is, Plotinus's doctrine, as well as Iamblichus's own doctrine—a doctrine which it is very important for us to understand if we are to make sense of his subsequent critique of the fourth doctrine.

Up to the end of Simplicius's report of and commentary on Archytas, that is, up to 290,25, the discussion is about "more" and "less" or—with closer reference to the lemma—about Aristotle's intimation that to admit more and less is *not* a particular feature of quality, but rather a common feature of several categories;[19] only the like and the unlike are unique to quality.[20] After 290,25, and until the end of the commentary on the lemma, that is, 291,18, we therefore deal with this final aspect of the lemma, the question of πῶς ἴδιον τῆς ποιότητος τὸ ὅμοιον καὶ ἀνόμοιον. The answer is that quality ἐπείσακτός ἐστιν (290,27), and hence quality's specific kind of κοινωνία produces a sort of παράχρωσις. Simplicius explains that each of the categories features its very own kind of κοινωνία: in substance κοινωνία manifests itself as identity (ταὐτότης), quantity's sort of κοινωνία is equality (ἴσον), and quality's is of course similarity/likeness (ὅμοιον). Simplicius goes on (290,31-33) to explain that similarity is produced by a certain χαρακτήρ coming about somewhere in that which receives it thereby constituting (supervenient) quality (which thus has its ἰδιότης, its specific feature, κατὰ τὸ ὅμοιον καὶ ἀνόμοιον); and Simplicius defines (290,33-291,1) similarity as the supervenient participation in the same form, as is shown in the *Parmenides* (ἡ τοῦ αὐτοῦ εἴδους ἐπεισοδιώδης μέθεξις, ὡς δέδεικται ἐν τῷ Παρμενίδῃ).[21]

This extremely difficult and technical discussion should not distract us from one major point I wish to stress: not only could it be shown that the passage 290,1-291,1 which immediately precedes this reference to the *Parmenides* is closely linked to the context of the first reference to the *Parmenides*; and not only is Iamblichus most probably at the origin of important parts of the text in both cases—the two *Parmenides* references are even linked by κοινωνία, and quite literally so. The reference at 291,1-2 serves to support the definition of ὁμοιότης as ἡ τοῦ αὐτοῦ εἴδους ἐπεισοδιώδης μέθεξις—and, of course, similarity is only quality's specific form of κοινωνία. The first reference to the *Parmenides*, discussed above, relates Plato's One, extended as it is throughout all the hypotheses, to the

---

19. μὴ ἴδιον εἶναι τῆς ποιότητος τὸ ἐπιδέχεσθαι τὸ μᾶλλον καὶ ἧττον (Simplicius, *In cat.* 285,9-10) and τὸ μᾶλλον καὶ ἧττον ὡς κοινὸν τίθησι πλειόνων κατηγοριῶν (Simplicius, *In cat.* 286,5-6).

20. τῶν μὲν οὖν εἰρημένων οὐδὲν ἴδιον ποιότητος, ὅμοια δὲ καὶ ἀνόμοια κατὰ μόνας τὰς ποιότητας λέγεται (Aristotle, *Cat.* 11a15-16).

21. This is a reference to Plato's, *Parmenides* 139e8: ὅτι τὸ ταὐτόν που πεπονθὸς ὅμοιον.

one continuity of the primary and ultimate genera, the continuity that "extends the same κοινωνία and continuity of the genera, accomplishing all things with the unbreakable bonds of ὁμοιότης". Hence one may say that there is indeed a κοινωνία between the two passages: for there is a strong parallel between the One of the *Parmenides*—which expresses or represents the community and continuity of the genera/categories—and *similarity* (and dissimilarity)—which is quality's manifestation of κοινωνία in the same way that equality is for quantity and identity for substance (and in the case of quality at least it is the *Parmenides* that corroborates the definition of its specific feature [ἴδιον, ἰδιότης], i.e., similarity). The *Parmenides*, it seems, is used by the later exegetes in the context of categorial κοινωνία, whether this applies to all categories (i.e., vertically), or only to one (i.e., horizontally).

SECTION 2
THE HIDDEN INFLUENCE OF THE *PARMENIDES*
IN PHILO, ORIGEN, AND LATER PATRISTIC THOUGHT

11
EARLY ALEXANDRIAN THEOLOGY AND PLATO'S *PARMENIDES*

David T. Runia

When I was first asked to speak about Philo's interpretation of Plato's *Parmenides*, I was rather hesitant.[1] My initial response was to say that to my knowledge Philo never makes any reference to this particular Platonic dialogue and that it was hard to talk at any length about nothing. It must of course be agreed that not everyone finds this difficult in equal measure. Philosophers as a rule do not find it at all hard to speak about nothing. In fact some of them appear to revel in it. Theologians have a little more difficulty in doing this, and are not amused when people say that they do little else. Historians find it much harder, while philologists find it flatly impossible. Both of them, it would seem, need a subject on which to focus their musings. But perhaps on reflection it is possible to say something on the subject, if it is taken in a broader sense than just concentrating on direct use of the original Platonic text. This will be my approach in the remarks that follow.

By the "early Alexandrian theology" of my title I mean the Judaeo-Christian thought that developed in Alexandria in the first two centuries of the common era. I will concentrate largely on the great Jewish exegete and philosopher Philo of Alexandria, but will also say something about his Christian successor, Clement of Alexandria. Of course Origen is usually mentioned in one breath with his two Alexandrian predecessors, but I leave the theme of his use of the *Parmenides* to the paper devoted to that very subject by Mark Edwards.

---

1. I dedicate this contribution to the memory of my mentor and friend Eric Osborn, who read an early version before his death and engaged me in a valuable discussion of its main themes. Abbreviations of Philonic treatises in the notes follow the conventions of *The Studia Philonica Annual*.

Philo of Alexandria

There are no references to Plato's *Parmenides* in the extensive corpus of Philo's works and also no identifiable quotations or allusions to that work. Indeed Philo never actually refers to Parmenides himself in his extant Greek works, but there are three references to the Eleatic philosopher in that part of *On Providence* that is only extant in an Armenian translation. These texts discuss the fact that he wrote his theology in the form of poetry and his doctrine of the eternity of the universe.[2] They do not touch on the subject matter of Plato's dialogue. The most extensive general study on Philo's Platonism is still the Chicago dissertation of Thomas Billings, supervised by Paul Shorey and published in 1919 (Billings 1919). In his chapter on "Philo's conception of the ultimate reality" Billings makes about ten references to the *Parmenides*,[3] but on closer inspection none refer to direct identifiable usage of the dialogue. We can certainly agree with Henry Chadwick when he says that "Philo betrays no special interest ... in the *Parmenides*" (Chadwick 1967, 145).

This result need not surprise us. Philo is writing in the fourth and fifth decades of the first century C.E. Comparable contemporary authors are scarce. The best author to compare him with is Plutarch, born some fifty years later. In contrast to Philo, Plutarch regarded himself as a Platonist. In his case we can make use of the excellent index of Helmbold and O'Neill (Helmbold and O'Neill 1959, 58). It seems that in the vast Plutarchean corpus there is but a single direct reference to the *Parmenides*, at *On brotherly love* 484C, where Plutarch notes that Plato gives his (half-)brother Antiphon a role in the dialogue. There is also a possible allusion to 131b4 in *Platonic Questions* 3 1002D, but the allusion is far from compelling.[4] It would seem, therefore, that in the first century C.E. the *Parmenides* was not in the forefront of academic study. But that need not mean that Philo was not acquainted with the dialogue. In the research of recent years the polymathic scope of Philo's philosophical knowledge has become more and more clear. I think it quite unlikely that Philo was unaware of the existence of the *Parmenides*, even if he has not referred to it explicitly or made allusions to it. There are three themes that we should investigate further in order to gain a more accurate idea of whether he was indebted to the dialogue.

(1) Firstly, there is the discussion of the knowability of the ideas. Parmenides suggests at 132b3 that each of the ideas might be a thought (νόημα) that is located

---

2. *Prov.* 2.39, 42, 48. In the case of the last text one might wonder whether it refers to the doctrine of the eternity of the universe or of matter. But in the doxographer Aëtius Parmenides is one of the representatives of the doctrine of the eternity of the cosmos; see Runia 2008, 40.

3. See the index prepared by Geljon and Runia (1995, 169–85).

4. See the note in Cherniss's edition of this work in the LCL edition of Plutarch's *Moralia*, 1976, vol. 13.1:45.

nowhere else than in souls. This suggestion is later developed into the proposition that if anyone were to have knowledge of the forms, it would be a god (τινα ... θεόν, 134b11). We would surely expect Philo to read this sympathetically, for the doctrine that the ideas are the thoughts of God is one of his most characteristic doctrines. The further consequence, however, that the gods would have no knowledge of anything in our world, would be wholly unacceptable. For Philo the ideas, and also knowledge of them, are very much linked to the existence of the cosmos and its creator. God, whose Logos is the locus of the ideas, first created the noetic cosmos as a model (παράδειγμα) for the physical cosmos (*On the creation of the cosmos according to Moses* 16–25). The *Parmenides* rejects the notion of the forms as models (132d2, παραδείγματα ἐν τῇ φύσει), but Plato notoriously takes up the idea again in the *Timaeus*, the dialogue that was Philo's main inspiration in trying to understand the Mosaic doctrine of creation.[5]

(2) Secondly, as is well known, Philo is the earliest author to exhibit an elaborate negative theology, including the extensive use of alpha-privative epithets such as ἀκατάληπτος, ἄγνωστος, ἀκατονόμαστος, ἄρρητος and so on. Claims that Philo was the originator of this kind of theology have generally been met with scepticism.[6] But let us entertain the possibility that a reading of the *Parmenides* may have aided Philo in developing his thought in this area. How might it have helped?

In the first place we might point out that the dialogue will not have given Philo any direct help in developing the characteristic terminology cited above. None of these terms are found in the second dialectical part of the dialogue. Only the term ἄγνωστος is found in the first part (133c1, 134b14, 135a5). But this is no doubt too narrow a view. It would not have been difficult to develop these terms on the basis of the conclusion of the first hypothesis, making use of terminological advances made in the Hellenistic period.

But what about this conclusion itself, together with the diametrically opposed conclusion of the second hypothesis? What might Philo have gained from them? For convenience I quote Cornford's non-dialectical translation (1939, 129, 192–93):

> 1.141e7–142a7: There is, accordingly, no way in which the One has being. Therefore the One in no sense *is*. It cannot, then, "be" even to the extent of "being" one; for then it would be a thing that is and has being. Rather, if we can trust such an argument as this, it appears that the One neither is one nor is at all. And if a thing is not, you cannot say that it "has" anything or that there is

---

5. On the doctrine of the ideas as thoughts of God and the noetic cosmos as model for the physical cosmos see Runia 1986, 158–74.

6. Especially as claimed by Wolfson 1968, 2:94–164. Radice 2003, 167–82, is more circumspect. For a recent sound survey of the issues see Calabi 2002, 35–54; 2008, 38–56 for English translation.

anything "of" it. Consequently, it cannot have a name (ὄνομα) or be spoken of (λόγος), nor can there be any knowledge or perception or opinion of it. It is not named or spoken of, not an object of opinion or of knowledge, not perceived by any creature.

2.155c8–e3: Now, since the One is in time and has the property of becoming older and younger, it has a past, a future, and a present. Consequently the One was and is and will be; and it was becoming, is becoming, and will become. Also, it can be said to have something, and there can be something of it; in fact we are now exercising all these activities with respect to it. Further, it will have a name (ὄνομα) and can be spoken of (λόγος); indeed it actually is being named and spoken of. And all the other characters which belong to any other things of which the above statements are true, belong equally to the One.

It is not hard to give a theological reading of these two passages as Philo would have understood them. Identifying the One with God would have been *de rigueur*, even if Philo can equally say that God is superior to the one. Diverse texts in which he says this explicitly are often quoted, for example, by Dodds in his famous article on Moderatus and the interpretation of the *Parmenides*.[7] He records that Philo states at *On the contemplative life* 2 that the Therapeutae worship "Being (τὸ ὄν), who is superior to the good and purer than (the) one (ἑνός) and more primal than a monad (μονάδος)." But this text is fundamentally unclear. Does Philo refer to the One here, or is he in fact alluding to the numerical unit? Another text at *Allegories of the Laws* 2.3 suggests the latter: "God has been ranked in accordance with the one and the monad, but rather (we should say that) the monad has been ranked in accordance with the one God. For every number is younger than the cosmos, as is time also, but God is older than the cosmos and He is its creator." Dodds saw here a reference to "the Neopythagorean identification of God with the supreme Monad" (Dodds 1928, 132 n. 1), but even if this is correct, it is quickly trumped by the creationism of the *Timaeus* as aligned with Mosaic scripture.

To say, however, that the One in no way *is*, as Plato does, would be quite unacceptable in the light of the Mosaic theology of Being based on Exodus 3:14, as would also be the alternative that the One was and is and will be in a state of becoming. Philo would have been attracted to the thought that God does not have a (real) name, yet does have names such as θεός and κύριος. The reference to the term *logos* would have also had appeal. But what about an interpretation in terms of two hypostases? Even leaving aside the issue of being versus beyond being, Philo would have surely had serious reservations in the light of his adherence to Jewish monotheism. To be sure, he does often speak about God and his Logos in a

---

7. See Dodds 1928, 129–42, esp. 132 n. 1. I analyze his argument in Runia 2007, 483–500.

way that seems to resemble the language of hypostasization, notoriously when the Logos is called God's "first-born son" (cf. *On the confusion of tongues* 63,146).[8] There are plenty of indications, however, that this is not the mode of speaking about God that most closely approximates the heart of his theological thought. In my reading of Philo—and it must be readily confessed that every Philonist has to exercise a certain degree of selectivity here—the heart of his theological thought lies in the simple yet profound distinction which he makes between God in his essence on the one hand and God in his existence and in the way that we can think and speak about him on the other.[9] A fascinating text in this connection is found at *On rewards and punishments* 39–40. Jacob, the spiritual athlete, becomes Israel, the man who sees God, and receives as his special reward the supreme vision. But what does this involve?[10]

> The Father and Saviour, seeing his yearning and longing, took pity on him. He granted power to the penetration of his sight and did not begrudge him the vision of Himself, to the extent that it was possible for a created and mortal nature to contain it, not a vision of *what* He is, but (only) *that* He is. §40. For in the case of that (entity) which is superior to what is good and more venerable than a monad and purer than a unit, it is impracticable that He be seen by someone else, because to Him alone is it permissible to know Himself.

In this text Philo again uses the language of extreme transcendence, claiming that God is beyond all ethical or mathematical categories. As noted above, it is not impossible to see a reflection of theological interpretation of the first hypothesis of the *Parmenides*. But he combines it with the theme of God's impenetrable essence, which in my view is scarcely compatible with the dialectics of the dialogue. It is just possible that this theological scheme could be read *into* the first two hypostases of the *Parmenides*, but it certainly cannot be derived *from* it. I conclude, therefore, that interpretation of Plato's dialogue did not lead Philo into the heart of his theological thought.

This is not to say, however, that Philo's theological pronouncements are unable give us information about currents of interpretation in his time. The scholar who has argued this the most persuasively, to my knowledge, is the late John Whittaker. In his article "Neopythagoreanism and the Transcendent Absolute" he affirms that Eudoran, Philonic, Clementine, and Hermetic texts that state that the ultimate principle transcends any form of dualism of opposites and even

---

8. The best discussion is by Winston 1985, esp. 9–25, 49–50.

9. See for example his presentation of the theme of human knowledge of God at *Spec.* 1.32–50, which is dominated by this central distinction.

10. Translations of Philo are my own, with debts to the translations of the LCL and Winston 1981.

unity itself go back to early Neopythagorean thought (Whittaker 1973, 77–86). Whittaker concludes (p. 83):

> At the close of the first hypothesis of the *Parmenides* Plato had indicated that the One, under the terms of that hypothesis, was not really one at all (141 E 12): τὸ ἓν οὔτε ἕν ἐστιν οὔτε ἔστιν. It is hardly conceivable that the Neopythagorean advocates of the doctrine which we have been considering were unaware of the similarity between that doctrine and the conclusion of the first hypothesis of the Platonic dialogue.

John Dillon too entertains the idea that "the influence of the first hypothesis of the *Parmenides* ... was already at work in Alexandrian Platonism before Philo's time" and he further refers to the highest transcendent principle in the thought of Eudorus. But he immediately adds that "the nature of the evidence does not permit of certainty."[11] The *caveat* is surely sound. Plausible as Whittaker's position may be, ultimately the conclusion cited above is a piece of rhetoric. It does not tell us anything about the interpretation of the *Parmenides* in Philo's time or before his time, because the connection it makes is the work of the modern scholar.

(3) There remains a third aspect of Plato's dialogue that I would briefly like to dwell on in relation to Philo's theological thought, namely the dialectical categories that Plato uses to unpack the logical implications of the eight hypotheses involving the one and the many. These are, of course, the group of eight antithetical pairs: whole–part, limit–unlimited, in same–in another, rest–motion, same–different, similar–dissimilar, equal–unequal, older–younger. Are there any traces of such dialectics in Philo's thinking about God?

Every reader of Philo's allegories will recall that he often uses these or similar categories in arguing about the nature of God. We can mention whole–part, containing–contained, without–with shape, standing–in motion, unchanging–changing, without–with qualities, without need–in need, older–younger and so on.[12] None of these arguments, to my knowledge, use exactly the same argumentation as in the theorems of the *Parmenides*. More importantly, their method and intent differ. Let me give two examples from the *Allegories of the Laws*, both using argumentation involving the part–whole relation. The first text is provoked by the biblical text in Gen 2:8, in which "God plants a paradise in Eden towards the east" (*Leg.* 1.43–44):

---

11. Dillon 1977, 155. On Philo and Eudorus see now Bonazzi 2008, 232–51.

12. I give a by no means exhaustive list of examples: whole–part *Leg.* 2.2–3; *Post.* 3; *Spec.* 1.208; containing–contained *Leg.* 1.44; *Sobr.* 63; *Fug.* 75; *Somn.* 1.63; without–with shape cf. *Deus* 59; *Fug.* 8; standing–in motion *Post.* 19, 23; unchanging–changing *Cher.* 90; *Deus* 22; *Mut.* 46; without–with qualities *Leg.* 1.36; 3.206; *Deus* 55; without need–in need *Cher.* 44; *Post.* 4; *Deus* 7; older–younger cf. *Deus* 31–32.

> Let not such great impiety take hold of human thought as to suppose that God tills the soil and plants paradises, since we would be at a loss to discover his motivation. It would not be in order to supply himself with pleasant refreshments and pleasures. Such mythical inventions should never enter our mind. §44. Not even the entire cosmos would be a worthy place and abode for God, since God himself is His own place and He is filled by Himself and is sufficient for Himself, filling and containing other things which are needy and empty and void, whereas He Himself is not contained by another else, seeing that He is Himself One and the All.

The second text reflects on the biblical text in Gen 2:18, "it is not good for the human being to be alone." Why is this the case, Philo asks. Three answers are given, each involving a comparison between the human being and God (*Leg.* 2.1–3):[13]

> (1) Because, he says, it is good that the Alone is alone. But God, being One, is alone of His own accord and there is nothing similar to God. As a result, since it is good that the one who is (τὸν ὄντα) is alone—for indeed goodness relates to him alone—it would not be good for the human being to be alone. §2. (2) But the aloneness of God can also be understood as follows. Neither before creation was there anything with God, nor once creation had occurred is anything ranked together with him. For there is absolutely nothing which He needs. (3) But a still better explanation is this. God is alone and a unity (ἕν). His nature is simple, not a composite, whereas each one of us and all other created beings are pluralities. I, for example, am a plurality consisting of body and soul.... God, however, is neither a composite nor consists of many parts, but is unmixed with anything else. §3. For whatever is added to God is either superior or inferior or equal to Him. But there is nothing equal or superior to God, and it is certainly not the case that anything inferior is added to Him, for then He will be diminished, and if this happens, He will be perishable, which in his case is not even permissible to think. God therefore has been ranked in accordance with the unit and the monad, or rather (we should say that) the monad has been ranked in accordance with the one God. For every number is younger than the cosmos, as is time also, but God is older than the cosmos and He is its creator.

In two respects Philo's theological thought is more concrete than the logical abstractions of Plato's dialectics. Firstly, as the two examples above show, the pretext for Philo's arguments is very often questions that arise from the biblical text and these mostly focus on the relation between God and humankind (or another aspect of created reality). Philo seldom engages in theological speculation for its own sake. Secondly, I would argue that the basic paradigm for Philo's theology is the relation between creator and created reality. Once again this point is

---

13. Note that the final part of the text has been cited above in connection with Philo's possible reading of the first two hypotheses.

illustrated by the two texts cited above. It meant that the fundamental Platonic dialogue for Philo had to be the *Timaeus*, not the *Republic* or the *Parmenides* or the *Sophist*. It was most convenient for his project of giving commentary on Mosaic scripture that during his lifetime it was the *Timaeus* that provided the dominant influence in Platonic interpretation.[14] A history of Platonism could be written in terms of the struggle between the *Republic*, the *Timaeus* and the *Parmenides* for that dominant position. By the third century the tide had turned in favor of the *Parmenides*. But the antithesis between the two dialogues should not be seen as too absolute. Long ago Robert Brumbaugh pointed out rather persuasively that the Demiurge in a sense applies the dialectic of theorems to the concrete case of the cosmos in his planning for how the cosmos should be (Brumbaugh 1961, 206). I cite his list of parallels:

God plans the world as	Parmenides' theorems
ONE	ONE-MANY
WHOLE	PART-WHOLE
SPHERE	SHAPE: ROUND, STRAIGHT OR MIXED
SELF-CONTAINED	IN SELF-IN OTHER
ROTATING	MOTION: ROTATION OR TRANSLATION
UNALTERED	OR ALTERATION
UNAGING	OLDER-YOUNGER
WITH ORGANS OF TIME	SHARING IN TIME
SO BROUGHT INTO BEING	EXIS-
TENCE	

This convergence can explain why some of Philo's theological arguments may remind us of the Parmenidean dialectics, even though it is rather unlikely that he makes any conscious use of them.

Clement of Alexandria

Between Philo and Clement there is a fascinating interplay of continuity and difference. The most important direct link between the two Alexandrian thinkers is the fact that Clement is the first author after Josephus to name Philo explicitly and make abundant and detailed use of his works.[15] It was most likely in the milieu frequented by Clement that Philo's writings were saved for posterity.[16] Yet unlike Philo, Clement was not a Jew and also not an Alexandrian by birth. He

---

14. This is a point made in a somewhat exaggerated fashion by H. Dörrie in various publications, e.g., 1974, 13–29; see further Runia 1986, 49.

15. On the relation between Philo and Clement see Van den Hoek, 1988; Runia 1993, 132–56; Osborn 2005, 81–105.

16. See further Van den Hoek 1997, 59–87.

was, we assume, of Greek descent and only travelled to Alexandria as part of his life-long intellectual pilgrimage. Most importantly, Clement at some stage prior to his arrival in Alexandria converted to Christianity. He thus showed the same loyalty to the biblical tradition as Philo did, but approached it from a different and radically new perspective. By the time Clement received his philosophical training, more than a century had passed since Philo's death.[17] Our task is now to track what Clement can tell us about the interpretation of Plato's *Parmenides*, with our findings on Philo forming a valuable backdrop for purposes of comparison.

Like Philo, Clement makes no explicit references to Plato's dialogue. He is well aware of the importance that the philosopher Parmenides has for Plato, for at *Stromateis* 5.112.2 he tells us that Plato in the *Sophist* gives him the epithet "the great" (237a4). He also cites verses from Parmenides' poem on five occasions.[18] It is possible that the description of the idea as ἐννόημα τοῦ θεοῦ goes back to *Parmenides* 132b4, but Clement certainly does not make this explicit.[19] This is the only reference that Stählin makes to the dialogue in his edition,[20] but there are two important passages in which we can be quite certain that theological interpretation of the *Parmenides* is lurking in the background. These passages have been well studied by Osborn and Le Boulluec,[21] but in the context of our investigation it will be worthwhile to go over the details again.

(1) We take the text relating to the theme of God's transcendence first. It is part of Clement's exposition of the mysteries of theology. Plato and Moses (and Philo as well, we might add[22]) agree that knowledge of God is not available to human beings and is hidden from them (*Strom.* 5.78). This is confirmed by John the Evangelist when he writes (1:18): "No one has ever seen God; the only begotten God who exists in the bosom of the Father, that one has made Him known (cited at 5.81.3)." "Bosom" (κόλπος) indicates the invisible and ineffable nature of God and it has led some (i.e., the Valentinians) to call God "abyss" (βύθος) because He embraces all things while Himself being unattainable and without limit. In the choice of this last term we already perhaps discern the interpretation of the *Parmenides* entering Clement's associative mind. At any rate, he continues (5.81.4–6):[23]

---

17. Clement is thought to have been born ca. 145 C.E. Philo's death is usually placed before 50 C.E.

18. *Strom.* 5.15.5, 5.59.6, 5.112.2, 5.138.1, 6.23.2.

19. The fact that it is stated in the introduction to a quote from the *Phaedrus* militates against a reference.

20. D. Wyrwa in his valuable study of Clement's debt to Plato (1983) also makes no further reference to the *Parmenides*.

21. Osborn 1957, 25–31; Le Boulluec 1981, 2:263–65.

22. *Strom.* 5.78.3 follows *Post.* 14 in citing Exod 20:21.

23. My translation is based on that of Osborn in his 1957 study.

§4. Indeed this question concerning God is the most difficult to treat. For since the first principle of every matter is difficult to find, the first and oldest principle is all the more difficult to demonstrate, that principle which is the cause of all things coming into being and remaining in existence. §5. For how could that be spoken of which is neither genus nor difference nor species nor individual nor number, but on the other hand is neither accident nor that to which an accident pertains? Nor can anyone describe him correctly as "whole," for wholeness is ranked with magnitude and He is the Father of the whole world. §6. Nor are any parts to be ascribed to Him. For the One is indivisible. For this reason it is also infinite, not in the sense of non-traversibility, but in the sense of being without dimension or limit, and therefore also without shape and without name.

For Clement God is unambiguously the first and oldest principle, cause of all becoming. This is still partly the language of the *Timaeus* (reiterated in §5 when He is called Father), though that dialogue never calls the Demiurge "first principle." But in the remainder of the passage metaphysical and dialectical themes take over. Various Aristotelian categories cannot be applied to him. "Wholeness" is first taken in terms of quantitative magnitude, which cannot apply to Him from whom the physical world is derived. But a whole can also be a unity consisting of parts. In §6, then, the direct use of the *Parmenides* begins. Clement's compressed account refers to five themes from three theorems:

(i) No parts are to be ascribed to the first principle because it is One: cf. *Parm.* 137c5–d3, where the One has no parts, but also is not a whole (cf. what Clement has just said in §5, but in the context of a different approach). Clement's alpha-privative term ἀδιαίρετος (indivisible) is the first of six such terms in this single section. Of these only ἄπειρος and ἀσχημάτιστος are found in Plato (the latter is used of true being at *Phdr.* 247c6, cited by Clement at 5.16.4). But the use of these terms in interpretation of the first hypothesis was a natural development.

(ii) The first principle is infinite (ἄπειρος): cf. *Parm.* 137d6, where the One is infinite, without beginning or end. I take the following phrase, in which Clement rules out the possibility that the first principle is κατὰ τὸ ἀδιεξίτητον νοούμενον, to refer to taking infinity in a spatial sense, which does not apply to God as a spiritual entity.[24]

(iii) Infinity for the first principle thus means being without dimension or limit: cf. *Parm.* 137c6–8, where end and beginning are agreed to be "limit" (πέρας) and not applicable to the One. This adds little to the previous point except the notion of being dimensionless (ἀδιάστατος), which is not found in Plato's text but is consistent with it, since what has no dimensions has no limits, like a point.

---

24. I agree here with Le Boulluec (1981, 1:161), who paraphrases as "non au sens d'une étendue qu'il est impossible de parcourir," against Osborn on this point.

(iv) The first principle is without shape (ἀσχημάτιστος): cf. the next theorem at *Parmenides* 137d8, the One is "without shape." The link that Clement makes with the previous theorem (therefore, τοίνυν) is not in Plato, but again it is natural enough, since shape is determined by limits.

(v) The first principle is without a name (ἀνωνόμαστος): cf. *Parmenides* 142a3. Clement now jumps to the very conclusion of the hypothesis, where Plato draws various conclusions about the One if it is the case that it neither exists or is one (cited above). Unlike in Plato, no argument is given, but it follows on from the earlier theorems, since if the first principle has no traits except negative ones, how can a name be given it which describes its proper nature? In the section that follows (5.82.1) Clement goes on to analyse what happens if we do give God names, such as in the case of the term God (θεός) itself.[25]

In this passage, then, Clement uses the dialectical argumentation of the first hypothesis of the *Parmenides* to develop a negative theology of absolute transcendence. There is nothing in what Clement writes that Philo would have disagreed with. But contrary to what we found in Philo's case, we may be certain that by the second half of the second century the *Parmenides was* being used for purposes of negative theology. There is nothing surprising in this, for, as was pointed out by Lilla (see Lilla 1971, 214–15), there is an excellent parallel for the Clementine passage in the Middle Platonist handbook of Alcinous (cf. Didask. §10, 165.5–7, 12–16 Whittaker-Louis). This work, however, cannot be dated with any accuracy, which makes Clement's evidence all the more valuable for the historian.

(2) The second passage is found in an earlier section of the *Stromateis*, at 4.156, where Clement is setting out the perfection that a human being can attain through knowledge and love. But how can this happen if knowledge of the first principle is unattainable? Does this not mean that our knowledge is necessarily imperfect? Yet it is claimed that the true gnostic, as Clement conceives him, can attain perfection and "live as a god among men." The solution to this conundrum lies in the role of the Son:[26]

> §1. God, then, since He is not the object of demonstration, is not the object of knowledge. But the Son is wisdom and knowledge and truth and all that is related to this. Indeed of him both demonstration and explication can be given. All the powers of the spirit, taken together and forming one single reality, contribute to the same being, the Son, but He is not describable in terms of the conception of each of his powers. §2. Indeed He is not simply unity (ἕν) as unity, nor multiplicity (πόλλα) involving parts, but as unity involving totality (ὡς πάντα ἕν). From this He is also the totality. For He Himself is the circle of all the powers gathered together and unified into unity.

---

25. This passage is indebted to Philo, as I argue in my article 1988, 86–87.
26. In my translation I have made good use of A. van den Hoek's French version (SC 463).

The passage begins with an affirmation of the negative theology that Clement will set out in more detail in book 5. But there is also positive theology, which is focused on the Son, identified in scripture with wisdom and knowledge and truth. He too is God, as the Johannine passage cited in 5.81.3 will make clear (cited above). In the case of the Son the dialectic of unity and multiplicity takes a different turn. §2 contains a double reference to the *Parmenides*. The phrase "simply unity as unity" must be a reference to the first hypothesis. We might compare the statement at 142d2, "therefore it [the one] will neither be a whole nor have parts, if the one is to be one." For the role of the Son the phrase "multiplicity (πόλλα) involving parts" might be a reference to the argument at 145a2–3, "so the one that exists is surely both one and many, a whole and parts, and limited and unlimited in multitude." But Clement baulks at the idea of using multiplicity to speak about the Son, since multiplicity holds an ill-defined middle position between unity and totality. Here too argumentation from the *Parmenides* can come to the rescue. Unity is opposed to multiplicity, but as soon as unity is unpacked in terms of a whole with parts, multiplicity can become totality. The phrase "unity involving totality" may allude to the argument at 145c2 that "the one is all the parts of itself, and not any more or less than all (πάντα)." It could also refer to the conclusion of the fourth hypothesis at 160b2, "thus if the one is, the one is all things." However this may be, Whittaker's comment on this passage that "it is difficult to believe that an interpretation of the first two hypotheses of the Parmenides has not influenced Clement at this point" is fully justified.[27]

Once again the historian will be happy with this result. Clement's text is an additional indication that the hypotheses of the *Parmenides* were used to found a metaphysics of distinct hypostases. To my knowledge it is the first clear evidence after the famous text of Moderatus on which Dodds based his article.[28] It is all the more interesting because it can be seen as a striking anticipation of the lucid schema that Plotinus uses at *Enneads* 5.1.8 to explain the Platonic background of the doctrine of the three hypostases.[29]

But there are also matters of interest for the philosopher and the theologian. For, unlike in the case of the negative theology discussed earlier, we can be less sure that Philo would have been happy with the conclusion reached by Clement. To be sure, for Philo the Logos can be regarded as the totality of the ideas or the divine powers (cf. *On the creation of the cosmos* 20). The Logos is also identified with wisdom (and by implication knowledge). The question is whether Philo

---

27. Whittaker 1969, 91–104 (quote at 99); repr. 1984.
28. Moderatus at Simplicius *In Phys.* 230.34–231.12 Diels, cited at Dodds 1928, 136.
29. *Enn.* 5.1.8.24–27: "But Parmenides in Plato speaks more accurately, and distinguishes from each other the first One, which is more properly called One, and the second which he calls 'One-Many' and the third 'One and Many.' In this way he too agrees with the doctrine of the three natures."

would have so boldly separated God and the Logos as Clement does in *Stromateis* 4.156. This may rightly be doubted. As Eric Osborn has shown in his two monographs,[30] Clement grapples with central philosophical and theological problems in this text. God is beyond human knowledge, but scripture tells us that he can be known through the Son (John 1:18, cited above). How can there be a God beyond God, yet also a God beside God? And how can the Son–Logos, "through whom all things were made" (John 1:3), form a bridge to the multiplicity of created reality? The solution lies firstly in the identification of God with unity and of the Son with unity as totality, and secondly in the affirmation of the reciprocity of Father and Son in the doctrine of the Holy Trinity. The age-old problem of the one and many, most trenchantly formulated by Plato in the hypotheses of the *Parmenides*, is thus given a theological solution that does not involve a hierarchy of gods, even if in the mystery of the Trinity the Father does generate the Son. And the added bonus for Clement is that the Son is the Christ who is also the Savior of humankind.[31]

As we noted at the outset of this section, more than a century separates Clement from his Alexandrian predecessor Philo. Although both wished to stand in the Judaeo-Christian tradition of scriptural thought, their understanding of its central doctrines was strongly influenced by contemporary currents of Middle Platonic and Neopythagorean philosophy. Philosophy did not stand still during this period, even if the advances were not spectacular. Just as there was a shift from a strong concentration on the *Timaeus* to a broader reading of Plato's dialogues, so Clement moves beyond Philo's strong emphasis on the relation between God and cosmos to a broader and more developed theological doctrine. It may be concluded that developments in the interpretation of the enigmatic second half of the *Parmenides* aided him in this achievement.

---

30. Osborn 1957, esp. 17–44; 2005, esp. 111–53.

31. As Osborn humorously notes (1957, 44), it is difficult for us to rouse any feelings whatever towards "one thing as all things," but Clement does manage to attach genuine religious feeling towards this notion.

12

CHRISTIANS AND THE *PARMENIDES*

Mark Edwards

It may be felt that the present paper achieves too little even for an exercise in negative theology. Not only does it leave a great deal unsaid that was suggested by its title, but it proposes to unsay at least part of what has been said admirably by others. If in addition I seem to be sweeping away with the left hand even the crumbs of positive speculation that are seen falling here and there from my right—this much, it may be granted, is in the spirit of the *Parmenides*, though my simile may be more Christian than Platonic. Even without this pretext, it is enough to plead that time and knowledge are finite (as Plato recognized, though not in the *Parmenides*) to explain my failure to canvass more than two topics in this paper. The first is the use of a formula, ἄρρητος καὶ ἀκατονόμαστος, which I believe to be not so much of a commonplace in Platonic literature as is generally supposed. The second concerns the provenance of the only text, the *Anonymus Taurinensis* or *Commentary on the Parmenides*, which contains this phrase but does not belong avowedly to that circle for which the Bible is the sole canon of theological speculation. While my proposals may not agree with those advanced by any other scholar at this meeting, it should be evident that I can scarcely be said to disagree with anyone when my principal thesis is that there is barely a conjecture on either topic that can be proved untenable.

NAMELESS AND INEXPRESSIBLE

Perhaps the most hyperbolical assertion of divine ineffability in Greek literature is the saying of Basilides, an early Christian whom we loosely describe as Gnostic, that to pronounce the highest deity ἄρρητον or inexpressible is to bind him, and that in strict truth neither this term nor its antonym should be used of one who is "loftier than every name that is named" (Hippolytus, *Refutation* 7.20).[1] The same God he styled elsewhere the inexpressible and unnamable (ἀκατονόμαστον) One

---

1. This section is primarily a response to Whittaker 1983, 303–6; 1969, 91–104.

who is not (1.7.26). John Whittaker notes that the Naassenes—true Gnostics and (as Hippolytus thinks) contemporaries of Basilides—yoked the same terms in calling the Son of God ἀκατονόμαστος καὶ ἄρρητος (5.9.1), and that they form a couple once again in a brief list of heretical locutions from the fourth century (*Const. ap.* 6.10.1). Clement of Alexandria, though he reserved the honorific label "Gnostic" for the orthodox, was steeped in the literature of the Basilideans, and will have known that only heretics could provide a Christian pedigree for such epithets as ἄρρητος and ἀνωνόμαστος (nameless) when he applied them to God at *Stromateis* 5.12.81. Origen may be credited with an equally conscious desire to rebaptize these terms when he amplified Hebrews 1.3 to make Paul say that the Son is the "image and stamp of the inexpressible, unnamable and unutterable hypostasis of the father" (*Princ.* 4.4.1). The words ἀκατονόμαστος and ἄρρητος recur at *Contra Celsum* 7.43, where he is rebutting his adversary's appeal to Plato; only the second adjective, however, is attributed here to Celsus. All these authors would no doubt have traced the words nameless and unnamable to Paul's eulogies of Christ as the one whom the Father has blessed with the name above every name (Phil 2.9) and has set above every name that is named (Eph 1.21); yet Whittaker, while noting the biblical precedents, observes that the One in the first hypothesis of the *Parmenides* is said to admit of no name while the notion that the first principle is ῥητός or expressible is vigorously denied in the Seventh Letter.[2] The language of Clement at least is undoubtedly colored by reminiscences of the *Timaeus*, and the cognate term to ἄρρητος (Whittaker argues) is to be sought not in the New Testament but in the second letter of Plato. The term ἄπειρος (infinite), which stands between the other two at *Stromateis* 5.12.81 also finds its antecedent in the first hypothesis of the *Parmenides*. For evidence of the currency of phrases drawn from this part of the dialogue—though not of the attribution of infinity to God—we may turn to the handbook or epitome of Alcinous,[3] which is assigned to the second century by the consensus of modern scholarship. The *Parmenides* therefore takes its place with the other Platonic dialogues for apologists in search of metaphysical securities for the truths revealed apodictically in scripture.

We cannot deduce, however, that the authors named above had read the *Parmenides* in its entirety, or even that they had encountered any passage of substance from this dialogue in a florilegium. Whereas a long quotation from the second letter of Plato is ascribed to Valentinus, and Christian variants on the most famous aphorisms in the *Timaeus* could fill a book, the *Parmenides* does not figure in Miroslav Marcovich's index of citations in his edition of Hippolytus, and there is nothing more to be gleaned from the copious indices to Koetschau's edition of Origen *On First Principles* or Stählin's edition of Clement. The impres-

---

2. *Parm.* 142a3 and *Ep.* 7.41c5 cited by Whittaker 1983, 304–5.
3. Alcinous/Albinus, *Didask.* 10.164.31–165.16 Hermann, cited by Whittaker 1969, 99.

sive studies of Förster on Mark the Mage and Wucherpfennig on Heracleon are bare of any allusion to the *Parmenides*, while Lohr on Basilides finds occasion to mention it only in recapitulating the work of another scholar (Förster 1999; Wucherpfennig 2002; Löhr 1996). Even such a learned spoiler of philosophical archives as Eusebius of Caesarea can show only two citations, both made inadvertently in the course of excerpting Atticus. Jean Daniélou, observing the frequency with which the Platonic texts appear in the Greek apologists, has reconstructed a florilegium in which the *Timaeus* predominates, while the *Republic, Phaedrus, Sophist, Gorgias, Laws* and *Meno* are also represented, but the *Parmenides* leaves no trace (Daniélou 1964).

This ignorance or neglect is not peculiar to the Christian world: our commentaries on the Hermetica and the *Chaldaean Oracles* seem to make no use of it. Dillon remarks, however, that in Philo's treatise *On Dreams* (1.67), the familiar terms "inexpressible" and "unnamable" are predicated of God, and adds that neither is "applied to God before his time in any surviving source" (Dillon 1977, 156; cf. Whittaker 1983, 303). We have no documentary evidence that he knew the first hypothesis of the *Parmenides*; which in any case would have offered him only the thought that is expressed by the terms ἄρρητος and ἀκατονόμαστος . Our evidence suggests that the second adjective was an Epicurean coinage,[4] though we can hardly suppose that Philo was a close reader of Epicurus; nor, for that matter, was it Epicurus who prompted Origen to introduce this term at *Contra Celsum* 7.43 when it seems, as I noted above, to have no counterpart in the words of his Platonizing interlocutor. There seems no reason not to say of Origen what we must surely say of Philo: his allusion to an unnamable and inexpressible God does not betoken a debt to any one text, but a readiness to choose from the *lingua franca* of philosophy in his day whatever terms he found most congruent with the biblical notion of God.

If then there must be an audible beginning to the theology of silence, why should we look for it in Alcinous rather than in Philo? No one in antiquity, after all, can be shown to have read, whereas borrowings from Philo in Christian literature are ubiquitous and often undisguised. It is argued that in the handbook of Alcinous there are passages of the same tenor—though far from identical in phrasing, either with Philo or with the *Parmenides*—which lend color to the suspicion that he and Philo were drawing on an older synthesis; but even granting this, there is nothing to show that their common precursor was a Platonist (and not, for example, a Stoic) or that he favored the *Parmenides* above other writings in the Platonic corpus. As David Runia has shown in these proceedings, Clem-

---

4. LSJ cites Epicurus frg. 314 Usener. A further point (which cannot be pursued here) is that in Jewish texts such privative terms may indicate not that the subject has no name, but that he conceals or forbids the use of it. Hence the quest for the secret name of God, and for an alternative to the name Yahweh in transcription or pronunciation of canonical Hebrew.

ent's term ἄπειρος can be tied to the *Parmenides* with philological evidence of the kind that has not been offered on behalf of ἄρρητος καὶ ακατονόμαστος. We might also—though at the risk of turning the cloud of witnesses into a fog—propose the *Sophist* as the source of the word ἄφθεγκτος (unutterable) when it joins the other terms in Origen's *De Principiis* 4.4.1.[5] Such an argument seems to me more tenable than one that brings the *Parmenides* into the tale without being able to prove any use of common terms; if putative affinities in thought will suffice, we will hardly avoid ascribing an intimate knowledge of the *Parmenides* to the author of Eph 1:21.

We should not expect, of course, that the most abstruse of all the dialogues would be a favorite with logomachists who seldom exhibit more than a second-hand and anecdotal knowledge of any work by Plato. And certainly we could not expect that the incidence of allusion or citation would be higher in Christian authors than in the dedicated Platonists of the same epoch. Of these perhaps only Moderatus of Gades can be shown to have spent any thought on the second half of the dialogue; Plutarch, though he would surely have perused the text with sympathy, never quotes this portion of it. Of Numenius we can say only that his Christian amanuenses have preserved no passage in which he makes explicit reference to the Parmenides. Albinus, in his division of the Platonic corpus, counts it among the elenctic or interrogative texts, while even in Alcinous, who approaches the reasoning of the first hypothesis in his adumbration of negative theology, verbal echoes are infrequent and debatable.[6] He mentions the dialogue once by name, and here again as an exercise in logic. Nor is it clear that Alcinous sets the precedent of treating the One as God, for his theology, as we call it, is in fact a discourse on the nature of *nous* or intellect. He dares to surmise that there may be a God above intellect, and we meet the same thought in Celsus (Origen, *Contra Celsum* 7.42); but this was not yet a truism for Christians as we see from the usage of Origen. While he concedes that God may be superior to *nous* in his answer to Celsus, he flatly informs the Christian readership of *De Principiis* 1.1.1 that God is mind—invisible, impassible, incorporeal, yet not infinite in capacity, since logic forbids us to posit a real infinity in the world over which he presides.

Clement and the Gnostics were more hospitable to the notion of an infinite deity; Gregory of Nyssa, a century later, preserved the analogy without trespassing on the infinity of God, by declaring even the human mind to be unfathomable.[7] Nevertheless the example of Origen demonstrates that Christians could make free with privative terms, yet not be driven to the antinomian logic of the *Parmenides*.

---

5. Juxtaposed with ἄρρητος at *Soph.* 238c.

6. On the classification of the *Parmenides*: Whittaker (1969) juxtaposes Albinus, *Intr.* 3 (148 Hermann) with Alcinous, *Didask.* 6 (p. 159), here ascribing them to the same author, Albinus.

7. Infinity of mind: Gregory of Nyssa, *Opif. hom.* 11.

Indeed it would be more politic to avoid it if one held that the "maker and father of this world" was also the God of Jesus Christ. The theology of negation was the result of an attempt to divine the properties of the First Cause by reason alone; Christians, on the other hand, maintained—against all reason—both that the Father cannot be known without revelation, and that this revelation proves him to be capable of love, of will, of punishing and rewarding, of creating a world from nothing and of perfecting the individual through time.

Gnostics, Victorinus, and the Anonymus Taurinensis[8]

In *Zostrianos*,[9] a Gnostic text known only from Coptic fragments found some sixty years ago at the Egyptian site of Nag Hammadi, we hear of a "single one who exists before all these who really exist in the immeasurable and undivided spirit." The subject so described is thus superior to all determinate being, and the epithets "invisible" and "undivided" represent Greek terms that are applied in the first hypothesis of the *Parmenides* to the One. Luc Brisson detects the other attributes that are accorded to higher principles in the *Timaeus* and the *Phaedrus*, but observes that these negative predicates are succeeded within a short page by a more "positive theology," one that implies a higher degree of objectivity in the referent than Plotinus would have granted to the One.[10] This remark, as Brisson intimates, need not imply that the treatise antedates Plotinus, any more than the marriage of apophatic and kataphatic theology in the works of the Areopagite proves that the author was unfamiliar with Proclus. It is not, in any case, clear that the treatise assigns these properties to the highest principle, for its subject in this passage is the threefold operation of spirit as intellect, vitality and existence. This is the same triple unity of being, life and mind that Neoplatonists after Porphyry discover in the noetic or intelligible realm, the first hypostasis after the One.

Thus it is not impossible that the author of this treatise, like Plotinus and his successors, has culled what he dares to say about the first principle from the *Parmenides*, while characterizing the second in terms adapted from the *Sophist*. Was it the Gnostics or the Neoplatonists who first performed this synthesis? The first possibility cannot be excluded, since Plotinus, in his treatise against the Gnostics (*Enn.* 2.9) speaks of his adversaries as lost friends, thereby hinting that he had known them in the school of Ammonius Saccas. The Coptic rendering of *Zostrianos* survives in a manuscript of the fourth century, but the archetype

---

8. On the date of the commentary see Hadot 1968, vols. 1–2; Bechtle 1999a; 2000, 393–414.

9. On Platonism at Nag Hammadi see Turner 1992, 425–60; Kenney 1992, 187–206; Majercik 1992, 475–88; Brisson 1999b, 173–90.

10. Brisson 1999b, 178; on positive determinations of the One, see G. Leroux's (1990) commentary on *Enn.* 6.8.

is at least a century older, as it was among the Gnostic texts which are said by Porphyry to have exercised Plotinus and his associates in Rome. Even our present version clearly antedates the philosophical treatises of Marius Victorinus against the Arians, some passages in which have now been shown by Michel Tardieu to have almost perfect counterparts in the Gnostic treatise.[11] Dare we conclude that Victorinus, who saw himself as a patron of the catholic cause against Arius, had consciously looked for allies in a quarter that lay outside the bounds of Christendom for both catholics and Arians? Brisson, answering tersely that "we cannot see why he would have used Gnosticism to combat Arianism," infers that the matter common to the treatise and Victorinus was adapted from the same "middle Platonic text."[12]

In fact, however, reasons for "using Gnosticism to combat Arianism" may not be far to seek. In a letter by Arius, Valentinus is named as one of four heretics whose errors can be confuted by assigning a creaturely status to the Son.[13] In the polemical usage of this epoch a Valentinian was one who multiplied gods. This charge was laid against Origen soon after his death by those who inferred, when he made the Son coeternal with the Father, that he was positing two unbegotten principles of equal rank or deriving one from the other by material emission.[14] After the Nicene Council of 325 it could be pressed a little more cogently against champions of the watchword *homoousios*, which had entered the ecclesiastical lexicon under quarantine, as a Valentinian term denoting the consubstantiality between members of the same embodied species.[15] For Origen, for the Platonists and for many Christians even after Nicaea, the word could signify only the unity of a substrate, a divisible stuff or a congeries of material particulars. When the arch-homoousian, Apollinarius of Laodicea, maintained that Christ is consubstantial in flesh with all humanity and in spirit with the Father, he was taxed with the same confusion of flesh and spirit that was thought to be the characteristic vice of every Gnostic speculation. Thus it was not quite ludicrous for the Arian to allege that the homoousian was a Gnostic under his mitre.[16] Seasoned churchmen would of course disavow the kinship even when they borrowed from the Valentinian lexicon;[17] but it is possible that a layman would have thought

---

11. Tardieu 1996. See further Turner 2006, 9–64.

12. Brisson 1999b, 179. On Gnostic tenets in Victorinus see Tommasi Moreschini 1998, 11–46.

13. Letter of Arius to Alexander of Alexandria in Epiphanius, *Pan.* 69.7; Athanasius, *Syn.* 16.

14. Origen as Gnosticizing materialist: Edwards 1998, 578–90.

15. *Homoousios* in Valentinus: Irenaeus, *Adv. Haer.* 2.14.4; cf. 1.11.3, where the consubstantial entities are aeons of the pleroma. See further Stead 1977, 193–98.

16. Perhaps we should add the allusion to the Anomaeans (bugbears of "Nicene" theology in the late fourth century) at Nag Hammadi Codices VI.4.40.

17. Cf. Tertullian, *Val.* 12 on the term *prolatio*.

it merely prudent to make a friend of his enemy's enemy—not least when the layman was, like Victorinus, a rhetorician of long experience but a neophyte in the quarrels of the Church.

The Gnostic treatise therefore could have been the source for Victorinus where the two coincide, and we may dispense with the hypothesis of a "middle Platonic" ancestor. This is not to say, however, that his *Zostrianos* or the one known to Porphyry was identical in all respects with ours. Our Coptic *Zostrianos* would appear to be not only a translation but an abridgment of the Greek, as it is not of a length to warrant the refutation in forty books which the original is said to have elicited from Amelius, and there is nothing in the present text to account for the coupling of the names Zoroaster and Zostrianos in the title.[18] It has therefore been proposed that it was revised in the catholic interest during the Arian controversy of the fourth century. If that is so, no single element in it can be securely said to antedate Plotinus unless, like the sibilant incantations and the myth of Sophia's fall from the *pleroma*, it is expressly impugned in *Enn*. 2.9. Since this text contains no allusion to the noetic triad, we are free to suppose that it entered *Zostrianos* at some time between the composition of *Enn*. 2.9 and the conversion of Victorinus a century later. The interpolation could have been designed to reconcile Platonists or to prove to the episcopal church that Gnostic thought, in contrast to that of Platonists, could accommodate the Trinity. The Gnostics of third-century Rome were both Platonists and Christians, and for all that we know remained so; but unless we are satisfied on other grounds that the triad of being, mind, and life was a formal premiss of Platonic exegesis before Iamblichus, there is no hope of deducing this from a source so incomplete as our present text of the *Zostrianos*.

The integrity of the *Anonymous Commentary on the Parmenides* is not open to the same doubts. Since this was not a canonical text, it would not have been subject to the revisions and increments that such texts must undergo to keep pace with changes in the philosophy of their adepts. The authorship and date of the work remain in doubt, but the hypothesis that commands the assent of the largest body of scholars—if only for want of any tangible alternative—is still that of Pierre Hadot, who in 1968 identified Porphyry as the author (Hadot 1968, vol. 2, etc.). If I am still not of this party, it is because I believe that the history of ideas should give more weight to an author's words than to the paraphrases obtruded upon his words by modern scholars. Hadot ascribes to Porphyry the earliest formulation of the noetic triad—being, life, and mind—that is expounded at length in the *Anonymous Commentary*. Yet the only noetic triad that can be shown to have been a formal postulate of Platonism before Iamblichus is that of the *Chaldaean Oracles* (a text familiar both to the commentator and to Porphyry), which

---

18. On the *Zoroaster, Zostrianos* and *Allogenes* in the third century see Porphyry, *Vit. Plot.* 16.

has for its middle term not life but power or δύναμις. The terms life and power are clearly not interchangeable in all latter attestations of the triad—not in Proclus, for example, when he explains that life is the property that belongs to all sentient beings in contradistinction to those which merely possess existence (*Inst. Theol.* 101). If we surmise instead that Porphyry might have derived one triad from the *Oracles* and the other from the *Sophist*, we concede that his being shown to have posited one would not suffice to prove that he posited the other. Iamblichus—no mean innovator in other fields—is also the earliest writer in whom the noetic triad demonstrably assumes the form that it bears in the *Anonymous Commentary*. If, with the majority of scholars, we assume that its appearance in *Zostrianos* cannot have preceded its first occurrence in the writings of a true Platonist, we now possess firm evidence, in addition to the circumstantial arguments quoted above, that this is a doctored text, which cannot serve as a testimony to Christian use of any text, the *Parmenides* included, before the fourth century.

But I promised to take away with the left what I gave with the right, so let us return to the hard fact that Plotinus was acquainted with a prototype of the *Zostrianos* and attributed it to a school of errant Platonists.[19] Is it altogether impossible that the Platonists of his own school met the triad first in the works of their adversaries; that, declining to borrow openly, they adopted it under camouflage; and that after a generation, when the quarrel had died, Iamblichus restored the initial nomenclature in the same eirenic spirit that induced him to add the Gnostics to his catalog of authorities on the cause of the soul's descent?[20] For him the noetic triad in the *Sophist* is identical with that of the *Chaldaean Oracles*, which are generally held to antedate Plotinus and to have issued, like the books of the Roman Gnostics, from a Platonic *demi-monde* in which philosophy took the form of apocalyptic. It is generally agreed that they were also known to the author of the *Anonymous Commentary on the Parmenides*, though he treats them with a reserve would have set him apart from other Platonists even in the third century. The case for assigning the text to the second century is at its strongest when its advocates are prepared to look for companion texts outside the works of those whom the Neoplatonists acknowledged as their forebears. Bechtle, for example, seeking analogues to the *Anonymous Commentary*, maintains that both the ineffable One of the first hypothesis and the One-existent of the second hypothesis can be found in close proximity in the Coptic *Allogenes* from Nag Hammadi—another treatise on Porphyry's index, or at least a descendant of it.[21] If this is so, reflection on the *Parmenides* was perhaps more characteristic of the Christian philosopher than of the less religious Platonist. Once we have gone so far, it is not

---

19. Gnostics of Plotinus as Platonists: *Enn.* 2.9.6.
20. Iamblichus, *An.* 357 Wachsmuth.
21. Bechtle 2000, 410–11; cf. Turner 1992, 430–39 and Hancock 1992, 174–80.

absurd to ask whether the *Anonymous Commentary on the Parmenides* exhibits any trace of Christian thought.

In our inventory of privative terms in the first half of the paper, we discovered only two authors, Philo and Origen, who had juxtaposed the terms ἀκατονόμαστος and ἄρρητος in their theology. They are paired again in the *Anonymous Commentary on the Parmenides*, but not, so far as I can ascertain from the scholarly literature, in any text securely attributed to a pagan author. I do not know whether any pagan text can supply a parallel to the word κένωμα on the following page; Hadot does not offer one, and when he encounters the complementary term πλήρωμα finds a perfect counterpart only in Hermetic literature.[22] Yet the second is endowed with a variety of meanings in the Valentinian system, while the first appears as its negative in Clement of Alexandria's catena of excerpts from the Valentinian Theodotus. Again it should not be forgotten[23] that the locution "god above all" (ὁ ἐπὶ πᾶσι θεός), which Hadot regards as eminently Porphyrian, is still more characteristic of his older contemporary the Christian Origen. Those who deny that a Christian of the second or early-third century could have undertaken a commentary on Plato must take care not to overlook the periphrastic and adulterated version of a passage from the *Respublica* that continues to puzzle students of the Nag Hammadi texts.[24]

This text, with its talk of gods and its allusions to older Platonists by name, would be an anomalous piece of Christian writing even on the most liberal definition of the term "Christian." I am therefore inclined to guess, not so much that the author was a Christian as that he occupied an intellectual hinterland, unknown to Irenaeus, in which free trade between pagan and Christian was the norm. The triumph of the episcopal church under Constantine put an end to this traffic, except for those, like Marius Victorinus, whose conversion was preceded by a longer than usual dalliance in the schools of pagan learning. What he owed to the tradition represented by the *Anonymous Commentary* has been amply demonstrated by Hadot; what is not (in the nature of proof) so easily proved is that the *Anonymous Commentary* itself was among his sources. After all, we must look to the *Sophist* rather than the *Parmenides* for the germ of his distinction between the *esse*, the absolute being, of the Father and the qualified being or essence of the Son; and again it is the *Sophist*, not the *Parmenides*, that inspired his (somewhat erratic) correlation of being, life and mind with Father, Son and Spirit.[25] We are not required to prove, if we could, that the *Anonymous Commentary* was the vehicle for any theological postulate that could just as well have reached him

---

22. *Anon. in Parm.* 1.3 and 2.15; Hadot 1968, 2.65–69.

23. As I did when writing this paper; Serge Cazelais informs me that he has found the phrase over eighty times in Origen.

24. NHC VI.5; J. M. Robinson 1988, 318–20.

25. Noetic triad in Plato: *Soph.* 248c–e, *Tim.* 39e with Aristotle, *Metaph.* 1027b27–31.

through the Gnostic *Zostrianos* or *Allogenes*. We need only conclude that, whatever was in his library, it is in his work that the stream of orthodoxy rejoins a subterranean current in which Platonic and Christian elements are mingled inextricably, the *Parmenides* cannot be separated from the *Sophist* in exegesis, and the noetic triad holds the mind in precarious suspense above the abyss of unity.

13
ORIGEN'S PLATONISM: QUESTIONS AND CAVEATS[1]

Mark Edwards

That Origen was a Platonist is still the first information that a student receives in a typical lecture on him.[2] If the student knows as little as most theologians do about Plato and his progeny, this epithet becomes a Procrustean bed for all that is subsequently learned about Origen's doctrine or career—that he was born in Alexandria, for example, or held the oneness of God as an axiom, hard though it is to find any pagan Platonist of whom both these are true. The representation of early Christian thinkers as philosophers enables the discipline known as patristics to pass itself off as a branch of Classics, a far more respectable subject than theology; Classicists also gain by this transaction, as their claim to be the custodians of two languages that have shaped the mind of Europe is barely credible unless they can bring the Church within the orbit of their studies. In one respect, however, these parties differ. Classicists are apt to commend the Platonism or Origen and to lament his divagations from the original, which they generally assume to proceed from ignorance; theologians, who are conscious that Origen bears the stigma of heresy, blame his Platonism not only for those opinions which the Church condemned in 553, but also for any traits in him which they themselves condemn, including some that are common to all early Christian writers. And in fact it has been repeatedly urged by Protestant and liberal theologians that the orthodoxy of the ancient Church, no less than its heresies, is the fruit of a coy liaison with the Greek schools, whose pronouncements were always inimical to the Gospel of Christ, have never been intellectually coherent and are now

---

1. Reprinted with permission from *ZAC* 12 (2008), 20–38 (© Walter de Gruyter 2008).
2. Thus McGuckin 2004, 5 n. 32 asserts that he is "technically a Christian Middle Platonist," though the sentence that this annotates asserts that he "technically an eclectic in his own philosophic tradition." Contrast Tzamalikos 2007, 17: "the claim of Platonism in Origen appears so baffling that argument would be needed to establish not its incoherence, but its coherence." I have defended a similar view in Edwards 2002, to which I refer at a number of points below to avoid duplication and prolixity.

regarded as anachronisms in the secular academy. While therefore the catholic, orthodox or oecumenical scholar treats Platonism as the peculiar vice of Origen and his retinue, the modernist replies that Origen's a priori reasoning and his fanciful permutations of the scriptures are peculiarly virulent symptoms of a general plague.

These theories have been maintained by some in spite of two developments that should have rendered them untenable. One is a more critical and dispassionate understanding of Platonism in late antiquity, a sort of unbaptizing that has rescued men like Plotinus and Proclus from their Christian dragomans and has shown that they not merely failed to embrace but conscientiously abhorred the Christian doctrines of creation, redemption, providence, and the transcendent unity of a personal God. The other is a more liberal estimate of early Christian hermeneutics, which is now perceived to be not so much an arbitrary dethronement of the original sense in favor of their own doctrines as a disciplined effort to vindicate the canon by deriving an equal measure of edification from every verse. These trends, where they have been noticed, have not so much laid the old fallacies to rest as laid to rest scholarly discussion of the philosophy of Origen. The many works devoted to his exegesis seldom represent this as a philosophical enterprise, though they may parenthetically credit him with the importation of a few thoughts from Plato. Meanwhile those works that credit him with an ontology, a cosmology or a psychology that are not simply biblical or ecclesiastical have refined but not abandoned the traditional view that every thought that he entertained on such matters had been pre-empted by a Greek, most commonly Plato. This bifurcation in scholarship can be overcome if we acknowledge that exegesis and philosophy need not be at war, that Origen conceived his systematic and harmonious exposition of the scriptures as the substrate for a Christian philosophy that would match the pagan schools in scope and rigor without subscribing to the chimerical pretence of self-sufficiency.

In the following paper I hope to show first that borrowing and dependence are inadequate terms to characterize the relation between philosophy and theology in Origen, and then that his reflection on Christian axioms in the light of philosophical disputes concerning the provenance of the soul did not (as is often thought) confirm his adherence to Plato, but on the contrary led him at least far from any Greek norm as from the prevailing canons of orthodoxy in the Church.

Seven Experiments with Greek Philosophy

To begin, then: What relations, other than borrowing and dependence, could obtain between Christian literature and the philosophical schools of late antiquity? I propose to distinguish seven, though conflations and additions might be imagined and the taxonomoy has no precedent in Origen or any Christian writer of antiquity. I begin with those that seem to me least characteristic of Origen, while the last two, the catalytic and dialectic, receive the most detailed illustration because they were of most service to him in the construction of an autonomous philosophy.

1. Formal. Origen does not imitate any literary form from Plato, unless the compilers of the *Philocalia* were right to attribute to him a dialogue in the elenctic or Socratic mode, which purports to show that the notion of a material substrate, destitute of all qualities yet hospitable to all, gives rise to insoluble contradictions. The ascription of the same work to Bishop Methodius of Olympia flatters his talents, but in its favor it can at least be said that Methodius, who managed a fair pastiche of Plato's style in his dull *Symposium*, was the harbinger of a Christian humanism that prized the ancient not only as repertories of knowledge but as models for imitation. Origen, by contrast, cultivates literary forms unknown to the classical tradition, fearing perhaps that to ape these self-reliant thinkers in externals would be to put abroad the notion that there are other means of seeking God than those disclosed to his prophets and apostles.

2. Obsequious. The use of philosophy may be deemed obsequious when a tenet is accepted, without inquiry or reflection on one's own account, because it enjoys the patronage of a great name. There is something of this in the mediaeval deference to Aristotle, a great deal more in the writings of those moderns who assume that those who live after Freud and Wittgenstein must think like Freud and Wittgenstein, whatever the Gospel might say to the contrary. There is little of it in early Christian writers, least of all in Origen: his references to Plato in the *Contra Celsum* are frequent enough to indicate some esteem for his philosophy, but the praise is always tempered and the criticisms invariably presuppose the superior authority of the scriptures. For all that, there are passages in which he seems, without naming him, to take Plato's side on a question that continued to divide the pagan schools. Platonists, Aristotelians and Stoics had come to no consensus in the identification of cardinal virtues, but the same four whose priority is assumed to be axiomatic in the *Respublica* of Plato—wisdom, courage, temperance, and justice—furnish the scaffolding for the early chapters of Origen's *Exhortatio ad Martyrium*. Wisdom, according to Plato, is the virtue of the reasoning faculty, courage of spirit or *thumos,* temperance of the desiderative or epithumetic element, and justice of the entire soul in which spirit and desire are duly subordinate to reason (Plato, *Resp.* 449e; *Phaedr.* 246a–b). While Origen does not embrace this scheme in its entirety, he subscribes to this threefold anatomy of the inner man. Yet it is one thing to be a Platonist in psychology—a topic on which, as Origen himself avers, the apostles left few teachings (Origen, *Princ.* 1.5)—and another to read the articles of faith through an alien lens. When Origen plots the stages of deliverance from the mortal sphere, or finds in the human composite a model for his polyphonic interpretation of scripture (Origen, *Princ.* 2.11.6; 4.2.4), he does not appeal to Plato's anthropology but to the Pauline triad of body, soul, and spirit, which has no true antecedent in the Greek schools.

The equation of God with mind, in the *De Principiis* and elsewhere, is an innovation of Christian usage but a commonplace in the pagan thought of late antiquity. One might think of the second-century Platonist (or Pythagorean) Numenius, if there were more than inferential proof of Origen's acquaintance with his cosmogony (Origen, *Princ.* 1.1; Numenius, frg. 11 des Places 1973). At the same time, the tenet is one that an Aristotelian might have claimed as the shibboleth of his own school, whereas the characteristic name for the highest principle among Platonists (he might argue) is the Good, or perhaps the One. Again, it may be no more than a verbal preference that separates the Stoic identification of Zeus with Logos from the deification of *nous* in the older systems. Were it not for the Epicureans, who were polytheists and held that the gods were accurately portrayed in dreams and sculptures, it could be said that the philosophers were at one in regarding intellect as the essence of divinity. For those who could entertain the notion of incorporeal being, its familiar if unfathomable paradigm was intellect; for those who could not, the analogy held so long as God was credited with a hegemonic and providential function in the universe. That Origen did not surrender his judgment to any one school is evident from his occasional hints that *nous* falls short of God—a tenet that, if we insist upon the name of God, is anticipated only in Philo, another biblical philosopher. But even when he embraced the more quotidian theology, he embraced it as a Christian. With the majority of his co-religionists, he opined that there can be no resurrection on the last day unless an incorporeal soul survives to guarantee the identity of the self between embodiments; that God is mind—or something akin to mind, or something greater than mind—was then entailed by the putative demonstration of his incorporeality from the scriptures. Only a hidebound Christian would have resisted this deduction because some unbaptized philosopher had arrived at it before him.

Certain tenets, now outmoded and consequently chaperoned in academic literature by the names of those who first enunciated them or defended them most eloquently, had become quotidian maxims in Origen's time. Those who held that all material bodies were compounded from the four elements did not consider themselves Empedocleans or Aristotelians, any more than we consider ourselves Copernicans because we hold that the earth goes round the sun. Today one must be a "Platonist" (or a "Cartesian") to postulate the soul as a thinking subject in apposition to the body; in the ancient world, however, even those who held that the elements or particles of bodies also constitute the soul conceived the latter as something as something more than a congeries of somatic functions, and believed that this substantial entity either survives the body or is dispersed immediately in its hour of death. It would not have entered a Christian's head to question these assumptions merely because they were not peculiarly Christian. This is not to say that Christianity was incapable of autonomous speculation: it was indeed the merit of its apologists, and of Origen in particular, to show that certain platitudes, which had functioned as subliminal assumptions in all disputes between philosophical sects, were in fact contestable. One such presupposition was the plurality of gods (which remained compatible for all Greeks with the asseveration of one transcendent fountainhead of being). Another was the necessity of matter as a substrate for the corporeal, which Origen (whether or not he wrote the dialogue assigned to him at *Philocalia* 24)[3] certainly contests in the *De Principiis*.[4] He presses his objections tentatively, and hints that others before him had urged that this empty concept is in fact a concept of nothing; nevertheless, he is the first known author to say so much in a systematic treatise, and this observation suffices to show that his debt to the philosophers was that of a critic rather than a disciple.

3. Metaphrastic. Most common, in Origen as in other early Christian authors, is the metaphrastic substitution of Greek philosophical terms for the more homely or poetic idiom of the sacred text. Without such expedients it would have been impossible to preach the Word with vigor to the Gentiles. Even the plebeian style of Paul and the evangelists is not, like that of the Septuagint, a calque on the Hebrew and Aramaic of the elder scriptures, but a living tongue, informed by the practice (if not the formal teaching) of Greek rhetoric and employing terms that had no counterpart in the languages of Palestine. The apologists of the first three Christian centuries aimed not only to express the Gospel in their own vernacular, but to endow it with the clarity of an intellectual system. While some modern academics hold the strange view that subtlety, urbanity, and roundness of vision represent a cheapening of the Gospel, it was inevitable that thinkers of the early Church would adopt the philosopher's lexicon. To do otherwise was to confess themselves mere malcontents, for it was only the philosopher in the Roman world whose trade entitled him to harangue a multitude, abstain from marriage and mock the puerility of the civic cults. Philosophy gave a man the right to differ in antiquity, and the assumption of the cloak was thus at once a provocative and a protective measure, calculated to excite derision rather than persecution, except in cases where the populace was estranged or its governors openly defied.

Some technical locutions pass into general parlance; others retain indelible traces of their origin. Only a fraction of those who speak of "natural law" or "the common good" are acquainted with the history of these terms; few, on the other hand, would fail to associate Freud with the "Oedipus complex," Marx with the "dictatorship of the proletariat." Our knowledge of Greek conventions is for the most part insufficient to tell us when the coinage of a particular school passed into the intellectual vulgate. We may be certain that in Origen's day the expression *to eph' hêmin* (that which lies within our power) was common tender and could be used without reference to the deliberations of Aristotle or the Stoics.[5]

---

3. On the authorship see *The Philocalia of Origen*, the text revised with a critical introduction and indices by J. A. Robinson 1893, xl–xlix; Barnes 1979, 47–55; Harl 1983.

4. Origen, *Princ.* 4.4.7, though the existence of (created) matter seems to be assumed at Origen, *Princ.* 2.1.4.

5. See especially Origen, *Princ.* 3.1.1.

No doubt it would have been harder to detach the word *monas* from the Pythagoreans, but when Origen applied it to the Godhead he may have been conscious of a Christian precedent in Athenagoras.[6] It is an index of his sympathies that he also co-opts the noun *henas*, which was not in use outside the Pythagorean and Platonic schools; but the truth that it adumbrates, the ineffable oneness of the Godhead, was in Origen's view concealed from the Platonists by their own presumption.[7] Perhaps, then, the suitability of the term lies not so much in its pedigree as in its rarity, which excludes a mundane interpretation, hinting that the unity of material particulars is a poor approximation to that of God. The privatives which are freely bestowed on God in Origen's writings, as in those of his predecessors, are drawn predominantly from the philosophic schools, but never without some warrant in the sacred text. Even if God were not said at 1 Tim 6:16 to dwell in "invisible light," we should deduce his invisibility from the prohibition of images in the Decalogue. His timelessness is the necessary precondition of his infallibility in prediction, while his incorporeality is to be inferred from his indestructibility, as well as from his power of being everywhere and nowhere as he pleases. His impassibility is the guarantee that he cannot be coerced, seduced or baffled by another agent. If the Bible avers that God is faithful and steadfast in defence of his elect, philosophy underwrites these promises by showing that it is the characteristic of one who is truly divine to be free of change and trepidation. No more than his predecessors or contemporaries could Origen see that any harm accrued from a mode of speech that reinforced prophecy with proof and made it possible to say openly what God had communicated to a younger world in riddles.

4. Supplementary. The supplementary use of the pagan classics is the one that Origen himself commends in a latter to Gregory Thaumaturgus—the same disciple who informs us that Origen's syllabus in Caesarea commenced with an introduction to the chief philosophic schools.[8] The letter twins philology with philosophy—the first because the Spirit has elected to speak in a human tongue, the second because a peculiarly subtle understanding of the natural creation has been vouchsafed by this same Spirit to the Greeks. It is, of course, a principle of all modern exegesis that the obscurities of biblical Greek are amenable to the same tools that are deployed in the elucidation of pagan literature. On the other hand, the progress of the intellectual disciplines has superannuated every claim to infallibility—that of scripture no less than that of Aristotle—and professional commentators on the New Testament no longer assume that its authors were omniscient or subject the results of science and history to their arbitration. In

---

6. Origen, *Princ.* 1.1.6; Athenagoras, *Leg.* 6.2 (reporting Pythagoras with approval).

7. Origen, *Princ.* 1.1.6; Origen, *Cels.* 7.42.

8. Origen, *Philoc.* 13. Gregory's *Panegyrica* attests the propaedeutic use of Greek philosophy in the school of Origen.

Origen's time no Christian exegete could doubt that whatever can be known was already known, to the Spirit at least, at the time of composition; to his mind, the perfect commentator will be at once a philologist, who defines the semiological function of each term in the scriptures, and a philosopher, who identifies that real thing which the term signifies in the order of creation.

We have seen above that Origen does not lightly reject the consensus of the schools, though at the same time he does not think even such a common postulate as matter wholly immune to dubitation and refinement. When philosophers disagree, the Christian's choice between them will be determined by the evidence of the scriptures. Thus, when Origen has to construe the term ἐπιούσιος in the Lord's Prayer (which is generally agreed to mean "supersubstantial" in Greek sources, rather than "daily" or "for tomorrow," as in the west"), he inquires for other specimens of it in Greek literature, and having ascertained that there are none, decides for himself that the radical element *ousia* connotes existence rather than locomotion (Origen, *Or.* 3.7). He proceeds to ask which of the current significations of this noun has the stronger warrant in the Bible, and appears to aim for a middle course between those who affirm that nothing truly exists but the intelligible, in opposition to those who hold that all existence requires a material substrate.[9] These parties correspond to the gods and giants of Plato's *Sophist*, though the materialists have sometimes been identified as Stoics.[10] If Origen shows some bias towards the contrary view, this is not because he is a Platonist, but because this view is sanctioned by one Tutor from whom no Christian can appeal.

5. Strategic. A strategic use of precedents and analogues enables the Christian to say *tu quoque* to anyone who brings a charge of folly, turpitude or equivocation against his faith. Thus the shrewd apologist for the doctrine of the Trinity can say "you too believe in a *deuteros theos*," though this phrase does not appear in works intended only for Christians, and it seems to intimate not that Christ is inferior to the Father, but only that he is second in the order of revelation and ecclesiastical prayer.[11] Another trope, which the Church learned from Josephus, was to scoff at the dissensions of the schools and urge that only the certitude of inspiration can bring peace to this cacophony. Or one can maintain that the philosophers themselves are unwitting heralds of the Gospel: Clement's *Stromateis* is a compendious exercise in the demonstration of homologies between Greek and Christian thought. Origen's *Contra Celsum*, the earliest text to speak of Christ

---

9. Markschies 2007, 183–87. On Origen's refusal to wear a borrowed livery see Rist 1983, 228–38.

10. On the possibility that Origen used the lexicon of Herophilus see Cadious 1932, 271–85, with the animadversions of Markschies 2007, 175–83.

11. See Edwards 2006, 191–95. Justin quotes the pagan accusation that Christians grant a man second place to God at *1 Apol.* 13 and at 22 he likens the Word to Hermes, son of Zeus.

as *deuteros theos*,[12] acknowledges that a Christian will find much of his creed in Plato; characteristic of the same work, however, is a new strategy, the reprobation of pagan usages that other Christians might have assimilated to their own practice. The collection of Platonic affidavits to the truth of Christianity is only half of Origen's case; the other half consists in the demonstration that even such a man could err for want of the intellectual sureties that can be furnished only by a revelation from above.

Allegory was the palliative applied by generations of philosophers before Origen to the enormities of Greek myth, and in particular to the faults that Plato himself condemned in Homer. Similar arts had been employed to preserve the reader of the Old Testament from scandal and temptation, and the symbolic interpretation of the gnomic sayings attributed to Pythagoras was expressly adduced by Clement of Alexandria as a charter for his expulsion of anthropomorphisms from texts that speak of God (see , e.g., Clement, *Strom.* 5.11.67). Even where the plain meaning of the Septuagint was innocent, however, the mere fact that this was a book in which every syllable was held to be inspired supplied both matter and motive for readings that were neither literal nor prophylactic. Philo looked for a deeper sense in narratives that would otherwise have been veridical but not edifying; for Paul and the evangelists the Torah is a mine of elusive testimonies to the mission and reign of Christ. What we now call typology is in the main coterminous with the spiritual or mystical interpretation of scripture in Origen's writings for other Christians; this reading is withheld from pagan critics in the *Contra Celsum*, as though to intimate that neither the few anomalies in the sacred text nor the remedies for them are of a piece with those that exercise the apologist for Homer.[13] For the most part, he argues, even the veneer of scripture is evidently less dangerous to the soul than that of a Homer, a Hesiod or a Pherecydes; to sponge every fault from texts like these would be too long an endeavor, even if Platonists were not forced to admit the presence in their master's work of irredeemable blemishes, such as the paradoxical rape of Plenty by Poverty in the *Symposium*.[14] The Bible does not require cosmetics; the vices of the Greek canon will not bear them. It need hardly be said that anyone who styled himself a Platonist in Origen's day would have credited Plato's dialogues with an authority not far short of that which Origen accords to the impeccable and infallible word of God.

6. Catalytic. *Catalysis* occurs when a philosopher's resolution of his own difficulties is of no use to the Christian, in whose eyes the problem requires no answer

---

12. Origen, *Contra Celsum*. V 39; VI 61, where Origen seems to take up a locution from his adversary; cf. *heteros theos* at Origen, *Dial.* 1.25–33.

13. See Origen, *Cels.* 4.45 on the rape of Lot by his daughters; on pagan antecedents see Bendinelli 2005, 133–56.

14. Origen, *Cels.* 4.39, alluding to Plato, *Symp.* 203b–d.

or a different one, but makes it possible for the Christian to arrive at an analogous resolution of some problem which has arisen within his own system. A familiar example is the distinction which the Platonist Calvisius Taurus drew between two senses of the adjective *gen(n)êtos* in the *Timaeus*: the sense to which he awarded the double consonant implied a beginning in time, while he reserved the spelling *genêtos* for that state of mere contingency or dependence which can hold between an eternal object and its eternal cause (Dillon 1977, 242–44). To Christians, who believed that Plato and scripture concurred in assigning a temporal origin to the universe, this antithesis was redundant and sophistical; those, however, who found it necessary to differentiate the eternal Sonship of Christ from the creation of the world by fiat performed the same orthographic trick in a mirror by allotting the epithet *gennêtos* to the Son, or second person of the Trinity, reserving *genêtos* for his mortal handiwork (see further Stead 1964, 16–31; 1998, 671–84). Thus *gennêtos* signifies eternity to the Christian, temporality to the Platonist, and each attaches the opposite meaning to the term *genêtos*. The catalytic action of cosmology on Trinitarian doctrine is equally visible in the Arian tenet that both the Son and the world are "out of nothing," though in this case it was not the new doctrine but the negation of it that became dogma.

Such influence being by nature latent, unavowed and frequently unconscious, we cannot hope to discover incontestable signs of its presence in Origen. No doubt the most likely evidence—and our own judgment must be the measure of this likelihood—will be found in his exhibition of superfluous ingenuity when interpreting familiar texts from scripture. Few readers of Heb 1:3, where the Son is styled the radiance of the Father's power or *dynamis*, would reify this *dynamis* to produce a triad in which it sits between the first and second hypostases of the Trinity. Origen concludes, however, that Christ is a ray "not of God but of his glory [...] not of the Father, but of his power, an unsullied emanation of his almighty glory" (Origen, *Comm. Jo.* 13.25.153). In his times the closest analogue is not Christian: paternal intellect, *dynamis* and filial intellect form a ubiquitous triad in Porphyry's exposition of the *Chaldaean Oracles*. Augustine later attempted to baptize it by equating *dynamis* with the Holy Spirit,[15] but it is clear that Origen's aim is not to supplement a lacuna in the apostolic teaching, not to produce a strategic vindication of Christian doctrine from its pagan antecedents, and still less to augment the teaching of the apostles with an obsequious borrowing from profane philosophy. Had he not been required to gloss this one text from the New Testament, he would not have devised the triad; on the other hand, this gloss would perhaps have seemed as stilted to him as it does to us were he not aware of a precedent in Greek philosophy.

---

15. Augustine, *Civ.* 10.23–26, though this seems to me a disingenuous reading.

Origen's designation of the Father as *autotheos* (God in himself), in contradistinction to the Son who is *theos* only by derivation from the Father,[16] is perhaps another example of catalysis. This neologism (as it appears to be) is evidently modeled on such compounds as *autoanthropos* and *autohippos*, which in the usage of some Platonists denote the species or transcendent paradigms by virtue of which all entities of one kind possess the same essence.[17] Origen is not of their school, however, as he will not admit a plurality of referents for the term *theos* any more than for *autotheos;* the relation between the first god, the *autoagathos*, in Numenius and his second god, who is *agathos* by participation in the *autoagathos*, affords a closer parallel, though the substitution of adjective for noun may be no light matter. It is often held that Origen's nomenclature implies the subordination of the Son to the Father, making him a "second god" according to the parlance of such Platonists as Numenius.[18] But if he means no more than the attributes of the Son belong primordially to the Father—that the Son is what the Father is only because the Father is already what the Son is—he is merely the first to say what was afterwards strongly affirmed by all proponents of the Nicene Creed, including some who expressly denounced the subordination of any member of the Trinity. Eusebius of Caesarea, who inherited the term *autotheos* from Origen, put his name—with deliberation, but with no avowed reluctance—to the Nicene proclamation of Christ as "true God from true God."[19] A letter ascribed to Basil of Caesarea (and to the equally orthodox Gregory of Nyssa) explains that the Son is God, in the only sense that this term bears, because he owes his being and attributes entirely to the Father.[20] In Latin we find equivalents for the compound *autotheos* both in Arnobius, a writer of uncertain orthodoxy, and in Augustine, who is generally considered unimpeachable. The latter protests that "he himself was not the one who died on the Cross, since what is divine cannot succumb to death; the latter upbraids the Manichees for their worship of a God who permitted himself to be taken captive and dismembered.[21] Both passages imply that what can be predicated of God incarnate cannot be predicated of God himself; Origen treats the locution "God himself" as a synonym for God the Father because (as I hope to have shown elsewhere; Edwards 2002, 70–71.) his concept of the Son, even as a person of the Trinity, is seldom divorced from that of the human form that the Son was destined to assume.

7. Dialectical. We may speak of a dialectical engagement with philosophy when the Christian accepts that the defence of his faith requires him to acknowl-

---

16. Origen, *Comm. Jo.* 2.3.20, the Son being designated *autologos* in the same chapter.

17. See Aristotle, *Metaph.* Z.1040b33; cf. A.991a29

18. Numenius, frg. 16,8–9 = 57 des Places 1973.

19. Addendum to Athanasius, *Decr.* For *autotheos* see Eusebius, *Eccl. Theol.* 2.14.6 (Eusebius 4:115,16 Klostermann 1972), and on his use of the prefix auto see Strutwolf 1999, 162.

20. Basil, *Ep.* 38.6. On the authorship see Zachhuber 2003, 73–90.

21. Arnobius, *Adv. nat.* 1.62; Augustine, *Faust.* 5.4.

edge the validity of the questions in dispute between the schools, to frame his answers in terms already received among philosophers, to vindicate them according to recognized principles of argument and to meet without evasion whatever may be pertinently urged against them. This does not preclude an appeal to scriptural authority, provided that it is reinforced by arguments cogent enough to disarm proponents of any other revelation and the sceptics who deny the need of any. Nor does it preclude either the creation of new terms or the usurpation of old term in some other sense than the one conferred on it by his interlocutors: it is a common fallacy in modern scholarship to assume that whenever a Christian fails to mean by Plato's words what Plato meant by them, he betrays some defect of memory or intelligence. In speculation as in life, the philosopher was the servant of his own conscience. His profession obliged him to be at odds not only with lay members of society, not only with the patrons of other schools, but with the apologists and patriarchs of his own where he could not reconcile his eye to their perceptions. Of course there was some expectation of fidelity to a master, and if the master was Moses or Paul, the claim was absolute. The object of the Christian philosophers was to show that, even it had not been absolute, the truths conveyed through Moses and Paul would be irresistible to any mind that was not corrupted by a previous allegiance.

Such an adaptation of dogma to the canons of philosophy is evident in Origen's account of the tenuous body which preserves the saint's identity after death. In *Contra Celsum* he affirms the Pauline doctrine of a spiritual body, but his own thesis, as he expressed it in a more esoteric work *On the Resurrection* (*De resurrrectione*) is that the bodily form, or *eidos*, is translated to the soul. This appears to mean that the soul will acquire an envelope of subtler texture than the palpable body that we now wear, and more docile to the promptings of the illuminated spirit. This is not a logical or organic deduction from any biblical teaching, but we can point to its counterpart in the Platonism of late antiquity. Alcinous speaks for many when he states that it is the indefeasible function of soul to animate a body; since it was an axiom for the Platonists that "all soul is immortal," this tenet entailed that the soul must possess a vehicle that it continues to inhabit during periods of enfranchisement from the lower world. It could be argued that this vehicle is represented by the chariot of the soul in Plato's *Phaedrus*, or that this is the organic body of which the soul is said to be the *eidos* in Aristotle. Plutarch holds that soul in Hades carries a simulacrum of its discarded husk, while Porphyry, in his essay *On the Styx* (*De Styge*; frgs. 372F-380F Smith 442–61) asserts that the liberated soul will bear a congelation of memories into the next life, thus ensuring that it remains conscious of its past and recognizable to others until the next embodiment. While Origen could not agree that the body which accompanies the soul in its ascent to God will be such a morbid accretion, it is unlikely that he was ignorant of all Platonic thought on the retention of the soul's domicile after death, and if he admits these teachings into his system through a Christian filter, it cannot be said that their influence on him is merely catalytic.

It is in his speculations on the causes of the soul's union with the body that origin is most Platonic, though at the same time he is demonstrably innocent of the copybook Platonism that is foisted on him by ancient and modern critics. The topic is one on which Platonists and Christians were inevitably at cross-purposes, since the latter maintained that God grants only a single probation on earth to every soul. To reconcile the eternal consequences of this pilgrimage with the justice of an omnipotent Creator was no easier in antiquity than today, and it was only with the assistance of the Platonists that a Christian could elicit a theodicy from his own scriptures or arrive at a view on the culpability of the embodied soul. Desultory and abstruse as Origen's conjectures are, they won him global influence and enduring notoriety; for this reason alone they merit examination in some detail. The inquiry will also lead us from analysis to synthesis, since Origen himself offers no anatomy of his principles, but allows the dialectical relation to coalesce with the supplementary and the catalytic, deeming one shift as useful as another so long as it helps to redeem the silence of the text.

The Vicissitudes of a Young Soul

Whether the soul exists before its sojourn in the present world was to Origen's contemporaries a difficult question, not foreclosed by any scriptural text. There is one verse—John 9.2—which might be thought to attest a previous existence, for what could prompt the conjecture that the man born blind is expiating his own sin but the belief that we enter the present world with a private cargo of merits and demerits? Basilides, one of the more intrepid Christian thinkers in Alexandria before Origen, is said to have maintained this doctrine on two grounds[22]: it reveals some other cause for inequalities in the condition of souls at birth than the will of an arbitrary creator, and it accounts for the conjunction of a mature soul with an embryonic body in the womb. The first argument is Platonic, and Basilides goes so far with this school as to posit the transmigration of souls not only from body to body but from one species to another. The Platonists, on the other hand, were not of one mind regarding the ensoulment of the foetus, and Porphyry, who professes to represent the most authoritative tradition, holds that any appetitive motions that it exhibits are the product of *phantasia* or of energies inherited from the parent.[23] In the Roman world it was Christians alone

---

22. On the questionable evidence for his teachings see Löhr 1996, 121–45.

23. In Porphyry. *Gaur.* 37–46 Kalbfleisch, Porphyry argues (a) that the functions manifested by the embryo are only those of the nutritive soul, which is the only principle of life in plants; (b) that it may appear that the foetus is capable of responding to "phantastic" stimuli, but in fact these motions are communicated by the mother; (c) that *phantasia* cannot shape the constitution of the agent who experiences it, but it can enable that agent to shape the constitution of another being. At pp. 46–52, he adds (d) that before the act of procreation, the sperm is governed by the vegetative power of the father and by his higher soul and (e) that if a particular

who held abortion to be a sin tantamount to murder,[24] and who were therefore obliged, when the question came before them, to maintain that the soul in the womb is already mature. This point deserves attention because it shows that an apologist who was not a disciple of Basilides might have cause to defend the rationality of the embryo even when he was not advancing any doctrine of a life before the present one. I have argued elsewhere that Origen regards the exultation of John the Baptist in the womb as proof that the soul is endowed with reason at conception, not as evidence for a previous life.[25] John could not have served as a paradigm for discussion of the latter topic,[26] as the theories that he was Elijah or an angel were not wholly devoid of scriptural warrant, as Origen concedes.[27]

In his *Commentary on John* he denies that a soul can pass from one human tenement to another.[28] Commenting on Rom 7:9, he observes that if the sin that "revived" in Paul had been committed, as Basilides argued, in a previous life, this cannot have been the life of a brute, as creatures devoid of rational discernment are incapable of sin.[29] This principle that only a reasoning agent can be deemed

---

soul has an affinity with one body rather than another, this will be either a consequence of the "former life itself" or a corollary of the universal revolution that draws like to like. At pp. 52–58 he concludes (f) that if the sperm has a soul, it need not be rational, as the fecundity is the product of our irrational powers; and (g) that even if the sperm is the joint issue of the imaginative (phantastic) and vegetative powers, it does not follow that these powers are communicated by the foetus.

24. Tertullian, *An.* 25.2–3; 26; *Diogn.* 5,6; *Did.* 2,2; 5,2; *Barn.*19,5; Jones 2004.

25. Origen, *Princ.* 1.7.4 (= 5:90,3–20 Koetschau 1913). Si hominis anima, quae utique inferior est, dum hominis est anima, non cum corporibus ficta, sed proprie et extrinsecus probatur inserta, multo magis eorum animantium, quae caelestia designantur. Nam, quantum ad homines spectat, quomodo cum corpore simul ficta anima videbitur eius, qui "in ventre" fratrem suam subplantavit, "id est Jacob" [Gen 25,22.26]? Aut quomodo simul cum corpore ficta est anima vel plasmata eius, qui adhuc "in ventre matris suae positus, repletus est spiritu sancto" [Luke 1,41]? Iohannem dico "tripudiantem in matris utero," et magna se exultatione iactantem pro eo quod salutationis vox Mariae ad aures Elisabeth suae matris advenerat [...]. Et quomodo effugiemus illam vocem, qua ait : "Numquid iniustitia est apud deum? Absit!", vel illud: "Numquid personarum acceptio est apud deum? [Rom 9,14]."

26. At least not in Origen. But see Theodotus, as reported by Clement, *Exc.* 50: The elder said that that which is in the belly is a living thing. For the soul enters into the womb, having been prepared through cleansing for conception, and set apart by one of the angels who presides over generation, who knows before hand the time appointed for conception and prompts the mother to intercourse. And when the seed is deposited, the spirit in the seed is, as it were, assimilated and taken up into the process of formation.... And in the Gospel [Luke 1,41] "the child leapt," as being ensouled.

27. Origen, *Comm. Jo.* 6.11. On his repudiation of the view that the Baptist was an angel see Origen, *Comm. Jo.* 1.31(34); 1.31(25).

28. Origen, *Comm. Jo.* 1.11; 6.14. On Origen's rejection of transmigration see Kruger 1996, 117–26.

29. Origen, *Comm. Rom.* 6.8.1.21, though he does not name his enemy here.

guilty, when applied to the law commanding the execution of an ass that has lain with a woman, might indeed afford an argument for the perambulation of souls between different species, were it not that the church expressly prohibits this inference. Thus he rejects the teaching of the Platonists Plutarch, Porphyry, and Celsus, partly because the attribution of rationality to beasts belies experience, and partly because this doctrine is countermanded by an infallible authority. A Platonist might have answered that the first argument is false, the second unconscionable, and that Origen is consistent only in his determination to reason independently of the pagan schools.

Nevertheless, both ancient and modern authors have repeatedly imputed to Origen the Platonic doctrine that the soul was created to be incorporeal, and that it fell into its material envelope, and that it wears its material corset as a punishment for satiety, loss of ardor or willful insurrection.[30] As I hope to have shown elsewhere, the evidence for his having held these views is almost wholly derived from his enemies: if we excise from Koetschau's edition of the *De Principiis* all the avowedly loose, calumnious and periphrastic accounts of Origen's teaching that are offered as Greek correctives to the Latin of Rufinus, we will find that Origen does indeed cite inward refrigeration and satiety as causes of sin, but only in the present life;[31] that he does indeed believe that angels fall and that the saints will be the heirs to their lost estate, but does not expressly say that human beings in this world are fallen angels;[32] that he does indeed regard the world as a nursery in which punishments are laid up for sins foreseen as well as for those already committed, but not necessarily as a place of retribution for trespasses in heaven.[33] In an infamous passage Origen informs us that the soul of Christ, in contrast to every other, burnt with undiminished ardor for the Logos *ab initio creaturae*; yet whether this means "the beginning of all creation" or "the beginning of its creation" I at least cannot determine from the Latin.[34] A descent of souls from earth to the hand of God is clearly asserted, both in the *De Principiis* and in the *Commentary on Ephesians*;[35] this descent, however, is clearly not a fall, and nothing is said that the soul exists without a body for more than the instant which precedes its insufflation. The body that we now possess is said in other works to be grosser

---

30. On the obscurity of his teaching see Harl 1987, 238–58; Laporte 1995, 159–61.

31. As is clear from the conclusion of Origen, *Princ.* 1.4.1, that if our backsliding is arrested at an early stage, it is possible to return to our original state of knowledge and alertness.

32. Origen, *Princ.* 1.8.1–4 and Origen, *Hom. Cant.* 20,8.

33. See Edwards 2002, 105 on Origen, *Princ.* 2.9.6.

34. Origen, *Princ.* 2.6.3. Cf. Edwards 2002, 94.

35. Origen, *Princ.* 3.5.4; Origen's commentary on Eph 5.29 is handed down to us only in Latin by Jerome (PL 26.567c–568a; Corpus Christianorum. Series Latina 79, 27,16–32 Lardet. See also Heine 2000, 478–514.

than that of Adam in his state of innocence,[36] but this does not entail that he was created without a body, and we have Origen's own admission at *De Principiis* I,6,4 that he does not know how the identity of any being other than the persons of the Trinity can be sustained without a material substrate.[37] We cannot even be certain that the flesh which now envelopes us is a punitive afterthought rather than a proleptic remedy for the foreseen effects of sin as it is in the work of Gregory of Nyssa *De Opificio Hominis* (*On the Creation of Humanity*).[38]

What is eminently clear is that, while Origen takes the word *koros* or satiety from the Platonists, while he accepts their derivation of the term *psukhe* from the adjective *psukhros* ("cool"), and while he accepts some correlation between the gravity of an agent's sin and the crassitude of his body, his presuppositions are those of the church, and his difficulties arise from the attempt to harmonize scripture with scripture or scripture with experience. Even when he vacillates he will find a text to corroborate each position, and among his presuppositions are the descent of all humanity from one man and its universal redemption by another, neither of which a Platonist can entertain. How far he believed that any of his conclusions could be reconciled with those of the Platonists we can only guess, for his representation of their philosophy is schematic, seldom conscious of its varieties and often anachronistic. The view that the soul descends but does not fall—that its fall results from its becoming too enamored of its new medium and betraying the mind to the senses—may sit poorly with the myth in Plato's *Phaedrus*, but is a fair approximation to the teaching of both Porphyry and Plotinus.[39] If a question forced on Origen by the scriptures had already been engaging the fertile intellects of the Platonic school for more than half a millennium, he was no more likely to find an answer that they had not considered than to stumble upon a fifth point of the compass.

The most cogent of all the passages adduced to show that Origen posits a previous embodiment of the soul is his justification of God's preference for Jacob over Esau, his elder brother. His choice cannot be determined (Origen argues) by a capricious partiality, and we must therefore presume that the dispossession of

---

36. Origen, *Comm. Jo.* 20.182 appears to say that the body is the penalty of the fall, but perhaps emans only that the peccability of our present body is inherited from Adam. Prinzivalli 2005, 374–79, observes that both the fashioning of the body from the earth at Gen 2.7 and the pristine creation of Gen 1.26–28 precede the remedial stitching of the coats of skins at Gen 3.21. The making or poiêma of the first man is supervenes on the fall of Satan, which in turn presupposes the ktisis or creation of the intelligibles in the Word: e.g., Origen, *Princ.* 2.1.5.

37. Cf. Tzamalikos 2007, 59–63. On the vehicle that preserves the soul's identity after death see Schibli 1992, 381–91.

38. See especially Gregory of Nyssa, *Opif. hom.* 15–18.

39. Augustine, *Civ.* 10.30 (satirically); Rist 1967, 121–45.

Esau was a penalty for his sin in a "former life."[40] This is pure Platonism, if we join the majority of commentators in taking "former life" to mean life in a different body, rather than a past episode of the same life, as when Paul speaks of his "former conversation." But if that is the sense, it fails to explain why God did not award the birthright to Jacob simply by making him the first to leave Rachel's womb. Rabbinic casuists urged that the wrong for which Esau suffers must have been committed between conception and birth: he was said to have been an idolater by instinct, who was always propelling his mother into foreign shrines, or else (in a story patently designed to annul his claim to primogeniture) to have threatened to cause her death if he were not the firstborn of the twins.[41] We cannot prove that Origen knew or would have endorsed such fables, but we have seen above—that he felt obliged, as a spokesman for the Church, to maintain the presence of a rational soul in the embryo. If it is uterine sin[42] that he attributes to Esau, Origen is reasoning not only independently of the Platonists, but against their view that the foetus is irrational, and hence not capable of a personal sin. If his meaning is that Esau was expiating a trespass committed in some previous body, he has turned to Platonism for the amelioration of difficulties that would not have troubled him but for his belief in the infallibility of a barbarous text.

---

40. Origen, *Princ.* 2.9.7 (171,3–8 Koetschau 1913): Igitur sicut de Esau et Iacob diligentius perscrutatis scripturis invenitur quia non est "iniustitia apud deum" [Rom 9,14], ut "antequam nascerentur vel agerent aliquid" [Rom 9,11], in hac scilicet vita, diceretur quia "maior serviete minori" [Rom 9,12], et ut invenitur non esse "iniustitia" quod et "in ventre fratrem suum supplantait Iacob," si ex praecedentis videlicet vitae meritis digne eum "dilectum esse" sentiamus a deo [proceeds to argue that celestial creatures are assigned to offices commensurate with their merit or demerit].

41. Ginzberg 1909, 313: "They strove to kill each other. If Rebekah walked in the vicinity of a temple erected to idols, Esau moved in her body, and if she passed a synagogue, Jacob essayed to break forth from her womb. The quarrels of the children turned upon such differences as these. Esau would insist that there was no life except the earthly life of material pleasures, and Jacob would reply 'my brother, there are two worlds before us [...]. If it please thee, do thou take this world, and I will take the other.' [...] Even the quarrel between the two brothers regarding the birthright had its beginning before they emerged from the womb of their mother. Each desired to be the first to come into the world. It was only when Esau threatened to carry his point at the expense of his mother's life that Jacob gave way."

42. See further Urbach 1979, 220, citing *Genesis Rabbah* 34,10.4. "Antoninus asked Rabbi, 'At which stage is the evil inclination instilled in man?' He replied 'from the moment that he is formed.' Thereupon (Antoninus) said to him, 'If so, it (the embryo) would dig its way from the mother's womb and go forth. The answer must therefore be when the soul had gone forth.' Rabbi admitted to him that his view was in accord with that of the Bible [...]. He further inquired, 'At which stage is the soul instilled in man?' Said Rabbi to him, 'As soon a sit leaves its mother's womb.' He replied, 'Leave meat without salt for there days: will it not become putrid? The answer must be: from the moment that he (the child) is commanded (to come into existence).' And Rabbi admitted to him that scripture also supports him." Cf. Urbach 1979, 243.

There is, then, nothing obsequious, nothing that would justify our labeling a Platonist, in Origen's speculations on the soul's history before the present life. They may be called supplementary in so far as they illuminate such texts as "Jacob I loved, but Esau have I hated": but even if he does not conceive the soul's pre-existence merely as a sentient life in the womb, he differs from the Platonists[43] in assuming that it entails such a life; he differs again from them, and from his Christian precursors, in denying any previous embodiment of the soul in the present world. The doctrine that he holds is designed to explain the inequalities of our one embodied life without recourse to any notion of transmigration, and thus stands in a dialectical relation to the philosophies of the schools, which, as a spokesman for the Church and God, he undertakes to conquer by a new philosophy.

Concluding Remarks

Whom should we call a Platonist? In antiquity he was one who, in contradistinction to the Stoics and Epicureans, maintained the reality of the incorporeal and the providential government of the cosmos; who, in contradistinction to Aristotle, held that the soul cannot die and that the Form subsists eternally, transcending the material particular; who, in contradistinction to the Pythagoreans, believed the Forms to be more primordial than number. In contradistinction to Christians (when he had heard of them), he denied that God can will or perpend an object that is not eternally necessitated, or that a book can be a source of infallible knowledge that could not have been attained by independent reasoning. He might agree with a Christian that the One is God (though not that God is one), and that the soul lives for ever (though Christians would not say that it is naturally immortal). But a Christian, even if he was aware that the Platonists held them, held these tenets on other authority than Plato's.

There is a moribund controversy regarding Origen's Greek tutors, which I do not propose to revive here.[44] That he was not the same Origen who studied with Plotinus under Ammonius Saccas has always been agreed among classical scholars, if only because the Christian Origen was forty-seven years old in 232 when Plotinus became a disciple of Ammonius. That there were two scholarchs of eminence named Ammonius is certain, and I do not know how to ascertain which, if either, was Origen's mentor in philosophy. For our purpose the question is of no great consequence, for Platonists and Aristotelians often held the same views and held that those of their founders were, for the most part, reconcilable. Unless he was a Christian (as Eusebius contends) the creed of Ammonius was not that

---

43. Alcinous, *Intr.* 25.6 assumes what Porphyry sets out to demonstrate, viz. that the body receives a rational soul after parturition.

44. For bibliography see Edwards 1993, 1–13.

of his pupil; the description of the latter as a Platonist is tenable only if we add the rider that he never appeals to Plato as an oracle, that (like Justin) he preferred the way of the book to the way of introspective ratiocination, and that where his opinions coincide with those of a contemporary Platonist, this may be an occasion when it is impossible to differ from one without cleaving to another. It would be as unjust to suppose that when he made use of philosophical ideas he stole them raw and added nothing. The true philosopher demonstrates his autonomy neither by robbing his predecessors nor by shunning them: he waters what they have planted in the hope of nurturing seed for other soils.

14

Plato's *Parmenides* among the Cappadocian Fathers: The Problem of a Possible Influence or the Meaning of a Lack?

Jean Reynard

Far from what one can see among contemporary Neoplatonic philosophers, it seems *a priori* difficult to find a direct influence of Plato's *Parmenides* in the writings of the Cappadocian Fathers. First, my paper will focus particularly on Gregory of Nyssa, who is rightly considered the most profoundly influenced by Plato and Neo-platonic interpretations. There is no explicit quotation of the dialogue in his works, but some themes exhibit a possible link with certain of its passages: for example, the spiritual ubiquity of God, participation as resemblance, or the impossibility of giving a name or definition of the first principle. But, whether the influence of this dialogue is direct or indirect seems difficult to say. Only a precise inquiry will allow one to confirm actual borrowings from the dialogue that are not merely general notions inherited from the Platonic tradition, and to indicate the possible influence of Neoplatonic references to the dialogue on Gregory.

I. An Influence on Gregory of Nyssa?

Since the dialogue is separated into two parts, the possible influence of the *Parmenides* will be examined in terms of the notion of participation and the problems it implies, and in terms of the elaboration of the hypotheses and of their Neoplatonic interpretations. The problem of participation is the center of the first part of the dialogue. For Gregory, this theme is related to the problem of the relationship between human nature and God, between the human individual and humanity, and between divine hypostases and the divine nature.

For a Christian, the first reason for the relationship between divinity and human being is the creation of man by God according to his image. It is a favorite topic of Gregory that, because the creature is similar to the creator, she can participate in him. It's not far from Plato, who associates participation and resemblance: participation can be spoken of also in terms of resemblance, according to *Parmenides* 132d: ἡ μέθεξις ... τῶν εἰδῶν οὐκ ἄλλη τις ἢ εἰκασθῆναι. Like Plato, Gregory employs the language of the doctrine of ideas and participation in intelligible reality: all the universe remains in a state of being, in the goodness that grants the power of becoming and of permanent being.[1] Being is sustained in being by virtue of its participation in goodness and in God. This passage can be compared to *Parm.* 130c–d. Gregory too considers this problem as an aporia: "How they can say that the intellective, immaterial and invisible (τὴν νοεράν τε καὶ ἄϋλον καὶ ἀειδῆ) nature, penetrating the humid, the soft, the warm and the solid, keeps beings in being (ἐν τῷ εἶναι συνέχειν τὰ ὄντα), whereas it has no relationship with those in which it takes place and is not unable, by its heterogeneity, to be in them?" (*An. res.* 24C; cf. *Parm.* 137e). Gregory discusses also in the same terms the concept of participation. For example, when he discusses the Beatitude: "Blessed are the poor in spirit, for theirs is the kingdom of the heavens," he opposes earthly wealth and spiritual wealth, which can be shared without diminution like the sun:

> The division of virtue (τῆς ἀρετῆς ἡ διαίρεσις) is like that: it is divided (διαμερίζεσθαι) between all those who work for it, and is there entire for every one (πᾶσαν ἑκάστῳ παρεῖναι), not diminished by being shared with the other participants (μὴ ἐλαττουμένην ἐν τοῖς συμμετέχουσιν). In the distribution of earthly wealth a person wrongs those entitled to an equal part (τοὺς ἰσομοιροῦντας) if he grabs too much for himself; he is sure to reduce (ἐλαττοῖ) the share of his partner (τὸ μέρος τοῦ συμμετέχοντος) if he increases his own. Spiritual wealth however behaves like the sun, sharing itself (ἑαυτὸν μερίζων) between all those who see it, and at the same time totally available to all (ὅλος ἑκάστῳ παραγινόμενος). Since then each has an equal hope of reward for his toil, let us all work equally together by our prayers towards our goal." (*Hom. Beat.* 1)

This passage shows links with *Parm.* 131b (ἓν ἄρα ὂν καὶ ταὐτὸν ἐν πολλοῖς χωρὶς οὖσιν ὅλον ἅμα ἐνέσται) where the image of the day is used—it recalls also the sun of *Resp.* 7, which is not diminished by those who partake of it—it

---

1. "The universe (τὸ πᾶν) is a continuous whole (συνεχὲς ἑαυτῷ) and the bond of reality (ἡ ἁρμονία τῶν ὄντων) admits no break (λύσιν); there is a sympathy (σύμπνοια) of all things with each other. The whole is not released (ἀπέσχισται) from connection (συναφείας) with itself, but all things stay in being (ἐν τῷ εἶναι) because they are held fast (περικρατούμενα) by the power of what really is (τοῦ ὄντως ὄντος)... This good, then, surely more than good (τοῦτο τὸ ἀγαθὸν ἤτοι ὑπὲρ τὸ ἀγαθόν) itself truly is and through itself has given and still gives power to existing things (τοῖς οὖσι) to come into being (τὴν τοῦ γενέσθαι δύναμιν), and continuance in being (τὴν ἐν τῷ εἶναι διαμονήν); but everything which is thought of (θεωρούμενον) as outside it, is unreality (ἀνυπαρξία); for what is outside what is, is not in being" (*Hom. Eccl.* 7.7).

is always the same even if it exists in several places at the same time. The expression (ὅλος ἑκάστῳ παραγινόμενος) is remarkable. It echoes the problem of the unity of the two natures of Christ who, in his glory, is omnipresent, is everywhere (ἀπερίγραπτος, πανταχοῦ ὤν) by being one with God: "The name of his humanity was Jesus. His divine nature, however, cannot be expressed (ἀπερίληπτος) by a name, but the two became one through their co-mingling (ἓν δὲ τὰ δύο διὰ τῆς ἀνακράσεως)."[2] We can compare this with Basil who writes about the Holy Spirit:[3] ὅλον ἑκάστῳ παρὸν καὶ ὅλον ἁπανταχοῦ ὄν. These expressions are inspired by the Platonic tradition, especially *Parmenides* 144c: πρὸς ἅπαντι ἑκάστῳ τῷ τῆς οὐσίας μέρει πρόσεστιν τὸ ἕν, οὐκ ἀπολειπόμενον οὔτε σμικροτέρου οὔτε μείζονος μέρους and 144d ἓν ὂν πολλαχοῦ ἅμα ὅλον ἐστι, but they are probably indirectly transmitted through Plotinus's *Enneads* and the philosophical tradition.

In his theological writings, when he discusses the unity of the divine nature and the plurality of hypostases, Gregory refers not to the *Parmenides* specifically, but, more generally, to Platonic discussions about the one and the many. He distinguishes the divine nature as being one and the three hypostases as being plural and he explains the unity of God and the plurality of the Trinity by the singular term "man" and the plural "individual men." First, he insists on the unity of the divine nature: "The nature is one, united in itself, a monad completely indivisible (ἀδιάτμητος), not increased by addition, nor diminished by subtraction (δι' ὑφαιρέσεως), but in what it is, it is one (ὅπερ ἐστὶν ἓν οὖσα) and remains one even if it is seen in a multitude. It is indivisible (ἄσχιστος), continuous, and complete (ὁλόκληρος), and not divided (συνδιαιρουμένη) alongside the particulars who participate (τοῖς μετέχουσιν) in it" (*Ad Abl.* 41.1–2). This unity is affirmed against the plurality of the physical world, since Gregory refers to the concept of multitude and assigns it to the phenomenal world: "Is only counted that which is considered in a particular circumscription. That which is not circumscribed is not counted and what is not counted cannot be considered in plurality"; for example, "we can say that gold is one, even if it can be divided in a plurality of coins (κἂν εἰς πολλοὺς διακερματίζηται τύπους, ἕνα καὶ εἶναι καὶ λέγεσθαι)" (*Ad Abl.* 53.9–10). It can be seen as a reminiscence of *Parmenides* 144d: ἄλλως οὐδαμῶς ἅμα ἅπασι τοῖς τῆς οὐσίας μέρεσιν παρέσται ἢ μεμερισμένον and 144e: τὸ ἓν αὐτὸ κεκερματισμένον ὑπὸ τῆς οὐσίας πολλά τε καὶ ἄπειρα τὸ πλῆθός ἐστιν (the one itself divided by being is an infinite plurality).[4] In the eighth hypothesis of the dialogue too, the other is conceived under the concept of the manifold and any quantum (ὄγκος) of it is an indeterminate manifold: the difference is among

---

2. *Antirrh.* 161.17.
3. *Spir. s.* 9.22.
4. See Cherniss 1930, 80, n. 33. Cf. also *Ad Abl.* 53.20: "The gold is said to be plural when it is considered in a quantum (πόλυς λέγεται ὅταν ἐν ὄγκῳ πλείονι θεωρῆται)." It is the property of physical nature to be divided in a plurality (*An. res.* 48.25).

itself and the result is an infinite plurality. It follows that everything that is and that we can posit in thought will necessarily crumble and break up, for it can only be taken as a mass without unity, cf. Parmenides 165b: θρύπτεσθαι δὴ οἶμαι κερματιζόμενον ἀνάγκη πᾶν τὸ ὄν, ὃ ἄν τις λάβῃ τῇ διανοίᾳ· ὄγκος γάρ που ἄνευ ἑνὸς ἀεὶ λαμβάνοιτ᾽ ἄν.[5]

Gregory explains the paradox that God as real being is at once one and many by the words "man" and "men." According to his analysis, all human beings are one substance, which is man: Peter is a man, Paul is a man. When we say they are men, we speak wrongly, by a catachrèsis: they are one man and according to the essence "man," they cannot be many for "the same in itself can't be one and plural" (*Graec.* 25.19). The use of the plural refers not to the nature of humanity, but to the individual and different characteristics of those who partake of the same nature. This theme too is close to the theory of Platonic Forms in the Parmenides where the question is: Is it possible to admit an Idea of man separate of the totality of empirical men and, more generally, the existence of Ideas for the other concrete individuals? Socrates wonders whether one may suppose a Form in itself of man, separate from us, of all men—*Parm.* 130c: ἀνθρώπου εἶδος χωρὶς ἡμῶν καὶ τῶν οἷοι ἡμεῖς ἐσμεν πάντων, αὐτό τι εἶδος ἀνθρώπου—by taking part in the Form Man, an eponymic Form, a single individual receiving the name man (*Parm.* 130e). This is also a problem of language, and Gregory proposes a similar analysis about the creation of Adam.[6] The problem is presented in *Ep.* 38: "For he who says "man" produces in the ear a somewhat scattered notion (ἐσκεδασμένην τινὰ διάνοιαν) on account of the indefiniteness of its signification, so that the nature is indicated from the name, but the subsisting thing (τὸ ὑφεστὸς πρᾶγμα), which is specifically indicated by the name, is not signified." The name directs our thoughts to a multiplicity of objects. The universal term "man" indicates the totality of human individuals. Its relation to the individual thing is that of a whole to its parts. The proper name is thought to separate the notion of an individual from that of a whole that the universal name conveys.[7] And by means of the

---

5. Plato compares this process to dreams that disappear and crumble and to the perspective in a drawing: for a distant spectator, everything appears one, identical and equal in quality, but when he steps up close, it will appear to be various and unequal: the unity constantly crumbles (*Parm.* 164d; 165c). But Gregory doesn't seem to use this image.

6. "When the word says that God made man it points out on account of the indefiniteness of its signification the entire human item. For the name Adam is not used here for the creature as the history says in the following; but the name given to the created man is not the individual (ὁ τις) but the universal one (ὁ καθόλου)" (*Opif. hom.* 185.16).

7. Cf. *Ep.* 38.2.19: "If now of two or more who are man in the same way, like Paul and Silas and Timothy, an account of the *ousia* of men is sought, one will not give one account of the *ousia* of Peter, another one of Silas and again another one of Timothy; but by whatever terms the *ousia* of Paul is shown, these same will fit the others as well. And those are *homoousioi* to

hypostasis,[8] he obtains a concrete idea of one individual thing including both its individual and its specific properties, a principle of individuation. Both the identity and unity of the individuals are safeguarded by the underlying unity of *ousia*, which is one in many. Therefore, *ousia* is one in the entire nature, yet whole in each individual. Even if it is necessary to introduce *ousia* as a further item beyond the hypostaseis, according to the Platonic approach to the problem of universals, the idea or form would be an independently subsisting entity in which individuals participate; and Plato in the Parmenides shows the problems that arise when one gives forms ontological priority over particular being. Gregory proposes an original view, considering the *ousia* is immanent in the individuals (Zachhuber 2000, 80). In spite of different developments and conclusions in another theological context, the Parmenides can be considered as the background for a part of these discussions.[9]

The speculation on being and not-being, the one and plurality, conceived as a development of the first part, constitutes the second part of the dialogue. A few themes can be presented as attesting a possible influence. For instance, there is the problem of the lie defined as representation of that which is not. H. Cherniss (1930, 87 n. 11) has shown that Gregory defines truth and falsehood in Platonic terms and establishes a parallel between his definition of the lie (ψεῦδος γάρ ἐστι φαντασία τις περὶ τὸ μὴ ὂν ἐγγινομένη) and that of *Parmenides* 166a (οὐδ᾽ ἄρα δόξα τοῦ μὴ ὄντος παρὰ τοῖς ἄλλοις ἐστὶν οὐδέ τι φάντασμα), where Plato says among other things that there is neither opinion nor representation of that which is not. If Gregory is hinting at this passage, he interprets it both in a moral and ontological way: "The knowledge of that which is (ἡ τοῦ ὄνος ἐπίγνωσις) purifies of the opinion about that which is not (τῆς περὶ τὸ μὴ ὂν ὑπολήψεως). In my opinion the definition (ὁρισμός) of truth is being free from error about the perception of reality (τὸ μὴ διαψευσθῆναι τῆς τοῦ ὄντος κατανοήσεως). A lie is a representation in the soul about what is unreal (ψεῦδος γάρ ἐστι φαντασία τις περὶ τὸ μὴ ὂν ἐγγινομένη), which suggests that what does not exist (τοῦ μὴ ὑπάρχοντος) in fact exists. Truth, on the other hand, is a firm perception (κατανόησις) of what really is. So anybody who has thought (ἐμφιλοσοφήσας) at

---

each other, who are described by the same formula of being." I follow here the commentary of Zachhuber (2000, 61–62).

8. "This then is *hupostasis*. It is not the indefinite notion of *ousia*, which finds no stability on account of the community of what is signified. It is that notion which sets before the mind a circumscription in one aspect of what is common and uncircumscribed by means of such properties as are seen with it" (*Ep.* 38.3.8).

9. Zachhuber in his study on the concept of human nature in Gregory of Nyssa can conclude: "In the trinitarian context, the item responsible for the unity of humanity was a kind of immanent form – in the *Epistle* 38, it was referred to as *ousia*. Its philosophical background is constituted by a fusion of Platonic, Aristotelian and Stoic notions of immanent forms or universal qualities" (2000, 151).

leisure in such high meditations will gradually perceive (κατανοήσει) what being (τὸ ὄν) really is, which has being of its own nature, and what non-being (τὸ μὴ ὄν) is, which exists only apparently (ἐν τῷ δοκεῖν εἶναι), without any substantial nature of his own (ἀνυπόστατον ἐφ' ἑαυτοῦ τὴν φύσιν)" (*Vit. Moys.* 2.22–24.). We can see here the traditional Platonic opposition between reality and being on the one hand, and appearance and illusion on the other, with a possible allusion to the *Parmenides*. These reflections are inspired by Gregory's meditation on Moses's experience of theophany. This experience was an experience of real being, not of the One beyond the being, but the being who exists without participation in Being in the sense that he is self sufficient whereas all others depend on him: "Neither those things grasped by senses nor those that the mind can contemplate have a real (τῷ ὄντι) existence, except the substance that is above all things (τῆς ὑπερανεστώσης οὐσίας), the cause of the All on which the All (τὸ πᾶν) depends (ἐξῆπται). Whatever else the intelligence (διάνοια) sees in existing things, in none of these does the *logos* discover (ἐνθεωρεῖ) the self-sufficiency (τὸ ἀπροσδεές) that enables it to exist without participation in being (δίχα τῆς μετουσίας τοῦ ὄντος). Always to exist in the same way (ὡσαύτως), never to be increased and never to be diminished (τὸ ἀναυξές, τὸ ἀμείωτον), to be totally beyond all change (πρὸς πᾶσαν μεταβολὴν ἀκίνητον), whether it be for the better or the worse ... to be participated in by all, yet to be in no way thereby diminished (παρὰ παντὸς μετεχόμενον καὶ ἐν τῇ μετουσίᾳ τῶν μετεχόντων οὐκ ἐλαττούμενον), that is truly the real being." In spite of evident differences, this text offers parallels with the characteristics of the One of the first hypothesis, particularly in the negative terminology employed.

The Negative Theology

The Cappadocians developed negative theology in response to the Eunomian conception of divinity. They reject Eunomius's doctrine of subordinationism and the conception that the idea of being ungenerated would be the correct and only conceptual expression of the divine substance. Against this, they affirm that the divine being is necessarily unknowable and there is no adequate conception by which his substance may be understood. According to Eunomius, there is an identity between the divine substance and the vocabulary used to define it: it is the word "unbegotten" (ἀγέννητος). God remains ἀγέννητος, whether humans call him such or not, and language provides a picture entirely faithful to reality: οὐσία and προσηγορία are the same; there is a close relationship between reality and language. The Cappadocian response is that a concept like *agennētos* applies not to the substance, but to the process of understanding (διάνοια, ἐπίνοια), which operates between the thought and the articulated word.[10] All these expres-

---

10. According to Basil, "every theological expression is inferior to the thought of the

sions of negative theology are situated in the tradition of Plato, who asserts that the good in itself can't be known (cf. *Parm*. 134b: ἄγνωστον ἡμῖν ἐστὶ καὶ αὐτὸ τὸ καλὸν ὅ ἐστι καὶ τὸ ἀγαθόν). Gregory amplifies this theme: "What really is, is goodness itself (αὐτοαγαθότης), or whatever name beyond this one conceives (ἐπινοεῖ) to denote (σημαντικόν) the indescribable nature (τῆς ἀφράστου φύσεως). How could anyone find a name for that which the divine voice of the Apostle says is "above every name" (Phil 2:9)? However, whatever word is actually found to explain (ἑρμηνευτικόν) the inexpressible (ἀνεκφωνήτου) power and nature, such a denotation is certainly good" (*Hom. Eccl.* 7.7; on Eccl. 3:7). The affirmation that the Good is ineffable can also be partly inspired by *Parmenides* 142a: no name, no definition, no science or opinion can be predicated of the one.[11] Gregory strongly insists on the transcendence of God, not only in his theological discussions, but also in his spiritual commentaries.[12] In order to understand the reasons for this inaccessibility, one must hold in mind the opposition between creator and creature, an opposition that is linked to Gregory's conception of movement.

The Idea of Movement

Gregory distinguishes two types of movement: translation (τοπικὴ μετάστασις) and alteration (ἀλλοίωσις, τροπή).[13] These two movements exist in the creation: the heaven is subject to translation, not to alteration, whereas the earth is motionless, but not without alteration. On the contrary, for the divinity, both movement (as translation) and alteration are excluded: οὐ θεότητος ὑπόληψιν σχοίη ὅπερ ἂν κινούμενον ἢ ἀλλοιούμενον τύχῃ. One of the most important themes of Gregory's thought is the total opposition between the immutability of God and the mutability of the creature. In the divine nature, itself separated in three hypostases, unity is preserved and the Father stays the same, immutable in his identity as Father, without alteration.[14] Already Plato, when he develops the implications

---

speaker, speech is naturally too weak a thing to serve perfectly the conceptions of our minds" (*Ep.* 7.C1). Whereas according to Eunomius the concept of "unbegotten" would be the adequate formulation of the divine substance, it is by his very silence that one gives honor to the mysteries of the Trinity (σιωπῇ τιμάσθω).

11. Between Plato and the Cappadocians, Clement of Alexandria already develops this theme, cf. Hägg 2006, 212–13, 260–68.

12. Cf. *Vit. Moys.* 2.234–35: "Since it is the special character of the divine nature to lie above all definition, whoever supposes that God is one of the things he knows, is himself without life, having turned aside from the real being to what is supposed to be grasped by a concept. For the real being is inaccessible to our understanding."

13. *Opif. hom.* 129.38. See Dolidze 2000, 428–29, 442.

14. Cf. *Ad Abl.* 55: "If the nature of the holy Trinity was altered (παρήλλακτο), there would be a plurality of gods and of essence (τὴν κατ' οὐσίαν ἑτερότητα), the divine nature would not

of the first hypothesis, presents the same two movements—translation being also defined as a circular rotation (*Parm.* 138c)—and explains that the one has neither movement nor alteration. It is not impossible to admit here that Gregory has the *Parmenides* in mind, but the argumentation is different: Gregory's theological point of view, which insists on the immutability of the divinity contrasts with the Platonic philosophical assumption that unity excludes parts and whole and the radical conclusion that the first one is neither motionless nor moved. On the other hand, this question of movement and of its contrary can be referred also to some paradoxical developments we find in the two authors. The second hypothesis shows that the one who is is necessarily moved and motionless. It results logically from the fact that, if the whole is not in itself in so far as it is not enclosed in its parts, it must be in an other. The conclusion is *Parmenides* 145e: ἀνάγκη καὶ κινεῖσθαι καὶ ἑστάναι. Far from this logical argumentation, but in the same terms, Gregory describes Moses, who can't see God face to face, but only his back part, and applies to him the paradox of movement that is also immobility: "'I will station you upon the rock': this is the greatest paradox of all, that the same thing is both stationary and on the move (τοῦτο δὲ τὸ πάντων παραδοξότατον πῶς τὸ αὐτὸ καὶ στάσις ἐστὶ καὶ κίνησις). For normally he who ascends never stays still, while he who stands still does not ascend. Yet, in this case, it is precisely through being still that the ascent occurs. The meaning of this is that the more firm and immoveable a person is in the good, so much the more does he accomplish the race of virtue" (*Vit. Moys.* 2.243-244). Since Moses is for Gregory not a simple man searching for God, but a figure who announces Christ, he can represent the Logos and, by consequence, he corresponds to the one of the second hypothesis who assumes the paradox of movement and immobility. Nevertheless, the important point is the transformation by Gregory of the logical argumentation in a mystical paradox of the soul's progress towards God, which results from the infinity of God.

The Infinity of God

It appears that Gregory, by his insistence on the idea of assimilation to God as an infinite process, stands in the Platonic tradition of *Parmenides*-interpretation: "Moses is instructed that the divine is itself infinite (ἀόριστον), circumscribed by no limit.... Whatever has a limit has a boundary.... If the divine were thought to have a boundary, this would imply the existence of a limit distinct in character from himself, and our arguments have shown that whatever limits is greater than that which it limits" (*Vit. Moys.* 2.236). According to the first hypothesis, the One has neither beginning nor end, nor limit; it is unlimited (*Parm.* 137d). According to Gregory too, the divine has no beginning or end, being unlimited

---

be simple and immutable (ἁπλῆ καὶ ἀναλλοίωτος)."

by temporal intervals like creatures, such that it is impossible to pass through it from side to side and to grasp it. Gregory's conception of infinity appears different from the classical, Platonic, or Aristotelian, point of view, as Mühlenberg has shown (1966). He conceived the infinity of God not only as the limit of human knowledge, but, in a positive sense, as the essence of divinity itself. Goodness in itself has no bounds because it could be bounded only by its opposite, just as strength is limited only by weakness; therefore, the nature of God, being in no way confined by the opposite of goodness, must be infinite. When Gregory discusses the conception of God as unlimited, he does not refer specifically to the *Parmenides*.[15]

In conclusion, it is difficult to find explicit references to the *Parmenides* in Gregory. In a few passages we can suppose an inspiration, yet this remains hypothetical. The themes that could have inspired Gregory of Nyssa are the following:

- The Parmenidean question of participation and resemblance in relation to the question of the relationship of human beings and God, the question of the unity of God and the plurality of hypostases, and also the double nature of Christ. In all his discussions, Gregory refers not to the *Parmenides* specifically, but to the Platonic tradition in general, particularly the theory of Platonic Forms. Although Cherniss has quoted the *Parmenides* as a possible source of inspiration for Gregory, the examples are very general and not completely convincing.

- The other theme is the negative theology: the Cappadocians are well known as promoters of this negative theology in continuity with Philo's thought. The apophatic dimension of the dialogue might be congruent with their preoccupations when they defend against Neo-arianism the idea that God is uncircumscribed and unattainable by concepts. The famous expressions that described the One of the first hypothesis could support their arguments;[16] nevertheless, when Gregory presents the same idea, he doesn't employ the same expressions, even if some terms can be compared. For example, he speaks about "that which is without form, definition, greatness and quantity (τοῦ ἀσχηματίστου καὶ ἀορίστου καὶ ἀμεγέθους καὶ ἀπόσου), I mean the

---

15. In order to conclude this development on the possible influence of *Parmenides* on Gregory's spiritual speculations, I merely mention the concept of contact that plays a role in both. The simple one of the first hypothesis who has no parts cannot have contacts with others (*Parm.* 138a). The one of the second hypothesis could have contacts with himself and with the others, cf. *Parm.* 148e: τῶν ἄλλων ἅπτοιτο ἄν ... αὐτοῦ ἅπτοιτο ἄν. In fact he has contact and no contact (*Parm.* 149d). There is perhaps a link between this contact of the One with itself and with the others and the importance of mystical contact between God and his creatures. But this link, if it exists, is rather a simple echo.

16. "The one in no sense is. It cannot be, even to the extent of being one. Consequently it cannot have a name or be spoken of, nor can there be any knowledge or perception or opinion of it."

Father, the Son and the Holy Spirit."[17] Finally, he defends the idea that the uncreated God has neither beginning nor end, is unlimited and introduces the idea of infinity in God (*apeiron*).[18]

The instances in which Gregory seems to have borrowed *Parmenides*' terminology and principles are not numerous, at least not sufficiently numerous as to justify the assumption that Gregory read the *Parmenides* itself. It is more likely that such reminiscences came to him through the doctrines that by his time had become the common property of many schools of philosophy, and probably through the Neoplatonic movement. As *Parmenides* contains a lot of Platonic themes, similarities can exist between some expressions of the dialogue and some expressions of Gregory. But it is impossible to affirm that they are borrowed directly from the dialogue or that some precise allusions betray some special interest for the *Parmenides* itself, even if he was perhaps inspired by it for his own speculations and probably did not ignore the role of this dialogue in the philosophy of his time, particularly given the fact that Neoplatonists extracted a triadic structure from the *Parmenides*. Anticipating pseudo-Dionysus, Gregory presents God as being at once transcendent, ineffable, beyond all knowledge and, at the same time, immanent and present in the universe. But his own doctrine never depends on the *Parmenides*.

---

17. *Opif. hom.* 185. His adversary Eunomius writes also: "If the unbegotten is unbegotten neither according to the concept nor the privation nor in part (μήτε κατ' ἐπίνοιαν μήτε κατὰ στέρησιν μήτε ἐν μέρει)—for God is indivisible (ἀμερής)—nor in himself as an other (μήτε ἐν αὐτῷ ὡς ἕτερον)—for he is simple, without composition (ἁπλοῦς καὶ ἀσύνθετος)" (in *Eun.* 2, frg. 65).

18. On this theme, I quote an extract of his *Homiliae in Canticum canticorum*: "The pure of heart will see God, according to the Lord's infallible word (Mt 5, 8), according to his capacity, receiving as much as his mind can sustain; yet the infinite and incomprehensible nature of the Godhead remains beyond all understanding. For the magnificence of his glory, as the Prophet says, has no end, and as we contemplate him, he remains always the same, at the same distance above us. The great David cried to God: Thou art the most High, and canst never seem smaller to those who approach thee for thou art always to the same degree higher and loftier than the faculties of those who are rising. This, then, is the doctrine that I think the Apostle is teaching about the ineffable nature of the Good, when he says that the eye doesn't know it even though it may see it. For the eye does not see it completely as it is, but only in so far it can receive it. So too, even though we may constantly listen to the Word, we do not hear it completely according to its manifestation…. For those who are rising in perfection, the limit of the good that is attained becomes the beginning of the discovery of higher goods. Thus, they never stop rising, moving from one new beginning to the next, and the beginning of ever greater graces is never limited of itself. For the desire of those who thus rise never rests in what they can already understand" (*Homily* 8, trans. Musurillo 2001, 212–13).

I would like now to treat the question in another way, the links of other Cappadocians, especially Basil, brother and master of Gregory, with Neoplatonism and Neoplatonic interpretations of the *Parmenides*.

II. THE INFLUENCE OF NEOPLATONISM ON BASIL: HIS USE OF *Enn.* 5.1 [10]

J. Trouillard has written that "Neoplatonism appeared after Middle Platonism when the Platonists began to search in the *Parmenides* for the secret of Plato's philosophy. Even if they don't agree in the interpretation of the hypotheses, all affirm that no one is a Platonist without having faced in this dialogue the mystery of the one" (Trouillard 1973, 83). With Plotinus, the dialogue was no longer a logical and dialectical exercise, but a theological revelation of the three Ones—the One, the Intellect, and the Soul—which correspond to the three hypotheses of the second half of the dialogue. And all the Neoplatonists after Plotinus considered this dialogue the source of inspiration of their doctrine, and developed the meaning of the hypotheses as a representation of the universe's structure. If the dialogue doesn't appear, at least clearly, among the Cappadocian Fathers, was its centrality known by them and how can we interpret the fact that it plays no role in their writings?

I introduce a very interesting text of Basil, for the evocation of an episode of his biography can be relevant for our subject. The first surviving letter of Basil is about his relationship with pagan philosophy. It is addressed to a philosopher, Eustathius of Cappadocia, one of the pupils of Iamblichus who lived in the middle of the fourth century. This letter is a piece of rhetorical art, without philosophical content, and describes how Basil, attracted by the reputation of Eustathius, moved from Athens, past Constantinople, probably to Caesarea, then to Syria and Egypt, probably in Alexandria where he remained at the time of writing, intending to return home. He says that he has tried to join Eustathius who has preceded him in the same places although he couldn't find him: destiny, necessity, and fortune didn't allow it. The references and time frame are not explicit and precise, but it seems that the journey had taken place during the years of Basil's youth, when he had just left the brilliant schools of Athens. He gives as the only motive for his journey a desire to follow Eustathius. We have the impression that following his friend was important, because in his mind such travel would be a form of philosophical instruction. Although the identity of the addressee—Eustathius the philosopher—has been questioned, R. Goulet has shown that nothing in the content merits its rejection. On the contrary, the mythological allusions and the pagan character of the letter are well explained by the influence of his early Athenian studies on the young man (Goulet 2000, 369–78). In fact, during this travel, he seems to have experienced a kind of conversion. Later Basil wrote a long letter where, he said, during his years at Athens, he "lavished much time on the vanity of the precepts of that wisdom made foolish by God." He creates the impression that he wants to describe a rejection of that Athenian experience and alludes to some dramatic conversion: "When one day arising as from a deep sleep, I looked out upon the marvelous light of the truth of the gospel and beheld the uselessness of the wisdom of the princes of this world, bemoaning much my piteous life, I prayed that there be given me guidance to the introduction to the teachings of religion.... I prayed that I might find some one of the brethren who has taken this way of life" (*Ep.* 223; cf. Rousseau 1994, 21–22). He goes on to refer to his journey of exploration in the East, but this time, returning home, he admires the ascetics he had found. These latter seem to exemplify the following continuity yet radical change: before his conversion he had desired to follow a philosopher, but after this moment he decided to follow holy men. Perhaps it is not exactly the reality he lived, but the letter he addressed to his friend, a pupil of Iamblichus, is a good testimony to his proximity to the philosophical currents of his time, and allows me to introduce a text he had probably written at the same period of his life, after he passed from philosophy to religion by the conversion he described, namely, the *De spiritu*. In this text he speaks as a theologian, even if he exhibits a remarkable knowledge of Plotinus, meditating on *Enn.* 10. Whether this text is a homily or a letter remains unknown.

The meditation on the Holy Spirit connected to a reading of *Enn.* 10 (5.1.2) is the proof that Basil has studied Plotinus. In his edition, P. Henry puts parallel passages from the two authors in two columns (Henry 1938, 185–96). Where Basil's text follows Plotinus, the differences are often only stylistic, as is demonstrated by the parallelism:

> Let us search with faith concerning the nature of the Holy Spirit: by him we shall try to obtain the knowledge of what we search, because he is the subject of the research and he gives the knowledge of himself.... And how he is purveyed to all things and to the separate beings (τίς δὲ ὁ τρόπος τῆς χορηγίας τοῦ εἶναι αὐτὸ ἕν τε τοῖς πᾶσι καὶ ἐν τοῖς καθ' ἕκαστον)[19] has to be conceived by a thought that has become worthy to behold.... Let not merely the enveloping body be at peace, the body's turmoil stilled, but all that lies around (ἥσυχον δὲ αὐτῆς ἔστω μὴ μόνον τὸ περικείμενον σῶμα καὶ ὁ τοῦ σώματος κλύδων, ἀλλὰ καὶ πᾶν τὸ περιέχον),[20] heaven, earth, sea and rational beings who live there; let the Spirit be conceived to fill all things, to roll inward at every point, penetrating, permeating, from all sides pouring in its light (καὶ νοείτω τὰ πάντα πληρούμενα καὶ παντόθεν εἰς αὐτὰ ἑστὼς τὸ πνεῦμα οἷον εἰσρέον καὶ εἰσχυθὲν καὶ παντόθεν εἰσιὸν καὶ εἰσλάμπον)."[21]

---

19. Cf. Plotinus: τίς δὴ ὁ τρόπος τῆς χορηγίας τοῦ ζῆν ἕν τε τῷ σύμπαντι ἕν τε τοῖς ἑκάστοις.

20. Cf. Plotinus: ἥσυχον δὲ αὐτῇ ἔστω μὴ μόνον τὸ περικείμενον σῶμα καὶ ὁ τοῦ σώματος κλύδων, ἀλλὰ καὶ πᾶν τὸ περιέχον. He speaks about ψυχή, Basil about διάνοια.

21. Cf. Plotinus: νοείτω δὲ παντόθεν εἰς αὐτὸν ἑστῶτα ψυχὴν ἔξωθεν οἷον εἰσρέουσαν καὶ εἰσχυθεῖσαν καὶ παντόθεν εἰσιοῦσαν καὶ εἰσλάμπουσαν. The soul of Plotinus becomes the Spirit for Basil.

After a quotation of Wisdom 1.7 (the Spirit of God filled the universe), Basil continues:

> He shines on everyone who deserves it. As the rays of the sun casting their brilliance upon a cloud make it gleam all gold (ἡλίου βολαὶ φωτίσασαι νέφος καὶ λάμπειν ποιοῦσι χρυσοειδῆ ὄψιν ποιοῦσαι),[22] so the Holy Spirit, entering the body of man, has given life, immortality, and holiness, and what was abject it has lifted up (οὕτω καὶ πνεῦμα ἅγιον ἐπελθὸν εἰς ἀνθρώπου σῶμα ἔδωκε μὲν ζωήν, ἔδωκε δὲ ἀθανασίαν, ἔδωκεν ἁγιασμόν, ἤγειρε δὲ κείμενον).[23] What is moved in endless motion by the Holy Spirit, has become an holy living being (τὸ δὲ κινηθὲν κίνησιν ἀίδιον ὑπὸ πνεύματος ἁγίου ζῷον ἅγιον ἐγένετο).[24] The Spirit domiciled within, man received the dignity of a prophet, of an apostle, of an angel, of God, where, before, he was earth and dust.
>
> The Spirit's power and nature will be brought out more clearly, more brillantly (γένοιτο δὲ ἂν φανερωτέρα καὶ ἐναργεστέρα τοῦ πνεύματος ἡ δύναμις καὶ ἡ φύσις),[25] if we consider next how it envelops and guides to its purpose the holy men and all the rational nature (ὅπως περιέχει καὶ ἄγει τῷ ἑαυτοῦ βουλήματι τοὺς ἁγίους καὶ πᾶσαν τὴν λογικὴν φύσιν).[26] For he has given himself upon all that multitude of heavenly powers (ἅπαντι μὲν γὰρ τῷ πλήθει τῶν οὐρανίων δυνάμεων ἔδωκεν ἑαυτό)[27] and all that multitude of the right people; and every hypostasis of them, whether they are big or small, angels or archangels, has been sanctified. The material bodies are made up of parts, each holding its own place, other powers holding no interval between themselves (ἄλλη μὲν καὶ ἄλλη κειμένων τῶν σωμάτων τοῦ μὲν ὧδε, τοῦ δὲ ὧδε καὶ τῶν ἄλλων δυνάμεων ἀπ'ἀλλήλων ἐχουσῶν τι μέσον).[28] The Spirit is in no such condition; he is not whittled down so that life tells of a part of the Spirit, each separate life lives divinely by his entire power (οὐ τὸ πνεῦμα οὕτως οὐδὲ μέρος αὐτοῦ ἑκάστῳ

---

[22]. Basil is very close to Plotinus: νέφος ἡλίου βολαὶ φωτίσασαι λάμπειν ποιοῦσι χρυσοειδῆ ὄψιν ποιοῦσαι.

[23]. The Plotinian world-soul becomes the Spirit (Basil adds ἁγιασμός); cf. Plotinus: οὕτω τοι καὶ ψυχὴ ἐλθοῦσα εἰς σῶμα οὐρανοῦ ἔδωκε μὲν ζωήν, ἔδωκε δὲ ἀθανασίαν, ἤγειρε δὲ κείμενον.

[24]. Cf. Plotinus: ὁ δὲ κινηθεὶς κίνησιν ἀίδιον ὑπὸ ψυχῆς ἐμφρόνως ἀγούσης ζῷον εὔδαιμον ἐγένετο. Basil extends to all things the action of the Spirit and introduces the idea of holiness (versus εὔδαιμον).

[25]. The parallelism soul/Spirit continues, cf. Plotinus: γένοιτο δ'ἂν φανερωτέρα αὐτῆς καὶ ἐναργεστέρα ἡ δύναμις καὶ ἡ φύσις.

[26]. Cf. Plotinus: ὅπως περιέχει καὶ ἄγει ταῖς αὑτῆς βουλήσεσι τὸν οὐρανόν. Basil developps the simple mention of heaven as indicating human beings and angels.

[27]. Cf. Plotinus about the soul: παντὶ μὲν γὰρ τῷ μεγέθει ἔδωκεν ἑαυτήν. Basil introduces at this time the mention of heavenly powers.

[28]. Cf. Plotinus: ἄλλου μὲν ἄλλη κειμένου τοῦ σώματος καὶ τοῦ μὲν ὡδί, τοῦ δὲ ὡδί ὄντος καὶ τῶν μὲν ἐξ ἐναντίας, τῶν δὲ ἄλλων ἀπάρτησιν ἀπ'ἀλλήλων ἐχόντων. Basil insists apparently more on the idea of discontinuity than on interdependence.

κατακερματισθὲν ζῆν ποιεῖ θείως, ἀλλὰ ἅπαντα ζῇ τῇ ὅλῃ αὐτοῦ δυνάμει),[29] omnipresent in the likeness of God who sent him, because he is and he is everywhere in all things in a similar way (καὶ πάρεστι πανταχοῦ τῷ ἐκπέμποντι θεῷ ὁμοιούμενον καὶ κατὰ τὸ εἶναι καὶ κατὰ τὸ πανταχοῦ καὶ ἐν πᾶσιν ὁμοίως εἶναι):[30] Gabriel announcing to Mary the good news, another doing the same to another holy man in another place, each prophet prophesizing, Paul in Rome, James in Jerusalem, Mark in Alexandria, one in a city, another in another place filled by Spirit, because no interval (διαστήματος) has made impossible the fact that the same grace should be present in the same Spirit, and for this reason each of the holy men is a god. For God said: "I've told you: you are gods and all of you are sons of the Most High" ...

So, the Spirit once seen to be thus precious, thus divine, you may hold the faith in such a reality (οὕτω δὴ τοιούτου ἀγαθοῦ καὶ θείου ὄντος κτήματος τοῦ πνεύματος πιστεύσας ἤδη τῷ τοιούτῳ) without hesitating to search out Christ who supplies him:[31] "No one can say: 'Lord Jesus,' if not in the Holy Spirit." The entire stream of life sent forth by the Spirit to the production of further being (ἣν προΐεται δὲ ζωὴν εἰς ἄλλου ὑπόστασιν τὸ πνεῦμα),[32] does not divide him, but looks like a fire which has outgoing heat for water and has also heat essentially inherent (ὥσπερ πυρὸς τὸ μέν ἐστιν ἡ συνοῦσα θερμότης, τὸ δὲ ἣν παρέχει).[33] So in himself he has life and those who have parts in him live divinely with a divine life.

For he [Spirit=Intellect] contains in himself all that is immortal, all intellect, all angel, all soul; and all beings dwell in him, he doesn't seek change (οὐδὲ ζητεῖ μεταβολὴν εὖ ἔχον): what need could he reach for, who holds all within himself (μετελθεῖν πάντα παρ'ἑαυτῷ ἔχον)? what increase can he desire, who stands utterly achieved (αὔξησιν ἐπιζητεῖ τελειότατον ὄν)? All his content, thus, is perfect (παρ' αὐτῷ πάντα τέλεια)[34]...

---

29. Cf. Plotinus: οὐχ ἡ ψυχὴ οὕτως οὐδὲ μέρει αὐτῆς ἑκάστῳ κατακερματισθεῖσα μορίῳ ψυχῆς ζῆν ποιεῖ, ἀλλὰ τὰ πάντα ζῇ τῇ ὅλῃ. In all this passage Basil expresses in very similar terms by identifying soul and Spirit. The *Parmenides* is in the background.

30. Cf. Plotinus: καὶ πάρεστι πᾶσα πανταχοῦ τῷ γεννήσαντι πατρὶ ὁμοιουμένη καὶ κατὰ τὸ ἓν καὶ κατὰ τὸ πάντῃ. The Plotinian Father is identified to God and Basil insists on the universal presence of the Spirit.

31. If we compare here with Plotinus (οὕτω δὴ τιμίου καὶ θείου ὄντος χρήματος τῆς ψυχῆς πιστεύσας ἤδη τῷ τοιούτῳ), we can see that Christ represents here Plotinus's Intellect and the Spirit the world-soul.

32. The Spirit is here for the Plotinian Intellect (cf. Plotinus: ἣν προΐεται ζωὴν εἰς ἄλλου ὑπόστασιν).

33. Cf. Plotinus: οἷον πυρὸς τὸ μέν ἡ συνοῦσα θερμότης, ἡ δὲ ἣν παρέχει.

34. In this passage Basil follows strictly Plotinus except when the latter writes that the Intellect περιέχει θεὸν πάντα. Basil is forced by his theological view to deviate from his model and says περιέχει ἄγγελον πάντα.

As a manifold, then, this divinity [Spirit=Intellect] exists within the rational soul (πολὺ οὖν τοῦτο τὸ θεῖον ἐν ψυχῇ λογικῇ ὑπάρχει),[35] unless by a deliberate apostasy it goes away (ἀποστατεῖν θέλοι). Bringing itself close to him, becoming, as it were, one with this (προσπελάσασα δὲ αὐτῷ καὶ οἱονεὶ ἓν γενομένη),[36] [the soul] hears: "Who is attached to the Lord is one spirit."

In this text, Basil follows Plotinus. In fact, *Ennead* 10 seems to have interested Christians for some generations, because, before Basil, a few sentences of it had been quoted by Eusebius of Caesarea (Aubin 1992, 21). In our text, much more deeply, Basil tries to understand the nature of Holy Spirit with the help of Plotinus, but in a very specific and Christian way: it is not simply a Plotinian cento. For example, he doesn't pay attention to the differences between Soul and Intellect, for he identifies the Holy Spirit successively with the world-soul and the intellect, the third and second entities of the Parmenidean hypotheses. Nevertheless, it is clear that Basil is aware that Plotinus follows these hypotheses. Plotinus clearly mentions the *Parmenides* in ch. 8 of the same *Ennead* and testifies that this dialogue was at the center of his philosophy:

The Platonic *Parmenides* is more exact: the distinction is made between the Primal One, a strictly pure Unity, and a secondary One which is a One-Many and a third which is one and many; thus he too is in accordance with our thesis of the three natures. (*Enn.* 5.1.8)

It is probably Plotinus who really initiated the theological interpretation of the hypotheses which indicates the different levels of the reality. If our text doesn't allude directly to the *Parmenides*, it exhibits some familiarity with it. The Holy Spirit for Basil has a kinship (οἰκείωσις) with the Father and the Son, but he hesitates to put him at the same level: he is in general reluctant to go beyond recognizing that the Holy Spirit was *theion*.[37] All this appears as a Christianization of Plotinus's ideas, in relation to the *Parmenides*. The text is also more precisely connected with themes of Plato's dialogue.

We can focus on a passage where in the first half of the dialogue Socrates asks how the form can be present in the many: "It is one and the same, complete, in the many … it is not separated from itself (ἓν ἄρα ὂν καὶ ταὐτὸν ἐν πολλοῖς χωρὶς οὖσιν ὅλον ἅμα ἐνέσται) like the day is present in a lot of places without being separated (ἡ αὐτὴ οὖσα πολλαχοῦ)." Parmenides objects that the unity of the form can't be preserved if it is divided (131a–b). When he discusses the second hypothesis (144b–c), the One-many, he explains that being (*ousia*) has been given to the whole of reality and is not lacking in any element, great or

---

35. Cf. Plotinus: πολὺς οὖν οὗτος ὁ θεὸς ἐπὶ τῇ ψυχῇ τῇδε ὑπάρχει. Here Basil refuses to follow Plotinus and to apply the term "God" to the Spirit who is only a divinity.

36. Cf. Plotinus: πελάσασα οὖν αὐτῷ καὶ οἷον ἓν γενομένη. Basil identifies Christian and Neoplatonic souls.

37. In our text, by following Plotinus he affirms only once that Spirit is God.

small (κατακεκερμάτισται ὡς οἷόν τε σμικρότατα καὶ μέγιστα καὶ πανταχῶς ὄντα, καὶ μεμέρισται καί ἐστι μέρη ἀπέραντα τῆς οὐσίας). The one is present in each part of being (πρὸς ἅπαντι ἑκάστῳ τῷ τῆς οὐσίας μέρει πρόσεστιν τὸ ἕν). These expressions are quoted by Plotinus and Basil. They are also employed by Gregory of Nyssa in his theological treatises when he insists on the unity of the divine nature: he says: "We can say that the gold is one, even if it can be divided in a plurality of coins," as we have seen. J. Pépin has shown that the rather complicated verb κατακερματίζω has an interesting history. Its meaning is "cut into pieces," its original meaning being "coin into money, change into smaller coin." It was employed by Plato not only in the Parmenides, but also in the Republic (7.525) in a philosophical context: "If you cut into pieces (κερματίζῃς) the One, the mathematicians do the contrary, for fear that the one should appear not as one, but as a plurality of parts." If Plotinus also employs this word, it seems that Porphyry would be particularly inclined to use it. The use of this term by Porphyry in the Sententiae suggests, according to Pépin, that he has directly read the Parmenides, and not only Plotinus (Pépin 2002, 327). Basil and Gregory can also depend here on Porphyry and Plato.

This meditation of Basil reveals a strong relationship with Plotinus's thought, and therefore with the *Parmenides*, even a kind of fascination. This text is nevertheless a text of youth and, during the second part of his life, he made only allusions, and rarely, to the *Enneads*, so that the authorship has been denied to him by John Rist who finds unlikely that the famous bishop of Cesarea could have written such a text and prefers to attribute it to Gregory of Nyssa (Rist 1981, 137–220). I am not sure he's right, but, as a matter of fact, this text is an exception among the works of the Cappadocians. Can we explain what happened and the reasons for their silence?

III. The Meaning of a Lack

One of the reasons for the Cappadocians' silence on the *Parmenides* is probably the fact that the Neoplatonic interpretation of the dialogue influenced Aetius and Eunomius, particularly Iamblichus. Since J. Daniélou (Daniélou 1956, 412–32), scholars have insisted on the Neoplatonic background of Neo-Arianism—particularly given the influence of Iamblichus—even if, here too, John Rist prefers to discard Daniélou's theory (see Rist 1981, 137–220). For example, J. Daniélou writes:

> The Eunomian system is a Neoplatonic system, an explanation of the birth of the multitude from the One. At the top of the hierarchy there is the *agennetos*, the divinity ineffable. This by the way of an *energeia*, which is called the Father, produces an *ergon*, which is the Son. The Son, by an *energeia* which is Spirit, produces the cosmos. The trinity is therefore reduced to a hierarchy of *hyposta-*

seis. Under a Christian appearance, this would be a Platonic system. (Daniélou 1956, 428)

There is an order of three principles, the triad, which explains the appearance of many, of becoming and of cosmos. In this system the transcendence and absolute simplicity of the first is maintained, because the *agennētos* is strongly separated from the inferior *ousia*: God is incomparable and greater than the Son, who has been brought into being by the Father; each successive hypostasis is inferior to the One. The concept of *agennētos*, a natural notion, is inspired by the transcendence and the simplicity of that which is One and cannot produce the many. Eunomius has excluded all form of community and comparison between *agennētos* and *gennētos*.[38] There is communication between the *ousiai* only through the *energeiai*, the activities. Only the activity of the *agennētos* includes, by producing an *ergon*, the reason for becoming. The Monogenes also is really one, even if, by his activities, he has part in the many. There are many activities for each substance, but these activities don't completely reveal the nature of each substance. So there is a similarity between the activity "Father" and the activity "Son," not between *gennētos* and *agennētos*. These aspects show analogies between the Neoplatonic interpretation of the three first hypotheses of the *Parmenides* (especially for Plotinus) and Eunomius, who seems to be near to Iamblichus's system (which excludes any relationship between the Principle and the triad whereas Porphyry accepts it). The difference is that, for him, the One is not beyond being, and, for this reason, can be known. He is simply *agennētos*; each intellect, including the human intellect, can perceive this characteristic that completely defines the first principle. For Eunomius, this is no mystery, whereas negative theology becomes the characteristic of orthodox, Cappadocian thought. If this parallel between Eunomius's and Iamblichus's conception of God can be sustained, they have also a common theory about names: for Iamblichus they are sacralized and linked to the nature of the beings they designate; if they are translated, they lose their power. This is his answer to Porphyry, who thought that the meaning of a word is self-sufficient and can be communicated in any language (Athanassiadi 2006, 159). Iamblichus seems to believe in a magical, mystical, and religious power of names. For Eunomius, names are natural, they have been applied to realities by God: the real being of things and their designation correspond strictly and do not result from human invention. The divine origin of the unique name that expresses completely the nature of God allows one to maintain his transcendence even if it seems threatened by his accessibility to human understanding: Alone of all similar privative terms and of all the attributes of God, unbegottenness indicates the *ousia* of God. Even if one prefers to see only the influence of the biblical

---

38. "The similitude or the comparison or the community referred to the substance excludes superiority and difference, and clearly causes equality" (*Apol.* 11).

tradition on this theory, it seems to depend also on the mystical tradition of the Neoplatonism represented by Iamblichus.[39] This Eunomian system can explain, in part, the lack of references to the *Parmenides*. Since it was the most important dialogue read in the regular Platonic school curriculum laid down by Iamblichus, and considered as a recapitulation of all other dialogues and was placed at the summit of his canon, it is less surprising to find no mention of it even though its themes were often in resonance with the theological discussions of the fourth century.

The connections between the Eunomian system and Neoplatonism are generally admitted by scholars. Alternatively, the Cappadocians perhaps did not recognize the use of the dialogue among their opponents: "If the Fathers had understood that Neoplatonic systematization was hidden under the dialectical principles of Eunomius, they would have judged Eunomius's doctrine similarly; but furthermore they would have appreciated it in another way and would have more completely rejected it" (Vandenbussche 1945, 72). This opinion supposes that they were ignorant of the philosophical movements of their time, especially the role that the *Parmenides* played in it, and, in this case, their silence about this dialogue can be easily explained: it was not quoted in the manual they used and they paid no attention to it, so they saw no link between it and their own preoccupations.

This point of view is a possibility that cannot be excluded. Yet we can interpret this silence in a different way: it would be not a sign of ignorance, but could betray a strategy of omission. As we have seen, Plotinus seems to have been largely admired among the Christians of the fourth century, at least Basil and Gregory. Two facts played in his favor: 1) he was not an antichristian thinker: on the contrary having condemned the Gnostics, a Christian heresy, he could be considered an ally; and 2) his thought was flexible enough to be easily associated with the Christian elaboration of the Trinity, as we have seen with the *De Spiritu*. Furthermore, according to some critics, Basil and Gregory had adopted in their polemical treatises against Eunomius the Plotinian theory of infinity, when they affirmed that God is absolutely unknowable and that no concept can adequately define his substance. Cyril of Alexandria also used the original thought of Plotinus against the emperor Julian. Yet this positive reputation of Plotinus must be considered in relation to an important evolution of Neoplatonism towards mythology represented by Iamblichus, Julian's master: with him things changed, since he initiated a form of scholastics in the Neoplatonic school, and the consequence was a greater rigidity of thought compared to that of Plotinus's

---

39. See Mar Gregorios 1988, 217–35. According to Dörrie also, a *Plato christianus* doesn't exist, there is only *Platonismus partim receptus, partim confutatus*. Platonism has influenced heretical doctrines much more than orthodox ones. Dörrie has in mind the Platonic influence on Arius. The idea that Plato has influenced the heretics is already mentioned by Tertullian.

time. The conflict opposed two forms of Platonism, an original Platonism and a new Platonism, a form of modernism that gets rejected. The pagan mysticism of the new generation of philosophers, represented by a man like Iamblichus or even the emperor Julian, their anti-christianism, very different in orientation from Plotinus's philosophy, and the proximity of certain aspects of their theory to the speculations of the new and very influential heretics, were perceived as a danger. In this evolution, the role, more and more central and officially affirmed by Iamblichus[40] played by the *Parmenides* among these currents, together with its definitive transformation into a kind of theological scripture or, rather, holy scripture, and its connection, more obvious than in the past, with the pagan gods, all these factors have contributed to the same result for the Greek Fathers: the dialogue has been deliberately ignored.

Probably the Cappadocians were reluctant to quote and use a dialogue such as the *Parmenides*, because they recognized the deep relationship between the Eunomian heresy and Neoplatonism. Heresy was understood as a form of pagan thought, and they couldn't confess their interest in the dialogue without accepting the legitimacy of its Neoplatonic interpretation and, consequently, the legitimacy of a doctrine that was inspired by Neoplatonic schematism. It is only one century later that a Christian thinker will dare to follow Neoplatonic interpretations of the dialogue, yet it will be in another context.

---

40. Cf. Proclus, *In Tim.* 1; *Plat. Theol.* 56: according to Iamblichus, all the philosophy of Plato and all theology can be found in the *Parmenides*.

15
THE IMPORTANCE OF THE *PARMENIDES* FOR TRINITARIAN THEOLOGY IN THE THIRD AND FOURTH CENTURIES C.E.

Kevin Corrigan

On the surface, it seems unlikely that the interpretation of Plato's *Parmenides* might have had anything to do with Christian thought of the fourth century. How could a series of hypotheses about the one and the others have been of interest to Christian theologians? The unspoken consensus then has naturally been that there is little reflection of the *Parmenides* in the Church Fathers. One may argue, however, for a more nuanced view since the *Parmenides* formed an indirect context for the development of Trinitarian theology[1] and its interpretation was even decisive, we may say, for the formulation of Cappadocian Trinitarian thought.

For Athanasius, Basil, and Gregory Nazianzus, the Neoplatonic hypostases (interpreted by Plotinus as the first three hypotheses of the Parmenides—the "one" simply; the "one-multiple" (intellect); and the one and many (soul) are a possible, threatening parallel to their own Trinitarian theology that they are concerned to exclude. The Trinity is decidedly not "three gods." "Let no one think I am speaking of three originary hypostases," Basil observes in the *De Spiritu Sancto*, "or saying that the activity of the Son is imperfect (ἢ ἀτελῆ φάσκειν τοῦ Υἱοῦ τὴν ἐνέργειαν)," when he describes the Father as the principal or prokatarchtic cause (in Stoic terms), the Son as creative or demiurgic cause, and the Spirit as perfecting cause: "for the origin of beings is one, creating through the Son and perfecting in Spirit" (Ἀρχὴ γὰρ τῶν ὄντων μία, δι' Υἱοῦ δημιουργοῦσα, καὶ τελειοῦσα ἐν Πνεύματι) (16.38.136b).

---

1. My approach is in substantial agreement with that of Jean Reynard in this volume.

Basil

The problem for Basil, as already for Plotinus in 6.7 [38].1,[1] is that no activity of God can be imperfect (ἀτελῆ), like an Aristotelian *kinesis,* movement or potentiality that requires completion or actualization, or like an originated or derived reality that needs to be perfected by turning back or converting to its source or cause. Trinitarian inner causality is not like Plotinus's Intellect in relation to the One or Soul in relation to Intellect or, again, like the noetic, noeric, and psychic levels in Iamblichus that are perfect or complete in themselves as far as they go, but require additional perfection from a reality both greater than, and ontologically different from, themselves. Causality in the Trinity is really operative between the different persons, but this does not mean that they are substantially different realities or that they stand in need of each other: "The Father, creating by willing alone, could not be in need of the Son, but nevertheless he wills through the Son; nor could the Son need cooperation, in acting according to the likeness of the Father, but the Son too wills to make perfect through the Spirit" (*Spir.* 38.136b25–c3).

Athanasius

Athanasius makes a similar point prominently in his *Adv. Ar.,* 1.18, in arguing against the possibility that the "completeness of the doctrine of God is composed of additions" (as, one may argue, appears to be the case suggested by the language used in the second part of the *Parmenides*): "It is peculiar to the Greeks to introduce a generated triad and to equate it with generated things. For it is possible for generated things to admit defects and additions. But the Christian faith knows an unmoved, perfect ... blessed Triad. It neither adds something more to the Triad nor considers that it has a need—each of these impossibilities is impious. Therefore, it knows that the Triad does not mix with generated things" (PG 26 49b). Here Athanasius argues against the Arians (whom he mentions in the very next line), but he is also plainly thinking of the Neoplatonic derivative hypostases (that are invariably triadic)—derivative, that is, in terms of "additions" and "mixing with generated things." This is reminiscent of the first series of hypotheses in the *Parmenides,* where the "unspeakable" one of the first hypothesis becomes, in the second and the third, multiple by addition and by a form of dialectic that mixes the "one" with "generated" things or "the others" (see, e.g., *Parm.* 143d). In this passage, therefore, Athanasius is probably thinking of the *Parmenides,* although by itself this is inconclusive.

---

1. *Enn.* 6 [38]..1.45–48: Οὐ μὴν ἀλλ' εἰ δεῖ ἑκάστην ἐνέργειαν μὴ ἀτελῆ εἶναι, μηδὲ θεμιτὸν θεοῦ ὁτιοῦν ὂν ἄλλο τι νομίζειν ἢ ὅλον τε καὶ πᾶν, δεῖ ἐν ὁτῳοῦν τῶν αὐτοῦ πάντα ἐνυπάρχειν.

Gregory of Nazianzus

Gregory Nazianzus is much clearer. In his *Third Theological Oration* delivered in Constantinople (*Oratio* 29 in the collection), he discusses what he calls the three oldest opinions about God (anarchy, polyarchy, and monarchy) and determines that monarchy, the rule of one—as opposed to "no rule" (anarchy) or the rule of many (polyarchy)—is the only opinion to be honored, since anarchy and polyarchy involve lack of order in different ways. Monarchy in this sense, however, is not determined by one person, Gregory argues: " for it is possible that the one in dispute with itself comes into a state of many" (ἔστι γὰρ καὶ τὸ ἓν στασιάζον πρὸς ἑαυτὸ πολλὰ καθίστασθαι (PG 36, 76a–b; *Oratio* 29, 2, 7–8). Instead, it is a monarchy "composed of an equality of honor of nature, a concordant spirit of thought, an identity of motion, a convergence of things from it to the one, which is impossible for generated nature so that while it differs in number, it is not divided in substance. Because of this, a monad, moved from the beginning to a dyad, has remained stable up to a triad (ἀλλ' ἣν φύσεως ὁμοτιμία συνίστησι, καὶ γνώμης σύμπνοια, καὶ ταυτότης κινήσεως, καὶ πρὸς τὸ ἓν τῶν ἐξ αὐτοῦ σύννευσις, ὅπερ ἀμήχανον ἐπὶ τῆς γεννητῆς φύσεως, ὥστε κἂν σύννευσις, ὅπερ ἀμήχανον ἐπὶ τῆς γεννητῆς φύσεως, ὥστε κἂν ἀριθμῷ διαφέρῃ, τῇ γε οὐσίᾳ μὴ τέμνεσθαι. διὰ τοῦτο μονὰς ἀπ' ἀρχῆς εἰς δυάδα κινηθεῖσα, μέχρι τριάδος ἔστη. καὶ τοῦτό ἐστιν ἡμῖν ὁ πατήρ, καὶ ὁ υἱός, καὶ τὸ ἅγιον πνεῦμα (*Oratio* 29, 2, 8–13; PG 36. 76b).

This curious passage in context is a complex reflection upon the "second hypothesis" of the *Parmenides*, namely, upon the One as existent and participant in being. The language Gregory uses—"the one in dispute with itself comes into a state of many"—reflects the cases of polyarchy and anarchy as somehow derived from monarchy or, in the language of the *Republic*, how lesser forms of government, such as timocracy, oligarchy, democracy, and tyranny, emerge out of aristocracy through discord among the rulers. This is exactly, for instance, the principle Socrates asserts in *Respublica* 8.545c-d: "the cause of change in any government is to be found in the ruling group itself, whenever *stasis* occurs in this very group," whereupon Socrates goes on to examine how discord arises (πῇ στασιάσουσιν οἱ ἐπίκουροι καὶ οἱ ἄρχοντες) between auxiliaries and rulers "*in relation both to one another and to themselves*" (πρὸς ἀλλήλους τε καὶ πρὸς ἑαυτούς) (545c8–d7), a double relation that anticipates the basic strategy of the second half of the *Parmenides*. Gregory is evidently thinking of *both* texts in this context, linking the *Republic* to such passages in the *Parmenides* as the following: "The one, split up by existence is many and infinite in number" (Τὸ ἓν ἄρα αὐτὸ κεκερματισμένον ὑπὸ τῆς οὐσίας πολλά τε καὶ ἄπειρα τὸ πλῆθός ἐστιν) (144e; 144b-d; 143a). He is further concerned throughout this passage to argue: 1) that the one-triad cannot be divided as generated things are by time so that the cause becomes "older than that of which it is the cause" (δῆλον δὲ τὸ αἴτιον ὡς οὐ πάντως πρεσβύτερον τῶν ὧν ἐστιν αἴτιον) (*Oratio* 29, 3, 15–16; PG 36, 77b), as the language of the *Parmenides* suggests (namely, that the one becomes older and younger than itself); and b) that the triadic one is not arrived at by addition (namely, by qualitative or quantitative reckoning), as the *Parmenides* suggests concerning the second hypothesis or one-being: "But if each of them is one, by the addition of any sort of one to any pair whatsoever the total becomes three" (*Parm.* 143d: Εἰ δὲ ἓν ἕκαστον αὐτῶν ἐστι, συντεθέντος ἑνὸς ὁποιουοῦν ἡτινιοῦν συζυγίᾳ οὐ τρία γίγνεται τὰ πάντα;). By contrast for Gregory, "the perfect is not from addition" (οὐ γὰρ ἐκ προσθήκης τὸ τέλειον) (PG 36, 97a; 17, 18). Instead, he emphasizes something like the Plotinian principle of σύννευσις or convergence: "in intellect there is desire and convergence to its form (3.8 [30].11, 26[2]), that is, convergence to its own "one," which for Gregory—unlike Plotinus—is not "beyond being," but as in Plotinus and Porphyry respectively, convergence to the first moment of the pre-being of intellect in itself, which is unformed beauty just like the One's unformedness (for Plotinus; cf. 6.7 [38].32.24–39) or to the "Father" of the one and only noetic triad (for Porphyry; see Hadot 1968, 1:264–66).

So the question here for Gregory Nazianzus, against the series of hypotheses about the one and the others in the *Parmenides*, is this: can there be a procession that retains identity in difference? And his answer, of course, is affirmative, but expressed in very strange-sounding language, since he is conducting an implicit dialogue not only with the *Republic* and *Parmenides*, but with the entire pagan tradition, especially Plotinus and Porphyry: "a monad, moved from the beginning to a dyad, has remained stable up to a triad" (μονὰς ἀπ' ἀρχῆς εἰς δυάδα κινηθεῖσα, μέχρι τριάδος ἔστη) (PG 36, 76b).

Plotinus, I have argued elsewhere (2008, 114–34), has exactly such a triadic model of intellect, in which "cause" and "things caused" co-exist—language reflected in Gregory of Nyssa's several replies to Eunomius's rejection of co-existence (see Vaggione 1987, 44,10–46,19). Furthermore, in one work, *Enn.* 6.8 [39], Plotinus—on his own admission illegitimately—applies a triadic model to explicate his daring view that the One is "cause of itself" in such a way that its activity, substance and perfection (or making, self-hood and eternal generation) are "concurrent" (τὸ σύνδρομον) with itself (6.8 [39].20.17–25). It is precisely this self-causing triadic view that Iamblichus takes exception to, first, in positing a One beyond the One (i.e., to avoid any affirmative language of the One that would contaminate it with multiplicity) and, second, in arguing in his *De Mysteriis* that the only proper name of God is "Ungenerated," not any commixed form of hypostasis (τὸ σύμμικτον τῆς ὑποστάσεως εἶδος; *Mys.* 3.21.30). This latter view will find its way into Arianism and particularly the extant fragments of Eunomius.[3] Against it, Basil, Gregory of Nyssa and Gregory Nazianzus will suc-

---

2. Ἔφεσις γὰρ καὶ ἐν τούτῳ καὶ σύννευσις πρὸς τὸ εἶδος αὐτοῦ.

3. Cf. Basil, *Contra Eunomium* 1.5 (Sesboué 176, 79–81; 180, 124–29); 1.11 (Sesboué 208, 5–8); 1.16 (Sesboué 228, 17–20); 1.19 (Sesboué 238, 10–20); 1.19 (Sesboué 240, 25–29); Vaggione, 1987, 29.

cessfully apply Plotinus's *syndromos*-language to their descriptions of the Trinity[4] and, by extension, to the community of substance and individuality in human beings and other perceptible things.[5]

In this context, while the monas–dyas–trias language Gregory Nazianzus employs is the common heritage of Christians and pagans in the fourth century, the argument behind it is recognizably Platonic and, indeed, Plotinian. I give one similarly strange example from *Enn.* 6.7 [38].13: "In fact, if a simple being moves, it has that alone; and it is either itself and has not gone forward to anything, or if it has gone forward, another remains; so that there are two; and if this is the same as that, one remains and has not gone forward, but if other, it has gone forward with otherness and made from something same and different a third one" (6.7 [38].13.16–21).[6] However we are to interpret this,[7] Plotinus is speaking in the context of being and intellect and his argument provides something of a model for understanding how three "ones" can each be themselves and yet form an integral reality in which procession retains both identity and otherness, but as a function of internal creativity. I see this passage as a thought-parallel to Gregory Nazianzus's monad–dyad–triad explanation. This is also why, at the end of the immediate passage under discussion, Gregory takes pains to distance himself from accompanying elements in the Neoplatonic view, namely, the ideas that goodness "overflows" (οὐ γὰρ δὴ ὑπέρχυσιν ἀγαθότητος) "as if a bowl overflows" (οἷον κρατήρ τις ὑπερερρύη)[8] and that this is somehow "involuntary" (ἀκούσιον) "like some natural superfluity, hard to settle down" (οἷον περίττωμά τι φυσικὸν καὶ δυσκάθεκτον; 76c).

CAPPADOCIAN RESERVATIONS CONCERNING THE *PARMENIDES*

In other words, while precise language and argumentation in Cappadocian Trinitarian formulations is evidently inspired by Scripture and the Patristic tradition, there is also the natural concern of Athanasius, Basil, Gregory Nazianzus, and

---

4. For references see *PGL*.
5. See *ZAC* 2008, vol. 12/1, 133–34.
6. Ἁπλοῦν δὴ εἰ κινοῖτο, ἐκεῖνο μόνον ἔχει· καὶ ἢ αὐτὸ καὶ οὐ προὔβη εἰς οὐδέν, ἢ εἰ προὔβη, ἄλλο μένον· ὥστε δύο· καὶ εἰ ταὐτὸν τοῦτο ἐκείνῳ, μένει ἓν καὶ οὐ προελήλυθεν, εἰ δ᾽ἕτερον, προῆλθε μετὰ ἑτερότητος καὶ ἐποίησεν ἐκ ταὐτοῦ τινος καὶ ἑτέρου τρίτον ἕν. Γενόμενον δὴ ἐκ ταὐτοῦ καὶ ἑτέρου τὸ γενόμενον φύσιν ἔχει ταὐτὸν καὶ ἕτερον εἶναι· ἕτερον δὲ οὐ τί, ἀλλὰ πᾶν ἕτερον· καὶ γὰρ τὸ ταὐτὸν αὐτοῦ πᾶν. Πᾶν δὲ ταὐτὸν ὂν καὶ πᾶν ἕτερον οὐκ ἔστιν ὅ τι ἀπολείπει τῶν ἑτέρων. Φύσιν ἄρα ἔχει ἐπὶ πᾶν ἑτεροιοῦσθαι.
7. Plotinus warns, of course, about the incorrect use of language throughout; see, for example 6.8 [39].13.1–13.
8. Cf. Plotinus, *Enn.* 5.2 [2].1.6–11: ὃν γὰρ τέλειον τῷ μηδὲν ζητεῖν μηδὲ ἔχειν μηδὲ δεῖσθαι οἷον ὑπερερρύη καὶ τὸ ὑπερπλῆρες αὐτοῦ πεποίηκεν ἄλλο· τὸ δὲ γενόμενον εἰς αὐτὸ ἐπεστράφη καὶ ἐπληρώθη καὶ ἐγένετο πρὸς αὐτὸ βλέπον καὶ νοῦς οὗτος.

Gregory of Nyssa: first, to distance themselves from the Neoplatonic hypostases in the concrete knowledge that they are derived, in part, from Plato's *Parmenides*; second, to show that the Trinity cannot be conceived as functioning like some second hypothesis either by addition or by being cut up qualitatively or quantitatively into plurality; and third, to indicate that while the overall Neoplatonic worldview obviously has to be rejected, there is nonetheless a triadic causal procession of sameness and otherness in Plotinus and Porphyry that results in the hypostases or individual persons of the Trinity, as it were, being substantially included in divine substance rather than being cut up into a hierarchy of different substances.

CONCLUSION: TRINITARIAN THEOLOGY IN THE SHADOW OF THE *PARMENIDES*

I suggest therefore that the fourth-century Fathers were well aware of the second part of the Parmenides and that, in fact, this text was an indispensable backdrop, however indirect, for the formulation of Trinitarian theology in this century. But the impetus to Parmenides-interpretation, of course, goes farther back to Plotinus and Origen: to Plotinus, because as we know from 5.1[10].9, the first three hypotheses are coordinated with the famous Plotinian "hypostases"; and to Origen, because Parmenides-language is clearly part and parcel of the expression of his thought. I give one example, in which Origen is surely thinking not so much of the "one" as of "the others" considered in relation to themselves, if the one does not exist: "Nowhere is the monad, nowhere the harmony and the one; because of their dissension and quarreling, the one has abandoned them and they have become numbers, perhaps endless numbers"[9] (Origen, 785a, Von Balthasar; 5.5: Οὐδαμοῦ γὰρ ἡ μονάς, καὶ οὐδαμοῦ τὸ σύμφωνον καὶ ἕν, ἀλλὰ παρὰ τὸ διεσπάσθαι καὶ μάχεσθαι τὸ ἓν ἀπ' ἐκείνων ἀπώλετο καὶ γεγόνασιν ἀριθμοί, καὶ τάχα ἀριθμοὶ ἄπειροι).

---

9. Origen's language certainly reflects more than the *Parmenides* itself and the *Respublica*, as also in Gregory Nazianzus's *Third Theological Oration* cited above, since the terms are generally Neopythagorean, but the context of Prov 10.19 against *polulogia* resonates with the language of the *Parmenides* (e.g., 144a;144e; 145a; and in the case where "the one is not," 164d; 165c) and the *Resp.* 545c–d, cited above.

16
Pseudo-Dionysius, the *Parmenides*, and the Problem of Contradiction

Andrew Radde-Gallwitz

Denys and the Laws of Non-Contradiction (LNC) and the Excluded Middle (LEM): Two Interpretations

> Everything is real and not real.
> Both real and not real.
> Neither real nor not real.
> That is Lord Buddha's teaching.[1]

Recently, western philosophers interested in the Law of Non-Contradiction (LNC) and the Law of the Excluded Middle (LEM) have turned their attention to statements such as the tetralemma reproduced above from Nagarjuna, the third-century C.E. Indian Buddhist philosopher, which seems to undermine those laws.[2] The Christian theological tradition, which has so often been indebted to Aristotle and his classic formulations of the LNC and LEM, may not appear to be an obvious place to look for deconstructions of these laws. However, in this essay, I analyze a corpus of texts from Christian late antiquity that calls them into question, at least in the case of human language about ultimate reality, in a way that echoes the "Lord Buddha's teaching," though obviously from a very different cultural context.[3]

Sometime in the late-fifth or early-sixth century, a Christian author picked up on a philosophical tradition that some earlier Christian theologians had

---

1. Nagarjuna, *Mûla-madhyamaka-kârikâ* 18.8, trans. Garfield 1995, 102. In his commentary, Garfield argues that this tetralemma does not yield a genuine contradiction in that things are real and unreal in different senses (ibid., 250–51).
2. For general discussion, see Horn 2006.
3. On Denys and Buddhism, see the fascinating comparative study of J. N. Williams (2000).

engaged with, but which had decidedly taken a backseat during the recent and still ongoing Christological controversies. The tradition I am referring to is the theological interpretation of Plato's *Parmenides*. The fruit of our mysterious figure's recovery of this tradition is what we call the *Corpus Dionysiacum*, the works of Pseudo-Dionysius the Areopagite, whom I will simply call "Denys" for shorthand. For some time now, scholars have acknowledged the influence upon Denys of Neoplatonism generally, and of the Neoplatonist commentaries on the *Parmenides* in particular.[4] Eugenio Corsini's 1962 work on Denys and the *Parmenides* commentaries has garnered scholarly consensus. In this paper, I want to take up the issue of the influence of this commentary tradition upon Denys and frame some questions about Denys's use of the *Parmenides* commentary tradition and the impact this has on his view of the LNC and LEM.

In order to grasp the force of Corsini's interpretation, it is necessary first to rehearse in broad strokes the standard Neoplatonist interpretation of the second part of the *Parmenides*. When interpreted theologically, the first hypothesis of the second part leads to negative theology; the second hypothesis to affirmative theology. Platonist interpreters realized that if the hypotheses were read as dealing with the same "Ones," they would yield contradictions.[5] The dialogue would be affirming and denying the same predicates of the same being. Consequently, Platonists distinguished a simple One as the subject of the first hypothesis, a One-Many as the subject of the second, and so forth.[6] While the pagan Neoplatonist tradition distinguished the subjects of the first and second hypotheses, the standard scholarly line since Corsini has held that Denys attributes both the first and second hypotheses to the same level of divine being. As a defender of Nicene Trinitarianism, Denys simply cannot divide levels of divinity as the Platonists had done, or even as pre-Nicene Christians like Clement of Alexandria had done (see Lilla 1971, 212-26). There is ample evidence for Corsini's interpretation, some of which I will examine in a moment. For now, let us clarify the implications of this move in Denys. If he both affirms and denies the same predicates of the same divine being, how is he not guilty of the kind of contradiction that the Platonists were trying to avoid?

There are two possibilities for what Denys is up to on this point. Either he thinks that:

---

4. The influence of Proclus upon Denys was established in 1895 by Stiglmayr and Stiglmayr 1895, 253-73, 721-48; Koch 1895, 438-54. The first to note the influence of the *Parmenides* upon Denys (so far as I know) was Ivanka 1964, 234-35. The classic statement of the influence of the Neoplatonic commentaries on the *Parmenides* upon Denys is Corsini 1962. See also Lilla 1994, 117-52.

5. Cf. Proclus, *In Parm.* 6.1040-41, trans. Morrow and Dillon 1987, 401.

6. Cf., e.g., Plotinus, *Enn.* 5.1.8.23-26.

A. LNC and LEM are not valid in the case of God, or
B. LNC and LEM are valid in the case of God.

Both of these options have been taken by scholars. If A is true, then Denys can make apparently contradictory claims, affirming and denying the same predicates of the same God, without this causing any problem. However, some have tried to save Denys from contradiction, and have assumed that this is something he would have wished to be saved from—that is, they have endorsed B.

The most sophisticated version of B, which has been endorsed by Corsini and Salvatore Lilla, is what I will call the "Causal Interpretation." It asserts that, while Denys does attribute the first and second hypotheses to the same God, he nonetheless attributes them to different *aspects* or *moments* of God. Specifically, the first hypothesis and consequently negative theology corresponds to the divine μονή or "abiding," that is, God in so far as God remains in himself. The second hypothesis and consequently positive or cataphatic theology corresponds to the divine πρόοδος or "procession," that is, God in so far as God proceeds *ad extra*, God as Creator. I call this the Causal Interpretation because it distinguishes the hypotheses, not on the basis of their divine referent, but on the basis of divine causality. God in God's self bears no attributes; God *qua* cause bears all attributes.

The interpretation that embraces option A is what I will call the "Transcendent Interpretation." This interpretation has been advanced in some form by Raoul Mortley, Janet Williams, and Denys Turner. The interpretation states that, according to Denys, language about God is not subject to the LNC and the LEM in the sense that it is *beyond* them; talk about God transcends their scope.

As stated, these two interpretations are plainly incompatible. However, in what follows, I will argue that, when properly understood, the Causal Interpretation not only is compatible with the Transcendent Interpretation, it in fact implies it. My argument requires me to attend primarily to Denys's affirmative theology, that is, his use of the Second Hypothesis, since a great deal depends on what it means for him to affirm predicates of God.

The Causal Interpretation

In an excellent paper on Denys's notion of infinity, Salvatore Lilla argued for the Causal Interpretation. His analysis of the notion of infinity led him to conclude that Denys uses it in equivocal ways: in one sense, infinity (ἀπειρία) is identified with God; in another, God is above infinity as its cause. Lilla argues that "there is no real contradiction" here: the former "must be referred to God's μονή," the latter "is the expression of the divine emanation or πρόοδος" (Lilla 1980, 103). Understood in terms of God's "abiding" or μονή, ἀπειρία is one of the negative attributes drawn from the first hypothesis of the *Parmenides*. Understood in terms of God's causality, it is an attribute of the intelligible realm that God brings into being. Lilla provides a clear statement of the Causal Interpretation's motivation: namely, the desire to avoid contradiction. For him, the apparent contradiction of attributing both the First and Second Hypotheses to the same God is dissolved when one "take[s] into account a fundamental law of Dionysius's system—namely the law of μονή and πρόοδος, the two distinct stages of God's existence" (Lilla 1980, 103).

The Causal Interpretation draws its strength from its tidiness. By assimilating the two kinds of theological language—negation and affirmation—to "two distinct stages of God's existence," it appears to sweep away the messiness of contradiction. But it is not at all clear that there can be "two stages of God's existence," especially in light of the doctrine of divine simplicity, which Denys clearly endorses. Moreover, in the passages where he discusses these "two stages," they do not seem to be "stages" at all, but rather "simultaneous" and mutually implicating. God abides in his proceeding and proceeds while abiding.[7] As he says, "That one-being is said to be multiplied by producing from himself the many beings, while he nonetheless remains one as he is multiplied and united in the procession and full in the division."[8] Again, "when [the divine peace and rest] enters into itself and makes itself multiple, it does not abandon its unity, but proceeds towards all things while remaining whole in itself through the superiority of its unity which surpasses all things."[9] Denys seems almost consciously to be deconstructing any attempt to divide God's "abiding" and God's "proceeding." It is not simply that there is no sense to speaking of "two distinct stages of God's existence"; it is that the phrase fails accurately to capture the apparent intentionality of Denys's vastly more ambiguous phrasing.[10]

Moreover, there is a basic ambiguity in the Causal Interpretation that needs to be addressed. If Denys attributes the affirmations of the Second Hypothesis to God on the basis of God's causality (and that alone), then two options present themselves. Either

C. These attributes name intrinsic properties of God, or

D. They do not name intrinsic properties of God, but only name relations of other things to God.

---

7. In addition to the passages in the next two notes, see *Div. nom.* 5.10 (ed. Suchla 1990, 189,12; PG 3, 825B), as well as *Div. nom.* 2.4 = 126–127 Suchla; PG 3, 640D–641A, which discusses Trinitarian abiding and proceeding.

8. *Div. nom.* 2.11 = 136,2–5 Suchla; PG 3, 649B: πολλαπλασιάζεσθαι λέγεται τὸ ἓν ὂν ἐκεῖνο τῇ ἐξ αὐτοῦ παραγωγῇ τῶν πολλῶν ὄντων μένοντος οὐδὲν ἧττον ἐκείνου καὶ ἑνὸς ἐν τῷ πληθυσμῷ καὶ ἡνωμένου κατὰ τὴν πρόοδον καὶ πλήρους ἐν τῇ διακρίσει.

9. *Div. nom.* 11.1 = 218,10–13 Suchla; PG 3, 949AB: οὔτε εἰς ἑαυτὴν εἰσιοῦσα καὶ πολλαπλασιάζουσα ἑαυτὴν ἀπολείπει τὴν ἑαυτῆς ἕνωσιν, ἀλλὰ καὶ πρόεισιν ἐπὶ πάντα ἔνδον ὅλη μένουσα δι' ὑπερβολὴν τῆς πάντα ὑπερεχούσης ἑνώσεως.

10. See Lilla's comments (1994, 118), where he seems to reject this view. If he did not proceed on 119–20 and 136 to re-endorse the position (inexplicably), one could take his initial rejection as a genuine *volte-face* from his 1980 article.

Let us take an example of properties that Denys attributes to God on the basis of the fact that they come from him, in order to decide whether these are merely Cambridge properties or real properties of God. Denys attributes the "beginning, middle, and end" of things to God on the grounds that God causes the beginning, middle, and end. Now, he also denies these of God on the grounds of God's transcendence.[11] But in his affirmation of them, does he merely mean that other things have God as their beginning, middle, and end, or that God really contains these, whatever that would mean? That is, do the effects "beginning, middle, and end" pre-exist in their source? Or, to take another example, when he says that God is "all things," does he mean merely that "all things come from God" and so bear some relation to their Source, or that God contains all things?[12] These questions are relevant to the broader issue of Denys's interpretation of the LNC and LEM. Remember that the Causal Interpretation was initially invoked in order to absolve Denys of contradiction, assuming that the LNC is valid in theology. Yet, if C is true, then this makes it implausible that he actually believes the LNC is valid in the case of God, since if C is correct, Denys is attributing properties to God as real properties and denying these very properties of God. And, I will suggest, C is the correct reading of Denys.

C and D are plainly incompatible and were taken to be so in Denys's time by Proclus. Proclus endorses D, putting this forth over against C, a position he attributes to some unnamed Platonists. It will be worthwhile to look at how Proclus describes his opponents' position, for, while we cannot identify them precisely, their view is in line with Denys's—they may even be his sources. Proclus is discussing the first hypothesis, which denies that the One has "beginning, middle, and end," on the grounds that it is partless and these are parts. He notes that this appears to conflict with what the Athenian Stranger says in *Laws* 4: "there is a god who holds in his hands the beginning and end and middle of all things...." In typical fashion, Proclus discusses three solutions to the problem, the first two of which are at least partially unsound, and the last of which corresponds to Proclus's viewpoint, that is, to his master Syrianus's viewpoint. The first solution, which Hadot has attributed to Porphyry and Dillon to Iamblichus, reads as follows:

> There are some, again, who say in reply to this difficulty that the first principle both possesses beginning and middle and end and does not possess them; for it possesses them in a hidden mode, whereas it does not possess them distinctly; for it contains everything within itself in a manner inexpressible and inconceivable to us, but knowable to itself. Once again, we will not accept these theorists, since they in their turn are multiplying the One to some extent or other; for this

---

11. *Div. nom.* 5.10 = 189.13 Suchla; PG 3, 825B: οὔτε ἀρχὴν ἔχων ἢ μέσον ἢ τελευτὴν.
12. E.g., *Div. nom.* 5.8 = 187.10 Suchla; PG 3, 824B.

hidden and undivided multiplicity belongs to some other order of secondary entities and not to the primal entity itself, which is pure of all multiplicity.[13]

Syrianus and Proclus prefer another solution, taking "beginning, middle, and end" as naming relations of "other things" to God, rather than intrinsic properties of God. They say that the *Laws* passage

> teaches what relation God has to others, and not what his relation is to himself. Of other things, then, the first principle is beginning and middle and end, but he is not himself divided into beginning and middle and end; for he is the beginning of all things because all things proceed from him; and their end because all things are directed towards him; ... and he is the middle because all the centres of existent things ... are established in the One.[14]

Denys himself is somewhat less than clear on this point. Sometimes he appears to give the same account of "beginning, middle, and end" that Proclus endorses. At *Divine Names* (*De divinis nominibus*) 5.10, he says that God is "beginning as cause, and end as that for the sake of which."[15] However, elsewhere it is not so clear. Just two pages earlier in Suchla's edition, he says that God "contains beforehand in himself the beginnings, middles, and ends of beings in a non-relative and transcendent manner."[16]

The term I have translated "in a non-relative ... manner" is ἀσχέτως. It appears rather frequently in late Platonist authors like Proclus, but what does it mean?[17] In the *Institutio Theologica*, it is a predicate for the kind of causal productivity that something engages in when it effects a cause simply by virtue of being what it is: "everything that acts in virtue of its being acts without relation (ἀσχέτως)."[18] When X acts on Y simply in virtue of being X, Y bears a relation to X, but X does not stand in a reciprocal relation.[19] This is what it means to

---

13. Proclus, *In Parm.* 6.1114.1–10, trans. Morrow-Dillon, 457.

14. Ibid., 1115.25–36, trans. Morrow-Dillon, 459.

15. *Div. nom.* 5.10 = 189,7–8 Suchla; PG 3, 825B: ἀρχὴ μὲν ὡς αἴτιος, τέλος δὲ ὡς τοῦ ἕνεκα ...

16. *Div. nom.* 5.8 = 187,14–15 Suchla; PG 3, 824B: ἀρχὰς καὶ μέσα καὶ τέλη τῶν ὄντων ἀσχέτως καὶ ἐξῃρημένως ἐν ἑαυτῷ προειληφὼς ...

17. The account here differs from the placing of the Dionysian passages in the entry under ἄσχετος in *PGL* 253. Lampe places Denys under sense 3 "unlimited, boundless ... esp. in *Dion. Ar.* [ps-Dionysius Areopagita] of what pertains to God, *illimitable, incomprehensible*." I prefer placing Denys with the texts under Lampe's sense 4 "not relative, unconditioned, absolute." Luibheid's translation of ἄσχετοι at *DN* 2.5, "irrepressibly" takes it in either sense 1 ("not to be controlled or held") or 2 ("unrestrained, unchecked"): Luibheid 1987, 62.

18. *Inst. Theol.* 126 (108,15–16 Dodds, trans. altered): πᾶν δὲ τὸ τῷ εἶναι ποιοῦν ἀσχέτως ποιεῖ.

19. And, according to Denys, God does act as cause simply in virtue of being: *Div. nom.* 1.5 = 117,11–15 Suchla; PG 3, 593D.

act ἀσχέτως; but Denys says, not that God acts in this way, but that he *contains* beginning, middle, and end ἀσχέτως. This must mean that he contains these, but not by virtue of standing in any sort of relationship to anything else.[20] This is confirmed by what the scholiast says of another instance of ἀσχέτως slightly earlier in *De divinis nominibus*: "without relation, for the divine has no relation or commonality with beings either formally, conceptually, or in reality."[21] It is relatively safe, therefore, to conclude that by saying that God contains beginning, middle, and end ἀσχέτως, Denys means that God contains them "independently" or "absolutely." And if God's containing beginning, middle, and end is not a function of his relation to other things, then it is an intrinsic property of God. That is, Denys cannot endorse the kind of interpretation Proclus gives of the *Laws* passage as the final word. God does not merely possess beginning, middle, and end in a way relative to the world he causes.

Moreover, when Denys discusses other attributes from the *Parmenides*, he does not give the kind of interpretation that Proclus and Syrianus prefer. In fact, his language sounds a great deal like the position they oppose. For both Denys and Proclus's opponents, the apparently diverse attributes of God are united in a way that is transcendent and mysterious. They claim that God is X, Y, and Z, but in such a way that these are not really distinct; the incongruity is smoothed over by appealing to hiddenness and mystery. It is clear that the anonymous interlocutors that Proclus opposes also used this kind of interpretation for other attributes in addition to "beginning, middle, and end." When Proclus first mentions the interpretation, the point is quite general.

> There are other authorities, however, who have said that since the first principle is cause of all things, situated above Life, above Intellect, above Being itself, it possesses within itself in some way the causes of all these things unutterably and unimaginably and in the most unified way, and in a way unknowable to us but knowable to itself; and the hidden causes of all things in it are models prior to models, and the primal entity itself is a whole prior to wholes, not having need of parts.[22]

Here, the theory covers Life (ζωή), Intellect (νοῦς) and Being itself (αὐτὸ τὸ ὄν). These, in slightly modified form, are three of the "divine names' that Denys discusses in his work of that name. The interpretation of these names rejected by Proclus corresponds reasonably well to Denys's view. There are not so much exact

---

20. Cf. the phrase ἄσχετοι μεταδόσεις at *Div. nom.* 2.5 (129,1 Suchla; PG 3, 644A). Here it means that God gives life, being, and wisdom in such a way that is non-reciprocal: the gifts are participated in, but do not themselves participate.
21. PG 4, 321B: ἄσχετον· οὐδενὶ γὰρ λόγῳ, ἢ νοήματι, καὶ πράγματι ἔχει τὸ θεῖον τὴν πρὸς τὰ ὄντα σχέσιν τε καὶ κοινωνίαν.
22. Proclus, *In Parm.* 1107.9–17, trans. Morrow-Dillon, 452.

verbal parallels as congruity of ideas: for both views, God contains apparent multiplicity, but in some incomprehensible way this diversity is unified in God.

Denys uses a number of evocative, but entirely traditional, images to describe this unity-in-diversity. I will discuss one of these, the image of the sun, in a moment. But first let me pause and state what I think has been shown thus far. Denys attributes properties such as "beginning, middle, and end" to God on the grounds that God is the cause of these. But these are not *merely* relative names, but are intrinsically and non-relatively true of God. In other words, version C of the Causal Interpretation is correct. As we have seen, this separates Denys from Proclus, and suggests a different Neoplatonic source for his position (though he may have learned the position from reading Proclus). The fact that a position much like Denys's is reported and rejected in Proclus should lead us to be suspicious of Corsini's claim that Denys's reading of the first two hypotheses is original to him.

Denys's "Sun" and Socrates' "Day"

Denys uses a number of images to describe the unity-in-diversity he attributes to God. The sun, he believes, is a particularly apt image for this. The sun "transcendently contains within itself as a unity the causes of the many things which participate in it."[23] There is a clear analogy here: the sun is to the rest of the sensible world as Being or God is to all things. I want to dwell on this analogy, for it appears that Denys has conflated two distinct sets of questions. Thus far, I have focused on what he has to say about the second part of the *Parmenides*. However, Denys's way of describing the unity-in-diversity in God and the images he uses for this owe something to the first part of the *Parmenides* and the history of discussion it inspired. Specifically, I would suggest that Denys's "sun" image echoes Socrates' "day" image.

At *Parm.* 131b, the young Socrates likens the presence of the Forms to sensible objects to the simultaneous presence of a day in many places. This metaphor provokes the notorious "sailcloth dilemma." The dilemma is intended to force poor Socrates to admit that the Forms are divisible, thereby wrecking the theory of Forms entirely. When multiple things participate in the Form of F they do so by a relation to either (A) a part of the Form or (B) the Form as a whole. The sailcloth dilemma is motivated by Socrates' analogy of the day, which claims the latter (B), namely, that multiple, spatially separate participants all share in the Form of F as a whole. The problem is that this produces what appears to be an insoluble contradiction: if one and the same Form is present as a whole in more

---

23. *Div. nom.* 5.8, trans. Luibheid 1987, 102, altered = 188.2–3 Suchla; PG 3, 824C: καὶ τὰς τῶν πολλῶν μετεχόντων ὁ εἷς ἥλιος αἰτίας ἐν ἑαυτῷ μονοειδῶς προείληφε. "Transcendently" is my attempt to capture the force of the *pro-* suffix in *prolambanein*.

than one place, then it will be "separate from itself" (131b2: αὐτὸ αὑτοῦ χωρὶς ἂν εἴη), which is absurd. Socrates is then forced to admit that the Forms appear divisible, and that participants share in only a part of the Form, which has equally catastrophic consequences.

The language of Denys's sun image is similar to Socrates' description of the day. Socrates claims that it is "one and the same day" that is present in many places simultaneously. Denys says that "Each thing participates in *one and the same sun* in a way proper to itself." Parmenides charges Socrates with saying that although the Form is one and the same, it is present to many things as a whole. Denys says that the sun possesses "the causes of the many things that participate in it as a unity." Furthermore, there is reason to believe that Platonists before Denys had already merged Socrates' "day" analogy with the "sun" of *Respublica* book 7. Proclus mentions such an interpretation. [24]

I withhold judgment as to the historical sources for Denys's sun image, though I will make two notes in passing. First, Plotinus uses the same image to illustrate the omnipresence of being to its participants and hence to solve the sailcloth dilemma (Plotinus, *Enn*. 6.3.7). Second, some of Denys's language appears in the emperor Julian's *Hymn to King Helios*, which Julian himself claims to be derived from Iamblichus. Whatever the precise historical story, Denys uses the sun image (and other images) for the exact same purpose Socrates invokes the day analogy; namely, to explain the simultaneous participation of many things in Being. The problem is that this is something of a red herring for Denys's purposes. For the argument of the passage is that God is a unity-in-diversity; the image ought to be an illustration of this. But rather than explain this, he instead explains how multiple things can participate in a unity. And these are distinct questions.

Consider the context of the sun image. Denys has just listed attributes of God, considered under the name "Being." If God is Being, in accordance with the Second Hypothesis, then he is "all things," "all things belong to him," and

---

24. Proclus, *In Parm.* 4.862, trans. Morrow-Dillon, 228: "Socrates here thinks he has found something that can be present to many separate things at the same time, viz. the day, which is present to all things under the same meridian, the same day, but simultaneously present to many different things. If you say further that the Good is analogous to the Sun, and the forms analogous to the day and its light (for they illuminate the darkness of Matter, and each of them is a light, just as Matter is darkness) and its dependence on its own principle (even as they are dependent on the One), you could say that the likeness is very apt." This could be related to Denys's sun-image, though note that, for Proclus, the Sun corresponds to the Good, and the day to the forms. Denys's description of the realm of Being as analogous to the Sun may be another example of him denying the distinction between the levels of the One and the Intelligible Realm.

"all things may be simultaneously predicated of him."[25] Denys invokes the sun image to explain how this can be. However, he actually draws two conclusions from the image: first, "Each thing therefore has, in its own way, a share of the one and the same sun," and second, "and the one sun contains within itself as a unity the causes of all the things which participate in it."[26] The second is what Denys should, based on the context, be trying to establish. But the image seems more apt to provide the first. And the second does not follow from the first.

The fact that Denys confuses these two lines of inquiry is clear from what follows shortly after, where he says, "In its total simplicity it disowns all duplicity and it encompasses everything in the same way in its super-simple infinity. It is participated in a unified way by all in the same way that one and the same sound is participated as a unity by numerous ears."[27] We have here an inference from the hypothesis that God is a simple unity-in-diversity to the view that God is participated in indivisibly. But the relation between these two is not at all clear. Here, the image is not the sun, but the voice. This image had been used to explain the undivided presence of Being to participants before Denys. So had some other images he uses, such as the center of a circle and its radii.[28] With all these images, Denys appears to be thinking of discussions of the first part of the *Parmenides* and the problem of participation, while at the same time addressing the problem of God as a unity-in-diversity which stems from the second part of the dialogue.

To say, as Denys does, that everything within the sun's scope shares in "one and the same sun," seems relatively uncontroversial, less controversial than Socrates' claim that everything shares in "one and the same day." But Denys's claim that the sun actually *contains* the causes of things is controversial, when understood properly. Denys describes the sun's causality as follows:

> It is a single illuminating light, acting upon the essences and the qualities of the many and various things we perceive. It renews them, nourishes them, protects them and perfects them. It establishes the differences between them and it unifies them. It warms them and makes them fruitful. It makes them exist, grow, change, take root, burst forth. It quickens them and gives them life.[29]

---

25. *Div. nom.* 5.8 = 187.10–13 Suchla; PG 3, 824B;): πάντα ἐστιν ... Διὸ καὶ πάντα αὐτοῦ καὶ ἅμα κατηγορεῖται ...

26. *Div. nom.* 5.8 = 188.1–3 Suchla; PG 3, 824C.

27. *Div. nom.* 5.9 = 189.3–6 Suchla; PG 3, 825A: κατὰ μίαν ἁπλότητος ὑπερβολὴν πᾶσαν διπλόην ἀπαναινομένη, πάντα δὲ ὡσαύτως περιέχει κατὰ τὴν ὑπερηπλωμένην αὐτῆς ἀπειρίαν καὶ πρὸς πάντων ἑνικῶς μετέχεται, καθάπερ καὶ φωνὴ μία οὖσα καὶ ἡ αὐτὴ πρὸς πολλῶν ἀκοῶν ὡς μία μετέχεται.

28. See Plotinus, *Enn.* 6.5 [23].5.1–23.

29. *Div. nom.* 5.8, trans. by Luibheid, 101–2 = 187–88 Suchla; PG 3, 824BC; cf. the fuller account at *Div. nom.* 4.4.

It would be easy for us to assume that these are merely functions of some kind of relation between the sun and earthly things. The sun's warming a stone is not something that the sun "contains," is it? Surely the sun's warming a stone is merely a Cambridge property of the sun. But if this is true, then Denys seems to be endorsing a view like Proclus's view, D, above. However, this cannot be correct, because Denys describes the sun as "containing" these causes. In some sort of analogous way, then, God must contain causes that appear to be merely relative. Yet, the analogy has raised more questions that it has clarified. Denys's sun has failed to illuminate.

Negation and the Transcendent Interpretation

Thus far, I have focused on the Causal Interpretation and upon Denys's positive or cataphatic theology. But for every predicate he affirms of God, he also denies it. For instance, at *Divine Names* 5.10, he says that God "is both at rest and in motion, and neither at rest nor in motion."[30] Compare the tetralemma with which we began. This use of the First and Second Hypotheses for the same level of divine being is what generates the apparent contradictions in his theology. I have discussed one attempt to dissolve the contradiction and found it wanting. To be sure, Denys attributes positive properties to God because God is the cause of these properties in things, but they are also real properties in God. Yet, Denys also denies them. So, either he is being perverse, or he does not think that language about God is subject to the LNC and the LEM. Assuming a charitable interpretation of Denys, it seems that we are constrained to believe that he thinks discourse about God is not subject to these logical rules. In other words, when properly understood, the Causal Interpretation, together with Denys's negative theology, implies what I have called the Transcendent Interpretation. If Denys believes God is all things and believes God is none of these things, then Denys must believe that the LNC and LEM do not apply in theology.

And Denys is fortunately explicit on this point. At *Myst. theol.* 5, he says:

> In general, there is neither affirmation nor negation of (the Cause of all). Rather, we make affirmations and negations of the things that come after it; but of it, we make neither affirmation nor negation, since the perfect and unitary cause of all is beyond every affirmation and the transcendent cause of absolutely everything without qualification is beyond every negation and beyond everything.[31]

---

30. *Div. nom.* 5.10 = 189.12–13 Suchla; PG 3,825B: καὶ ἑστὼς καὶ κινούμενος καὶ οὔτε ἑστὼς οὔτε κινούμενος ....

31. *Myst.* 5 = 150.5–9 Suchla; PG 3, 1048B): οὔτε ἐστὶν αὐτῆς καθόλου θέσις οὔτε ἀφαίρεσις, ἀλλὰ τῶν μετ' αὐτὴν τὰς θέσεις καὶ ἀφαιρέσεις ποιοῦντες αὐτὴν οὔτε τίθεμεν οὔτε ἀφαιροῦμεν, ἐπεὶ καὶ ὑπὲρ πᾶσαν θέσιν ἐστὶν ἡ παντελὴς καὶ ἑνιαία τῶν πάντων αἰτία καὶ ὑπὲρ

If language about God is beyond the opposition between affirmation and denial, then God-talk is beyond the scope of the LNC, or as Denys Turner has put it, "what is demonstrated by this apophaticism is the failure of distinction itself" (Turner 1995, 44). However, it is striking that what Denys says here does not fit with his practice. For he does *not* make affirmations and denials only of what "comes after" God. Rather, he makes affirmations and denials of God, even though the logic of speaking about God is beyond the entire system of *thesis* and *aphairesis*. As such, we can view his use of the first and second hypotheses as a kind of ouroboric maneuver. Just as the snake Ouroboros ate its own tail to sustain its life, so too do Denys's apophatic and cataphatic theologies live only by ending in their own destruction. One advocate of the Transcendent Interpretation, Janet Williams, has in fact reserved the label "apophatic" for specifically this aspect of Denys's thought: not the denial that is opposed to affirmation, but the denial of both negations and affirmations together (J. N. Williams 1999, 157–72). And to deny this is to deny that the LNC and the LEM are valid in theology.

πᾶσαν ἀφαίρεσιν ἡ ὑπεροχὴ τοῦ πάντων ἁπλῶς ἀπολελυμένου καὶ ἐπέκεινα τῶν ὅλων. See *Myst.* 2 (PG 3:1000B; 143 Heil-Ritter).

REFERENCES

Abramowski, L. 1983. Marius Victorinus, Porphyrius und die römischen Gnostiker. *ZNW* 74:108–28.
———. 2005. Nicänismus und Gnosis im Rom des Bischofs Liberius: Der Fall des Marius Victorinus. *ZAC* 8:513–66.
———. 2007. "Audi ut dico": Literarische Beobachtungen und chronologische Erwägungen zu Marius Victorinus und den "platonisierenden" Nag Hammadi-Traktaten. *ZKG* 117:145–68.
Armstrong, A. H. 1966–1988. *Plotinus*. Text with an English Translation by A. H. Armstrong. 7 vols. LCL 441. Cambridge, Mass.: Harvard University Press.
———. 1971. Eternity, Life and Movement in Plotinus' Accounts of Nous. Pages 67–76 in *Le Néoplatonisme*. Colloques internationaux du CNRS à Royaumont du 9–13 Juin, 1969. Edited by P. M. Schuhl and P. Hadot. Paris: CNRS.
Atkinson, M. 1983. *Plotinus, Ennead V. 1: On the Three Principal Hypostases: A Commentary with Translation*. Oxford: Oxford University Press.
Athanassiadi, P. 2006. *La lutte pour l'orthodoxie dans le platonisme tardif de Numénius à Damascius*. Paris: Les Belles Lettres.
Aubin, P. 1992. *Plotin et le christianisme, Triade plotinienne et Trinité chrétienne*, Paris: Beauchesne.
Baltes, M. 2002. *Marius Victorinus: Zur Philosphie in seinen theologischen Schriften*. Beiträge zur Altertumskunde 174. Munich: Sauer.
Baltzly, D. 2006. Cathartic Virtue in Proclus' *In Timaeum*. Pages 169–84 in *Reading Plato in Antiquity*. Edited by D. Baltzly and H. Tarrant. London: Duckworth.
Barnes, T. D. 1979. Methodius, Maximus and Valentinus. *JTS* 30:47–55.
Barry, C., W.-P. Funk, P.-H. Poirier, and J. D. Turner 2000. *Zostrien (NH VIII, 1)*. BCNH 24. Québec: Presses de l'Univerité Laval; Louvain: Peeters.
Beatrice, P. P. 1992. Porphyry's Judgement on Origen. Pages 351–67 in *Origeniana Quinta. Papers of the 5th International Origen Congress, Boston College, 14–18 August 1989* Edited by R. J. Daly. Bibliotheca Ephemeridum Theologicarum Lovaniensium 105. Leuven: Presses universitaires de Louvain.
Bechtle, G. 1999a. *The Anonymous Commentary on Plato's "Parmenides."* Berner Reihe Philosophischer Studien 22. Bern: P. Haupt.
———. 1999b. Göttliche Henaden und platonischer Parmenides. Lösung eines Mißverständnisses? *Rheinisches Museum für Philologie* 142:358–391. Repr. pages 135–59 in *Iamblichus – Aspekte seiner Philosophie und Wissenschaftskonzeption*. Studien zum späteren Platonismus. Sankt Augustin: Academia, 2006.
———. 1999c. Das Böse im Platonismus: Überlegungen zur Position Jamblichs. *Bochumer*

Philosophisches Jahrbuch für Antike und Mittelalter 4:63–82. Repr. pages 1–14 in *Iamblichus – Aspekte seiner Philosophie und Wissenschaftskonzeption*. Studien zum späteren Platonismus. Sankt Augustin: Academia, 2006).

———. 2000. The Question of Being and the Dating of the Anonymous "Parmenides" Commentary. *Ancient Philosophy* 20: 393–414.

———. 2006. A Neglected Testimonium on the Chaldaean Oracles. *CQ* 56:563–81.

Bendinelli, G. 2005. Il Commento a Giovanni e la Tradizione Scolastica dell' Antichita. Pages 133–56 in *Il Commento a Giovanni di Origene. Il testo e suoi contesti, Atti dell' VIII convegno del Gruppo Italiano di Ricerca su Origene e la Tradizione Alessandrina (Roma, 28–30 settembre 2004)*. Edited by E. Prinzivalli. Biblioteca di Adamantius 3. Villa Verucchio: Pier Giorgio Pazzini.

Berchman, R. 2005. *Porphyry Against the Christians*. Ancient Mediterranean and Medieval Texts and Contexts 1. Leiden: Brill.

Bidez, J. 1913. *Vie de Porphyre: Le philosophe néo-platonicien*. Hildesheim: Georg Olms. Repr. 1980.

Billings, T. H. 1919. *The Platonism of Philo Judaeus*. Chicago: University of Chicago Press.

Bonazzi, M. 2008. Towards Transcendence: Philo and the Renewal of Platonism in the Early Imperial Age. Pages 232–51 in *Philo of Alexandria and Post-Aristotelian Philosophy*. Edited by F. Alesse. Studies on Philo of Alexandria 5. Leiden: Brill.

Brisson L., et. al. 1982. *Porphyre, La vie de Plotin. Études d'introduction, texte grec, et traduction française, commentaire, notes complémentaires, bibliographie*. 2 vols. Histoire des doctrines de l'antiquité classique 16. Paris: Vrin.

———. 1987a. Amélius: Sa vie, son oeuvre, sa doctrine, son style. *ANRW* 36.2:793–860. Berlin: de Gruyter.

———. 1987b. *Platon. Lettres. Translated, with introduction and notes, by Luc Brisson*. Paris: Flammarion.

———. 1994. *Platon. Parménide. Translated, with introduction and notes, by Luc Brisson*. GF 688. Paris: Flammarion. 2nd rev. ed. 1999.

———. 1999a. The Platonic Background in the *Apocalypse of Zostrianos*: Numenius and Letter II attributed to Plato. Pages 173–88 in *The Tradition of Platonism: Essays in Honour of John Dillon*. Edited by J. J. O'Cleary. Aldershot, UK: Ashgate.

———. 1999b. Qualche aspetto della storia del Platonismo. *Elenchos* 20:145–69.

———. 2000. Castricius Firmus. *Dictionnaire des Philosophes Antiques* 3:425.

Bussanich, J. 1996. Plotinus' Metaphysics of the One. Pages 38–65 in *The Cambridge Companion to Plotinus*. Edited by Lloyd P. Gerson. Cambridge: Cambridge University Press.

Busse, A. 1887. *Isagoge et in Aristotelis categorias commentarium*. CAG 4.1. Berlin: Reimer.

Cadious, R. 1932. Dictionnaires antiques dans l'oeuvre d'Origène. *REG* 45:271–85.

Calabi, F. 2002. Conoscibilità e inconoscibilità di Dio in Filone di Alessandria. Pages 35–54 in *Arrhetos Theos: l'ineffabilità del primo principio nel medio platonismo*. Edited by F. Calabi. Pisa: ETS (coll. Filosofia. 55)..

———. 2008. *God's Acting, Man's Acting: Tradition and Philosophy in Philo of Alexandria*. Studies in Philo of Alexandria 4. Leiden: Brill.

Cazelais, S. 2005. L'expression HO EPI PASI THEOS de l'Ancienne Académie à Origene et dans le *Commentaire* anonyme sure le *Parmenide*. *Science et Esprit* 57:199–214.

Chadwick, H. 1967. Philo and the Beginnings of Christian Thought. Pages 137–92 in *The Cambridge History of Later Greek and Early Medieval Philosophy* Edited by A. H.

Armstrong. Cambridge: Cambridge University Press.
Charrue, J.-M. 1978. *Plotin, Lecteur de Platon*. Paris: Les Belles Lettres. Repr. 1987.
Chase, M. 2003. *Simplicius. On Aristotle's Categories 1-4*. The Ancient Commentators on Aristotle Series. Ithaca, N.Y.: Cornell University Press.
Cherniss, H. 1930. *The Platonism of Gregory of Nyssa*, Berkeley and Los Angeles: University of California Press.
———, trans. 1976. On the Generation of the Soul in Plato's Timaeus. Pages 133-345 in *Plutarch's Moralia*, vols. 13.1 (999C-1032F) and 13.2 (1033A-1036B). Cambridge, Mass.: Harvard University Press; London: Heinemann.
Clarke, E. C., J. M. Dillon, and J. P. Hershbell. 2003. *Iamblichus: On the Mysteries*. Atlanta: Society of Biblical Literature.
Cornford, F. M. 1939. *Plato and Parmenides. Parmenides' Way of Truth and Plato's Parmenides Translated with an Introduction and a Running Commentary*. New York: The Humanities Press; London: Routledge & Kegan Paul.
Corrigan, K. 1987. Amelius, Plotinus and Porphyry on Being, Intellect and the One. A Reappraisal. *ANRW* 35.2:975-93. New York: de Gruyter
Corrigan, K. 2000a. Platonism and Gnosticism: The Anonymous Commentary on the Parmenides: Middle or Neoplatonic?" in *Gnosticism and Later Platonism: Themes, Figures, and Texts*. Edited by J. Turner and R. Majercik. SBLSymS 12. Atlanta: Society of Biblical Literature, 141-77.
———. 2000b. Positive and Negative Matter in Later Platonism: The Uncovering of Plotinus's Dialogue with the Gnostics. Pages 19-56 in *Gnosticism and Later Platonism: Themes, Figures, and Texts*. Edited by J. Turner and R. Majercik. Society of Biblical Literature Symposium Series 12. Atlanta: Society of Biblical Literature.
Corsini, E. 1962. *Il Trattato De Divinis nominibus Dello Pseudo-Doinigi e i Commenti Neoplatonici al Parmenide*. Univerità di Torino Pubblicazioni della Facoltà di Lettere e Filosofia XII,4. Torino: Giappichelli.
Cousin, V. 1864. Pages 617-1244 in *Procli commentarium in Platonis Parmenidem*. Procli Philosophi Platonici. Opera inedita, pars 3. Paris: Durand. Repr. Hildesheim: Olms, 1961.
Daniélou, J. 1956. Eunome l'Arien et l'exégèse platonicienne du Cratyle. *REG* 69:412-32.
———. 1964. *Message Évangelique et Culture Hellenistique*. Tournai: Brepols.
de Falco, V., ed. 1922. *[Iamblichi] theologoumena arithmeticae*. Leipzig: Teubner, 1-87.
De Haas, F. A. J. 2001. Did Plotinus and Porphyry Disagree on Aristotle's Categories? *Phronesis* 46:492-526.
Dehnhard, H. 1964. *Das Problem der Abhängigkeit des Basilius von Plotin*. Berlin: de Gruyter.
des Places, E. 1966. *Jamblique: Les Mystères d'Égypte*. Collections des Universités de France. Paris: Les Belles Lettres.
———. 1973. *Numénius: Fragments*. CUF-Association Guillaume Budé. Paris: Les Belles Lettres.
Deuse, W. 1973. *Theodoros von Asine, Sammlung der Testimonien und Kommentar*. Palingenesis 6. Wiesbaden: Steiner.
Diehl, E. 1965. *Procli Diadochi in Platonis Timaeum commentaria*. 3 vols. Leipzig: Teubner, 1904. Repr. Amsterdam: Hakkert.
Diels, H. ed. 1882. *Simplicius. In Aristotelis physicorum libros quattuor priores commentaria*. CAG 9. Berlin: Reimer.

Dillon, J. M. 1973a. *Iamblichi Chalcidensis In Platonis Dialogos Commentariorum Fragmenta*. Philosophia antiqua 23. Leiden: Brill.

———. 1973b. *In Platonis dialogos commentariorum fragmenta*. With text, translation and commentary. Philosophia antiqua 23. Leiden: Brill.

———. 1977. *The Middle Platonists, 80 B.C. to A.D. 220*. Ithaca, N.Y.: Cornell University Press.

———. 1987. Iamblichus of Chalcis (c. 240 - 325 A.D.). *ANRW* 36.2:862–909. Part 2. Berlin: de Gruyter.

———. 1992. Porphyry's Doctrine of the One. Pages 356–66 in ΣΟΦΙΑΣ ΜΑΙΗΤΟΡΕΣ: *Chercheurs de sagesse: Hommage à Jean Pépin*. Edited by M.-O. Goulet-Cazé, G. Madec, and D. O'Brien. Collection des Études Augustiniennes: Série Antiquité 131. Paris: Institut d'Études Augustiniennes.

———. 1996. *The Middle Platonists, 80 B.C. to A.D. 220*. Rev. ed. Ithaca, N.Y.: Cornell University Press.

———. 1997. Iamblichus' Νοερὰ Θεωρία of Aristotle's *Categories*. Pages 65–77 in *Iamblichus: The Philosopher*. Edited by H. J. Blumenthal and J. F. Finamore. Syllecta Classica 8. Iowa City: University of Iowa Press.

———. 2003. *The Heirs of Plato: A Study of the Old Academy, 347–274 B.C.* Oxford: Oxford University Press.

Dodds, E. R. 1928. The Parmenides of Plato and the Origin of the Neoplatonic "One." *CQ* 22:129–42.

———. 1963. *Proclus: The Elements of Theology: A Revised Text with Translation, Introduction and Commentary*. Oxford: Clarendon.

Dolidze, T. 2000. Der ΚΙΝΗΣΙΣ-Begriff der Griechischen Philosophie bei Gregor von Nyssa. Philosophie bei Gregor von Nyssa. Pages 221–45 in *Gregory of Nyssa. Homilies on the Beatitudes*. Proceedings of the Eighth International Colloquium on Gregory of Nyssa, Paderborn, 14–18 September 1998. Edited by R. Drobner and A. Viciano. Supplement to *Vigiliae Christianae* LII. Leiden: Brill.

Dörrie, H. 1959. *Porphyrios' Symmikta Zetemata*. Monographen zur Klassischen Altertumswissenschaft 20. Munich: Beck.

———. 1970. Der König. Ein platonisches Schlüsselwort, von Plotin mit neuem Sinn erfüllt. *Revue International de Philosophie* 24:217–35. Repr. Dörrie, H. *Platonica minora*. Studia et testimonia antiqua 8. Munich: Fink, 1976, 390–405.

———. 1974. Le renouveau du platonisme à l'époque de Cicéron. *Revue de Philosophie et de Théologie* 8:13–29.

———, and M. Baltes. 1999. *Der Platonismus in der Antike: Grundlagen–System–Entwicklung* V. Stuttgart: Frommann; Bad Cannstatt: Holzboog.

Drecoll, V. H. In press. Marius Victorinus. In *Reallexikon für Antike und Christentum*.

Edwards, M. J. 1990. Porphyry and the Intelligible Triad. *JHS* 110:14–25.

———. 1993. Ammonius, Teacher of Origen. *Journal of Ecclesiastical History* 44:1–13.

———. 1998. Did Origen Apply the Term *Homoousios* to the Son?" *JTS* 49:578–90.

———. 2002. *Origen against Plato*. Ashgate Studies in Philosophy and Theology in Late Antiquity. Ashgate: Aldershot.

———. 2006. Nicene Theology and the Second God. *Studia Patristica* 40:191–95.

Festugière, A. J. 1966–1968. *Proclus: Commentaire sur le Timée*. 5 vols. Paris: Vrin.

Finamore, J. F. 1985. *Iamblichus and the Theory of the Vehicle of the Soul*. Chico, Calif.: Polebridge.

———, 1997. The Rational Soul in Iamblichus' Philosophy. Pages 163–76 in *Iamblichus: The Philosopher*. Edited by H. J. Blumenthal and J. F. Finamore. Syllecta Classica 8. Iowa City: University of Iowa Press.

———, and Dillon, J. M. 2002. *Iamblichus De Anima: Text, Translation, and Commentary*. Leiden: Brill.

Förster, N. 1999. *Marcus Magus*. WSNT 114. Tübingen: Mohr Siebeck.

Fowler, H. N., trans. 1925. *Plato in Twelve Volumes*. Vol. 9 translated by Harold N. Fowler. Cambridge, Mass.: Harvard University Press; London: Heinemann.

Funk, W.-P. 2004. Texte Copte. Pages 189–238 in *L'Allogène (NH XI, 3)*. Edited by W.-P. Funk et al. BCNH 30. Québec: Presses de l'Univerité Laval; Louvain: Peeters.

———, and P.-H. Poirier. 2004. Notes philologiques. Pages 241–57 in *L'Allogène (NH XI, 3)*. Edited by W.-P. Funk et al. BCNH 30. Québec: Presses de l'Univerité Laval; Louvain: Peeters.

———, P.-H. Poirier, M. Scopello, and J. D. Turner. 2004. *L'Allogène (NH XI, 3)*. BCNH 30. Québec: Presses de l'Univerité Laval; Louvain: Peeters.

Garfield, J. 1995. *The Fundamental Wisdom of the Middle Way: Nâgarjuna's Mûlamadhyamaka-kârikâ*. Oxford: Oxford University Press.

Gatti, M. L. 1996. Plotinus: The Platonic Tradition and the Foundation of Neoplatonism. In *The Cambridge Companion to Plotinus*. Edited by Lloyd P. Gerson. Cambridge: Cambridge University Press, 10–37.

Geljon, A. C., and D. T. Runia. 1995. An Index locorum to Billings. *Studia Philoncia Annual* 7: 169–85.

Gill, M. L., and P. Ryan. 1996. *Plato: Parmenides*. Translated by Mary Louise Gill and Paul Ryan. Introduction by Mary Louise Gill. Indianapolis: Hackett.

Ginzberg, L. 1909. *The Legends of the Jews*. Vol. 1. Trans. H. Szold. Philadelphia: Jewish Publication Society of America.

Goulet, R. 1977. Porphyre, Ammonius, les deux Origènes et les autres.... *Revue d'histoire et de philosophie religieuses* 52:483–84.

———. 2000. Eustathe de Cappadoce. Pages 369–78 in *Dictionnaire des Philosophes Antiques*, vol. 3. Paris: CNRS.

———. 2003. Galien de Pergame. Pages 440–66 n *Dictionnaire des Philosophes Antique*, vol. 3. Paris: CNRS.

Gourinat, J.-B. 2001. La dialectique des hypothèses contraires dans le *Parménide* de Platon. Pages 233–61 in *La philosophie de Platon*. Edited by M. Fattal. Paris: L'Harmattan.

Gurtler, G. M. 1992. Plotinus and the Platonic *Parmenides*. *International Philosophical Quarterly* 32:443–57.

Hadot, P. 1957. Etre, vie, pensée chez Plotin et avant Plotin. Pages 105–57 in *Les Sources de Plotin*. Geneva: Fondation Hardt.

———. 1960. *Marius Victorinus: Traitées théologiques sur la Trinité: texte établi par Paul Henry, introduction, traduction et notes par Pierre Hadot*. 2 vols. Sources chrétiennes 68–69. Paris: Cerf.

———. 1961. Fragments d'un commentaire de Porphyre sur le Parménide. *REG* 74:410–38.

———. 1962. L'image de la Trinité dans l'âme chez Victorinus et chez Saint Augustin. *Studia Patristica* 6:409–42.

———. 1966. La métaphysique de Porphyre. Pages 127–57 in *Porphyre*. Entretiens sur l'antiquité classique 12. Geneva: Fondation Hardt.

———. 1968. *Porphyre et Victorinus*. 2 vols. Paris: Institut des Études Augustiniennes.

———. 1971. *Marius Victorinus. Recherches sur sa vie et ses oeuvres*. Paris: Institut des Études Augustiniennes.

———. 1996. Porphyre et Victorinus. Questions et hypotheses. Pages 115-25 in *Res Orientales* IX. Bures-sur-Yvette: Groupe pour l'Étude de la Civilisation du Moyen-Orient.

Hägg, H. F. 2006. *Clement of Alexandria and the Beginnings of Christian Apophaticism*. Oxford: Oxford University Press.

Halfwassen, J. 1993. Speusipp und die metaphysische Deutung von Platons "Parmenides." Pages 339-73 in *EN KAI ΠΛΗΘΟΣ - Einheit und Vielheit, Festschrift für Karl Bormann zum 65. Geburtstag*. Edited by L. Hagemann and R. Glei. Religionswissenschaftliche Studien 30. Würzburg: Echter.

Hancock, C. L. 1992. Negative Theology in Gnosticism and Neoplatonism. Pages 174-80 in *Neoplatonism and Gnosticism*. Edited by R. T. Wallis and J. Bregman. Albany: SUNY Press.

Harl, M. 1983. *Origène, Philocalie 1-20 sûr les Écritures*. Introduction, texte, traduction et notes par M. Harl. Sources Chrétiennes 302. Paris: Cerf.

———. 1987. La préexistence des ames dans l'oeuvre d'Origène. Pages 238-58 in *Origeniana Quarta. Die Referate des 4. Internationalen Origeneskongresses*. Edited by L. Lies. Innsbrucker Theologische Studien 19. Innsbruck-Wien: Tyrolia.

Hegel, G. W. F. 1807. *Phänomenologie des Geistes (Selbstbewusstsein)*, Werke 3. Frankfurt am Main: Suhrkamp, 1973.

Hegel, G. W. F. 1807. *The Phenomenology of Spirit*. Translated by A. V. Miller. Oxford: Oxford University Press, 1977. Reprinted 1981.

Hegel, G. W. F. 1955. *Lectures on the History of Philosophy*. Translated by E. S. Haldane. 3 vols. London: Kegan, Paul, Trench, Trübner, 1892, 1894, 1896. Repr. London: Routledge, Kegan & Paul.

Hegel, G.W.F. 1971. *Vorlesungen über die Geschichte der Philosophie*. Berlin : Duncker und Humblot, 1833-1836. Repr. Theorie-Werkausgabe Vol. 18. Frankfurt: Suhrkamp.

Heil, G., and A. M. Ritter, eds. 1991. *De coelesti hierarchia, De ecclesiastica hierarchia, De mystica theologia*. Patristische Texte und Studien 36. Berlin: de Gruyter.

Heine, R. 2000. Recovering Origen's Commentary on Ephesians from Jerome. *JTS* 51, 478-514.

Henry, P. 1938. *Études plotiniennes I. Les états du texte de Plotin*. Bruxelles: Desclée de Brouwer.

Henry, P., and H.-R. Schwyzer, eds. 1977. *Plotini Opera: Tomus II: Enneades IV-V*. Oxford: Clarendon.

Hermann, C. F. 1850-1853. *Platonis Dialogi secundum Thrassylli tetralogias disposili. Ex recognitione Caroli Frederici Harmanni*. Leipzig: Teubner.

Hoek, A. van den. 1988. *Clement of Alexandria and His Use of Philo in the Stromateis: An Early Christian Reshaping of a Jewish Model*. Vigiliae christianae Supplements 3. Leiden: Brill.

———. 1997. The "Catechetical" School of Early Christian Alexandria and Its Philonic Heritage. *HTR* 90:59-87.

———, and C. Mondésert. 2001. *Clément d'Alexandrie, Les Stromates: Stromate IV*. Sources Chrétiennes. Paris: Cerf.

Hoffmann, P. 1994. Damascius. Pages 540-93 in *Dictionnaire des philosophes antiques*, 2.

———, et al. 2001. *Simplicius. Commentaire sur les Catégories d'Aristote. Chapitres 2-4*,vol.

2. Edited by I. Hadot. Trans. P. Hoffmann. Notes by C. Luna. Paris: Les Belles Lettres.
Horn, L. 2006. Contradiction. In *The Stanford Encyclopedia of Philosophy (Fall 2006 Edition)*. Online: http://plato.stanford.edu/archives/fall2006/entries/contradiction/. Cited 4 Sept. 2009.
Ivanka, E. 1964. *Plato Christianus: Übernahme und Umgestaltung des Platonisms durch die Väter*. Einsieldeln: Johannes Verlag.
Jackson, B. D. 1967. Plotinus and the *Parmenides*. *Journal of the History of Philosophy* 5:315–27.
Jonas, H. 1993. *Gnosis und spätantiker Geist: Zweiter Teil: Von der Mythologie zur mystischen Philosophie: Erste und zweite Hälfte: Herausgegeben von Kurt Rudolph*. Göttingen: Vandenhoeck & Ruprecht.
Jones, D. 2004. *The Soul of the Human Embryo. An enquiry into the status of the human embryo in the Christian tradition*. London: Continuum.
Kalbfleisch, K., ed. 1907. *Simplicius: In Aristotelis categorias commentarium*. CAG 8. Berlin: Reimer.
Kalligas, P. 1991. *Porphyriu Peri tu Plotinu biu kai tēs taxeōs tōn bibliōn autu*. Bibliothēkē A. Manusē 1. Athens: Akademia Athenon.
Kasser, R., and P. Luisier. 2007. P. Bodmer XLIII: Un feuillet de *Zostrien*. *Le Muséon* 120:251–72.
Kenney, J. P. 1992. The Platonism of the Tripartite Tractate. Pages 187–206 in *Neoplatonism and Gnosticism*. Edited by R. T. Wallis and J. Bregman. Albany: SUNY Press.
King, K. L. 1995. *Revelation of the Unknowable God with Text, Translation, and Notes to NHC XI,3 Allogenes*. CCL. Santa Rosa, Calif.: Polebridge.
Klibansky, R. and Ch. Labowsky, eds. 1953. *Parmenides usque ad finem primae hypothesis nec non Procli commentarium in Parmenidem, pars ultima adhuc inedita, interprete Guillelmo de Moerbeka*. Vol. 3 of *Plato Latinus*. London: Warburg Institute; Leiden: Brill.
Klostermann, E., ed. 1904. *Eusebius' Werke* 3.1. GCS 11.1. Leipzig: Hinrichs.
Koch, H. 1895. Proclus als Quelle des Pseudo-Dionysius Areopagita in der Lehre com Bösen. *Philologus* 54:438–54.
Koetschau, P. 1899. *Origenes Werke I. Contra Celsum I–IV*. GCS 2. Leipzig: Hinrichs.
———. 1899. *Origenes Werke II. Contra Celsum V–VIII, De oratione*. GCS 3. Leipzig: Hinrichs.
———. 1913. *Origenes Werke V. De principiis*. GCS 22. Leipzig: Hinrichs.
Kroll, W. 1892. Ein neuplatonischer Parmenides-kommentar in einem Turiner Palimpsest. *Rheinisches Museum für Philologie* 47:599–627.
Kruger, M. 1996. *Ichgeburt. Origenes und die Entstehung der christlichen Idee der Widerverkorperung in der Denkbewegung von Pythagoras bis Lessing*. Philosophische Texte und Studien 42. Hildesheim: Olms.
Lacombrade, C., ed. 1964. *L'empereur Julien. Oeuvres complètes*, vol. 2.2. Paris: Les Belles Lettres.
Laporte, J. 1995. *Théologie liturgique de Philon d'Alexandrie et Origène*. Liturgie 6. Paris: Cerf.
Lardet, P., ed. and trans. 1982. *Sanctus Hieronymus, Contra Rufinum*. 3 vols. Corpus Christianorum. Series Latina 79. Turnhout: Brepols.
Le Bonniec, H. 1982. *Arnobe: Contre les gentils, livre I*. Paris: Les Belles Lettres.
Le Boulluec, A. 1981. *Clément d'Alexandrie: Les Stromates*. Stromate V, Tome II. Commen-

taire, bibliographie et index. Sources Chrétiennes 279. Paris: Cerf.
Leroux, G. 1990. *Commentary on Enneads* VI.8. Paris: Éditions du Cerf.
Lilla, S. R. C. 1971. *Clement of Alexandria: a Study in Christian Platonism and Gnosticism.* Oxford Theological Monographs, Oxford: Oxford University Press.
———. 1980. The Notion of Infinitude in Ps.-Dionysius Areopagita. *JTS* 31:93–103.
———. 1997. Pseudo-Denys L' Aréopagite, Porphyre et Damascius. Pages 117–52 in *Denys L' Aréopagite et sa Postérité en Orient et en Occident.* Edited by Y. de Andia. Actes du Colloque International, Paris, 21–24 septembre 1994. Paris: Études augustiniennes.
Linguiti, A. 1995. Commentarium in Platonis "Parmenidem." Pages 3.63–202 (text, translation, commentary), 601–12 and 649 (indices) in *Testi e lessico nei papiri di cultura greca e Latina.* Studi e Testi per il Corpus dei Papiri Filosofici. Firenze: Olschki.
Logan, A. 1996. *Gnostic Truth and Christian Heresy: A Study in the History of Gnosticism.* Peabody, Mass.: Hendrickson.
Löhr, W. A. 1996. *Basilides und seine Schule: Eine Studie zur Theologie- und Kirchengeschichte des zweiten Jahrhunderts,* Wissenschaftliche Untersuchungen um Neues Testament 83. Tübingen: Mohr Siebeck.
Luibheid, Colm, trans. with Paul Rorem and Rene Roques. 1987. *Pseudo-Dionysius: The Complete Works.* New York: Paulist.
Madec, G. 1989. § 564 C. Marius Victorinus. Pages 342–55 in *Restauration und Erneuerung: Die lateinische Literatur von 284–374 n.Chr.* Edited by Reinhart Herzog and P. L. Schmidt. Handbuch der Lateinischen Literatur der Antike 5. Handbuch der Altertumswissenschaft. Munich: Beck.
Majercik, R. 1989. *The Chaldean Oracles: Text, Translation, and Commentary.* Studies in Greek and Roman Religion 5. Leiden: Brill.
———. 1992. The Existence–Life–Intellect Triad in Gnosticism and Neoplatonism. *CQ* 42:475–88.
———. 2001. Chaldaean Triads in Neoplatonic Exegesis: Some Reconsiderations. *CQ* 51:265–96.
Mar Gregorios, P. 1988. Theurgic Neo-Platonism and the Eunomius-Gregory Debate. An Examination of the Background. Pages 217–35 in *El "Contra Eunomium I" en la produccion literaria de Gregorio di Nisa.* Edited by L. Mateo-Seco and J. Bastero. Pamplona: Colleción Teológica de la Universidad de Navarra.
Markschies, C. 2007. Was bedeutet οὐσία? Zwei Antworten bei Origenes und Ambrosius und deren Bedeutung für ihre Bibelerklärung und Theologie. Pages 173–93 in C. Markschies. *Origenes und sein Erbe. Gesammelte Studien.* Texte und Untersuchungen zur Geschichte der altchristlichen Literatur 160. Berlin: de Gruyter.
McGuckin, J. A., ed. 2004. *The Westminster Handbook to Origen.* The Westminster Handbooks to Christian Theology. Louisville, Ky.: Westminster.
Morrow, G. R., and J. M. Dillon. 1987. *Proclus' Commentary on Plato's Parmenides.* Princeton: Princeton University Press.
Mühlenberg, E. 1966. *Die Unendlichkeit Gottes bei Gregor von Nyssa.* Göttingen: Vandenhoek & Ruprecht.
Musurillo, H. 2001. *From Glory to Glory: Texts from Gregory of Nyssa's Mystical Writings.* New York: St. Vladimir's Seminary Press.
Narbonne, J.-M. 1999. L'*ou ti* de Plotin. *Les Cahiers philosophiques de Strasbourg* 8:23–51.
Narbonne, J.-M. 2001. The Origin, Significance and Bearing of the ἐπέκεινα Motif in Plotinus and the Neoplatonic Tradition. *Proceedings of the Boston Area Colloquium in*

Ancient Philosophy 17:185-97.
Natorp, P. 1903. Platos *Ideenlehre: Eine Einführung in den Idealismus*. Leipzig: Durrheim.
O'Brien, D. 1992. Origène et Plotin sur le roi de l'univers. Pages 317-42 in ΣΟΦΙΗΣ ΜΑΙΗΤΟΡΕΣ. *Chercheurs de sagesse: hommage à Jean Pépin*. Edited by M.-O. Goulet-Cazé, G. Madec, D. O'Brien. Collection des Études Augustiniennes 131. Paris: Institut d'Etudes Augustiniennes.
Onuki, T. 1989. *Gnosis und Stoa: Eine Untersuchung zum Apokryphon des Johannes*. Novum Testamentum et Orbis Antiquus 9. Freiburg Schweiz: Universitätsverlag.
Osborn, E. F. 1957. *The Philosophy of Clement of Alexandria*. Texts and Studies N. S. 3. Cambridge: Cambridge University Press.
Osborn, E. F. 2005. *Clement of Alexandria*. Cambridge: Cambridge University Press.
Owen, G. E. L. 1965. The Place of the Timaeus in Plato's Dialogues. Pages 313-38 in *Studies in Plato's Metaphysics*. Edited by R. E. Allen. London: Routledge & Kegan Paul.
Owen, G. E. L. 1966. Plato and Parmenides on the Timeless Present. *The Monist* 50:317-40.
Patillon, M., and L. Brisson 2001. *Longin, Fragments, Art rhétorique. Rufus, Art rhétorique.* Edited and translated by Michel Patillon and Luc Brisson. Collection des Universités de France publiée sous le patronage de l'Association Guillaume Budé. Paris: Les Belles Lettres.
Pearson, B. 1990. *Gnosticism, Judaism, and Egyptian Christianity*. Studies in Antiquity and Christianity. Minneapolis: Fortress.
Pépin, J. 2002. Le Parménide dans les Sentences de Porphyre. Pages 323-28 in *Il Parmenide di Platone e la sua tradizione*. Edited by M. Barbanti and F. Romano. Catania: Università di Catania.
Pleše, Z. 2006. *Poetics of the Gnostic Universe: Narrative and Cosmology in the Apocryphon of John*. Nag Hammadi and Manichaean Studies 52. Leiden: Brill.
Preuschen, E. 1903. *Commentarii in evangelium Joannis (lib. 1, 2, 4, 5, 6, 10, 13)*. Edited by Erwin Preuschen. [= *Der Johanneskommentar*. Origenes Werke 4. Die Griechischen christlichen Schriftsteller der ersten drei Jahrhunderte 10. Leipzig: Hinrichs.
Prinzivalli, E. 2005. L'uomo e il suo destino nel Coomento a Giovanni. Pages 374-79 in *Il Commento a Giovanni di Origene. Il testo e suoi contesti, Atti dell' VIII convegno del Gruppo Italiano di Ricerca su Origene e la Tradizione Alessandrina (Roma, 28-30 settembre 2004)*. Edited by E. Prinzivalli. Biblioteca di Adamantius 3. Rome: Villa Verucchio: Pazzini Stampatore.
Radice, R. 2003. The "Nameless Principle" from Philo to Plotinus: An Outline of Research. Pages 167-82 in *Italian Studies on Philo of Alexandria*. Edited by F. Calabi. Studies in Philo of Alexandria and Mediterranean Antiquity 1. Leiden: Brill.
Rasimus, T. 2009. *Paradise Reconsidered in Gnostic Mythmaking: Rethinking Sethianism in Light of the Ophite Evidence*. Nag Hammadi and Manichaean Studies. Leiden: Brill.
Rasimus, T. in press. Stoic Ingredients in the Neoplatonic *Being-Life-Mind* Triad: An Original Second-Century Gnostic Innovation? In *Stoicism in Early Christianity*. Edited by T. Rasimus, T. Engberg-Pedersen and I. Dunderberg. Peabody, Mass.: Hendrickson.
Rist, J. M. 1962. The Neoplatonic One and Plato's *Parmenides*. *Transactions and Proceedings of the American Philological Association* 93:389-401.
Rist, J. M. 1967. *Plotinus: Road to Reality*. Cambridge: Cambridge University Press.
———. 1981. Basil's "Neoplatonism": Its Background and Nature. Pages 137-220 in *Basil of*

Caesarea, Christian, Humanist, Ascetic. Edited by P. J. Fedwick. Toronto: Pontifical Institute of Mediaeval Studies.

———. 1983. Beyond Stoic and Platonist. A Sample of Origen's Treatment of Philosophy (Contra Celsum IV. 62–70). Pages 228–38 in *Platonismus und Christentum: Festschrift für Heinrich Dörrie*. Edited by H.-D. Blume and F. Mann. Westfalen: Aschendorff.

Robinson, J. A. 1893. *The Philocalia of Origen, the text revised with a critical introduction and indices*. Cambridge: Cambridge University Press.

Robinson, J. M. 1988. *The Nag Hammadi Library in English*. 2nd rev. ed. San Francisco: Harper.

Rousseau, P. 1994. *Basil of Caesarea*, Berkeley and Los Angeles: University of California Press.

Ruelle, C. É. 1899. *Damascii successoris dubitationes et solutions. De primis principiis in Parmenidem*. 2 vols. Paris: Klincksieck. Repr. Brussels: Culture et Civilisation, 1964; Amsterdam: Brepols, 1966.

Runia, D. T. 1986. *Philo of Alexandria and the Timaeus of Plato*. Philosophia Antiqua 44. Second edition. Leiden: Brill.

———, ed. 1995. *The Studia Philonica Annual: Studies in Hellenistic Judaism 7*. Atlanta: SBL.

———. 2007. The Rehabilitation of the Jackdaw: Philo of Alexandria and Ancient Philosophy. In *Greek and Roman Philosophy 100 BC–200 AD*. Edited by R. Sorabji and R. W. Sharples. London: Duckworth, 483–500.

———. 2008. Philo and Hellenistic Doxography. In *Philo of Alexandria and Post-Aristotelian Philosophy* Edited by F. Alesse. Studies in Philo of Alexandria, 5. Leiden: Brill, 13–52.

Saffrey, H. D. 1984. Le "Philosophe de Rhodes": est-il Théodore d'Asine. Pages 65–76 in *Mémorial André-Jean Festugière: antiquité paienne et chretienne: vingt-cinq études*. Paris: Cramer.

———. 2000. *Le néoplatonisme après Plotin*. Histoire des doctrines de l'Antiquite classique 24. Paris: Vrin.

———, and L. G. Westerink, eds. and trans. 1968–1997. *Proclus, Theologie Platonicienne*. 6 vols. CUF–Association Guillaume Budé. Paris: Les Belles Lettres.

———, and A.-Ph. Segonds 2001. *Marinus, Proclus ou Sur le bonheur*. Texte établi, traduit et annoté par H. D. Saffrey et A.-Ph. Segonds, avec la collaboration de C. Luna. Collection des universités de France publiée sous le patronage de l'Association Guillaume Budé. Paris: Les Belles Lettres.

———, and L. G. Westerink 1968–1997. *Proclus, Théologie Platonicienne. Texte etabli et traduit par H.D. Saffrey and L.G. Westerink*. 6 Vols. Collection des universités de France. Paris: Les Belles Lettres.

Sayre, K. M. 1996. *Parmenides' Lesson: Translation and Explication of Plato's Parmenides*. Notre Dame: University of Notre Dame Press.

Schenke, H.-M. 1974. Das sethianische System nach Nag-Hammadi-Handschriften. *Studia Coptica*. P. Nagel. Edited by Berliner Byzantinistiche Arbeiten 45. Berlin: Akademie-Verlag, 165–73.

———. 1981. The Phenomenon and Significance of Gnostic Sethianism. Pages 588–616 in *The Rediscovery of Gnosticism*. Vol. 2: *Sethian Gnosticism*. Edited by B. Layton. Studies in the History of Religions 41 (Supplements to Numen). Leiden: Brill.

Schibli, H. 1992. Origen, Didymus and the Vehicle of the Soul. Pages 381–91 in *Origeniana Quinta. Historica, text and method, biblica, philosophica, theologica, Origenism and later developments.* Edited by R. J. Daly. Papers of the 5th International Origen Congress (Boston College, 14–18 August 1989). BETL 105. Leuven: Leuven: Presses universitaires de Louvain and Peeters.

Scolnicov, S. 2003. *Plato's Parmenides.* Berkeley and Los Angeles: University of California Press.

Segonds, A.-P. 2003. *Proclus: Sur le Premiere Alcibiade de Platon.* 2 vols. Collection des Universités de France. Paris: Les Belles Lettres.

Segonds, A.-Ph., and H. D. Saffrey. 2001. *Marinus, Proclus ou Sur le bonheur.* Texte établi, traduit et annoté par H. D. Saffrey et A.-Ph. Segonds, avec la collaboration de C. Luna. CUF–Association Guillaume Budé. Paris: Les Belles Lettres.

Sels, L. 2009. *Gregory of Nyssa. De hominis opificio. O obraze cloveka. The Fourteenth-Century Slavonic Translation. A Critical Edition with Greek Parallel and Commentary.* Bausteine zur slavischen Philologie und Kulturgeschichte. Neue Folge. Reihe B. Köln, Weimar, Wien: Böhlau.

Sesboué, B. 1982. *Basile. Contre Eunome.* SC 299. Paris: Cerf.

Shaw, G. 1995. *Theurgy and the Soul: The Neoplatoism of Iamblichus.* University Park, Penn: Pennsylvania State University Press.

Sinnige, Th. 1984. Gnostic Influences in the Early Works of Plotinus and in Augustine. *Plotinus amid Gnostics and Christians: Papers Presented at the Plotinus Symposium Held at the Free University, Amsterdam on 25 January 1984.* Edited by D. Runia. Amsterdam: VY Uitgeverij/Free University Press, 73–97.

Sleeman, J. H., and G. Pollet. 1980. *Lexicon Plotinianum.* Leuven: Presses universitaires de Louvain; Leiden: Brill.

Smith, A. 1987. Porphyrian Studies since 1913. *ANRW* 36.2:717–73. Edited by H. Temporini and W. Haase. Berlin: de Gruyter.

———, ed. 1993. *Porphyrii philosophi fragmenta.* Stuttgart and Leipzig: Teubner.

Sodano, A. R. 1964. *Porphyrii In Platonis Timaeum Commentariorum fragmenta.* Naples, Istituto della Stampa.

Stead, G. C. 1964. The Platonism of Arius. *JTS* 15, 16–31.

———. 1977. *Divine Substance.* Oxford: Clarendon Press.

———. 1998. The Word "from Nothing." *JTS* 49, 671–684.

Steel, C. 1978. *The Changing Self: A Study on the Soul in Later Neoplatonism: Iamblichus, Damascius, and Priscianus.* Verhandelingen van de Koninklijke Academie voor Wetenschappen, Letteren en Schone Kunsten van België, Klasse der Letteren ; jaarg. 40, nr. 85. Brussells: Paleis der Academien.

———, ed. 1982. *Proclus. Commentaire sur le Parménie de Platon.* Trans. G. de Moerbeke. AMP 1.3. Leuven: Presses universitaires de Louvain; Leiden: Brill.

———. 2002. A Neoplatonic Speusippus? Pages 469–76 in *Hénosis kaì philía = Unione e amicizia : omaggio a Francesco Romano.* Edited by M. Barbanti, G. R. Giardina and P. Manganaro. Introduced by E. Berti. Catania: CUECM.

———, ed. 2007–2009. *Procli In Platonis Parmenidem Commentaria.* 3 vols. Procli in Platonis Parmenidem Commentaria. Oxford: Oxford University Press.

Stiglmayr, J. 1895. Der Neuplatoniker Proclus als Vorlage des sog. Dionysius Areopagita in der Lehre vom Übel. *Historisches Jahrbuch* 16, 253–73, 721–48.

Strange, S. K. 1992. *Porphyry.* On Aristotle's Categories. Ithaca, N.Y.: Cornell University

Press.

Strutwolf, H. 1999. *Die Trinitätstheologie und Christologie des Euseb von Caesarea. Eine dogmengeschichtliche Untersuchung seiner Platonismusrezeption und Wirkungsgeschichte.* Forschungen zur Kirchen- und Dogmengeschichte 72. Göttingen: Vandenhoeck und Ruprecht.

Suchla, B. R. 1990. *Corpus Dionysiacum I: Pseudo-Dionysius Areopagita. De divinis nominibus.* Patristische Texte und Studien 33. Berlin: De Gruyter.

Szlezák, T. A. 1979. *Platon und Aristoteles in der Nuslehre Plotins.* Basel: Schwabe.

Tardieu, M. 1984. *Écrits Gnostiques: Codex de Berlin.* Paris: Cerf.

———. 1987. Une diatribe antignostique dans l'interpolation Eunomienne des Recognitiones. Pages 325–37 in *ALEXANDRINA: Hellénisme, judaïsme et christianisme à Alexandrie. Mélanges offerts au P. Claude Mondésert.* Paris: Cerf.

———. 1996. Recherches sur la formation de l'apocalypse de Zostrien et les sources de Marius Victorinus. Pages 7–114 in *Res Orientales* IX. Bures-sur-Yvette: Groupe pour l'Etude de la Civilisation du Moyen-Orient.

———. 2005. Plotin citateur du Zostrien. Unpublished paper, Collège de France seminar "Thèmes et problèmes du traité trente-trois de Plotin contre les Gnostiques."

Tarrant, H. 1993. *Thrasyllan Platonism.* Ithaca, N.Y.: Cornell University Press; London: Duckworth.

———. 2000. *Plato's First Interpreters.* London: Duckworth and Ithaca, N.Y.: Cornell University Press.

Till, W. 1955. *Die gnostischen Schriften des Koptischen Papyrus Berolinensis 8502, herausgegeben, übersetzt und bearbeitet.* Berlin: Akademie.

Tommasi Moreschini, C.O. 1998. L' androginia di Cristo-Logos: Mario Vittorino tra platonismo e gnosi. *Cassiodorus* 4:11–46.

Tornau, C. 2000. Die Prinzipienlehre des Moderatus von Gades: Zu Simplikios in Ph. 230,34–231,24 Diels. *Rheinisches Museum für Philologie* 143, 197–220.

Trouillard, J. 1973. Le Parménide de Platon et son interprétation néoplatonicienne. *RThPh* 23:83–100

Turner, D. 1995. *The Darkness of God: Negativity in Christian Mysticism.* Cambridge: Cambridge University Press.

Turner, J. D. 1990. NHC XI,3: *Allogenes*: Introduction, Translation, and Notes to Text and Translation. Pages 243–67 in *Nag Hammadi Codices XI, XII, XIII.* Edited by C. W. Hedrick. NHS 28. Leiden: Brill.

———. 1992. Gnosticism and Platonism: The Platonizing Sethian Texts from Nag Hammadi in Their Relation to Later Platonic Literature. Pages 425–60 in *Neoplatonism and Gnosticism.* Edited by R. T. Wallis and J. Bregman. Albany: SUNY Press.

———. 2000a. Commentary. Pages 483–662 in *Zostrien (NH VIII,1).* BCNH 24. Edited by C. Barry, W.-P. Funk, P.-H. Poirier, and J. D. Turner. Quebec: Presses de l'Université Laval; Louvain: Peeters.

———. 2000b. The Setting of the Platonizing Sethian Treatises in Middle Platonism. Pages 179–224 in *Gnosticism and Later Platonism: Themes, Figures, and Texts.* Edited by J. D. Turner and R. Majerick. SBLSymS 12. Atlanta: Society of Biblical Literature.

———. 2001. *Sethian Gnosticism and the Platonic Tradition.* BCNH 6. Québec: Presses de l'Université Laval and Louvain-Paris: Éditions Peeters.

———. 2004. Introduction. Pages 1–188 in *L'Allogène (NH XI,3).* Edited by W.-P. Funk, P.-H. Poirier, M. Scopello, and J. D. Turner. BCNH 30. Québec: Presses de Université Laval; Louvain: Peeters.

———. 2005. Sethian Gnosticism and Johannine Christianity. Pages 399-433 in *Theology and Christology in the Fourth Gospel: Essays by the Members of the SNTS Johannine Writings Seminar*. Edited by G. van Belle et al. Bibliotheca Ephemeridum Theologicarum Lovaniensium 184. Leuven: Presses universitaires de Louvain and Peeters.

———. 2006. The Gnostic Sethians and Middle Platonism: Interpretations of the *Timaeus* and *Parmenides*. *VC* 60:9-64.

———. 2008. The Chaldaean Oracles and the Metaphysics of the Sethian Platonizing Treatises. *ZAC* 12:39-58.

———, and O. Wintermute 1990. Allogenes: Transcription and Translation. Pages 192-241 in *Nag Hammadi Codices XI, XII, XIII*. Edited by C. Hedrick. NHS 28. Leiden: Brill.

Tzamalikos, P. 2007. *Origen. Philosophy of History and Eschatology*. Supplements to Vigiliae Christianae 85. Leiden: Brill.

Urbach, L. 1979. *The Sages. The World and Wisdom of the Rabbis of the Talmud*. London and Cambridge, MA: Harvard University Press.

Urmson, J., and L. Siorvanes, trans. 1992. *Simplicius, Corollaries on Place and Time*. Ithaca, N.Y.: Cornell University Press.

Usener, H., ed. 1887. *Epicurea*. Leipzig: Teubner.

———. 1889. Variae lectionis specimen primum. *Jahrbücher für Klassische Philologie* 139:369-97.

———. 1991. *Epicurus, the Extant Remains, with Short Critical Apparatus*. Trans. C. Bailey. New York: Hyperion.

Vaggione, R. P. 1987. *Eunomius. The Extant Works*. Oxford: Oxford University Press..

Vandenbussche, E. 1945. La part de la dialectique dans la théologie d'Eunome le technologue. *RHE* 40:47-72.

Von Balthasar, H. U. 1984. *Origen, Spirit and Fire: A Thematic Anthology of His Writings*. Trans. R. Daly. Washington, D.C.: Catholic University of America Press.

Vorwerk, M., ed., trans., and comm. 2001. *Plotins Schrift "Über den Geist, die Ideen und das Seiende," Enneade V 9 (5)*. Beiträge zur Altertumskunde 145. Munich and Leipzig: Sauer.

Waldstein, M., and F. Wisse, eds. 1995. *The Apocryphon of John: Synopsis of Nag Hammadi Codices II,1; III,1; and IV,1 with BG 8502,2*. Nag Hammadi and Manichaean Studies 33. Leiden: Brill.

Weber, K. O. 1962. *Origenes der Neuplatoniker*. Zetema. Monographien zur klassischen Altertumswissenschaft, 26. Munich: Beck.

Westerink, L. G. and J. Combès. 1997-2003. *Damascius: Commentaire du Parménide de Platon*. 4 Vols. Collection des universités de France publiée sous le patronage de l'Association Guillaume Budé. Paris: Les Belles Lettres.

Whittaker, J. 1969. ΕΠΕΚΕΙΝΑ ΝΟΥ ΚΑΙ ΟΥΣΙΑΣ. *VC* 23:91-104.

———. 1973. Neopythagoreanism and the Transcendent Absolute. *Symbolae Osloenses* 48:77-86.

———. 1983. Ἄρρητος καί ἀκατονόμαστος. *Jahrbuch fur Antike und Christentum* 10:303-6 (Festschrift for H. Dörrie)

———, and P. Louis. 1990. *Alcinoos. Enseignement des doctrines de Platon*. Introduction, texte établi et commenté par J. Whittaker et traduit par P. Louis. CUF. Paris: Les Belles Lettres.

Williams, J. N. 1999. The Apophatic Theology of Dionysius the Pseudo-Areopagite. *Down-*

side *Review* 117:157-72.

———. 2000. *Denying Divinity: Apophasis in the Patristic Christian and Soto Zen Buddhist Traditions.* Oxford: Oxford University Press.

Williams, M. 1985. *The Immovable Race: A Gnostic Designation and the Theme of Stability in Late Antiquity.* NHS 29. Leiden: Brill.

Winston, D., ed. 1981. *Philo of Alexandria: The Contemplative Life.* The Giants and Selections. The Classics of Western Spirituality. New York: Paulist.

———. 1985. *Logos and Mystical Theology in Philo of Alexandria.* Cincinatti, Ohio: Hebrew Union College Press.

Wire, A. 1990. Introduction: NHC XI,3: Allogenes, 45,1-69,20. *Nag Hammadi CodicesXI, XII, XIII.* Edited by C. Hedrick. NHS 28. Leiden: Brill, 173-191.

Wolff, G. 1983. *Porphyrius: De philosophia ex oraculis haurienda librorum reliquiae.* reprint of 1856, Hildesheim: Georg Olms.

Wolfson, H. A. 1968. *Philo: Foundations of Religious Philosophy in Judaism, Christianity and Islam.* 2 Vols. 4th edition. Cambridge, Mass.: Harvard University Press.

Wolfson, H. A. 1957. Negative Attributes in the Church Fathers and the Gnostic Basilides" *HTR* 50:145-56.

Wrobewl, J., ed. 1876. *Platonis Timaeus interprete Chalcidio cum eiusdem Commentario.* Leipzig: Teubner.

Wucherpfennig, A. 2002. *Heracleon Philologus: Gnostische Johannesexegese Im Zweiten Jahrhundert.* Wissenschaftliche Untersuchungen zum Neuen Testament 143. Tübingen: Mohr Siebeck.

Zachhuber, J. 2000. *Human Nature in Gregory of Nyssa: Philosophical Background and Theological Significance.* VCSup 46. Leiden: Brill.

Zachhuber, J. 2003. Nochmals: Der 38. Brief des Basilius von Caesarea als Werk des Gregor von Nyssa. *ZAC* 7:73-90.

Zintzen, C. 1967. *Vita Isidori reliquiae.* Bibliotheca graeca et latina suppletoria 1. Hildesheim: Olms.

CONTRIBUTORS

Sara Ahbel-Rappe is Professor of Greek and Latin in the Department of Classical Studies at the University of Michigan (Ann Arbor). She is the author of *Reading Neoplatonism* (Cambridge University Press, 2000), *Socrates: A Guide for the Perplexed* (Continuum, 2009), *Damascius' Problems and Solutions concerning first Principles* (Oxford, in press), and co-editor of *Companion to Socrates* (Blackwell, 2006).

Gerald Bechtle teaches Classics at the University of Bern, Switzerland. His research interests include the Aristotelian and Platonic traditions and he has published widely on a range of topics from the Presocratics to late-ancient thought and beyond. His most recent book is *Iamblichus: Aspekte seiner Philosophie und Wissenschaftskonzeption: Studien zum späteren Platonismus* (Academia Verlag, 2006).

Johanna Brankaer, who holds the PhD in Philosophy from the Vrije Universiteit Brussel, is a Coptologist and an expert on the reception of Graeco-Roman philosophy in late-antique Egypt. She has recently been a post-doctoral research fellow at the Fonds National de Recherche Scientifique in Belgium, and curretly serves as an assistant in Church History at the Friedrich-Schiller-Universität in Jena. She is author of *A Coptic Learning Grammar (Sahidic)* (Harassowitz, 2009) and with Hans-Gebhard Bethge is editor of *Codex Tchacos: Texte Und Analysen* (Texte und Untersuchungen zur Geschichte der altchristlichen Literatur 161; de Gruyter, 2007).

Luc Brisson is Director of Research at the National Center of Scientific Research (CNRS, UPR 76-Centre Jean Pépin, Paris-Villejuif, France). He has translated works by Plato, Plotinus, Porphyry, and Iamblichus, and has published many books on the history of Greek philosophy and religion, as well as a bibliography on Plato, appearing periodically. Among his recent books are *Plato, The Mythmaker*, (University of Chicago Press, 1999); *How Philosophers Saved Myths* (University of Chicago Press, 2004); *Porphyre, Sentences* (Vrin, 2005); *Platon, Œuvres complètes* (Flammarion, 2008).

Kevin Corrigan is Samuel Candler Dobbs Professor of Interdisciplinary Studies and Director of the Graduate Institute of the Liberal Arts, Emory University, Atlanta, Georgia. His most recent book publications are *Plato's Dialectic at Play: Structure, Argument and Myth in the Symposium* (with Elena Glazov-Corrigan; Pennsylvania State University Press, 2004); *Reading Plotinus: A Practical Introduction to Neoplatonism* (Purdue University Press, 2004); *Platonisms: Ancient, Modern and Postmodern* (2 vols., edited with John D. Turner; Brill, 2007); *Reading Ancient Texts: Essays in Honor of Denis O'Brien*. Vol. 1: *The Presocratics and Plato*; Vol. 2: *Aristotle and Neoplatonism* (edited with Suzanne Stern-Gillet; Brill, 2007); and *Evagrius and Gregory: Mind, Soul and Body in the 4th Century* (Ashgate, 2009).

John Dillon is Regius Professor of Greek (Emeritus) at Trinity College, Dublin, and Director of the Dublin Centre for the Study of the Platonic Tradition. Among his publications are *The Middle Platonists* (Duckworth, 1977); *Alcinous: The Handbook of Platonism* (Oxford University Press, 1993); and *The Heirs of Plato: A Study of the Old Academy 347-274 B.C.* (Oxford University Press, 2004).

Volker Drecoll is Professor of Church History and Ephorus of the "Evangelisches Stift" at the Eberhard Karls University of Tübingen. His recent books include *Die Entwicklung der Trinitätslehre des Basilius von Cäsarea: Sein Weg vom Homöusianer zum Neonizäner* (Vandenhoeck & Ruprecht, 1996); *Die Entstehung der Gnadenlehre Augustins* (Mohr Siebeck, 1999); *Pneumatologie in der Alten Kirche* (with W. D. Hauschild; Lang, 2004). He is editor of the Augustinhandbuch (Mohr Siebeck, 2007), of the bilingual edition "Augustinus. Opera - Werke" (Schoeningh, Paderborn) and, since 2006, main editor of the *Zeitschrift für Antikes Christentum*. He is currently working on critical editions of Augustine's *De gratia et libero arbitrio*, *De praedestinatione sanctorum* and *De dono perseverantiae for the Corpus Scriptorum Ecclesiasticorum Latinorum* series (Verlag der Österreichen Akademie der Wissenschaften).

Mark Edwards has been Lecturer in Patristic Theology at Oxford University (Oxford, UK) since 1993. His doctoral thesis (1988) was entitled "Plotinus and the Gnostics," and his books include *Neoplatonic Saints* (Liverpool University Press, 2000), *Origen Against Plato* (Ashgate, 2002), and *Culture and Philosophy in the Age of Plotinus* (Duckworth, 2006).

John F. Finamore is Professor of Classics at the University of Iowa. He has published extensively on the Platonic tradition, including two books on Iamblichus: *Iamblichus and the Theory of the Vehicle of the Soul* (Scholars Press, 1985) and *Iamblichus's De Anima: Text, Translation, and Commentary* (with John Dillon; Brill, 2002).

CONTRIBUTORS

Noel Hubler is the chair of the Department of Religion and Philosophy at Lebanon Valley College, near Hershey, PA. He is a specialist in ancient Greek metaphysics, epistemology, and political theory. He has a forthcoming book entitled *Truth and Power in Ancient Greece* concerning the relations between epistemology and political theory from Plato to Plotinus.

Alain Lernould is Research Fellow at the National Center of Scientific Research (CNRS–UMR 8163, "Savoirs, textes, Langage," Université Charles-de Gaulle, Lille3). He has published *Physique et Théologie. Lecture du Timée de Platon par Proclus* (Presses Universitaires du Septentrion, 2001) and, recently, *Études sur le Commentaire de Proclus au premier livre des Éléments d'Euclide* (Presses Universitaires du Septentrion, 2010). He is currently working in collaboration with Carlos Steel (KUL–Leuven) on a critical edition and translation in french of Proclus's commentary on Euclid.

Zlatko Pleše, Ph.D. (1996) in Classics, Yale University, is Associate Professor of Greco-Roman Religion and Early Christianity at the University of North Carolina at Chapel Hill. He has published on Plutarch, Middle Platonism, Gnosticism, Hermetic writings, apocryphal gospels, and Coptic literature. Recent monographs include *Poetics of the Gnostic Universe: Narrative and Cosmology in the Apocryphon of John* (Brill, 2006) and *The Apocryphal Gospels* (in collaboration with Bart D. Ehrman; Oxford University Press, in press).

Andrew Radde-Gallwitz is Assistant Professor of Theology at Loyola University Chicago. He is the author of *Basil of Caesarea, Gregory of Nyssa, and the Transformation of Divine Simplicity* (Oxford University Press, forthcoming).

Tuomas Rasimus, Ph.D., Th.D. (2006–7), earned his doctorates from a joint degree between Université Laval and the University of Helsinki. He has published articles related to Gnosticism, New Testament, and Neoplatonism, and is the author of *Paradise Reconsidered in Gnostic Mythmaking* (Brill, 2009), as well as the editor of *The Legacy of John* (Brill, 2010). He is currently an Academy of Finland Research Fellow at the University of Helsinki

Jean Reynard, Ph.D. 1998, EPHE/Paris-Sorbonne, is Research Fellow at the Christian Sources Research Center (Lyon) in CNRS (French National Center for Scientific Research), specializing in Gregory of Nyssa. His most recent book is *Grégoire de Nysse, Sur les titres des Psaumes* (Sources Chrétiennes, Les Éditions du Cerf, 2002).

David T. Runia is Master of Queen's College and Professorial Fellow in the School of Historical Studies at the University of Melbourne, Australia. He has written extensively on the writings and thought of Philo of Alexandria, including

Philo of Alexandria and the Timaeus of Plato (Brill, 1986), *Philo in Early Christian Thought* (1993), and *Philo of Alexandria On the Creation of the Cosmos according to Moses: Translation and Commentary* (SBL, 2001). He has also published studies on the ancient doxographical tradition (*Aëtiana: The Method and Intellectual Context of a Doxographer*, with J. Mansfeld; 2 vols.; Brill, 1997 and 2009) and a translation of Book 2 of *Proclus, Commentary on Plato's Timaeus* (with M. Share; Cambridge University Press, 2008).

Thomas A. Szlezák (Ph. D. Berlin 1967, Habilitation Zurich 1976) has served as Professor of Classics at Universität Würzburg, Professor of Greek Literature at Universität Tübingen (now Emeritus), and is currently Honorary Professor of Philosophy at the Pontificia Universidad Católica del Perú. He is also a Fellow of the Braunschweigische Wissenschaftliche Gesellschaft and an Honorary Citizen of Syracuse (Italy). He is the author of *Pseudo-Archytas über die Kategorien* (de Gruyter, 1972), *Platon und Aristoteles in der Nuslehre Plotins* (Schwabe, 1979), *Platon und die Schriftlichkeit der Philosophie* (de Gruyter, Teil I, 1985, Teil II 2004), *Reading Plato* (Routledge, 1999), *Le plaisir de lire Platon* (Cerf, 1996), *Die Idee des Guten in Platons Politeia* (Akademie, 2003), and *Aristoteles, Metaphysik* (Akademie, 2004).

John D. Turner, Cotner Professor of Religious Studies and Charles J. Mach University Professor of Classics and History at the University of Nebraska-Lincoln, specializes in the study of ancient Gnosticism, in particular the restoration, conservation, translation, and interpretation of the thirteen papyrus codices from Nag Hammadi, Egypt in December 1945. Author/editor of ten books, including *Sethian Gnosticism and the Platonic Tradition* (Peeters, 2001) and English- and French-language critical editions of seven of the Nag Hammadi texts, and ninety articles, he was the organizer of two Society of Biblical Literature's seminars, "Gnosticism and Later Platonism," and, with Kevin Corrigan, "Rethinking Plato's Parmenides and Tts Platonic, Gnostic, and Patristic Reception" (whose proceedings constitute these two volumes).

Matthias Vorwerk teaches ancient philosophy at the Catholic University of America in Washington D.C. He specializes in Platonic, particularly Neoplatonic philosophy, and is the author of a commentary on Plotinus's *Ennead* V.9, *Plotins Schrift "Über den Geist, die Ideen und das Seiende" (Enneade V.9)* (Saur, 2001). He holds memberships in the International Plato Society, the International Society for Neoplatonic Studies, and in the Academia Platonica Septima Monasteriensis.

Subject–Name Index

Abramowski, L. 7, 9, 19, 66, 72n16, 74n18, 75n21, 81n23, 86n32, 99n85
abstraction 47
activity 68, 75n20, 79, 139, 148–54, 233, 237, 238, 240
addition 16, 31, 73, 77, 79, 200, 219, 238, 240, 242
Aetius 16, 109, 232
Aëtius 176n2
agennetos 222, 232, 233
akatonomastos 189, 190, 192, 197
Albinus 115, 190n3, 192, 192n6
Alcinous 9, 14, 19, 38, 46, 116, 170, 185, 190, 190n3, 191, 192, 192n6, 209, 215n43
Alexandria 5, 18, 49, 86, 143, 175, 176, 180, 182, 187, 194n13, 199, 210
Alexandria 199, 215
allegory 206
Allogenes 6–8, 15, 18, 69, 82, 88n37, 89n41, 92, 93n54, 96, 97n70, 97n71, 97n72, 98n74–78, 99, 99n79–83, 100–104, 106n98, 107, 108, 195n18, 196, 198
Amelius 3, 11, 12, 18, 28n21, 37–40, 43, 44, 46n8, 48, 54, 61, 61n46, 95n67, 97n74, 102n91, 104, 104n93, 105n96, 117, 144, 146, 195,
Ammonius Saccas 193, 215
anarchy 239
angel 13, 14, 37, 77, 119, 120, 125, 126, 127, 129–31, 131n30, 136, 145, 211n26, 212, 229, 229n26, 230
anthropomorphism 206
antitupoi 104
ἀνωνόμαστος 185, 190
aphthegktos 192
Apostolic Constitutions vii, 190
Aramaic 203
arche 39. See principle.
archetypal 138, 139, 165n9
Arianism 16, 19, 109, 109n111, 194, 195, 207, 225, 232, 240,
Aristotle 1, 4, 9, 13, 14, 19, 30, 31, 38, 59, 74, 95, 11, 112, 112n4, 116, 117, 117n9, 139, 149, 157, 158, 158n2, 159, 159n4, 160, 161, 162, 162n7, 164, 167n12, 170, 171, 171n20, 197n25, 201, 203, 204, 208n17, 209, 215, 243
Armstrong, A. H. 35n1, 57n41, 95n69, 102n91, 255, 257,
Arnobius of Sicca vii, 106, 106n99, 208, 208n21
ἄρρητος 16, 177, 189, 190, 191, 192n5
ἄσχετος 248–49, 248n17, 248n18
Athanasius 16, 194n13, 208n19, 237, 238, 241
Athanassiadi, P. 233
Athenagoras 204, 204n6,
Athenian Stranger 247–48
Atkinson, M. 27n13, 27n14, 30n31, 144n2
Aubin, P. 231

-273-

Augustine of Hippo 7, 65, 85, 85n26, 87, 94, 94n60, 105n97, 109n110, 207, 207n15, 208, 208n21, 213n39
autoagathos 208
Autogenes 96–97, 97nn70&74, 98, 99n79, 101, 101n89
autotheos 208, 208n19

Baltes, M. 32n35, 65n2
Balthasar, H. von xiii, 242, 267
Baltzly, D. 155
Barbelo 6–8, 18, 96–97, 97n71, 97n73–74, 98n76–77, 100–102, 102n91
Barnes, T. D. 203n3
Barry, C. 65n3, 82n6
Basil of Caesarea viii, 14, 16, 208, 208n20, 219, 226–28, 228n20.21, 229n22–24, 229n26–29, 230n30&34, 231, 231n35–36, 232, 234, 237, 238, 240, 240n3, 241, 264
Basilideans 190, 191, 210
Beatrice, G. 49n4
Bechtle, G. vi, 2, 3, 7, 9, 10, 12, 14, 18, 19, 38, 59n44, 69, 81n3–4, 85–86, 86n28, 94, 95n67, 157, 166n9, 193n8, 196, 196n21
being *passim*. *See also* substance.
　absolute 55–56, 61, 95, 107n102, 107n103, 197
　architecture of 133–41
being-life-mind 8, 15, 19, 68–69, 75, 76, 77–79, 82, 83, 84, 88, 89, 90, 98, 99, 102, 107, 107n104, 136, 195–96
being/becoming 5, 35
　categories of 157–72
　determinate 9, 83, 84, 95
　divided 219
　existence-life-beatitude 73, 75, 91, 97, 101, 102
　enneadic structure of 6, 8, 13–14, 83–84, 85, 87, 88, 94, 97, 98, 98n76–77, 102, 136
　infinitival/substantive 12, 67, 69, 72
　Mosaic Theology of 178
　non-being 142–56
　non-being above being 61, 92, 98, 98n77, 99, 99n80, 100. *See also hyparxis.*
　one-being 24, 91, 133, 137
　participation in 32, 44, 53, 56, 121, 145, 218, 222, 239
　pre-being 240
　pure act of 60, 67, 68, 107n103, 145
　realm of 142–56
　triadic model of 84, 87, 97n74, 136, 140, 240, 241
　undetermined 83, 84, 88, 95, 97, 98
Bendinelli, G. 206n13
Berchman, R. 109n110
Bible 189, 190, 204–6, 214n42
Bible, interpretation of 181
Billings, T. H. 176
blessed(ness) 84, 91, 96–97, 98n76, 99n79, 101, 101n89, 102, 107
body 37–38, 40, 43–46, 103, 104, 105n96–97, 107n100, 131, 201–2, 209–10, 211n23, 212–13, 213n36, 215n43
Bonazzi, M. 180n11
Brisson, L. 3, 8–11, 13, 18–19, 23n1–2, 27n13, 49, 50n4, 51n15.22, 52, 54, 54n29, 57n40, 58n43, 61n46, 86n31, 87n34, 100, 104n93, 109, 111, 115n8, 193, 193n9–10, 194, 194n12
Buddhism 243n3
bulk/mass 41–43, 220,
Bussanich, J. 27n15, 256

Cadious, R. 205n10
Calabi, F. 177n6
Calvisius Taurus 207

Cappadocians 9, 14–16, 222, 223n11, 225–26, 232, 234–35
categories vi, 1, 9, 14–15, 19, 38, 46, 59, 124, 150, 157–72 *passim*, 179–80, 184, 257, 258, 261, 265
causal Interpretation (Second Hypothesis) 17, 245–54
cause 10, 17, 27, 27n15, 28–29, 32, 54, 58, 61, 70, 89, 134, 155, 184, 193, 237–40, 245, 247–54
Cazelais, S. 26, 81n4, 86, 86n29, 90, 197n23
Celsus 86n29, 191, 192, 201, 205–6, 209, 212
Chadwick, H. 176
Chaldaean Oracles 89n43, 91, 93, 93n54, 94, 100, 102, 108, 191, 195, 196, 207, 256, 262
Charrue, J. M. 10, 25, 25n10, 26, 32n36, 33, 33nn37–38
Chase, M. 19, 49n1, 117, 163
Cherniss, H. 176n4, 219n4, 221, 225
Christians 15, 103, 103n92, 189–97, 199–216, 231, 234, 241, 244, 256, 265
circle, image of 42, 185, 252, 252n28
Clarke, E. C. 126n14
Classics, as discipline 199
Clement of Alexandria 15, 175, 179, 182–87, 190–92, 223n11, 244, 260, 262, 263
  Excerpts from Theodotus 197, 211n26
  Stromateis 106, 190, 205–6, 261, 262
Combès, J. 122n6, 123, 123n8, 124n11, 124n12
Combès, J. (and L. G. Westerink) 50n5, 83n14, 84n16, 85, 85n26, 87, 88, 91, 91n48, 105,97, 119n2, 120n3, 120n4, 121n5, 130n18, 130n19, 137, 146, 146n5, 148, 151, 155

consciousness 47–48, 136n11, 153–55
consubstantiality 73, 194, 194n15
convergence 182, 239–40
Copernican theory 202
Coptic 8, 82, 82n8, 89n41, 92, 99, 99n80, 100, 193–96
Cornford, F. M. 177
Corrigan, K. 2, 7, 9–12, 16–19, 35, 61n46, 81n4, 83n15, 85–86, 86n28, 87, 90n47, 93n55, 95n67, 97n70, 103, 104n94, 106n100, 108n105, 237
Corsini, E. 244, 244n4, 245, 250
Cousin, V. 23n1, 30n32, 49n3, 56, 76n26, 91, 135, 135n6

daemon 13, 14, 119, 120, 120n14, 122–23, 125–32, 136, 145
Damascius 2–3, 10, 13–14, 49–52, 56, 56n38, 57n42, 68n8, 83, 84n16, 85, 85n26, 87–88, 91, 105n97, 119–23, 126–32, 137, 143, 146–56, 159n3
  Plato 137
  remaining-procession-return 137, 138
Daniélou, J. 191, 232, 233
De Falco, V. 108n107
De Haas, F.A. 167n12, 169n15
demiurge 11, 28, 28n24, 31–32, 56, 60, 93n55, 97n74, 124, 182, 184. *See also* Ialdabaoth.
descent 121, 123, 125, 127–32, 151, 155, 183, 196, 212–13
Des Places, E. 27n17, 28, 28n21, 29n29, 87, 90n46, 97n74, 126n14, 202, 208n18
Deuse, W. 60n43
deuteros theos 205–6
dialectic 13, 15, 23, 40, 47, 54, 56, 114–16, 177, 179–82, 184–86, 200, 208, 210, 215, 227, 234, 238
Diehl, E. 55n32, 60, 85, 87, 88, 95, 97n74, 99n84, 105n97, 136n9

Diels. H. 24n5, 58, 86n27, 145, 155n9, 186n28
Dillon, J. M. 3, 10, 13–15, 24n6, 37n4, 46n8, 62n47, 81n3, 84, 86n27, 119, 119n11–12, 120n13–14, 123n17, 126n24, 129, 130, 130n28, 133, 144n3, 145, 145n4, 146n5, 169n15, 180, 180n10, 191, 207, 244n5, 247, 248n13–14, 249n22, 251n24, 258, 259, 262, 272
Diotima 13, 128
Divine names 248, 250, 253
Dodds, E. R. 5, 10, 24, 24nn3–6, 25–26, 54n30, 88n35, 124n21, 136, 145, 178, 178n6, 186, 186n27, 248n18, 258
Dolidze, T. 233n13
Dörrie, H. 32n35, 27n17, 95n66, 182n13, 234n39
Drecoll, V. H. 1, 7, 8, 13, 19, 65n2, 66n4
dynamis 196, 207
dyad (indefinite) 4–5, 24, 67, 108n107, 133, 138, 139n18, 140n22

Edwards, M.J. 15–16, 18, 86n33, 89n38, 90n45, 92n51, 93n57, 175, 189, 194n14, 199, 199n2, 205n11, 208, 212n33–34, 215n44, 258
Egypt 193, 227
enmattered form 40, 43
Empedocles 30, 202
enneadic structure 6, 8, 83–85, 88, 94n65, 97, 98, 102, 105n97. See also triads.
Epicureans 191, 202, 215
epiousios 205
Er 106
Esau 213–15
eternity 5, 35, 78, 101, 137, 137n14, 150, 176, 176n2, 204, 207
Eudorus 2, 5–6, 18, 179–80, 180n10
Eunomius 16, 222, 223n10, 225n17, 232–34, 240
Eusebius of Caesarea 104n93, 105n97, 191, 208, 208n19, 215, 231
evil 44–45, 90, 104, 105n97, 107n100, 108, 124, 149, 214n42
ἐξαίφνης 152, 155
excluded Middle, law of 152, 243–45, 247, 253–54
existence 6, 8, 18, 38, 44, 54–56, 58–60, 68, 71–73, 75, 83–84, 91, 96–98, 98n76–77, 99n79, 101–2, 107, 137, 146, 182, 193, 205, 215, 220, 222, 239, 240, 246. See also *hyparxis*.

Father–Power–Intellect triad 83, 84, 87, 91, 94, 102
Father/Son distinction 72–75, 77–78, 96–97, 101, 101n90, 102, 185–87, 190, 193, 197, 207, 208, 225, 231–33, 237–38
Festugière, A. J. 124n13, 130n19
Finamore, J. F. 13, 123n7, 126n14, 130n18, 149, 151
first hypothesis 4, 6–9, 11, 15, 17–18, 23–26, 32–33, 46, 56–57, 59, 62, 134–35, 143, 145, 147, 177, 179–80, 184–86, 190–93, 196, 222, 224–25, 225n15, 238, 244–45, 247
Forms/forms 3, 4, 37–38, 43–44, 50–57, 107n101, 114, 116, 121, 123, 135, 137–39, 145, 147–48, 167n12, 177, 215, 220, 225, 250–51
Essential Living Being 138
Förster, N. 191, 259
Fowler, H. N. 107n102
freedom 47–48
Freud, S. 201, 203
Funk, W.-P. 82n6, 99n80

Garfield, J. L. 243n1, 251
Gatti, M. 26n11

SUBJECT-NAME INDEX

Geljon. A. C. (and D. T. Runia) 176n3
genêtos, gennêtos 207, 233
Gill, M. L. (and P. Ryan) 112n1, 147
Ginzberg, L. 214n41
Gnostic(s) 2, 6–10, 12–13, 18–19, 58, 61, 66, 68, 80–82, 82n5, 86, 86n33, 89n42, 92, 93n54, 99–101, 103–4, 104n92, 105, 106nn98&100, 107, 107n104, 108, 108n108, 109, 109n109, 109n111, 110, 117, 153, 185, 189–90, 192–94, 194nn12&14, 195–96, 196n19, 198, 234, 257, 260–68. *See also* Sethian Gnosticism.
God/god(s) 5, 8–9, 10, 12, 13–15, 16, 17, 27, 28, 37, 56, 59, 60, 62, 67, 70, 72, 73, 77, 78, 87, 89–90, 93, 93n54, 94, 99, 100, 120, 122, 125–40, 135n4, 145–47, 149, 152, 155, 159, 163, 165n9, 177, 177n5, 178, 179, 179n9, 180–82, 187, 189–92, 194, 197, 200–202, 204–8, 212, 213, 217, 218, 220, 222–54
   above all (ὁ ἐπὶ πᾶσιν θεός) 12, 86, 90, 197
   aloneness/one 181, 182, 192, 199, 215, 219
   and humanity 62, 125, 128–29, 181, 217, 219, 225
   autotheos 208
   concept of 192, 200–204, 208
   eros 128–29
   essence and existence 179, 246
   existence–life–beatitude 72, 73, 78
   the Good 163
   hierarchy of 12, 13–14, 27, 28, 28n21, 62, 67, 87, 125–45, 187, 208
   hypercosmic/encosmic 136, 146
   idea of being 90, 90n46, 91, 100
   infinity of 184, 190, 192, 224–25, 245
   intelligible/intellective 136, 137, 139, 140, 147, 147n6, 163
   knowledge of 93, 93n54–55, 136, 139, 177, 179n8, 183, 185, 187
   leader-gods 123, 123n10, 124–26, 132
   name of 178, 185, 191n4, 202, 240
   pneuma-tridynamos-makarios 89–91, 99, 102
   simplicity 91, 91n48, 98nn76–77, 100
   Son of 179, 185–87, 190, 207–8, 233
   transcendence of 179, 183, 185, 223, 233, 247
   Trinity 175–254 *passim*
   unbegotten 222, 226, 233
   visible 126, 129
Good, the 4, 11, 24, 27, 28, 29, 31, 42, 45, 50, 53, 56, 60, 87, 96n69. 107n103, 163, 178, 202, 218, 223, 224, 226n18, 251n24. *See also* the One.
   as God 163
   beyond being/intellect 29, 32 and *passim*
   goodness 87, 218
   idea of 24, 27, 29, 32, 33, 60
   ineffable 223, 226n18
   "itself" 50, 53, 223
   Limit of 226n18
Goulet, R. 49n4, 57n37, 227
Gourinat, J.-B. 115n8
Gregory Nazianzus 16, 237, 239–41, 242n9,
Gregory of Nyssa 14, 16, 192, 192n7, 208, 213, 213n38, 217, 221n9, 225, 232, 240, 242
Gregory Thaumaturgus 204
Gurtler, G. 24n3, 259

Hadot, P. 2, 7–10, 12–13, 18, 50, 59, 59n44, 60, 65–110 *passim*, 136n8,

Hadot, P., *cont'd.*
    193n8, 195, 197, 197n22, 240, 247, 259
Hägg, H. F. 223n11
Halfwassen, J. 24n6, 260
Hancock, C. L. 196n21
Harl, M. 203n3, 212n30
hebdomad (intellective) 14, 136, 140, 147, 147n6
Hebrew 191n4, 203
Hegel, G. W. F. 11, 46-48
Heil, G. (and A. M. Ritter) 254n31
Heine, R. 212n35
henads 37-38, 56, 135, 137
    Iamblichus 135n4, 136
    Intelligible realm 136, 137-38
    Porphyry 136
    Plotinus 136
    Being-Life-Intellect 136
Henry, P. 108n107 (and H.-R. Schwyzer) 228
heresy 109n109, 199, 234-35
Hermann, C. F. 190n3, 192n6
Hermetica 15, 179, 191, 197
hero(es) 13-14, 37, 119-20, 123, 125-27, 127n25, 129-32, 136, 145
Hesiod 95n69, 206
    Orphic Poems 134n3
    Chaldaean Oracles 134, 140
    Proclus 134, 135, 137, 139-40
Hestia 89
Hippolytus of Rome 189-90
Hoek, A. van den 182n15, 183n16, 185n26
Hoffmann, P. 49n2, 159n3, 165n9
Holy Spirit 73-75, 77-78, 204-5, 207, 219, 225, 228-31
Homer 206
homoousios 194, 194n15
Horn, L. R. 243n2, 261
humanism 201
Hymn to King Helios 251
hyparxis 83, 84, 91, 96, 97, 98, 98nn76-77, 99nn79-80, 101, 102, 107
hypostases 3-5, 11, 14, 16-17, 23, 25-33, 35-37, 58-59, 62, 85, 85n97, 89, 104-5, 105n97, 144, 163, 165n9, 178-79, 186, 207, 217, 219, 223, 225, 237-38, 242
hypotheses 1, 3-4, 6-7, 11-12, 14-17, 23-25, 30, 32-33, 33n38, 35-48, 51, 58-59, 62-63, 115, 119-20, 122n16, 133, 134, 142, 143, 145-48, 153, 156, 163, 165n9, 171, 180, 180, 181n12, 186-87, 217, 227, 231, 233, 237-38, 240, 242, 244-46, 250, 253-54

Ialdabaoth 103
Iamblichus 3, 6, 11-14, 16, 25n8, 37, 55n34, 61-63, 67, 108n107, 117, 119-32, 135, 135n4, 136, 136n9, 146, 149-54, 164-71, 195-96, 196n20, 227-28, 232-35, 238, 240, 247, 251
idea of being 90, 91, 100, 222
ideas. *See also* Forms.
    knowability of 176
    thoughts of God 177
immaterial form/quality 163, 166n10, 167, 167n12, 168, 218
infinite 45, 47, 101, 138, 184, 192, 219, 220, 224-26, 234, 239, 245, 252
    being infinitival 8, 12, 67, 68, 69, 78
    deprivation of unity 45
    divisible 41, 42, 44
    freedom 48
    life 72
    mind 192
    self-consciousness 47
instant 14, 152-55, 212
intellect 6, 9, 14, 18, 23, 24, 25, 27, 28, 31, 32, 33, 35, 37, 38, 40, 54, 55, 56, 59, 60, 67-69. 83, 84-99, 102,

105, 107, 108, 121, 127, 134, 136, 139, 140, 145, 146, 147, 148, 149, 153, 163, 165, 192, 202, 218, 227, 230, 230nn31-32, 231, 233, 238, 240
and Good/One 28-29, 56, 84
and henads 38
and hypostases 23-48, 85-86, 134, 144, 165, 227
and hypotheses 23-48, 59, 62, 148
and life 108
and soul 32, 163, 165n9, 231, 238
Barbelo 6, 18, 96-97, 97n71, 97n73-74, 98n76-77, 100-2, 102n91
being and idea 28, 29, 32
being-life-mind 8, 15, 19, 68-69, 75-79, 82-84, 88,-90, 98, 99, 102, 107, 107n104, 136, 195-96
cause 28, 29
demiurgic 28, 29
depth 61
enneadic structure 6, 8, 13-14, 83-84, 85, 87, 88, 94, 97, 98, 98n76-77, 102, 136
Father-Power-Intellect 10, 83, 84, 87, 88, 91, 91n48. 94, 102, 207
Hebdomad 14, 136, 140, 147, 147n6
human 148, 233
intelligible-intellective structure 14, 38, 54, 61, 62, 74-75, 105, 134, 136, 139, 140, 146
limit of 90n47
One-Being 24, 91
One-Many 25n9, 237
participation 95n67
Plotinian 33, 238, 240, 241
prefiguration 84, 87-89
procession-reversion 5, 8, 94, 102n90, 108, 136-37, 148, 153, 207, 245
second One 67-69. 83

self-generation 89
super-intellectually 88
triadic model of 84, 87, 97n74, 136, 140, 240, 241
Invisible Spirit 90, 96, 97, 97n71, 98, 98nn76 & 77, 99n83, 100, 102, 103
Irenaeus of Lyons 15, 82n8, 92n53, 106n98, 109n109, 194n15, 197
Ivanka, E. 244n4

Jackson B. D. 25, 25n8-9, 32n36, 33, 261
Jacob 94n65, 179, 211n25, 213-15
John the Baptist 211
Jonas, H. 108n6
Jones, D. 211n24
Josephus 106n98, 182, 205
Julian the Emperor/Apostate 91, 234-35, 251
Juliani 94

Kalligas, P. 57n38
kaluptos-protophanês-autogenês triad 96, 97, 97nn70 & 74, 97, 98, 99n79
katabolê 212, 213
Kasser, R. 82n6
Kenney, J. P. 193n9
kinesis 238
Klostermann, E. 208n19
Koch, Hugo 244n4, 261
Koetschau, P. 74n17, 190, 210, 211n25, 212, 261
Kroll, W. 67n7, 81n3
Kruger, M. 211n28

Lacombrade, C. 91
Lampe, G. W. H. 248n17
Laporte, J. 212n30
Lardet, P. 212n35
Le Bonniec, H. 106
Le Boulluec, A. 183, 183n20, 184n23, 262
learned ignorance 93n54, 107, 108

Leroux, G. 193n10
Lilla, S. 185, 244, 244n4, 245, 246, 246n10
Linguiti, A. 59n42, 67n7
Logan, A. 82n8
logos 41, 90, 168, 202, 222
Logos of God 177–79, 186–87, 212, 224
Löhr, W. 191, 210n22, 262
Lord's Prayer 205
Luibheid, C. 248n17, 250n23, 253n29

Madec, G. 65n2, 81n3
magnitude 41, 44–47, 184
Majercik, R. 68n8, 83, 83n13, 84n16, 86, 86n32, 89n40, 90n44, 91, 99n84 & 85, 100, 102, 193n9
Manichees 208
Marcovich, M. 190
Mar Gregorios, P. 234n39
Marius Victorinus 7–9, 12–13, 18, 60, 65–80, 81, 81n2, 84–92, 95–96, 97n70, 99–100 102, 108–10, 193–95, 197, 255, 258, 259–60, 262,
Mark the Mage 191
Markschies, C. 205n9–10
Marx, K. 203
matter 11, 29, 35, 37, 39–41, 43–46, 56, 95, 96n69, 105n97, 107n100, 108–9, 127–31, 133, 147–48, 161, 162n7, 163, 166, 176n1, 203, 203n4, 205, 251n24, 257
McGuckin, J. 199n2, 262
Membrane 14, 136
metanoia 104
Methodius of Olympia 201
Middle Platonism 2, 6, 8, 11, 59–60, 196, 199, 227, 266, 273
mixture (Stoic theory of) 95, 95n66
Moderatus 1–6, 18, 24–25, 24n5, 27, 27n17, 57–58, 85, 85–86n27, 133, 145, 178, 186, 186n27, 192, 266
monad 4, 53n26, 83, 89n43, 94, 108n107, 139n18, 140n22, 145, 178, 179, 181, 219, 239–42
monarchy 239
monê 245
Morrow, G. R. 115, 144n3, 146n5, 244n5, 248n13–14, 249n22, 251n24, 262
Mortley, R. 245
Moses 106, 177, 183, 209, 222, 224, 274,
motion 16, 71–75, 77, 78, 107, 107nn102–103, 151, 153–54, 168, 180, 180n11, 182, 205, 210, 210n23, 223–24, 229, 239, 253
movement 35, 47, 60, 74n20, 75, 94, 94n62, 103, 107n103, 223–24, 238, 255
Mühlenberg, E. 225
mutual implication 84, 85, 88, 98, 108
myth 8, 13, 30n31, 101n90, 104, 105, 109, 122, 124–25, 132, 181, 195, 206, 213, 227, 234, 261, 263, 271, 272, 273

Nag Hammadi 6, 15, 65, 82, 107n104, 193, 193n9, 194n16, 196, 197, 255, 263, 264, 266, 267, 268, 274
Nagarjuna 17, 243, 243n1, 259,
Narbonne 25n7, 54n27, 263
Natorp, P. 38n7, 263
nature 4, 11, 30, 32–33, 35, 44, 51, 55, 55n34, 70, 95, 102–3, 104, 105n97, 106–7n100–101, 116, 121, 124, 127–28, 130, 133, 134, 135n4, 138, 151–53, 155, 179, 180–81, 183, 185, 186n28, 192, 207, 217–23, 219n4, 221n9, 223nn12.14, 225, 226n18, 228–29, 231–33, 239, 264, 268
negation 48, 101, 145, 146, 148, 193, 207, 246, 253–54
negative theology 15–16, 48, 71, 93, 177, 185–86, 189, 192, 222–23,

225, 233, 244, 245, 253–54, 260
negative/apophatic theology 189, 193
negativity 3, 47
Neoplatonism 1, 2, 6, 7, 8, 12, 13, 16, 19, 59, 60, 68, 82, 83, 85, 87, 110, 146, 227, 234, 235, 244, 250
Neopythagoreanism 2–8, 12, 18, 24, 25, 57, 58, 108n107, 178, 179–80, 187, 242n9
New Testament 190, 204, 207
Nicaea, Council of 194, 208
Nicene Trinitarianism 244
noetic cosmos 177
noetic triad 195–97
non-being above being. 92, 98, 98n77, 99, 99n80, 100. *See also hyparxis*.
non-Contradiction, law of 243–45, 247, 253–54
nous 44, 46, 135, 136, 138, 146, 192, 202. *See also* intellect
number 3–4, 42, 44, 45, 55, 125, 133, 139–40, 151, 178, 181, 184, 215, 239, 242
    divine 139
    female/male 140n22
    generation of 3, 139, 139n18, 145n4
    natural 133
    of the infinite 45
    same in 151
    unlimited 42
    younger 178, 181
Numenius 1, 7, 9, 10, 12, 27, 29, 31, 85, 86, 87, 90, 90n46, 94n62, 95n67, 97n74, 102n91, 105n97, 108, 108n108, 192, 202, 208

O'Brien, D. 27n17
One, the 3, 5, 11, 12–19, 23–34, 35–47, 50–70 passim, 83, 84, 88, 89, 90, 95, 98, 98n76, 101, 108, 111–17, 120, 133, 137, 138, 143–48 *passim*, 163, 164, 165n9, 169, 172, 177, 180, 192, 199, 202, 215, 219, 221, 223, 224, 227, 233, 238, 240, 247, 248, 251. *See also* the Good; the others. *Cf.* henad; monad.
    absolute, simple 30, 38, 58
    all and none 43, 186
    aloneness/one 181, 182, 192, 199, 215, 219
    and categories 169, 172
    and first hypothesis 9, 12, 35–47, 56, 58, 62, 145, 180, 190, 193, 196, 222, 224, 225, 247
    and hypostases 23–47, 144, 163, 164, 165n9, 193, 233
    and hypotheses 12, 14, 23, 35–47, 58, 62, 117, 134, 143–144, 146, 147–48, 163, 186, 224, 237
    and indefinite dyad 133
    as limit 90n47
    attributes of 95
    beyond being *passim*
    by genus 42
    cause of itself 240
    centers in 248
    convergence to 239
    deprived of 44, 45
    dispute with itself 16, 239
    divided 219, 232
    escape 42
    existence/non-existence 38–39, 40, 41, 45, 55, 56, 58, 134, 143–144, 146, 147, 148, 177, 178, 185, 186, 225n15, 239, 242, 242n9
    final cause 27n15
    first cause 54n28, 58
    first principle 6, 31, 54, 59, 184, 185
    generation from 84, 88, 89, 90, 108, 148, 232
    quantity denied of 46
    in *Allogenes* 98n76–77
    in time 111–17, 178

One, the, *cont'd.*
  indivisible 184
  infinite 180
  non-predicable 26, 58, 184, 223
One, and God 62, 163, 178, 202, 215
One beyond the One 240
One–Intellect–Soul 85, 85–86n27, 89
Oneness 199
One vs multiplicity 3, 5, 11, 15, 25, 33, 38–39, 50n7, 53n24. 140, 180, 187, 219, 221, 231, 237, 242
  one-triad 239
  monad 178
  mystery of 227
  mystical contact 225n15
  "nothingness" 93n55
  older/younger 239–40
  others, the 3, 39, 40–48, 50, 50nn7 & 8, 51, 51nn15 & 16, 51n18, 52–55, 136, 144, 148, 225n15, 237, 238, 240, 242
  positive determinations of 193n10
  potential existence/prefiguration in 84, 98n76, 108
  pre-principle 98n76
  presence 232
  procession/reversion 98, 102n90, 137
  splitting 140, 239
  unformedness 240
  vision of 93n54
Onuki, T. 103
Origen (Christian) 194, 197, 215. See also Index Locorum.
  as philosopher 199–210
  condemnation 199
Origen (Platonist) 215
Osborn, E. F. 183
others, the 3, 39, 40–48, 50, 59nn7 & 8, 51, 51nn15 & 16, 51n18, 52–55, 136, 144, 148, 225n15, 237, 238, 240, 242
Ouroboros 254

Parmenides of Elea 53, 176, 183
Parmenides *passim. See* Index Locorum.
paroikêsis 104
paronyms 12, 69, 76, 77, 79, 80, 84, 88, 89, 94, 99
part-whole relation 180
participation 16, 17, 44, 53, 53n24, 54, 95, 101, 171, 208, 217, 218–20, 22, 225, 251, 252
  intelligible 95, 95 n67
Patillon, M. 51n15, 51n20
Paul (Saint) 70, 90, 190, 201, 203, 206, 209, 211, 214, 230
  Ephesians 191, 192, 212
  Philippians 190
  Romans 211
  Hebrews 207
Pearson, B. 82n5, 99n85
perfection 101, 122, 140, 185, 226n18, 238, 240
Pherecydes 206
Philo of Alexandria 2, 10, 15, 16, 94n65, 95, 96, 175–82, 183, 186–87
Plato *passim. See* Index Locorum.
  and Origen 199–216
pleroma 194n13, 195
Plotinus 23–48, 81–83, 83n12, 84–85, 85n26, 86n27, 86–88, 88n37, 89–90, 90n47, 91, 93, 93nn54–55, 94n62, 95, 95n67, 95n69, 96, 97n70, 97n74, 98, 100, 102n91, 103–4, 104n92, 105, 105n96–97, 106, 100n100, 107, 107n104, 108, 108n108, 109–10, 111, 113, 117, 134, 136, 137n14, 144, 148, 149, 152, 161n6, 162n7, 164, 165n9, 166, 166n9, 167n12, 168, 169, 169n15, 170, 171, 186, 194, 196, 200, 215, 219, 228–32, 244n6, 251, 252n28
Plutarch of Athens 11, 78, 146–47

Plutarch of Chaeronea 5, 176, 192
pneuma 89, 89n43, 94–95, 99, 102–3
polyarchy 239
Porphyry 2–15, 16–18, 24, 28, 37, 39–40, 43–44, 46–48, 50, 54, 55, 57, 57nn38–39, 58–59, 61, 62–63, 65–69, 72, 75n21, 76, 79–96, 100, 102–6, 108–10, 113, 117, 123, 136, 144–46, 162n7, 164, 164n8, 165n9, 166–70, 207, 209–10, 212–13, 215n43, 232–33, 240, 242, 247
positive theology 243–54
pre-being 240
prefiguration 84, 86n27, 87–89, 94, 98, 101, 108
pre-principle 98n76, 98n77
Preuschen, E. 74n17
principle 2, 3, 4, 11, 16, 18, 25n7, 26–27, 31, 32, 38, 39, 40, 41, 51n17, 54, 55, 56, 58, 59, 62, 67, 69, 71, 74, 80, 82, 83, 84, 85, 86n27, 88, 89, 91, 92, 94, 96–98, 99n83, 100–103, 105n97, 107n103, 130, 143, 144, 145, 147, 158, 158n3, 159n3, 162, 168, 179–80, 184–85, 190, 193, 194, 202, 210, 210n23, 211, 217, 221, 226, 233, 234, 239, 240, 247–49, 251
Prinzivalli, E. 213n36
procession and return 9, 83, 87–88, 94, 98, 108, 137, 138, 145, 149, 151, 240, 241, 242, 245, 246
Proclus 1–3, 6, 9–11, 13, 17, 19, 23n1, 24, 30n32, 36, 38–40, 44, 46–47, 49–50, 54–56, 58, 60, 62, 76n26, 83n15, 84n16, 85, 87–89, 91, 95, 97n74, 99nn80 & 84, 105n97, 112n6, 113, 115, 117, 119, 120–21, 123–32, 134–40, 143–47, 149–50, 154, 165n9, 193, 196, 200, 235n40, 244nn4–5, 247–51, 253
proodos 245
προσεκτικόν 154

Pseudo-Dionysius (Denys) 243–54
pure soul 123–26, 129–32
Pythagorean 25, 25n8, 31, 57, 89n43, 94, 133, 145n4, 161, 202, 204, 215, 202, 204

Rabbinic thought 214
Radice, R. 177n6
Rasimus, T. 12, 13, 29, 82n5, 82n8, 94n60, 106n98
relative predominance 83–85, 88, 94, 98–99, 108
resurrection 209
Rist, J. M. 24–25
Robinson, J. A. 203n3
Robinson, J. M. 197n24
Rome 194, 196, 204
Rousseau, A. 93n53
Rousseau, P. 228
Ruelle, C. E. 83n14, 84n16, 85, 85n26, 87, 88, 91, 91n48, 105n97, 149, 150, 152, 153

Saffrey, H. D. 38, 144–46
Saffrey, H. D (and L. G. Westerink) 23n1, 24n5, 27n13, 27n17, 28n19, 31, 36n2, 37n4, 38, 49n3, 54n25, 55n35, 58, 65n1, 88, 119n2, 120n3, 135, 135n4, 137n12, 137n13, 138n15, 138n16, 139n17, 139n19, 140n23, 144n3, 146n5, 147, 147n6
Sayre, K. 147
Schenke, H.-M. 82n5
Schibli, H. 213n37
Scolnicov, S. 38n7, 39
Segonds, A.-P. 56n36, 124n12
Septuagint (Old Testament) 202, 206
Sesboué, B. 240n3
Seth 105, 106n98
Sethian/Classic Gnosticism 82, 82n5, 87–91, 96–97, 97n70, 98–99,
Sethian/Classic Gnosticism, *cont'd.* 99n83, 100, 102–3, 103–4n92,

105-6, 106n98, 107, 107n104, 108-9, 109n111, 110
Shaw, G. 151n7
Simplicius 2-5, 9, 13-14, 18-19, 24, 24n5, 50n10, 58, 86n27, 143, 155n9, 157-71, 186n28
  ps.-Simplicius 149, 151, 151n7, 154n8
Sinnige, Th. 107n100, 108n106
Skepticism 47
Smith, A. 24n5, 65n1, 81n4, 209
Socrates' "day" image 250-52; 251n24
Sodano, A. R. 136n7
Sophia 104, 195
Soul 4, 6, 9, 13, 14, 23, 25, 27, 28, 29, 31, 32, 33, 35, 37, 38, 39, 40, 42, 33, 46, 59, 61, 67, 71, 74, 85, 89, 105n96, 107, 108, 117, 119, 120, 122, 123, 124, , 133-42, 143-56, 163, 165n9, 177, 181, 196, 200, 201, 202, 206, 209, 210-14, 214n42, 215, 221, 224, 227, 228, 229n25-27, 230, 230n29, 231, 237, 238
  all soul 37, 43, 230
  and body 105n96, 131, 163, 181, 201, 209, 210-12
  and embryo 210, 210n23
  and hypotheses 32, 35-48, 59, 62, 119, 120, 122, 136, 143-56, 209
  and life 89
  and material world 67, 105n96, 125, 127
  and motion 107, 107n102
  and non-existence 44
  ascent/descent 121, 132, 148-52, 196, 209, 212, 213
  of Christ 212
  divine 145, 150, 152
  embodied 148, 149, 210-14
  entry to non-being 147
  essence 150-53
  fallen 104, 108, 132, 213

  generation of 28, 134n2
  higher/purified 123, 125-32, 149, 202, 209, 210, 212, 215
  human 62, 120, 122, 123, 124, 125-32, 151, 152
  hypostasis 23, 25, 25n9, 29, 35, 85, 85n27, 89, 144
  image of intellect 27
  individual 14, 28, 148, 149
  intellect 163, 165n9, 231, 238
  judgment of 106
  kinds of 28, 124-25, 129
  one-many 33, 121, 153, 237
  participated 150
  rational/irrational 37, 39, 40, 151, 214, 215n53
  root of 107n103
  transmigration 210-11, 215
  tripartite 122, 209
Speusippus 1, 2-4, 5, 17-18, 24, 90, 133, 139n18, 145n4
Stählin, O. 183
Stead, G. C. 194n15, 207
Steel, C. 17, 49n3, 76n26, 112n5, 112n6, 113, 114, 115, 120n4, 121n5, 122n6, 123, 123n8, 148, 149, 150, 151n7, 152, 153
Stiglmayr, J. 244n4
Stoics 12, 46, 59,67, 83, 84, 85, 89n43, 92-95, 95n66, 96n69, 100, 102, 103, 108, 115, 116, 129, 170, 191, 201-3, 205, 215, 221n9, 237
  categories 9, 92, 100, 103,
  cosmic cycle 103
  criterion of truth 9
  distinction between σύγχυσις/ παράθεσις 67
  division of philosophy 94n65
  ἔννοιαι/notion 89n43
  in Hegel 46
  intension 170
  matter 96n69
  mixture 95

physics 12, 84, 85, 93, 95, 95n66, 108,
physics/metaphysics 81–110 *passim*
prokatarchtic cause 237
quasi-existents
spermatikos logos 94
spirit/pneuma 89n43, 94, 102, 103
God 94
substance and paronyms 94
total blending 94
ὕπαρξις 94–95
Strange, S. K. 167n12
Strutwolf, H. 208n19
sublunary god 130
substance 17, 42, 43–44, 50–52, 60, 73, 77, 94, 138, 145, 150, 161, 166n10, 168, 171, 172, 220, 222–23, 233, 233n38, 234, 239–42
beyond 145, 202, 222
all humans as one 220
and categories 161, 163,
Christian notions 73, 77, 238, 239, 240, 241, 242
divine 17, 222–23
eternal 150
vs. *existentia* 72
infinitival/substantive 12, 67, 69, 72
Porphyry/Iamblichus 167, 168
proper/improper senses 50–52
sensible 43–44
Stoic view 94
substantial, vital, and intellectual 153
supersubstantial 202
threefold (Aristotle's *Metaphysics*) 161–62, 162n7
Trinity 239–42
substantiality 17, 43, 150, 151–53, 166n10, 168, 169, 202
and insubstantiality 98, 99n80, 222

Suchla, B. R. 246–54
sun, image of 250–53, 251n24, 252n25
superior classes 119, 122–32
syndromos 240–41
Syrianus 11, 13–14, 38, 95, 119–20, 123, 133–40, 144–46, 247–49
Szlezák, T. A 3, 4, 25, 25n8

Tardieu, M. 7, 21, 65n3, 66, 78n28, 81n4, 82n6, 82n8, 86, 86n30, 86n31, 87n34, 90, 92, 95n68, 96n69, 97n70, 100, 109, 109n111, 194, 194n11
Tarrant, H. 57n37, 145
tensile movement 94, 94n62, 103
the one (in dispute)
the other/the one
Theodore of Asine 12, 59, 60, 60n43, 61
Theodotus 197
theology 7, 15, 19, 55, 62, 73, 78, 79, 101, 117, 158, 162n7, 175–87, 189, 191–93, 197, 199, 200, 202, 222–23, 225, 237–42, 244, 247, 253, 254
henological 160n4
of logos 78–79
Mosaic 178
negative 15, 16, 19, 48, 71, 93n54, 177, 185, 186, 189, 192, 193, 222–23, 225, 273, 235n40, 237–42, 244–45, 253
Nicene 194n16
positive 15, 17, 19, 55, 62, 101, 193, 237–42, 244–45, 253
Trinitarian 17, 19, 65, 237–54
theurgy 11–13, 62, 63, 94, 132, 149, 155
Till, W. 82n5
time 5, 14, 32, 35, 77, 78, 101, 111–14, 20, 121–22, 148, 150, 152, 153–55, 178, 181, 182, 189, 204, 207
Tornau, C. 24n5
transcendent interpretation (first

hypothesis) 245, 253–54
triads 6, 8, 10, 12, 13–14, 16–17, 19, 60, 61, 68–69, 73, 75, 76, 76n22, 78–79, 79n29, 80–108 *passim*, 135–40, 146, 147, 195–96, 197, 198, 201, 207, 226, 233, 238–42
  being–life–mind 8, 15, 19, 68–69, 75, 76, 77–79, 82–84, 88–90, 98, 99, 102, 107, 107n104, 136, 195–96
  demiurgic 61
  enneadic structure 6, 8, 13–14, 83–84, 85, 87, 88, 94, 97, 98, 98nn76 & 77, 102, 136
  existence–life–beatitude 73, 75, 91, 97, 101, 102
  Father–Mother–Child 96–97, 102
  Father–Power–Intellect 10, 83, 84, 87, 88, 91, 94, 102, 207
  feminine 100, 102
  intelligible 61, 68, 88, 94, 98, 102, 135–36, 138–47, 195, 197 (in Plato)
  Invisible Spirit–Barbelo–Autogenes 96–97
  καλυπτός–προτοφανής–αὐτογενής 96, 97, 97nn70 & 74, 97, 98, 99n79
  monad, dyad, triad 241
  one-being 137
  ὀντότης–ζωότης–νοότης 77
  Pauline (body, soul, spirit) 201
  πνεῦμα–μακάριος–τριδύναμος 102
  Trinity 238. 239, 240
  Unity, potency, being 136
tridunamos 89, 89n42, 96, 99–102
Trinitarian thought/Trinity 187, 207, 213, 219–21
Trouillard, J. 227
Turner, D. 245, 254
Turner, J. D. 6, 7, 8, 10, 12, 18, 65n3, 69, 69n10, 76n22, 81n4, 82n5, 82n6, 82n8, 85, 86, 86nn27–28, 89n38, 92, 92n49, 96, 97n70, 97n74, 99n80, 99n85, 100n87, 101, 104n94, 104n95, 106n99, 108n105, 143n1, 193n9, 194n11, 196n21
Two Intellect-theory 10, 87, 102, 105n97, 108

undetermined being 83, 84, 88, 95, 97, 98
unformedness 240
unity. *See* the One/Good; the others.
unlimited 4, 15, 42, 101, 134, 138, 140, 180, 186, 224–26, 248n17
  and limit 15, 134, 140n22, 180, 186
Urbach, L. 214n42
Urmson, J. 155
Usener, H. 191n4

Vaggione, P. 240, 240n3
Valentinian(s) 92–93n53, 109n109, 183, 194, 197
Vandenbussche, E. 234
visible god 126, 129
voice, image of 252, 252n27
Von Balthasar, H. U. 242
Vorwerk, M. 10–11, 12, 28n24, 29n28

Waldstein, M. (and F. Wisse) 82n8
Weber, K. 54n25, 29n26
Westerink, L. G. (and J. Combès) 50n5, 83n14, 84n16, 85, 85n26, 87, 88, 91, 91n48, 105,97, 119n2, 120n3, 120n4, 121n5, 130n18, 130n19, 137, 146, 146n5, 148, 151
Westerink, L. G. (and H. D. Saffrey) 23n1, 24n5, 27n13, 27n17, 28n19, 31, 36n2, 37n4, 38, 49n3, 54n25, 55n35, 58, 65n1, 88, 119n2, 120n3, 135, 135n4, 137n12, 137n13, 138n15, 138n16, 139n17, 139n19,

140n23, 144n3, 146n5, 147, 147n6
Whittaker, J. 15, 46, 179, 189–92
Williams, J. N. 243n3, 245, 254
Williams, M. 81n3
Winston, D. 179n8, 179n10
Wire, A. 81n4
Wittgenstein, L. 201
Wolfson, H. A. 177n6
womb 210, 211, 211n26, 214, 214nn41 & 42, 215
Wücherpfennig, H. 191

Zachhuber, J. 208n20, 221, 221n7, 221n9
Zeus 122, 136n9, 202, 205
Zintzen, C. 56n36
Zoroaster 100, 104–6
Zostrianos 7, 21, 100, 104–6, 106n98–99
Zostrianos 6–9, 18, 65–66, 68–69, 72, 72n16, 73, 75, 78–79, 80, 82, 82nn5–7, 86, 87, 88, 88n37, 89, 89n41, 90, 91, 92, 93n53, 95, 96, 97, 98n76, 99, 99n82–83, 100–110, 193–98

Index Locorum

Auctores Graeci et Latini

Albinus

Isagoge
3	191n6

Alcinous

Didaskalikos (Hermann-Whittaker-Louis)
6	191n6
6.10	38, 46
6.158.20–22	116
6.158.23–27	116
6.158.32–33	116
6.158.34–35	116
6.158.40–41	116
6.159.7–8	116
6.158.35–36	116
6.159.15–16	116
6.159.20–21	116
6.159.27–28	116
10	185
10.164.31–165.16	190n3
25.6	215n43

Anonymus in Platonis Parmenidem Commentarium (ed. Hadot)

1.3	90, 197n22
2.15	197n22
4.32–35	93n55
7–8	111
8	116
8.1–21	111
8.21–35	111
8.29–30	115
8.30–31	117
9.1–4	91, 91n48
9.8–10	94
9–12	95
12.4	91
12.29–35	84nn20–21
12.32	90
13.27–14.4	95
14.6	84n21
14.12	90
14.15	84n21
14.17	84n21
14.18	84n21
14.23	84n21
14.25	84n21
14.15–26	88n37, 89n39
14.17–26	84nn18–19

Apuleius

Apologia
64	27n17

Aristotle

Categories
1b25–2a10	160
10b26–11a19	170
11a15–16	171n20

Metaphysics
A.991a29b	208n17
E.1027b27–31	197n25
Z.1035a1–2	162n7
Z.1040b33	208n17

DAMASCIUS

Corollary on Time (Urmson)
798, 30–35	155

De principiis (Westerink-Combès)
1.23	121
2.1.4–2.10	84n16, 85, 85n26, 87, 88, 91, 105n97
2.3.5–6	83n14
2.17.14–17	137
2.36.5–6	83n14
2.71.1–7	83n14
2.148.6–12	153
3.7–4.19	121
3.8–10	121
3.10–13	121
3.13–15	122
3.15–4.1	122
3.17–4.1	127
3.44.17–45.2	155
3.145.10–18	91, 91n48
4.1	122
4.1–7	122
4.7–13	122
4.13–19	122
4.19.9–18	128
4.19.14–18	128
4.24.1–7	131
§43–48 (Ruelle)	68n8
238 (Ruelle)	85n26

In Parmenidem (Steel)
11, 11–15	153
13, 1–5	150
15, 1–5	149
33, 10–15	152
83, 16	148
85, 15	148
84, 5–9	146

In Parmenidem (Ruelle)
252.7–15	150
253.19–21	151
253.25ff.	152
254.3–19	149
255.8–15	151

In Parmenidem (Westerink-Combès)
3.73–74	51
3.75, 1–18	50-51
4.125, 7–9	52
4.125, 1–14	51-52

In Phaedonem
1.271, 1–4	154
1.477.2	126
2.94.3–5	126

Vita Isidori (*Photius, Epitoma Photiana fragmenta* Zintzen)
244	56 n. 36, 57 n. 40

EPICURUS

Fragmenta (Usener)
314	191n4

EUNAPIUS

Vita Porphyrii   94n59, 105n97

HERMEIAS

In Platonis Phaedrum Scholia
8.14–20	115
162.29–163.19	123–24n10

HIEROCLES

In aureum carmen
20	99n84

INDEX LOCORUM

IAMBLICHUS

De Anima Fragmenta (Finamore-Dillon)
   6–7 (= Stobaeus, *Anthologium* 1.49.32, 61–81 Wachsmuth)   149
   Appendix D (= Priscianus <ps-Simplicius> *In Aristotelis libros de anima commentaria* 11.240.33–241.26 Hayduck)   151

De Anima Fragmenta (Wachsmuth)
   357   196n20

De Mysteriis
1.3.9.10–11	123n9
1.10, 33.12–15	123
1.10, 36.6–10	123
1.20.63.5–64.12	126
1.20.63.12–13	126
1.20.64.7–9	126–27
2.1.68.12–13	127
2.2.68.4	127n15
2.2.68.6–7	127n15
2.3	129n16
2.4.77.19–78.2	127n15
2.5.79.7	127
2.5.79.10	127
2.5.79.10–11	127
2.5.80.5–6	127n15
2.5.80.15–81.4	127
2.6.82.10–11	127
2.6.82.13–14	127

In Parmemidem fragmenta (Dillon-Finamore)
1	119
2.7–11	119–20
12	120
13	128, 129

In Phaedonem fragmenta (Dillon-Finamore)
   5   130

PS-IAMBLICHUS

Theologoumena arithmeticae
   9.4–6   108n107

JOSEPHUS

Antiquitates judaicae
   1.68–72   106n98

JULIANUS IMPERATOR

Oratio
   IV 5 [132cd]   91

JOANNES LYDUS

De mensibus
   4.94   88n36, 89
   4.122   85, 85n26, 87, 88, 105n97

JOANNES PHILOPONUS

In Aristotelis categorias commentarium
   49,23–50,3   162n7

JULIANUS IMPERATOR

Oratio
   IV 5 [132cd]   91
   Hymn to King Helios   251

MODERATUS

apud Simplicius, *In Aristotelis physicorum libros commentaria* (Diels)
   230.34–231.24 (= Porphyry frg. 236 Smith) 24n5, 186n28

Numenius

Fragmenta (des Places)
11	97n74, 202
12,2–3	29n29
12,12–13	27n17
12,13	28
12,13–14	29n29
13	97n74
15	97n74
15,4–5	28n21
16	97n74
16,8–9	208n18
17	87
19–22	87
20	90n46

Oracula Chaldaica Fragmenta (Majercik)
1	83n15, 93n54
2	83, 89n43, 100
3–4	91, 94
3	83
4	83
20	83n15
23	83
26	89n43, 100
27	83
28	83
29	83
31	83
84	83n15
84,3	68n12

Philo of Alexandria

Legum allegoriae
1.2–3	181
1.36	180n12
1.43–44	180–81
1.44	180n12
2.2–3	180n12
2.3	178
3.36	96n69
3.206	180n12

De mutatione nominum
46	180n12

De cherubim
46, 90	180n12

De confusione linguarum
63, 146	179

De vita contemplativa
2	178

De opificio mundi
16–25	177
20	186

De fuga et inventione
8	180

De Somniis
1.67	192

De posteritate Caini
3, 4, 14, 19, 23	180n12

De providentia
39, 42, 48	177n2

De praemiis et poenis
39–40	179

De sobrietate
63	180n12

De specialibus legibus
1.32–50	179n9
1.208	180n12

Quod Deus sit immutabilis
2, 7, 31–32, 55, 59	180n12

Plato

Clitophon
408c3–4	135

Epistulae
2.312d–e	27
2.312e	31
2.312e1–4	27n14
6.323d	28, 31
6.323d2–4	28n23
7.41c5	190n2

Parmenides
129b–d	53 n. 24

130c	218, 220	142d9	138
130d	218	143a	239
130d3–133a9	53	143a2–3	138
130e	220	143a3–144e7	139
131a	231	143d	238, 240
131a4–c11	53	144b1–2	31n34
131b	218, 231, 250–51	144c	85n26
131b4	176	144c–d	219, 231
132b3	176	144a	44
132b4	183	144b–d	239
132d	218	144e	32, 239
132d2	177	144e5	30, 35
133c1	177	144e8–145a4	116, 140
134b	223	145a2-b5	116
134b11	177	145c4–b5	140
134b14	177	146a9–147b8	50
135a2	117	148b2–3	52 n. 23
135a5	177	148e	225
137a–143a	59	149d	225
137c–142a	35	151e–155d	32
137c3	38	154e	224
137c3–142a6	23n2	155d	33
137c4–142a7	30, 143	155e	32
137c5–d3	184	155e3–157b4	23n2, 59
137c6–8	184	155e4	38
137d	224	155e4–156a4	120–21, 144
137d4–8	116	155e5	30, 35, 148
137d4–138a1	116	156b6–159b	144
137d6	184	157b5	38
137d8	184	157c	43
137e	116	159b–16b4	144
138a	225	159c2	52 n. 23
138c	224	160b–163b	144
139e8	171n21	159b2	38
141a5–d6	111, 112 n. 1	160b3	38
141d6–142a1	55 n. 33, 56	163b–164b	144
141e7–142a7	177–78	163b7	39
142a	58, 223	164c–d	42
142a1–b1	55 n. 31	164b6–c1	52 n. 23
142a3	185, 190n2	164b5–165e1	144
142b1–155e2	23n2, 143	164d	45, 220
142b3	38	165b	41
142c1–155e3	59	165b–c	220

Plato, *Parmenides, cont'd.*

165e2–3	39, 41
165e2–166c5	144
166a	221

Phaedo

114c26	130

Pheadrus

234d5–6	135
246a3–256e2	122
246a–b	201
247c6	184
248c3	122–23
252c3	122
252c4	123
252c5	123

Respublica

VII	218, 232, 251
5.449e	201
5.475e4	117
6.509b	24, 29, 31
6.509b7–8	29 n.27
6.509d2–3	27
6.509d5	147
8.545c–d	239
8. 545c8–d7	239
10.597e6–8	27n16
10.614a–621d	106

Sophista

237a4	183
238c	192n5
248c–e	197n25
248e	107n102
248e7–249d4	29n28
249a	107n102
248–249	107, 107n104
248–249a	107

Symposium

199c5–201c9	128
201d1–202d9	128
202d10–13	128
202d13–202e1	128
202e3–203a4	128
203b–d	206

Timaeus

28a2	147
28c	70
29a6	28n24
29a6–7	56
35ab	31
35a1–36b6	28
39e	89, 102n91, 197n25
39e7	28n24
39e7–9	29n28
30c6	139
37d6	137
41d	31
41d4–7	28
47e4–5	28n24

PLOTINUS

Ennead

1.2 [19].3	105n97
1.6 [1].7.11–12	88n37
1.6 [1].7.12	88n37
1.6 [1].9.36–39	29n26
1.7 [54].1.19–20	29n26
1.8 [51]	105n97, 106n100, 108
1.8 [51].2	107n103
1.8 [51].2.5–7	88n37
1.8 [51] 2.13	112 n. 2
1.8 [51].2.27–32	27n14
1.8 [51].14	44
2.2 [14]	74n19
2.2 [14].10–15	74n19
2.3 [52] 17.10	112 n. 3
2.4 [12].13	41
2.9 [33]	82n7, 104, 193, 196
2.9 [33].1	83n9, 102n91, 104
2.9 [33].1.1–16	32
2.9 [33].4	104
2.9 [33].6	102n91, 104, 107n104, 196n19
2.9 [33].6.1–3	104
2.9 [33].6.42–62	105
2.9 [33].8	104

INDEX LOCORUM

2.9 [33].9	104	5.1 [10].8.23	30
2.9 [33].10	104	5.1 [10].8.23–26	244n6
2.9 [33].10.19–33	104	5.1 [10].8.23–27	30n32, 31, 32
2.9 [33].14	104	5.1 [10].8.25–26	25n9
3.6 [26]	44	5.1 [10].8.26	33
3.6 [26].6.10–17	88n37	5.1 [10].8.30	148
3.6 [26].6.23–24	88n37	5.1[10].9	242
3.6 [26].7.7–8	88n37	5.2 [11]	78
3.7 [45].11	35	5.2 [11].1.1	43
3.8 [30].8.8–12	88n37	5.2 [11].1.1–18	108
3.8 [30].9.29–32	93n54, 108	5.2 [11].1.6–11	241n8
3.8 [30].10	93n55	5.2 [11].2	108
3.8 [30].10.1–2	88n37	5.3 [49].10–17	83n9
3.8 [30].11	26, 93n54, 107, 240	5.3 [49].15.26–35	108
3.9 [13]	87, 102n91, 105n97	5.3 [49].16.38–42	88n37
3.9 [13].1	97n74	5.4 [7]	83n9, 87, 102n91, 105n97
3.9 [13].3	105n97		
3.9 [13].6.3–6	88n37	5.4 [7].2	108
3.9 [13].9	93n55	5.4 [7].2.17–18	88n37
4.2 [4].2.52–55	25n9	5.4 [7].2.43–44	88n37
4.3 [27].1–8	29n25	5.5 [32]	91, 107
4.3 [27].7.8–12	29n25	5.5 [32].1.38	88n37
4.8 [6].5	105n97, 108	5.5 [32].7.31–34	97n70
4.8 [6].8	29n25, 149	5.5 [32].10.12–14	88n37
5.1 [10]	83nn9–10, 228–32	5.6 [24]	83n9
5.1 [10].1	108	5.6 [24].6.20–22	88n37
5.1 [10].1–2	29n25	5.8 [31].4	108
5.1 [10].3.13	75n20	5.8 [31].5	104n95
5.1[10].3.18	149	5.8 [31].7	93n55
5.1 [10].4.7	75n20	5.8 [31] 7.41–42	112 n. 2
5.1 [10].5.2	31n34	5.9 [5]	91
5.1 [10].8	26–31, 35, 85n27, 105, 186 &n29	5.9 [5].3.26	28n24
		5.9 [5].5.20	28n24
5.1 [10].8.1–4	27n12	5.9 [5].8.1–7	29n28
5.1 [10].8.1–9	31	5.9 [5].9.1–8	29n28
5.1 [10].8.1–14	31	5.9 [5].10	88n37, 107n103
5.1 [10] 8.1–27	58	6.1 [42].1.19–30	161n6
5.1 [10].8.4–9	28n22	6.1 [42].1.28–30	167n12
5.1 [10].8.9–14	29n30	6.1 [42].12.44–45	167n12
5.1 [10].8.11–15	144	6.1 [42].12.45	168
5.1 [10].8.14–23	30	6.1–3 [42–44]	162n7, 165
5.1 [10].8.14–27	31	6.2 [43].2.53–54	165n9
5.1 [10].8.14–9.32	30, 31	6.2 [43]	83n9

Plotinus, *Enneads*, cont'd.

6.2 [43].6	107n103
6.2 [43].8.23–25	90n47
6.2 [43].12.10	42
6.3 [44].7	251
6.3 [44].9	44
6.4–5 [22–23]	91
6.4 [22].3.31–35	88n37
6.5 [23].1.27	43
6.5 [23].5.1–23	252n28
6.6 [34].8	107n103
6.6 [34]	44, 45
6.6 [34].1	45
6.6 [34].8.1–2	88n37
6.6 [34].8.9–10	88n37
6.6 [34].8.11–13	88n37
6.6 [34].8.15–17	88n37
6.6 [34].8.17–23	88n37
6.6 [34].9.27–29	88n37
6.6 [34].9.29–32	88n37
6.6 [34] 11–13	55
6.6 [34].15.1–3	88n37
6.6 [34].18.35–36	88n37
6.6 [34].18.51–53	88n37
6.7 [38].1	238
6.7 [38].1–13	93n55
6.7 [38].1.45–48	238n1
6.7 [38].8.22–32	29n28
6.7 [38].11	42
6.7 [38].13.42–43	88n37
6.7 [38].13.16–21	241
6.7 [38].23.11–12	44
6.7 [38].23.22–25	88n37
6.7 [38].32	90n47
6.7 [38].32.24–39	240
6.7 [38].34	90n47
6.7 [38].36.15–16	93n54, 108
6.7 [38].37–42	83n9
6.7 [38].37.18–22	83n9, 108
6.7 [38].39.28–34	29n28
6.7 [38].41	93n54
6.8 [39]	193n10
6.8 [39].8	93n55
6.8 [39].11	95n69
6.8 [39].16	95n69
6.8 [39].16.34	29n26
6.8 [39].20.17–25	240
6.8 [39].21.25–33	93n54, 108
6.9 [9]	87, 102n91, 105n97
6.9 [9].1	45
6.9 [9].1.12	41
6.9 [9].2.24	88n37
6.9 [9].3–4	93n54, 107
6.9 [9].9	88n37, 107n103

PLUTARCH

On brotherly love
484C	176

Platonic Questions
3.1002D	176

PORPHYRY

Ad Gaurum (Kalbfleisch)
10.5	95n66
37–46	210n3

Ad Marcellam
13	93n54
15–16	93n54

De abstinentia
2.34	93n54

De antro nympharum
74.22	93n54

De Materia (*Fragmenta* Smith)
236	24

De regressu animae apud Augustine, *De civitate Dei*
10.9	94
10.9–10	94n60
10.16	94n60
10.18	94n60
10.21	94n60
10.23	94, 94n60
10.26–30	94n60
10.27	94

10.28	94	3	87
10.29	94	3.10–12.25	55 n. 29
10.32	94n60	3.29	57 n. 39
12.21	94n60	3.37	105 n. 96
12.27	94n60	4	109
13.19	94n60	7.24–29	57 n. 38
22.12	94n60	13	105 n. 96, 109
22.27	94n60	14	87

De Styge (*Fragmenta* Smith)
372–380   209

Historia philosophiae
15	91
18	88, 91

In harmonica Ptolemaei
17.20	90

In Aristotelis categorias exposition
88,13–15	162n7
138,24–29	167n12
138,30–31	168
138,30–32	167n12. 170n17

in Timaeum fragmenta (Sodano)
LXXIX	136

Isagoge
69.14–70.24	88

Sententiae
10	88
12	87, 89
21	87
25–26	88
25	93n54
26	92
26.3–6	92
27	93n55
31	88
33.5	95n66
35	90
40	87
41	88, 89
44	95

Symmikta Zetemata
69	95n66

Vita Plotini
1.1–2	105n97

14.4–7	162 n. 7
14.12	28 n. 20
14.20	57 n. 39
16	82 n. 7, 100, 103, 105, 117, 195 n. 18
17–18	87
17.1–6	28n20
17.4–6	28 n.21
18	105, 105n96, 107, 109

PRISCIANUS <PS-SIMPLICIUS>

In de anima Hayduck)
11.220.2–15	151n7
11.240.33–241.26	151

In Phaedonem
290.6–8	154n8

PROCLUS

Institutio theologica (Dodds)
11	54 n. 28
17	54 n. 28
29	150
101	196
103	99n80
126	248n11
166–167	150
185	123–24
191	150
216	136

In Platonis Parmenidem commentaria (Cousin + Klibanski-Labowsky)
1.630.37	115

Proclus, *In Parm.*, cont'd.

1.630,37–643,5	23 n. 1
1.631.21–632.27	115
1.631.21–632.27	115
1.631.36–632.6	115
1.634.6	115
1.640,17	145
4.862	251,n24
6.1040–41	244,n5
6.1049,37–1050,24	135
6.1051.34–1064.12	49
6.1051.35–1052.1	115
6.1052–1053	146
6.1052,31–1064,17	36n3, 144
6.1053,37–1054,10	91
6.1053–1056	146
6.1053,37–1054,37	37n5, 58
6.1054–1055	146
6.1054,17	40
6.1054,37–1055,25	37n6
6.1057,5–1064,17	38
6.1060–1061	147
6.1061,21	145
6.1061,31–1062,17	**134**
6.1064.21–1066.16	55
6.1070,15–30	84n16
6.1106,1–1108,15	76n26
6.1107,9–17	249,n22
6.1114,1–10	248,n13
6.1115,25–36	248,n14
6.1083	46
7.1215,10–11	99n84
7.1226.15–26	114
7.1240,32–37	30n32

In Platonis Parmenidem commentaria (Klibanski-Labowsky)

7.36.8–31	56
7.64.1–16	56

In Platonis Timaeum commentaria (Diehl)

1.110.22–114.21	124
1.111.14–19	124
1.131.27–132.5	124
1.152.28–30	55 n. 32
1.195.15–25	129 n.17
1.196.11–16	129
1.196.16–24	129
1.196.24–27	129-130
1.196.30–197.1	130
1.306.1–14	97n74
1.308.18-23	136
2.41.20	99n84
3.33.32–33	95
3.64.8–65.1	105n97
3.64.8–9	85, 87, 88
3.262.6–26	125
3.262.7–8	125
3.262.14–26	125
3.262.21–26	125
3.274.11	60

Theologica Platonica (Saffrey-Westerink)

1:11	88
1:42,4–9	23n1
2:31, 1–28	54-55
3–4	146
3:83,10–18	135
3:85,27–86,3	137
3:87,1–5	137
3:87,8–16	138
3:89,7–16	138
4:21	83n15
4:31, 1–28	55
4:36	140
4:79,1–80,6	139
4:81,3–82,11	139
4:89,6–91,26	140

SEXTUS EMPIRICUS

Adversus mathematicos

11–20	53 n. 24

INDEX LOCORUM

SIMPLICIUS

In Aristotelis categorias commentarium

1,3–7	158
1,7	158n3
2,3–29	169n15
2,9–14	169n15
9,4–13,26	158n3
12,13–13,11	159n3
73,13	160
73,15	161
73,15–28	161
73,29–74,3	161
73,29–74,17	164
74,3–5	164
74,3–17	161
74,18–19	161, 162n7
74,18-75,22	164, 169.
74,28–75,3	162
74,32–75,3	163
75,3–8	160 (bis)
75,5–8	165n9
75,6	157. 160.
75,6–7	165n9 (tris)
75,8–9	166
75,8–22	166
75,22	161
76,18–19	164n8
76,20–22	164n8
76,22–23	164n8
78,4–5	164n8
78,5–8	161n7
90,19–20	164n8
205,22–35	164n8
205,22–24	164n8
225,21–231,33	58
230.36–231.5	58
277,5–11	164n8
283,29– 284,11	170
283,29–291,18	170
284,12–13	170
284,13–17	170
284,17–32	170
284,32–285,1	170
285,1–3	166n10, 167n12
285,1–8	170
285,5–8	166n10
285,6–8	167
285,9–10	171n19
285,9–286,4	170
286,4	170n18
286,5–6	171n19
286,5–15	170
286,16–34	170
286,35–290,10	170
289,13–33	166. 171
289,21–33	167n11
289,23	168n13
289,28	168n13
290,1	171
290,1–3	166n10, 167n12
290,1–9	166
290,1-10	170
290,1–291,1	171
290,5–6	168
290,5–9	168
290,6	168
290,9–10	164n8 (bis)
290,10-25	171
290,12–15	168
290,16–17	168
290,21	168
290,24–25	168n14
290,25	170. 171 (bis)
290,27	171
290,31–33	171
290,33–291,1	171
291,1–2	169 (bis), 171
291,2	157. 160.
291,18	171
300,25–28	164n8
340,12–13	164n8

In Aristotelis physicorum libros commentaria (Diels)

9.230.36–40	145

Simplicius, *In phys.*, cont'd.
9.230.34–231.27	86n27
9:798,30–35	155

SYRIANUS

In Aristotelis Metaphysica commentaria (Kroll)
109, 12–16	95
124, 24–125, 8	139
130, 24–131, 8	139
131, 36	140
146, 5–9	139

PS-SIMPLICIUS   SEE PRISCIANUS

BIBLICA

VETUS TESTAMENTUM

Genesis
1:26	75, 77
1:26–28	213n36
2:7	213n36
2:8 (LXX)	180
2:18 (LXX)	181
3:21	213n36
4:25 (LXX)	106n98

Exodus
3:14 (LXX)	178
33:32	73

NOVUM TESTAMENTUM

Luke
1:41	211n26

John
1:3	187
1:18	183, 187
1:1	70
1:3	73
1:9	75
4:24	77
6:63	73
9:2	210

Romans
7:9	211
9:5	90n44
9:11–13	214n40
11:33	70
9:14	211n25

1 Corinthians
12:6–7	73
12:5	73

Philippians
2:9	190

Ephesians
1:21	190
4:6	90n44
5:29	212n35

Colossians
1:16	77

Hebrews
1:3	190, 207

1 Timothy
6:16	204

APOCRYPHA ET PSEUDEPIGRAPHA

Vita Adae et Evae
50.1–51.3	106n98

GNOSTICA

NAG HAMMADI CODICES

NHC II,1 *Apocryphon of John*
2.33	99n83
3.26–29	92n49
4.19–7.24	96
5.8	100, 101n88
5.12	99n83
5.28	99n83
6.13–18	101n89

7.11–33	97n70	123.23	99n81
7.14	99n83	124.18–20	98n77
8.32	97n70	124.26–27	98n78
9.13–17	101n89	125.25–33	99n79
19.10	100	125.28–32	88n37, 98n76
NHC III,1 *Apocryphon of John*		125.28	98n78
8.2–3	101n88	126.5	97n70
14.4	93n53	126.14–15	98n77
14.18	93n53	NHC VIII,1 *Zostrianos*	
14.21	93n53	2.21–30	98n78
14.23	93n53	3.8–13	86n30
15.8	93n53	3.8–11	98n78
21.1	93n53	3.9	89n41
21.8	93n53	8–10	104, 105n97
21.23–24	90	14.13–14	88n37
25.14	93n53	14.13	89n41, 98n78, 99n81
27.20	93n53	15.1–19	97
28.14	93n53	15.1–12	99n79
28.15	93n53	15.4–5	89n41
30.11	93n53	15.5–11	88n37
30.20	93n53	15.6–12	97n70
32.12	93n53	15.7	89n41
32.21	93n53	15.10–16	98n78
NHC IV,2 *Holy Book of the Great Invisible Spirit*		15.11	89n41
		15.13–17	86n30, 88n37
55.25	97n70	15.14	89n41
57.16	97n70	15.18–19	96, 99n81
60.2	97n70	16.1	98n78
NHC VI,4 *The Concept of Our Great Power*		16.11–12	98n78
		17.1–3	86n30
4.40	194n16	17.2	98n78
5	197n24	17.6–8	99n81
NHC VII,5 *Three Steles of Seth*		17.12–13	99n83
119.16	97n70	18.5–7	97n74
120.21–22	99n81	18.5–19	97n70
121.25–32	98n76	19.5–21	97n70
121.31–32	97n73, 99n81	20.2–15	98n76
122.14	97n70	20.4–9	97n70
122.19–25	88n37	20.15–18	97n72
122.19–23	89n41	20.16–19	99n81
122.23	99n82	20.17–18	99n83
123.1–5	97n70	20.18–19	98nn76–77
123.5–6	98n74	20.21–22	98n78

Zostrianos, cont'd.

20.22–24	88n37	67.20	91
21	91, 107	67.24–68.1	98n76
22.9–23.5	97n70	68.1–7	88n37
23.26	89n41	68.16–17	98n78
23.27	98n78	73.1	98n78
24.3–6	97n70	73.8–11	88n37
24.9–10	99n83	73.8	98n78
24.12–13	99n81	73.10	89n41
28.27	89n41	73.11	99n81
30.18	98n78	74	97
34.1	98n78	74.4–25	98n77
34.5	98n78	74.8–21	86n30
36.2	98n78	74.8–9	98n78
37.22	89n41	74.9	90
38.17–18	98n74	75.6–24	86n30
40.10–11	98n78	75.7–10	88n37
41	97n70	75.7	98n78
44.26–31	97n70	75.8	89n41
44.27–29	98n74	75.10	89n41
54.19–20	98n74	75.11	89n41
58.14–16	97n70	75.14	89n41
58.16–20	98n77	75.15	89n41
63.7–8	99n81	75.16	89n41
64.11–68.26	86n30	75.17	89n41, 99n81
64.14–16	98n77	75.19	89n41
64.14	91	76.13	89n41
64.22	91	77.8	93n53
65.6–7	98nn76–77	77.20–21	98nn76–77
65.23–66.3	98n76	78.4	98n78
66–68	97	78.11	98n78
66.14–67.4	98n76	79.5–20	98n78
66.14–18	99n81	79.10–15	88n37
66.14–20	99n79	79.10–81.20	98n75
66.16–19	98n78	79.14	89n41
66.16–17	88n37	79.15	89n41
66.17	89n41, 99n81	79.16–25	99n81
66.20	91	79.16–22	86n30
66.21	90	79.21	96
66.23–67.2	88n37	80.18	99n81
66.25	89n41	80.23	89n41
67.3	89n41	81.7–20	98n76
67.13–15	98n77	82.5–13	98nn76–77
		84.12–22	98nn76–77

84.13	89n41	9.7–25	99n81
84.16	98n78	10.8–11	99n81
84.18–22	86n30	14.22–23	99n81
85.14	89n41	15.1–3	99n81
85.22	89n41		
86.15–16	98n78	NHC XI,*3 Allogenes*	
86.15–22	88n37	45.9–46.35	97n71
86.18	89n41	45.13	99n81
86.21	89n41	45.21	99n81
87.10–14	99n81	45.30–46.23	97n70
87.12	89n41	45.33–35	98n74
93.7	99n81	46.7–12	98n78
95.5	98n78	47.7–11	99n81
95.16	98n78	47.10–14	98n76
97.2–3	99n81	47.25	98n78
97.4	89n41	47.35–36	93n54
98.5	98n78	48.16	98n78
99.2	98n78	48.17–19	98n77
107.3	98n78	48.36–38	98nn76–77
115–116	91, 107	49.5–21	107
117.6	89n41	49.7–14	98n75
118.9–16	98n76	49.9–10	99n83
118.9–12	99n81	49.26–38	88n37, 89n41,
118.11–12	99n83		98nn76–77, 99, 99nn79–80
122.4	99n83	49.30–31	99n80
123.18	89n41	49.34	99n80
123.18–19	99n81	51.8–9	97n72, 99n81
124.3–4	99n81	51.17–26	97n70
124.9	89n41	51.19–20	98n74
124.16	98n78	51.35	99n83
124.18–125.20	97n70	52.18–28	93n54
124.21–22	98n74	52.19	99n81
128.1–22	99n81	52.30–35	99n81
129.4–6	98n74	53.10–18	98n75
129.11–12	99n83	53.30–31	99n81
130.1–17	106n98	53.31	92, 98n78
NHC X,*1 Marsanes*		54.16	99n82
3.26–4.10	97n70	55.28–30	98n78
4.10–22	97n71	55.30	92
4.13–19	99n81	56–58	93n54
6.19	99n81	56.20	93n54
7.16–29	99n81	57.6	98n78
8.5–20	99n81	58.12–19	97n70

Allogenes, cont'd.		24.13–25.3	101
58.16–18	98n74	24.20–25.1	101
58.24–26	99n81	25.15–16	101
59.9–60.16	93n54	26.15	102
59.9–20	99n82	26.18	101
59.10–20	88n37	27.21–28.2	101
59.20	98n78	27.21–28.1	101n88
59.22–26	98n76	30.1–8	101n89
59.26–60.12	93n54, 108	31.5–9	101
60.16–37	88n37	*Codex Brucianus, Untitled*	
60.17–31	99n82	6.12–13	97n70
60.31	98n78	*Corpus Hermeticum*	
61.1–19	93n54, 108	6	93n53
61.6	99n81		

Judaica

Genesis Rabbah	
34.10.4	214n42

61.10–15	93n54		
61.19–20	99n81		
61.21	93n54		
61.32–39	69		
61.32–62.2	98nn76–77		
61.36–37	88n37		
61.37–38	98n78		

Patristica

Arnobius

62.19–23	88n37		
62.23	92, 98n78		
62.24–25	93n54	*Adversus nationes*	
62.28–36	101	1.52	106
63.1–24	101	1.62	208n21
63.14–16	93n54		
63.17–20	92	**Athanasius of Alexandria**	
63.35	93n54		
64.10–23	93n54	*Adversus Arium*	
64.34–35	99n81	1.18 (*PG* 26, 49b)	238
64.36	99n83	*De Decretis*	
65.19	93n54	appendix	208n19
65.29–33	98n78	*De Synodis*	
65.32–36	98n77	16	194
65.33	92		
66.27	92	**Athenagoras**	
66.28–30	98n76		
66.33–35	97n72, 99n81	*Legatio*	
68.32	93n54	6.2	204
BG 8502 *Apocryphon of John*			
24.2	101		
24.6–25.7	101		

INDEX LOCORUM

Augustine

Contra Faustum
5.4	208n21

De civitate Dei
10.9–10	94n60
10.9	94
10.16	94n60
10.18	94n60
10.21	94n60
10.23	85, 85n26, 87, 94, 94n60, 105n97
10.23–26	207n15
10.26–30	94n60
10.27	94
10.28	94
10.29	85, 85n26, 87, 94, 105n97
10.30	213n39
10.32	94n60
12.21	94n60
12.27	94n60
13.19	94n60
19.22	109n110
22.12	94n60
22.27	94n60

Barnabas

Epistula
19.5	211n24

Basil of Caesarea

Adversus Eumomium (Sesboüé)
1.5	240

De spiritu 228–31

De Spiritu Sancto
9.22	219
16.38.126b	237
16.38.136b25–c3	238

Epistulae
38.6	208n20
1	227
7	223
223	228

Eunomius

Apologia
11	233

Clement of Alexandria

Excerpta ex Theodoto	211n26

Stromateis
4.156	185
5.11.67	206
5.12.81	190
5.14.103.2–4	106
5.15	183n18
5.16	184
5.59	183n18
5.78	183, 183n22
5.81	183–84, 186
5.82	185
5.112	183, 183n18
5.138	183n18
6.23	183n18

Constitutiones Apostolicae

6.10.1	190

Didache

2.2	211n24
5.2	211n24

Epistula ad Diognetum

5.6	211n24

EPIPHANIUS

Panarion
26	109n111
31.12.5	93n53
40.7.1–2	106n98
69.7	194n13

EUSEBIUS

De Ecclesiastica Theologia
2.14.6	208n19

Praeparatio evangelica
4.23	105n97
11.18.26–19.1	104n93

GREGORY NAZIANSUS

Orationes (PG 36)
29, 2, 7–8	239
29, 2, 8–13	239
29, 3, 15–16	239
29, 3, 17, 18	240

GREGORY OF NYSSA

Ad Ablabium
41.1–2	219
53.9–10	219
53.20	219
55	223

De anima et resurrectione
24.29	218
48.25	219

Antirrheticus adversus Apolinarium
161.17	219

Epistulae
38	220, 221

Contra Eunomium libri
2	226
3.105	225

Ad Graecos, Ex communibus notionibus
25.19	220

Orationes de beatitudinibus
1	218

Homiliae in Canticum canticorum
8	226

Homilia in Ecclesiastes
7.7	218, 223

De Opificio Hominis
11	192n7
15–18	213n38
129.38	223
185.16	220

De vita Moysis
2.22–24	222
2.234–35	223
2.236	224
2.243–44	224

HIPPOLYTUS OF ROME

Refutatio
1.7.26	190
5.9.1	190
7.20	189

IRENAEUS

Adversus haereses
1.1–8	92n53, 109n109
1.1.23	92n53
1.1.48	92n53
1.2.19	93n53
1.2.57	93n53
1.2.59	93n53
1.2.65	92n53
1.2.72	92n53
1.2.95	92n53
1.2.100–101	92n53
1.3.1	92n53
1.3.57	92n53
1.3.88	92n53

1.4.1	92n53	NEMESIUS	
1.4.3	92n53		
1.4.6	92n53	*De natura hominis*	
1.4.13	92n53	70.6–71.4	94
1.4.87	92n53		
1.4.37	93n53	ORIGEN	
1.4.58	93n53		
1.5.27	92n53	*Commentarii in evangelium Joannis*	
1.6.84	93n53	(Koetschau)	
1.7.3	93n53	1.11	211n28
1.7.7	93n53	1.31	211n27
1.7.9	93n53	2.3.20	208n16
1.7.14	93n53	2.10.78.3	73
1.7.24	93n53	2.12.87	74n17
1.8.30	93n53	5.5.1.14–16	242
1.8.31	93n53	6.11	211n27
1.8.43	93n53	6.14	211n28
1.8.89	93n53	13.25.153	207
1.8.96	93n53	20.182	213n36
1.8.102	93n53	*Commentarii in epistulam ad Romanos*	
1.8.108–109	93n53		
1.8.125	93n53	6.8.1	212n29
1.8.173	93n53	*Contra Celsum*	
1.8.174	93n53	4.39	206n14
1.11.3	194 n.15	4.45	206n13
1.29	82n8	5.39	206n12
1.29–31	109n109	6.61	206n61
1.29.55–56	93n53	7.42	204n7
1.30	106n98	7.43	190, 191
2.14.4	194n15	*De Oratione*	
		3.7	205
JEROME		*De Principiis*	
		1.1	202
In Ephesios (CCSL)		1.1.1	192
79.27,16–32	212n35	1.1.6	204nn6, 7
		1.4.1	212n31
JUSTIN MARTYR		1.5	201
		1.8.1–4	212n32
First Apology		2.1.4	203n4
13	208n11	2.1.5	213n36
22	208n11	2.6.3	212n34
		2.9.6	212n33
		2.9.7	214n40

Origen, *Princ., cont'd.*
   2.11.6   201
   3.1.1   203n5
   3.5.4   212n35
   4.2.4   201
   4.4.1   190, 192
   4.4.7   203n4
Dialogus cum Heraclide
   1.25–33   206n12

Homiliae in Canticum
   20.8   212n38
Philokalia
   13   204n8
   24   203

PHILOSTORGIUS

Historia ecclesiastica
   3.15   232n111

PSEUDO-DIONYSIUS

Divine Names (Suchla)
   1.5   249n19
   2.4   246n7
   2.5   248n17; 249n20
   2.11   246n8
   4.4   253n29
   5.8   247n12; 248n16; 250n23; 252n25; 252n26; 253n29
   5.9   252n27
   5.10   246n7; 247n11; 248n15; 253; 253n30
   11.1   246n9
   PG 4.321b   149n21
De mystica theologia
   2   254n31
   5   253–54; 254n31

TERTULLIAN

Adversus Valentinianos
   1   109n109
   12   194n16
De Anima
   25.2–3   211n24

THEODORET OF CYRRHUS

Haereticarum fabularum compendium
   1.13   93n53

MARIUS VICTORINUS

Ad Candidum
   1   69–71
   1.4   69
   1.2.14–23   84n21
   1.6   70
   1.11–14   70
   2   70
   2.19–20   70
   2.21   88n37
   2.21–30   69–71, 88n373
   3.1–2   70
   4   70–71
   5   69
   6   70
   6.2   70
   6.5–13   70n13
   6.6–11   70
   6–11   70n13
   7   70
   7.1–7   84n24, 89n41
   7–8   71
   7–10   70–71
   7.1   70n13
   8.19–21   71
   9   71, 74n20
   9.4–7.18–19   75n20
   10   71

10.36	71	1.57	73–74
11	71n14	1.58	74
11–14	71	1.59	74
13.1–14.5	92	1.60	74
14.1	92	1.60–61	74
14.11–25	97n70	1.60–64	71
14.5–27	97n70	1.60.1–31	84n23
15	71 n.15	1.60.6–7	74n18

Adversus Arium

		1.60.6–8	74
1A	66	1.60.22–27	74
1B	66, 69, 71, 75–76	1.61	74–75
1.21.41–22.2	81n2	1.61.8–12	74n20
1.30.18–31	72, 84n21	1.62	75
1.30.8–9	81n2	1.63.16–64.8	88n37
1.32	71, 75–76	2.2.7–11	84nn18–19
1.32.16–26	88n37	3	66, 69, 71
1.32.16–78	75	3.1.10–34	84n20, 88n37
1.32.24–27	81n2	3.1.10–34	84n21
1.41.9–18	81n2	3.1.30–34	84nn18–19
1.48	73	3.4	71, 76
1.49–50	65–66, 72–73, 75, 80	3.4.6–46	75
1.49.4	78	3.4–5	76n23
1 49.7–50.21	86n30	3.4.6–22	84n23, 88n37
1.49.12	91	3.5	76
1.49.17–40	81n2, 86n30	3.7.22–28	84nn18–19
1.49.20	91	4	66, 69, 76, 79
1.49.9–17	81n2, 86n30	4.1–3	77
1.50	73	4.2.4–5	76
1.50.4–22	84nn19.23, 86n30, 88n37, 89, 99n84	4.3	76
		4.4	76–77
1.50.9	91	4.5	76–77
1.50.10	91	4.6–7	77
1.50.11	72	4.8	77
1.50.14	86n30	4.9	77
1.50.16	72, 90	4.9–10	77
1.52.18	73	4.10	77
1.52.1–17	88n37	4.10.45	77
1.53	72	4.11	77
1.54	73	4.11.10	77
1.55	73	4.11.25	77
1.56	73	4.12	77
1.56–57	71	4.13	77–78
1.56.4–5	99n84	4.14	78

Marius Victorinus, *Adv. Ar., cont'd.*

4.15	78
4.15.3	78
4.16.29–17.2	88n37
4.17	78
4.18.45–59	78
4.19	78
4.19–20	78
4.19–24	78
4.19.4–20	84n20
4.21	78
4.21.19–29.38	78n28
4.21.26–22.6	84nn22–24, 88n37, 89n41, 99n84
4.21.26–24.39	79n29
4.21.26–27	99n84
4.22–24	79
4.22.6–23.10	88n37
4.23.12–31	84n20, 88n37
4.23.31–45	88n37
4.24.1–29.11	84nn18–19
4.24.21–39	88n37
4.25	79
4.25.44–28.22	84n21
4.25.44–29.11	84n21
4.26	79
4.26–33	79
4.28.1–22	84n23, 88n37
4.29	79
4.29.1–11	88n37
4.29.3	79
4.29.20–21	75
4.5.23–6.17	84nn20, 22–24, 88n37, 89n41

Candidus ad Victorinem

1.2.14–23	84n21
1.1.11–17	81n2

INDO-IRANICA

NAGARJUNA

Mûla-madhyamaka-kârikâ

18.8	243n1